ARCHITECTURAL DRAFTING

by

WILLIAM J. HORNUNG
Director of Training ~ National Technical Institute

SECOND
EDITION

Englewood Cliffs, N.J. — **PRENTICE - HALL, INC.**

PRENTICE-HALL TECHNICAL-INDUSTRIAL-VOCATIONAL SERIES

Claude H. Ewing, *Editor*

L. C. Cat. Card. No. : 54:12496

First printing. . . . . . . January, 1955
Second printing. . . . . . October, 1955
Third printing. . . . . .June, 1956

Printed in the United States of America
04413

ARCHITECTURAL
DRAFTING

To the Members of
"OPUS INCERTUM"
and
Bond Street

*"As long as there is a common goal,
irregular shaped stones will find their
place in the foundation of achievement."*

PREFACE

This book has come to occupy an important place in the fields of architecture and construction since the publication of the original edition in 1949. The present edition retains all the best features of the first edition, with elaborations of this material where warranted; in addition, it contains two new sections, Parts II and III, which explain and illustrate the standard details of house construction and the planning of the house. The book therefore represents a complete teaching unit in itself, and contains a large number of drawing problems.

It is said that the creation of a building involves four phases: first, the development of the idea of the design of the building by the architect; second, the execution of that idea by the draftsman; third, the reading of the blueprints by the builder; and fourth, the fabrication of the parts comprising the physical structure. This book is concerned primarily with the second phase in the process, namely, the execution of the architect's idea by the draftsman.

Parts I and II embrace the study of construction principles and architectural details for both frame and masonry construction. Plates illustrating sill construction, frame wall sections, masonry wall construction, and window, door, and fireplace details are included.

Part III, on planning the house, was added to acquaint the reader with the problems of planning and its technique before he actually begins to prepare the house plans. Beginning with the problem of the selection of site and lot, we go on to consider other important factors such as the availability of public utilities, the convenience to schools and churches, and transportation and shopping center facilities.

The main areas of the house, used for eating, living, and sleeping, are studied in their proper relation so as to fit the desired budget. Each area is further planned in the placement of furniture and fixtures. Basic kitchen types, for example, are described in regard to fixture and cabinet arrangements. The dining space, with built-in cabinets, is planned to show how valuable floor space can be saved. The living room, the bedrooms, the bathroom, laundry and utility room are planned for maximum use and convenience.

Part IV deals with the preparation of a complete set of working drawings for a residence. These are more complete than usual to enable better visualiza-

tion and understanding of the complex arrangements of joists and rafters. The section on simple "two point perspectives" will round out the draftsman's ability.

Part V explains the commonly used heating systems, including a fully detailed study of the one-pipe hot-water system.

Part VI covers the layout of the plumbing system in all its details.

Part VII is a discussion of the electrical plans for the various requirements, together with the latest methods employed in lighting the home.

Part VIII presents a complete set of plans and specifications for an existing, contemporary, flat-roof house, with perspective renderings.

The entire course of instruction involves the preparation of a series of drawing plates, with the descriptive material preceding the drawing. Each plate has a definite objective and is developed in a step-by-step sequence to assist the student. Test problems are given with each part of the book to further assist both student and instructor.

The author is indebted to Professor R. Waite of the New York State Technical Institute of Long Island, to Mr. Joseph Steinberg of the New York State Institute of Applied Arts and Sciences, to Mr. Fred Heine, architect, of the firm of Frederic P. Wiedersum, and to Mr. Benjamin J. Nasaf, architectural designer of the firm of Harrison and Abramovitz, for their valuable advice and suggestions in the planning and preparation of this book.

Further thanks are extended to Mr. Raymond H. Wadsworth, P. E., instructor, National Technical Institute, for writing the section on residential heating, and to Richard Seabrook, industrial designer, for the preparation of the sketches and drawings, and to the following companies for supplying illustrations and reference material: The Trane Co., La Crosse, Wis.; National Lumber Manufacturers Association; John Wiley & Sons Inc., New York; Anderson Corporation, Bayport, Minn.; Weyerhauser Sales Company, St. Paul, Minn.; National Concrete Masonry Association, Chicago, Ill.; Westinghouse Electric Corporation, Pittsburgh, Pa.

Special mention goes to the members of the "Opus Incertum," who through their pleasant and inspiring association have indirectly contributed largely to the subject content and organization of the material.

William J. Hornung

CONTENTS

PLATES

PART I
CONSTRUCTION PRINCIPLES

Single-Stroke Architectural Lettering

Lettering is as important to the draftsman as the working plans of the building, because without legible explanatory notes, titles, and dimensions, the plans could not be understood.

To achieve good lettering, three factors must be considered:

1. The instrument with which the letter is to be made.

2. The form or shape of the letter.

3. The technique.

When pencil lettering is desired, a soft pencil must be used in order to make a dark line without too much pressure on the paper. With little pressure on the pencil the muscles in the fingers and hand are relaxed and a greater freedom of line is achieved. The quality of the paper determines the grade of hardness in the pencil to be used. For example, a hard pencil on a soft paper of high rag content will tend to dig into and follow the grain of the paper and produce a crooked line. A little experimentation will determine the best combination.

The second factor, the form and shape of the letter, must be studied not by merely looking at good examples of letters but also by actually trying to reproduce them. Placing tracing paper over the letters and copying them as they are is a good method but should not be attempted until the shapes and forms are familiar.

The third factor, the technique, is the most important part of lettering. Keep in mind that a line must have a beginning and a definite end. Lines must not fade out near the ends. The stroke of the letter must be rapid and also must be confined between the guide lines. Once the stroke is made, it is poor practice to go over the same line. For this reason this type of lettering is called *single-stroke lettering*. The hand and pencil should be held in a natural position, generally that which you use when writing a letter or signing your name. This position should never be changed even when horizontal strokes are drawn.

Ink lettering is always more difficult than pencil lettering, though in many instances the use of incorrect pens causes additional difficulty. Try various pens to find the one that suits your style best and produces the best general results. The B-6 Speedball pen and the No. 107 Hunt Crow quill have been found satisfactory. When tracing lettering in ink on tracing cloth from an original pencil drawing, do not forget to draw the pencil guide lines first; they help prevent irregularities in the letters and words.

[1]

PLATE 1
ARCHITECTURAL LETTERING

Objective

To study the form and shape of the single-stroke architectural letter and the method of achieving good results.

Procedure

1. On a standard size sheet of drawing paper, 17 x 22 in., draw a ½-in. border line. (*All plates in this text were originally laid out on paper of this size.*) Draw a horizontal line 1¼ in. from the bottom border. This space is to be used for the title block, which includes the name of school, the student's name, date. A 1¼ x 1¼-in. block in the lower right-hand corner will be used for the plate number.

2. Draw the horizontal guide lines instrumentally by first measuring off distances for the heights of the letters on the left side vertical margin line. Lay the 12-in. architect's scale on the left side border with the figure 12 directly in the upper left-hand corner at the intersection of the margin lines.

3. Once the scale is set in this position, do not move it until all points have been marked off on the

margin. This precaution may prevent cumulative errors in measuring. Through these points draw light horizontal guide lines with the T square.

4. Before attempting to letter Plate 1, practice strokes by placing a piece of tracing paper over the shapes and forms shown in Fig. 1 until you are satisfied with the results.

5. Remember that strokes must be rapid and confined between guide lines. Use a soft pencil such as F or HB, and apply equal pressure on the pencil for the full stroke of the line. The line should be of uniform thickness and when held against the light should be opaque and black.

Problems

1. Freehand letter the first two lines of lettering on Plate 1.

2. Letter the same two lines by memory.

3. Compare the memory lettering with Plate 1 and study the form and shape of each letter. Continue to letter as in Problems 1 and 2 until a good degree of similarity is obtained.

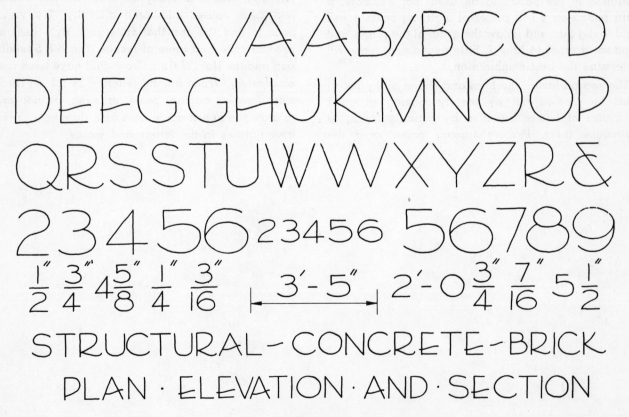

Fig. 1

ARCHITECTURAL LETTERING

ABCDEFGHIJKLMNOPQRSTUVWXYZ & 123456789O

& ABCDEFGHIJKLMNOPQRSTUVWXYZ

123456789O & ABCDEFGHIJKLMNOPQRSTUVWXYZ

SCALE $\frac{1}{4}$" = 1'-0"

THE LETTERING ON WORKING DRAWINGS IS CHARACTERIZED
BY LEGIBILITY AND SPEED. THE NECESSARY SKILL FOR
THIS CLASS OF WORK MAY BE ACQUIRED BY TAKING UP
SINGLE STROKE LETTERS, AS HERE REPRESENTED, AND
LEARNING THEIR SHAPES. THE LETTERS SHOULD BE PRACTICED
SEPARATELY, THEN COMBINED INTO WORDS AND SENTENCES,
FOLLOWING THE RULES FOR SPACING AND COMPOSITION.

NATIONAL TECHNICAL INSTITUTE SCHOOL OF DRAFTING
NEW YORK CITY

LETTERING

PLATES 2 AND 3
GEOMETRIC CONSTRUCTIONS

A review of the basic and the most important geometric constructions applied to architecture will be of great help. For this reason the constructions illustrated here are accompanied by actual applications.

Following is a step-by-step description in solving each geometric construction in Figs. 2 through 7 (Plates 2 and 3). Additional problems provided after these descriptions will serve as further practice. Suitable applications should be sought for each geometric construction.

To Construct a Tudor Arch (Fig. 2)

EXAMPLE APPLICATION. Entrance shown below Fig. 2.

Lay off the desired width and height of the arch AB and CD. Select any desired radius for the small arc, say AE and FB. With E as center for radius EF, swing the arc FG. Draw line EG extended to meet a perpendicular from F to meet this line at K. With E as center and radius EK swing an arc. With a radius equal to AE plus EK and D as a center describe the small arc intersecting the other arc at L. Draw line LE extended to M. Point E is the center for arc AM and point L the center for arc MD. Complete the arch similarly. A well-proportioned arch will be obtained when radius AE is approximately one-fourth of AB.

To Construct a Cylindrical Helix (Fig. 3)

EXAMPLE APPLICATION. Hand rail on circular stair.

Divide the circle of the top view into any number of equal parts, for example 12, and drop vertical lines from each point. Divide the pitch distance into the same number of equal parts and draw horizontal lines through the points. The intersection of the vertical line from a division of the circle with a horizontal line with the division of the pitch distance will locate a point on the helix. The procedure is the same for each of the corresponding points.

To Divide the Space between Two Given Lines into a Number of Equal Parts (Fig. 4)

EXAMPLE APPLICATION. Finding the number of risers for a stair within a given height.

Place the zero mark of the scale on one line and swing the scale around until a multiple of the desired number of spaces coincides with the other line. The drawing on Plate 2 shows the space between the two lines divided into four parts.

To Draw Lines Parallel to a Given Line (Fig. 5)

EXAMPLE APPLICATION. Guard rail on stair.

Line up the edge of the triangle with the given line AB. Place the T-square blade beneath the triangle and slide the triangle along to any desired point and draw the line RS along the edge of the triangle. Line RS will be parallel to line AB.

To Draw a Semiellipse by the Five-Center Method (Fig. 6)

EXAMPLE APPLICATION. Entrance shown below Fig. 6.

Assume the major axis AB and half the minor axis CO, and draw the rectangle ABDG. Draw AC, and from point G a line perpendicular to AC extended to intersect the perpendicular at P. Lay off OS equal to OC and with SB as a diameter draw the semicircle SMB. Measure OT equal to RM: then with P as a center and PT as a radius swing the arc as shown. With A and B as centers and a radius equal to ON swing arcs E and F. Through these points and center P draw lines PK and PQ. With L as center and radius LA draw arc AX. With E as a center and radius EX draw arc XK. Arc KCQ is drawn with PK as a radius. Complete arc similarly.

To Construct a Parabola by the Envelope Method (Fig. 7)

EXAMPLE APPLICATION. A municipal asphalt plant.

Lay off the desired span CD and the rise AE. On line AE extended lay off EB equal to AE. Connect points BC and BD. From point C erect a perpendicular of indefinite length, on which lay off any number of equal parts. Connect the last point on the perpendicular with point B on the triangle. Through each successive point on the perpendicular draw a line parallel to the line previously drawn, intersecting line CB and dividing it into a corresponding number of equal parts. Project the points on line CB to BD, locating similar points on that line. Starting at point B, with the figure 0, number the points on both sides of the triangle *inversely*, as indicated in Fig. 7. By connecting corresponding numbers on opposite sides of the triangle, an *outline* of the required parabola will be formed. With an irregular curve draw the parabolic line from point C to point D tangent to these lines.

Problems

1. Divide a given line AB into two equal parts. (Find suitable application for all constructions.)
2. Divide a line into any number of equal parts.
3. Divide a circle into six equal parts by the triangle method.

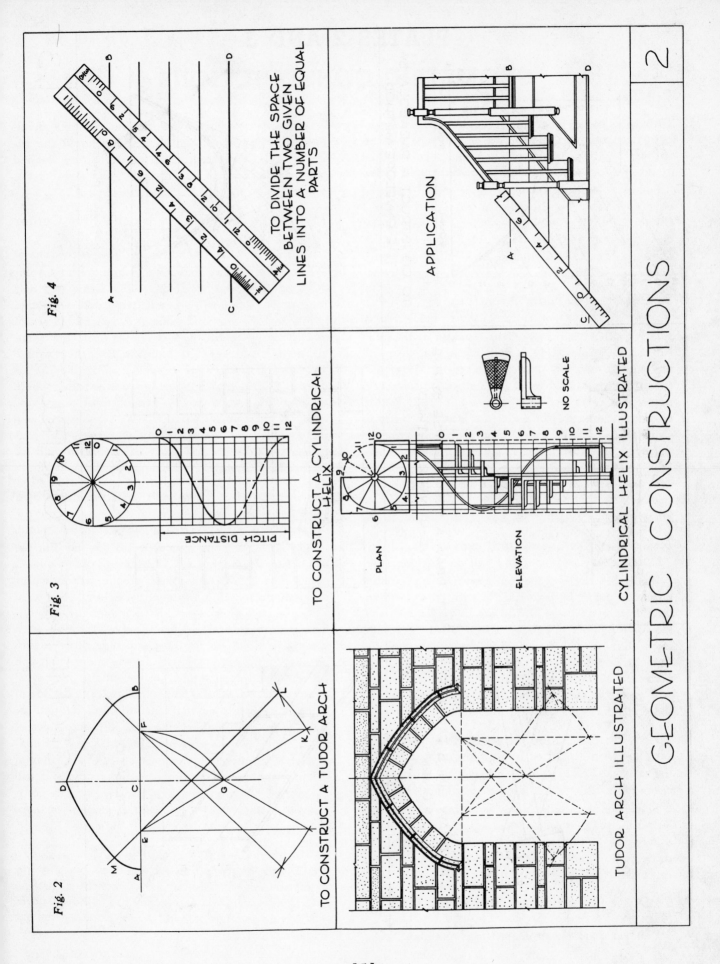

Fig. 4

TO DIVIDE THE SPACE BETWEEN TWO GIVEN LINES INTO A NUMBER OF EQUAL PARTS

APPLICATION

Fig. 3

TO CONSTRUCT A CYLINDRICAL HELIX

PITCH DISTANCE

PLAN

ELEVATION

NO SCALE

CYLINDRICAL HELIX ILLUSTRATED

Fig. 2

TO CONSTRUCT A TUDOR ARCH

TUDOR ARCH ILLUSTRATED

GEOMETRIC CONSTRUCTIONS

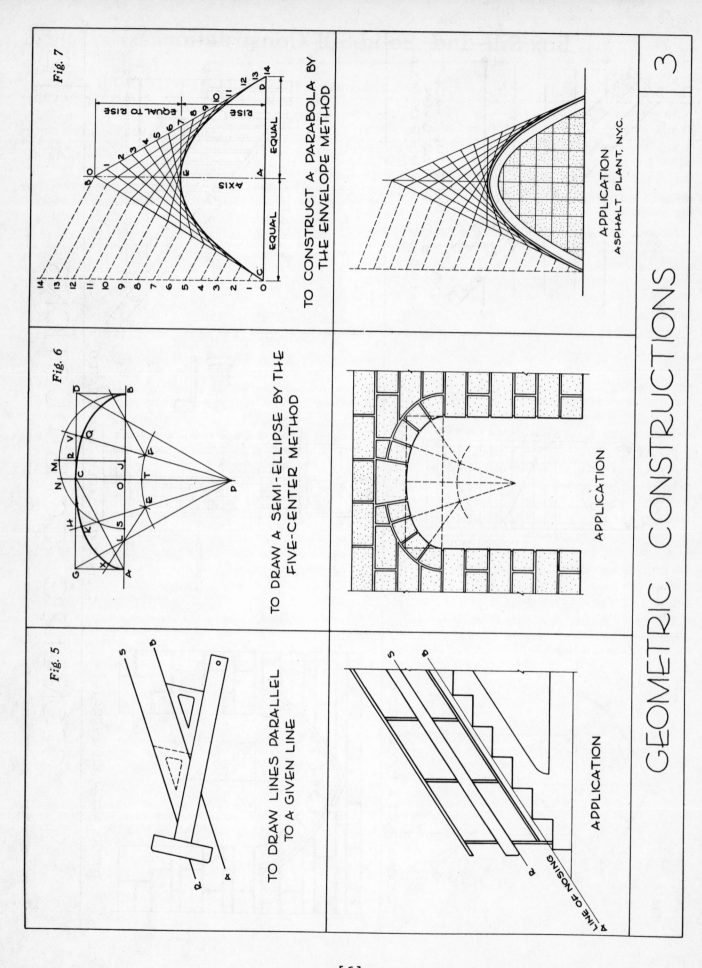

Fig. 7

TO CONSTRUCT A PARABOLA BY THE ENVELOPE METHOD

APPLICATION
ASPHALT PLANT, N.Y.C.

Fig. 6

TO DRAW A SEMI-ELLIPSE BY THE FIVE-CENTER METHOD

APPLICATION

Fig. 5

TO DRAW LINES PARALLEL TO A GIVEN LINE

APPLICATION

GEOMETRIC CONSTRUCTIONS

3

Box-Sill and Solid-Sill Construction

The Box Sill

All buildings have footings or foundations (see Fig. 8) which distribute the load transmitted to them over a larger ground area. They serve this purpose because flat objects cannot be driven as readily into the ground as sharp objects. The footing, being larger in area than the foundation wall, will distribute the weight of the building over a larger area.

Footings are generally made of concrete. This material is most desirable because it becomes one solid mass when dry. Steel reinforcing rods are sometimes employed in footings to add strength. When reinforcing is to be applied, the written specifications that accompany a complete set of drawings give the size and spacing.

Footings are employed all around the building under the foundation walls. When large beams are used to span outside walls, a column is used between the walls as an intermediate support. Such columns must have footings large enough to support the estimated load.

For small houses the depth of the footing is usually the same as the thickness of the wall but not less than 12 in. The portion of the footing that protrudes from the foundation wall is one-half of the wall thickness but not less than 6 in. The depth of footings in New York City, according to the building code, is at least 4 ft. below the ground level, in order to extend below the frost line. In states where the climate is warmer, such as Florida, the footing depth required by the building code is only 2 ft.

On top of the foundation wall is shown a piece of lumber, 4 x 6 in., called the sill. The sill is anchored to the foundation wall by means of anchor bolts ¾ in. in diameter, spaced approximately 6 to 8 ft. apart and extended at least 18 in. into the foundation. On the sill rest the header and joists, as shown on Fig. 9.

The joists are usually spaced 16 in. on center (o.c.). The ⅞-in. rough subflooring is then nailed to the joists and header. A double 2- x 4-in. secondary sill acting as a plate or sole for the 2- x 4-in studding is nailed to the flooring and the header (Fig. 10).

It is essential to understand the names of all the structural members used in this construction and to be able to make memory sketches of this detail.

The Solid Sill

The solid sill is very similar to the box sill, except that the studs rest directly on the sill. In the box sill the header is one continuous member, whereas in the solid sill it is cut and spaced between the joists. The header in this case acts as a fire stop and prevents any fluelike action between the walls in the event of fire. In Plate 4 the dotted line, the continuation of the joist on the solid sill passes behind the stud, indicating that the stud and joist are nailed together.

The advantage of the solid sill over the box sill is that there is less likelihood that the material will settle or shrink. It must be understood that when a new building is constructed it goes through a settling or shrinking period until the lumber is completely dry. Excess shrinking may mean cracks in the plaster walls, sagging floors, and ill-fitting doors. With the studs resting directly on the sill, the shrinkage factor is somewhat reduced.

PLATE 4
BOX-SILL AND SOLID-SILL CONSTRUCTION

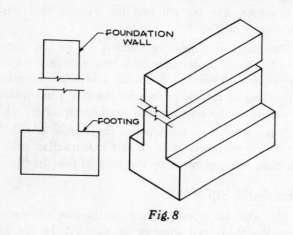

Fig. 8

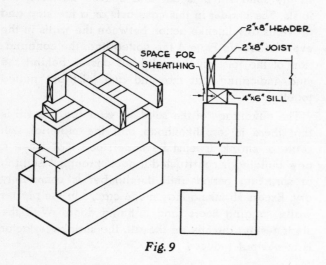

Fig. 9

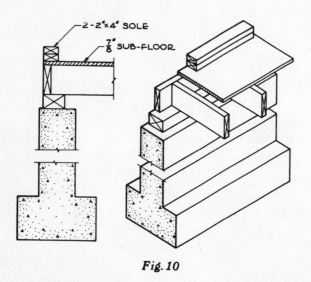

Fig. 10

Objective

To know the arrangement and the sizes of building materials used in the construction of the box sills and solid sills for the frame house.

Procedure

1. Lay out the footing and the foundation wall very lightly with a 2H pencil at a scale of 1 in. = 1 ft. (Fig. 8). *Note:* Draw the line first; then measure it.

2. Draw the 4- x 6-in. sill on top of the foundation wall ⅞ in. from the outside face of the wall. This space is allowed for the sheathing (Fig. 9).

3. Draw the 2- x 8-in. header and the 2- x 8-in. joist on top of the sill. Joists are generally spaced 16 in. on center (o.c.).

4. Next, draw the ⅞-in. subfloor, the double 2- x 4-in. sole, and then the 2- x 4-in. stud on top of the sole. Studs are generally spaced 16 in. o.c. Erase all excess line work.

5. Draw diagonals through sill, header, and sole. This is the symbol for end cuts on rough lumber. Cross-hatch the subfloor freehand, using 45-deg. lines spaced approximately $\frac{1}{16}$ in. apart (Fig. 10).

6. Darken in all object lines except "break" lines, which are somewhat lighter. Draw symbol for concrete—triangles for crushed stone and dots for cement particles when stone concrete is used. A uniform distribution of the concrete symbol is desirable. Label all members, using ⅛-in. single-stroke architectural letters. Draw guide lines before lettering.

7. Follow the above steps for the solid sill and note the arrangement of the framing members shown on Plate 4. Use scale 1 in. = 1 ft.

8. Draw the isometric of the two sill constructions, using dividers to carry off dimensions from the completed sections. (Study page 10.)

Test Problems

1. Draw the section of the box sill to a scale of ¾ in. = 1 ft.

2. Draw the section of the solid sill to a scale of ½ in. = 1 ft.

3. Make memory sketches of both constructions.

4. Draw the isometric of the box sill.

5. Draw the isometric of the solid sill. (See the following instructions on isometric drawing.)

[8]

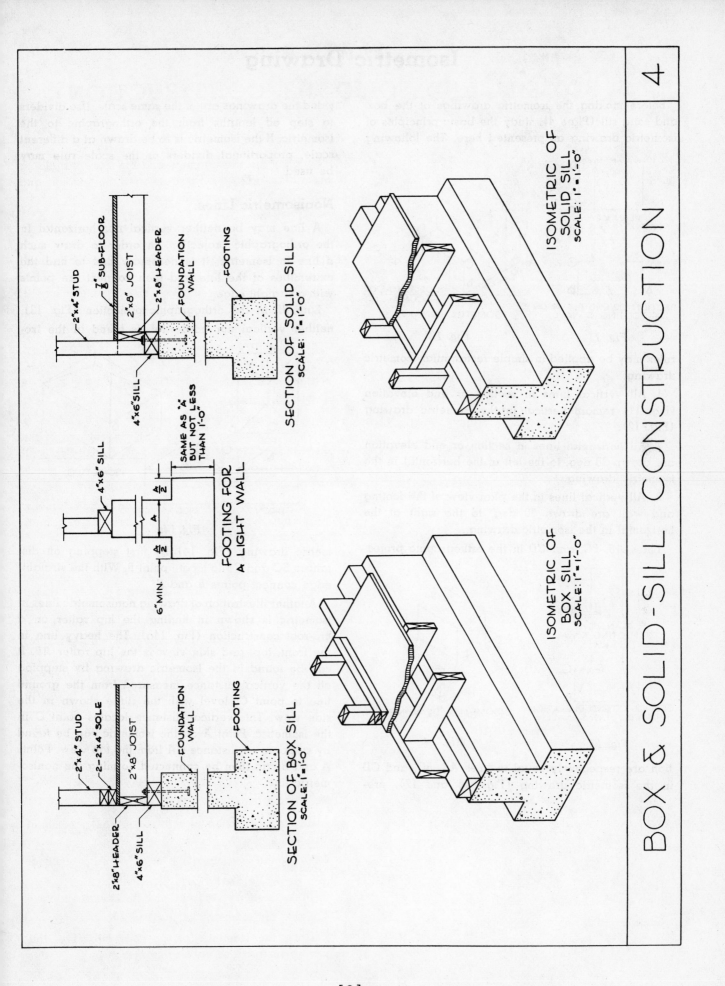

SECTION OF BOX SILL
SCALE: 1"=1'-0"

2"x4" STUD
2-2"x4" SOLE
2"x8" JOIST
2"x8" HEADER
4"x6" SILL
FOUNDATION WALL
FOOTING

4"x6" SILL

6" MIN.

A/2
A
A/2

SAME AS "A"
BUT NOT LESS
THAN 1'-0"

FOOTING FOR
A LIGHT WALL

SECTION OF SOLID SILL
SCALE: 1"=1'-0"

2"x4" STUD
7/8" SUB-FLOOR
2"x8" JOIST
2"x8" HEADER
4"x6" SILL
FOUNDATION WALL
FOOTING

ISOMETRIC OF
BOX SILL
SCALE: 1"=1'-0"

ISOMETRIC OF
SOLID SILL
SCALE: 1"=1'-0"

BOX & SOLID-SILL CONSTRUCTION

4

Isometric Drawing

Before making the isometric drawings of the box and solid sill (Plate 4), study the basic principles of isometric drawing as presented here. The following

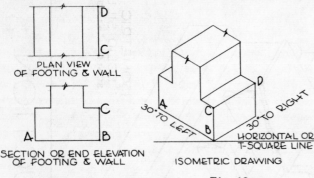

PLAN VIEW OF FOOTING & WALL

SECTION OR END ELEVATION OF FOOTING & WALL

ISOMETRIC DRAWING

Fig. 11   *Fig. 12*

rules may be applied in simple rectangular isometric drawing:

1. All vertical lines in section or end elevation (Fig. 11) remain vertical in the isometric drawing (Fig. 12).

2. All horizontal lines in section or end elevation are drawn 30 deg. to the left of the horizontal in the isometric drawing.

3. All vertical lines in the plan view of the footing and wall are drawn 30 deg. to the right of the horizontal in the isometric drawing.

Lines *AB*, *BC*, and *CD* in the orthographic projec-

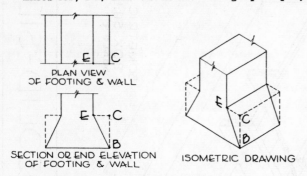

PLAN VIEW OF FOOTING & WALL

SECTION OR END ELEVATION OF FOOTING & WALL

ISOMETRIC DRAWING

Fig. 13   *Fig. 14*

tion are respectively equal to lines *AB*, *BC*, and *CD* in the isometric drawing (Figs. 11 and 12), pro-

vided the drawings are of the same scale. Use dividers to step off lengths from the orthographic to the isometric. If the isometric is to be drawn at a different scale, proportional dividers or the scale rule may be used.

Nonisometric Lines

A line may be neither vertical nor horizontal in the orthographic projection. In order to draw such a line in isometric, it is necessary first to find the extremities of the line and then connect the points with a straight edge.

Line *BE* in the orthographic projection (Fig. 13), neither vertical nor horizontal, is found in the iso-

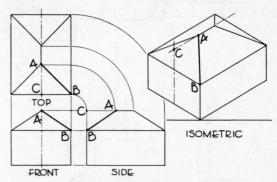

TOP

FRONT   SIDE

ISOMETRIC

Fig. 14a

metric drawing (Fig. 14) by first stepping off distances *EC* and *CB* to locate point *B*. With the straight-edge connect points *B* and *E*.

Another illustration of drawing nonisometric lines in isometric is shown in finding the hip rafter on a hip-roof construction (Fig. 14a). The heavy line in the front, top, and side view is the hip rafter *AB*. It can be found in the isometric drawing by stepping off the vertical distance measured from the ground line to point *C*, level with the ridge shown in the side view. This vertical distance locates point *C* in the isometric. Point *A* on the isometric can be found by stepping off distance *CA* from the top view. Points *A* and *B* can then be connected, forming the noniso-metric line.

The Brick-Veneer and the Solid-Brick Wall

The Brick-Veneer Wall

In studying brick-veneer construction (Plate 5) it will be seen that the framing is similar to the box-type construction. The only difference is that the foundation wall is thicker to make room for the stone water table, which in turn receives the face brick above. Heavy tar paper is nailed to the sheathing, as in other constructions, before the bricks are laid. In order to anchor the veneer wall to the framing, metal wall ties 24 in. apart are required after every fourth course of brick. The void left between the veneer wall and the sheathing is to provide "breathing space" to dry any moisture that might seep in between the brickwork.

Although this type of construction is widely used and is quite satisfactory, a still better construction can be made if a nonshrinking material, such as hollow tile, concrete block, or brick, is used for a backing instead of the framework. The brick veneer on frame may be used when remodeling older homes, in which the framing members are already set and in which the shrinkage factor has been eliminated.

Many builders prefer the use of the solid-type construction in conjunction with the brick veneer, because the small amount of horizontal-grain material in the wall construction decreases the shrinkage factor. For the same reason it is desirable to limit the thickness of the sill to 2-in. material.

The brick-veneer wall is generally 4 in. thick. It is not designed to carry any of the weight of the building but acts only as a covering.

Other materials, such as cut stone and 4-in. precast concrete slabs, may be used in place of the brick veneer.

The Solid-Brick Wall

When a solid-brick wall is used, the floor beams are bricked in solid in their respective positions. The rough flooring, butting against the wall and nailed to the joists, receives the grounds, which in turn are nailed to furring strips. (Furring is the fastening of wood strips, generally 7/8 x 1½ in., both vertically and horizontally to the entire inside face of the brick wall. The spacing of the furring strips is determined by the type and size of latch.) These act as nailing strips for the grounds and the metal lath, which in turn receives the plaster.

The ends of joists that are bricked into the wall are cut to an angle as represented by the dotted lines in Plate 5, with a minimum bearing surface of 4 in. The building code requires that beams be cut in this fashion, because in case of fire inside the building the beams will have a tendency to cave into the building and fall out of the wall socket. If the beams were not cut and they were too heavy in their sockets, the weight of the beams might topple the brick wall over and to the outside, endangering life and adjoining property (Fig. 16).

Most masonry construction is porous and permits the seepage of moisture or water, either through the material itself or through the mortar joints. To eliminate such seepage, the inside of the brick wall may be covered with a layer of hot pitch, otherwise the wall must be furred. Furring on the brick wall helps to prevent infiltration or leakage of air and prevents condensation on the interior.

[11]

PLATE 5
THE BRICK-VENEER AND THE SOLID-BRICK WALL

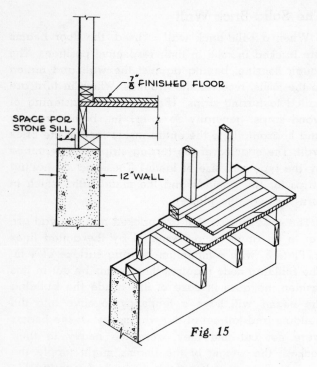

Fig. 15

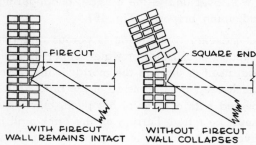

FIRECUT

SQUARE END

WITH FIRECUT
WALL REMAINS INTACT

WITHOUT FIRECUT
WALL COLLAPSES

Fig. 16

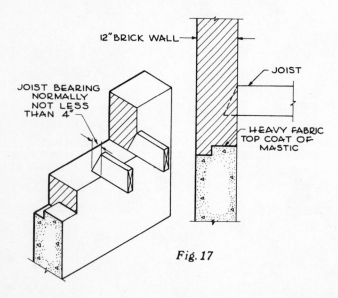

Fig. 17

Objective

To know the arrangement and the sizes of building materials used in the construction of the brick-veneer wall and the solid-brick wall.

Procedure

1. Lay out lightly the footing for a 12-in. foundation wall at a scale of 1 in. = 1 ft. (Fig. 15). Draw the 4- x 6-in. sill, the 2- x 10-in. header and joist, the ⅞-in. subfloor, the double 2- x 4-in. sole, and the 2- x 4½-in. stud. The ⅞-in. plaster with ⅞- x 1½-in. grounds and the baseboard with the ⅞-in. finished floor are drawn next. Add the ⅞-in. sheathing that is nailed to the studs, sole, header, and sill. A space on the foundation wall should be left to receive the stone water table and the brick veneer. The outside line of the brickwork must not extend beyond the line of the foundation wall (Plate 5).

2. Draw the stone water table with the brickwork above. Show the *wall ties* after every fourth course as shown on Plate 5. Cross-section the floors and the brickwork, and indicate all lumber end cuts by diagonals. Draw the symbols for concrete, plaster, and stone work. Darken in all object lines, dimension the footing and the foundation wall, and label all materials in name and size.

3. In drawing the solid-brick wall begin with a footing for an 8- or 12-in. foundation wall (Fig. 17). Since the top of the foundation wall is close to the grade line, a step arrangement is left in the concrete wall with a heavy top coat of mastic to prevent water seepage to the interior. Indicate the brickwork above the wall. Draw the 2- x 10-in. joist with anchor rod. Note the angle of cut at the end of the joist. Complete the section by drawing the ⅞- x 1½-in. furring strips, the ⅞-in. plaster, and the baseboard as shown on Plate 5.

4. Lightly lay out the isometrics of the sections, omitting the footings, at a scale of 1 in. = 1 ft. Use dividers for carrying dimensions from the sections to the isometric.

Test Problems

1. Draw brick-veneer section with frame backing. Use solid-type construction. Scale ¾ in. = 1 ft.

2. Draw section of solid-brick wall. Allow joists to rest on 10-in. foundation wall. Scale ¾ in. = 1 ft.

3. Make freehand memory sketches of the sections of the brick-veneer and the solid-brick wall. Dimension and label all materials.

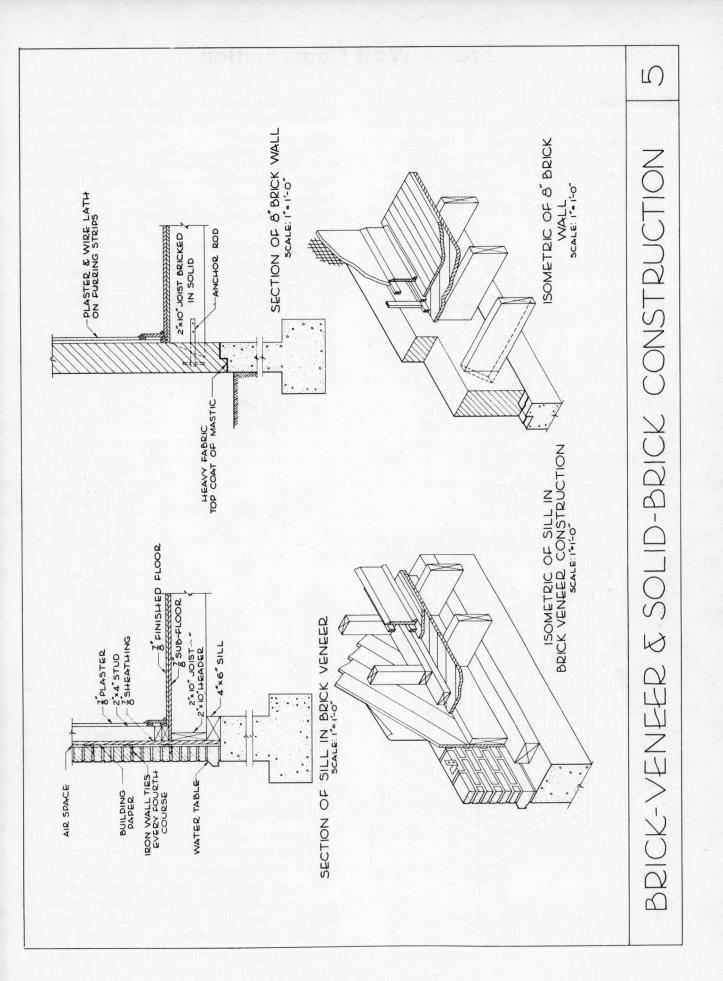

PLASTER & WIRE LATH
ON FURRING STRIPS

2"×10" JOIST BRICKED
IN SOLID

ANCHOR ROD

HEAVY FABRIC
TOP COAT OF MASTIC

SECTION OF 8" BRICK WALL
SCALE: 1"=1'-0"

ISOMETRIC OF 8" BRICK
WALL
SCALE: 1"=1'-0"

7/8" PLASTER
2"×4" STUD
7/8" SHEATHING

7/8" FINISHED FLOOR

7/8" SUB-FLOOR

2"×10" JOIST
2"×10" HEADER

4"×6" SILL

AIR SPACE

BUILDING
PAPER

IRON WALL TIES
EVERY FOURTH
COURSE

WATER TABLE

SECTION OF SILL IN BRICK VENEER
SCALE: 1"=1'-0"

ISOMETRIC OF SILL IN
BRICK VENEER CONSTRUCTION
SCALE: 1"=1'-0"

BRICK-VENEER & SOLID-BRICK CONSTRUCTION   5

[13]

Frame Wall Construction

Wood Sheathing

Sheathing is a covering nailed to the outside faces of studs. Its function is to enclose the framework, strengthen the structure, form a nailing base for siding or shingles, and act as an insulation material. In good construction, wood sheathing is generally laid diagonally because this adds additional strength to the framework (Fig. 17a).

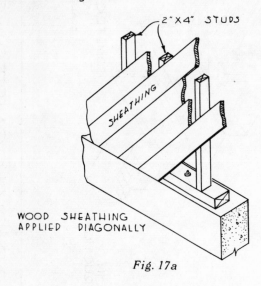

WOOD SHEATHING
APPLIED DIAGONALLY

Fig. 17a

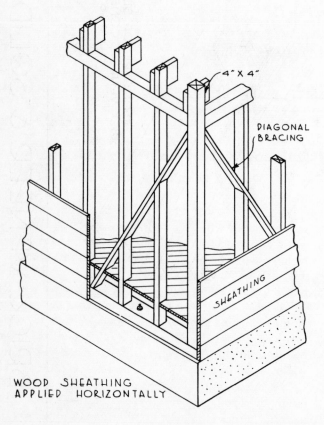

WOOD SHEATHING
APPLIED HORIZONTALLY

Fig. 17b

When sheathing is laid horizontally, a somewhat weaker structure results, but this method is more economical, since diagonal saw cuts are eliminated. To achieve the required rigidity of the framework, 2- x 4-in. braces are generally nailed diagonally at the corners of the structure, extending the full height between floor levels. Such corner braces are not required when diagonal sheathing is used (Fig. 17b).

Composition Sheathing

Composition sheathing (Fig. 17c) provides an effective and inexpensive method of sheathing and insulating frame structures. By its use, heat loss through the wall may be reduced as much as 20 to 40 per cent as compared with wood sheathing. Standard sizes are: 2 x 8 ft., 4 x 8 ft., 4 x 9 ft., and 4 x 10 ft. The long dimension may be placed horizontal or vertical.

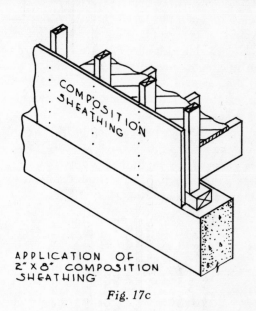

APPLICATION OF
2" X 8" COMPOSITION
SHEATHING

Fig. 17c

Certain types of composition sheathing have a better bracing strength than that of standard thickness wood sheathing laid horizontally, and are comparable with the bracing strength of standard wood sheathing laid on the diagonal.

Building Paper

Building paper, a heavy paper, is nailed to the sheathing to seal all the joints and cracks, acting as a barrier against the infiltration of wind (Fig. 17d).

Contrary to popular belief, building paper is not waterproof. A waterproof paper would prevent the wall from "breathing" and thus impede the escape of moisture condensed within the wall in cold weather.

Building paper is furnished in rolls 3 ft. wide.

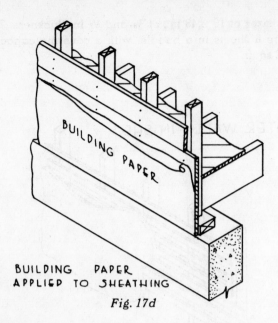

BUILDING PAPER

BUILDING PAPER
APPLIED TO SHEATHING

Fig. 17d

Shingles

Shingles are manufactured from a variety of materials, and in many pleasing shades and colorful styles. The wooden shingle (Fig. 17e), made of cedar, is made in lengths from 18 to 25 in., and in varying widths. The exposed end is about $\frac{3}{8}$ in. thick, and the tapered end about $\frac{1}{16}$ in. thick. Wood shingles are given a creosote dip, which acts as a preservative to prevent rot and decay. The amount of overlap depends on the size of the shingle. Usually 18-in. shingles are exposed 8½ in. to the weather, and up to 12 in. for the 25-in. shingle. The starting course is usually doubled in good construction.

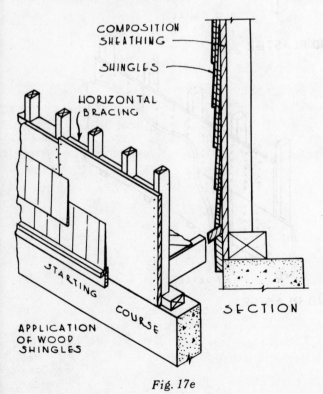

COMPOSITION
SHEATHING

SHINGLES

HORIZONTAL
BRACING

SECTION

STARTING COURSE

APPLICATION
OF WOOD
SHINGLES

Fig. 17e

Clapboard

Clapboards, which provide the exterior finish of a house, are laid horizontally, starting at the bottom of the given area to be covered. Each clapboard overlaps the preceding board by about 1 in. No nailing strips are used, and the clapboards are nailed directly to the sheathing with building paper in between (Fig. 17f).

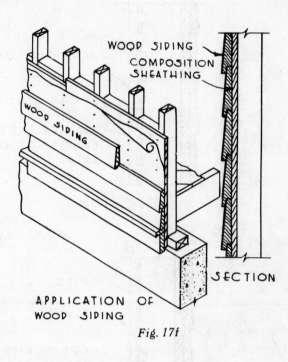

WOOD SIDING
COMPOSITION
SHEATHING

WOOD SIDING

SECTION

APPLICATION OF
WOOD SIDING

Fig. 17f

Vertical Siding

In place of clapboards, it is sometimes desirable, for reasons of design or appearance, to use vertical siding, which is available in a number of finishes and sizes.

Lath and Plaster Wall Finishes

The following illustrations show three methods of bonding plaster to walls. The first, involving the use of wood lath and plaster, has been largely replaced by the use of wire lath and sheet lath. Although the wood lath creates a good bond for the plaster, it has become too costly a labor item to warrant its use today. The second method, which uses wire lath and plaster, is far better and easier to apply. The wire or metal mesh creates an excellent bond for the plaster. Metal lath is manufactured in sheets 24 or 27 in. wide and 96 in. long. The 24 in. width is packed in 9-sheet bundles, having a total area of 16 sq. yd. The 27 in. width is packed in 10-sheet bundles containing 20 sq. yd. of material. The third method of bonding plaster to the wall involves the use of sheet lath. This material can be quickly applied and also serves as an additional insulator. The plaster when applied is pressed into the holes or keys, and acts as a tack when the plaster has hardened. Sheets are furnished in sizes of 16 x 48 in., of ⅜ and ½ in. thickness. There are 6 sheets in a bundle, with a covering capacity of 32 sq. ft.

TYPES OF LATH AND PLASTER WALL FINISHES

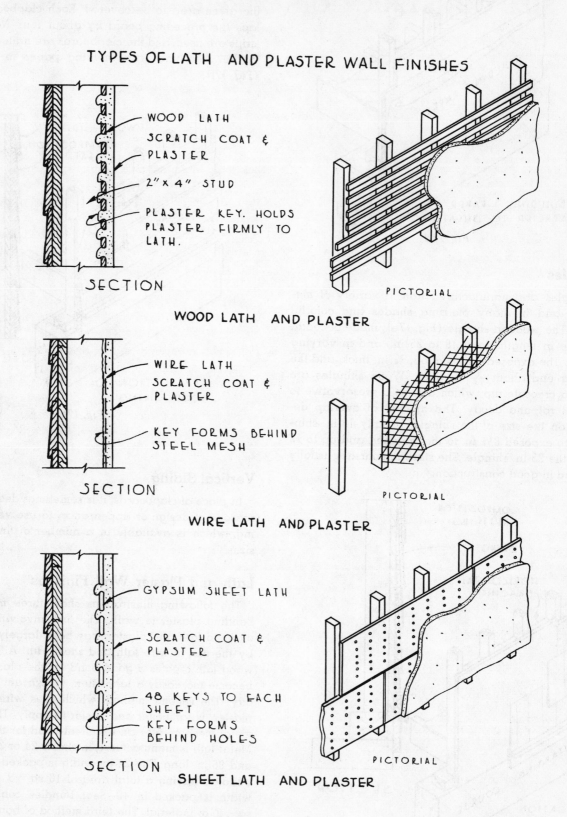

WOOD LATH

SCRATCH COAT & PLASTER

2" x 4" STUD

PLASTER KEY. HOLDS PLASTER FIRMLY TO LATH.

SECTION

PICTORIAL

WOOD LATH AND PLASTER

WIRE LATH

SCRATCH COAT & PLASTER

KEY FORMS BEHIND STEEL MESH

SECTION

PICTORIAL

WIRE LATH AND PLASTER

GYPSUM SHEET LATH

SCRATCH COAT & PLASTER

48 KEYS TO EACH SHEET

KEY FORMS BEHIND HOLES

SECTION

PICTORIAL

SHEET LATH AND PLASTER

PLATE 6
SILL CONSTRUCTION CARRIED TO CORNICE

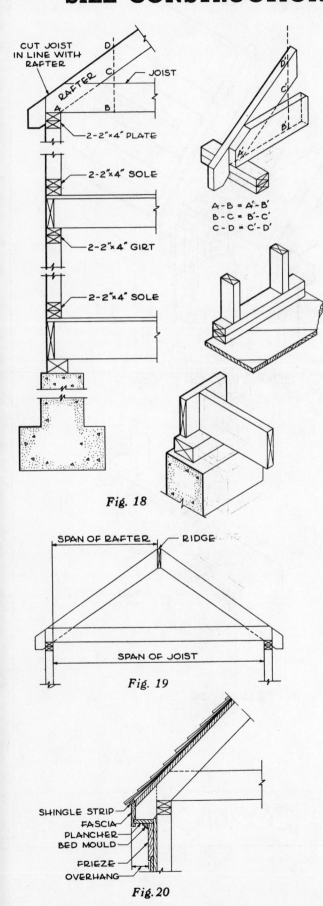

CUT JOIST IN LINE WITH RAFTER

RAFTER

JOIST

2-2"x4" PLATE

2-2"x4" SOLE

2-2"x4" GIRT

2-2"x4" SOLE

A - B = A'- B'
B - C = B'- C'
C - D = C'- D'

Fig. 18

SPAN OF RAFTER — RIDGE

SPAN OF JOIST

Fig. 19

SHINGLE STRIP
FASCIA
PLANCHER
BED MOULD
FRIEZE
OVERHANG

Fig. 20

Objective

To know the arrangement and the sizes of the building materials used in a complete frame house section.

Procedure

1. Lightly lay out the footing with a 10-in. foundation wall. Use box-type construction. Scale 1 in. = 1 ft. (Fig. 18). Carry the studs to first-floor ceiling and then draw the two 2 x 4's, called the girt, over the studs. The second-floor header, joist, floor, and sole are then drawn. These in turn receive the studs and the two 2 x 4's, called the plate. The isometrics in Fig. 18 help to visualize this construction.

2. The 2- x 8-in. ceiling beams and the 2- x 6-in. rafters rest on the plate. The angle of the rafters is determined by the general design of the building and the height of the ridge (Fig. 19). The sizes of joists and rafters are determined by the span or the distance from wall to wall and by the relative live and dead loads to which the beams are subjected (Refer to tables of joist and rafter sizes, pages 205-206 of this book.)

3. The rafters resting on the plate are notched for good seating. The top ends of joists alongside the rafters are cut to match the slope of the rafters.

4. The ends of the rafters are cut vertically and horizontally to receive the fascia and plancher (Fig. 20). The ends of the rafters may extend if greater roof overhang is desired.

5. Draw the isometric of the second-floor girt, joists, header, subfloor, sole, and stud. Use scale of 1 in. = 1 ft. (Plate 6).

6. Draw the isometric of the cornice, showing roof rafters, ceiling joists, plate and studs, roofing, fascia, plancher, frieze, and siding on sheathing (Plate 6).

Test Problems

1. Draw a complete frame section to the cornice at a scale of ½ in. = 1 ft. Use solid-type construction. Assume joist spans between supports to be 23 ft. 1 in., using Western hemlock with plastered ceiling. (Select proper joist sizes from the tables on joist spans, pages 205-206.) Rafter slope more than 20 deg. Give sizes of joists and rafters.

2. Make a freehand memory sketch of the complete section.

3. Make a freehand isometric sketch of the second-floor arrangement similarly to the isometric shown on Plate 6.

[17]

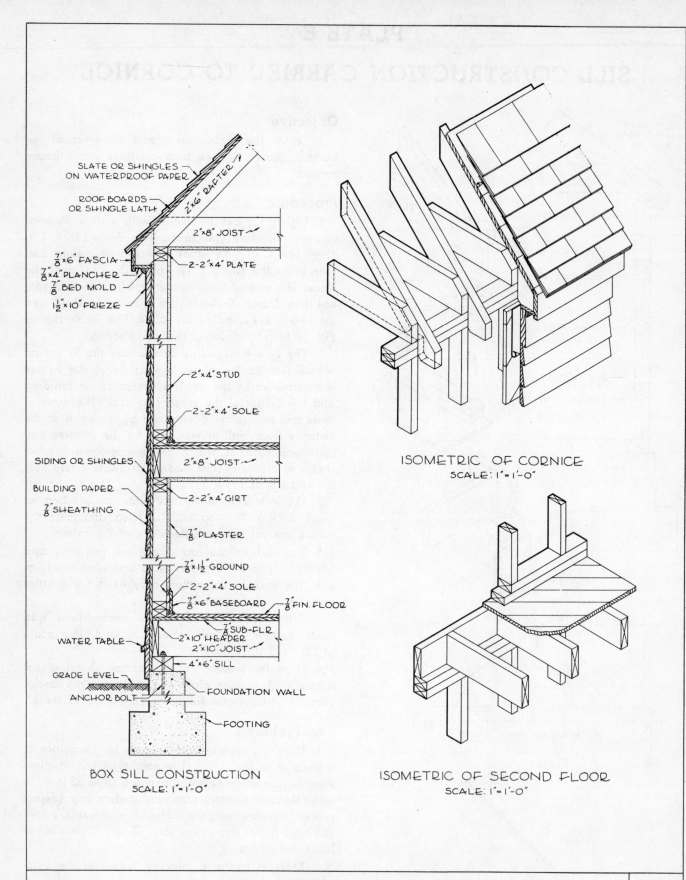

SLATE OR SHINGLES
ON WATERPROOF PAPER

ROOF BOARDS
OR SHINGLE LATH

$2"\times6"$ RAFTER

$2"\times8"$ JOIST

$\frac{7}{8}"\times6"$ FASCIA

2-$2"\times4"$ PLATE

$\frac{7}{8}"\times4"$ PLANCHER

$\frac{7}{8}"$ BED MOLD

$1\frac{1}{2}"\times10"$ FRIEZE

$2"\times4"$ STUD

2-$2"\times4"$ SOLE

SIDING OR SHINGLES

$2"\times8"$ JOIST

BUILDING PAPER

2-$2"\times4"$ GIRT

$\frac{7}{8}"$ SHEATHING

$\frac{7}{8}"$ PLASTER

$\frac{7}{8}"\times1\frac{1}{2}"$ GROUND

2-$2"\times4"$ SOLE

$\frac{7}{8}"\times6"$ BASEBOARD

$\frac{7}{8}"$ FIN. FLOOR

$\frac{7}{8}"$ SUB-FLR.

$2"\times10"$ HEADER

$2"\times10"$ JOIST

WATER TABLE

$4"\times6"$ SILL

GRADE LEVEL

FOUNDATION WALL

ANCHOR BOLT

FOOTING

BOX SILL CONSTRUCTION
SCALE: $1"=1'-0"$

ISOMETRIC OF CORNICE
SCALE: $1"=1'-0"$

ISOMETRIC OF SECOND FLOOR
SCALE: $1"=1'-0"$

SILL CARRIED TO CORNICE

6

[18]

The Window

Until recent years, the window was little more than a glazed opening in a wall for the main purpose of admitting light and air.

In cities, where many houses were built so close together, windows in adjacent buildings served mostly for ventilation. Certainly a window was not one of the outstanding architectural features of a room.

But today the role of the window is somewhat different. New ideas of living, new methods of heating, new materials, and new decorating techniques are among the factors which have brought forth a "New Look" in windows.

Following are some of the more common types of windows used:

Casement Window. A single window unit hinged at the side to open outward (Fig. 20a).

Double-Glazed Window. A patented window glass consisting of two layers of plate glass separated by an air space, and sealed around all sides to keep out moisture and dust. This glass permits large window areas of low heat loss.

Combination Sash. An additional exterior frame equipped with interchangeable glass- or wire screened panels, serving as a storm window in winter and a screen in the summer.

Picture Window. A large glass area, with part or all of its sash fixed, used to furnish an unobstructed view, and also to admit sunshine and light.

APPLICATION OF MODERN CASEMENT-TYPE STEEL SASH WINDOWS TO KITCHEN

Fig. 20a

Fig. 20b

A picture window of the casement type. Center sash fixed, end sash moveable. Each glass square is called a "light."

[19]

Residential Windows

Two types of residential windows are the casement (Fig. 20b), and double-hung.

Although there are many styles of each type, depending on the size and arrangement of the glass lights, all can be classified as either casement or double-hung. The term double-hung refers to the common type window with upper and lower sash, both movable. Both casement and double-hung windows are available in either wood or metal construction. Steel, and lately aluminum, are the most practical metal materials.

The architect or draftsman does not generally design the window, but selects the desired style and size from manufacturer's data. It is necessary, however, to indicate on the plans the location and sizes of sash openings.

The important task at this time, is to understand the detail construction of the window and the wall that receives it.

The following pages will describe the rough opening, the window frame that fits into it, and the sash that is set into the frame (Fig. 20c).

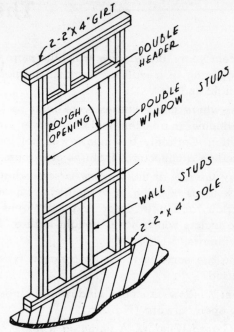

ROUGH FRAME OPENING FOR DOUBLE HUNG WINDOW

Fig. 20d

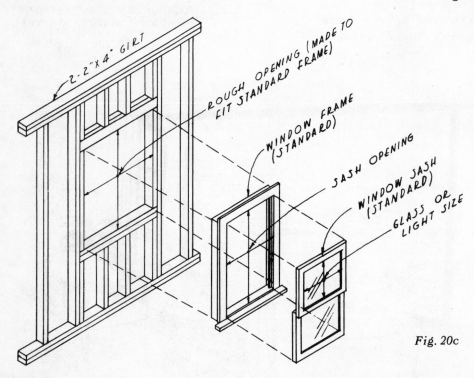

Fig. 20c

Rough Opening

The framing for window openings (Fig. 20d) in good construction must have double 2- x 4-in. window studs, double 2- x 4-in. header, and double 2- x 4-in. sill. Then 2- x 4-in. wall studs are nailed between the double sill and sole plate to support the sill. The distance between the inner faces of the window studs, the inner faces of the header and the sill, is called the

"rough opening."

Notice that the 2- x 4-in. members in the header are placed on their 2- in. dimensions, to give maximum stiffness in supporting the weight of the framework above. For larger openings, the headers may be 2- x 6-in., 2- x 8-in., 2- x 10-in., or 2- x 12-in. members. This is not necessary at the sill, since the only weight it supports is the weight of the window.

Residential Double-Hung Wood Windows

The following chart shows stock sizes of double-hung wood windows for residential use. The width and height of the glass pane is indicated by numbers such as 16/20, 20/12, and so forth.

The width of the sash and the rough opening are given across the top of the chart, while the height of the sash and the rough opening is given along the left side of the chart. For example, the window in the upper right corner has a glass pane 28 in. wide and 12 in. high, a sash 2 ft. 8 in. wide by 2 ft. 6 in. high, and requires a rough opening 3 ft. 2 in. wide by 2 ft. 9⅝ in. high.

Window Frame

Window frames are shop assembled and may be

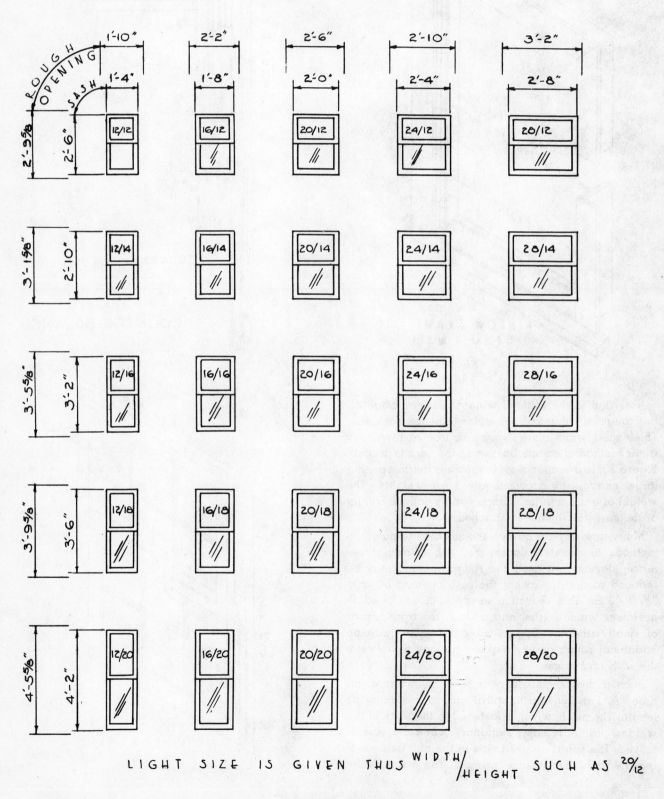

LIGHT SIZE IS GIVEN THUS WIDTH/HEIGHT SUCH AS 20/12

[21]

purchased ready made from the mill or dealer. The frame consists of the casing, the stool, and parting strip. The sides of the casing are known as pulley styles (Fig. 20e).

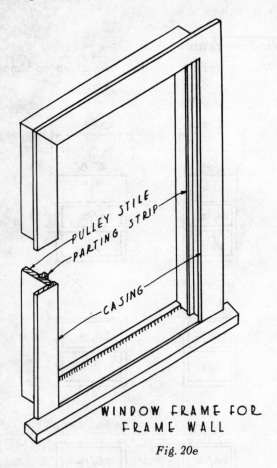

PULLEY STILE
PARTING STRIP
CASING

WINDOW FRAME FOR FRAME WALL

Fig. 20e

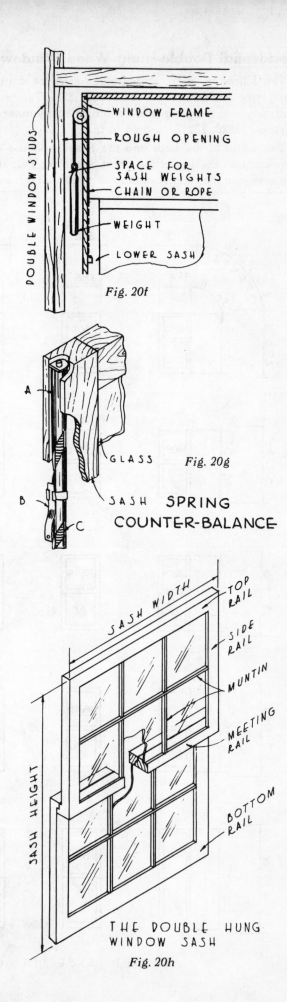

DOUBLE WINDOW STUDS

WINDOW FRAME
ROUGH OPENING
SPACE FOR SASH WEIGHTS
CHAIN OR ROPE
WEIGHT
LOWER SASH

Fig. 20f

A
GLASS   *Fig. 20g*
B
C   SASH   SPRING
COUNTER-BALANCE

SASH WIDTH
TOP RAIL
SIDE RAIL
MUNTIN
MEETING RAIL
SASH HEIGHT
BOTTOM RAIL

THE DOUBLE HUNG WINDOW SASH

Fig. 20h

Note that in the table of window sizes on page 21, the rough opening is 6 in. wider than the sash size. This excess width allows space for iron sash weights if this method of counterbalancing the sash is desired. Figure 20f is a sectional view showing rough opening large enough to accommodate sash weights. The weight of each counterbalance equals half the weight of the sash to which it is attached.

Many new devices now on the market use patented methods to counterbalance the sash. Where these newer devices are used, the rough opening may be reduced so that it exceeds the sash opening by only 2¼ to 3 in. This reduction in space makes possible narrower window trim, and adds to the appearance of small windows. Some sash balances require no additional rough opening space, as they fit between the sash and frame.

Such a device consists of a ⅝-in. diameter metal tube (A, Fig. 20g), with spiral groove cut along its length. The nut B, which is fastened to the track of the window frame, remains stationary when the sash is moved. The spiral groove twists in the nut, thus winding the preloaded torsion spring C. The action of the spring causes the window sash to remain in any position in which it is placed.

Window Sash

The double-hung window, Fig. 20h, is made up of an upper and a lower sash. The top rail and side rails, for both upper and lower sashes are generally 1⅜ in. thick and 2 in. wide, whereas the bottom rail is 1⅜ in. thick and 3 in. high. The wood strips which separate the glass panes are called "muntins." The window

ADDITIONAL WINDOW DATA
RESIDENTIAL DOUBLE-HUNG STEEL WINDOWS

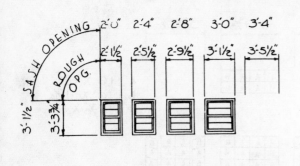

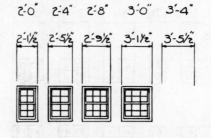

HORIZONTAL MUNTINS   HORIZONTAL & VERTICAL MUNTINS

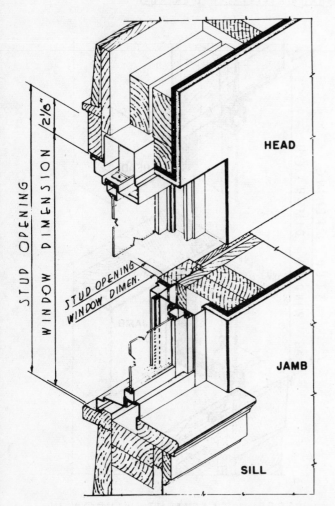

STEEL DOUBLE HUNG WINDOW
IN FRAME WALL CONSTRUCTION

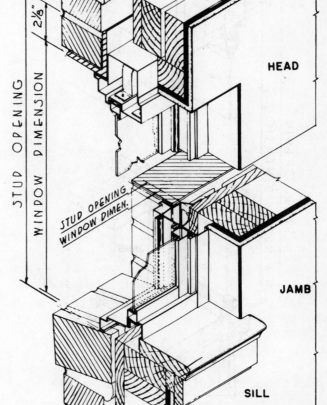

STEEL DOUBLE HUNG WINDOW
IN BRICK VENEER CONSTRUCTION

shown here is a 12-light window because it has 12 panes of glass. When we speak of the sash width and the sash height, we mean the distance between the outer faces of the side rails, and the outer faces of the top and bottom rails.

The frame opening is usually ⅛ in. wider and ⅟₁₆ in. higher than the actual sash dimensions. This clearance is necessary to allow the sash to slide freely in its track. However, a disadvantage of such clearance is that it allows cold air to infiltrate, and consequently some form of weather stripping should be used.

RESIDENTIAL CASEMENT-TYPE STEEL WINDOWS

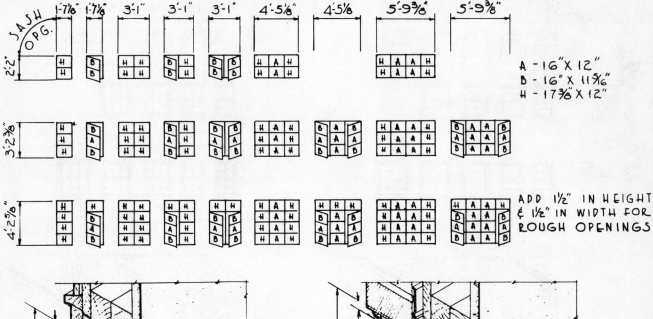

A - 16" X 12"
B - 16" X 11⅝₁₆"
H - 17⅜ X 12"

ADD 1½" IN HEIGHT
& 1½" IN WIDTH FOR
ROUGH OPENINGS

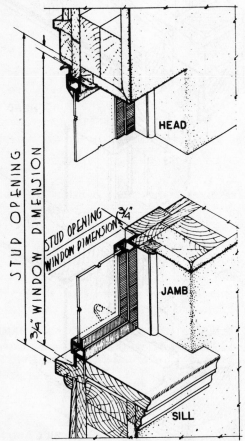

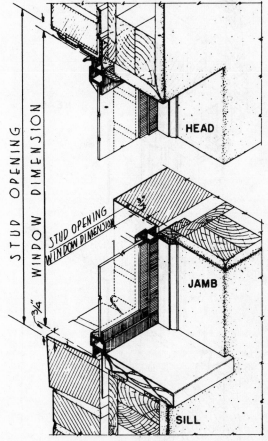

STEEL CASEMENT WINDOW
IN FRAME WALL CONSTRUCTION

STEEL CASEMENT WINDOW IN
BRICK VENEER WALL CONSTRUCTION

[24]

PLATE 7
THE DOUBLE-HUNG WINDOW

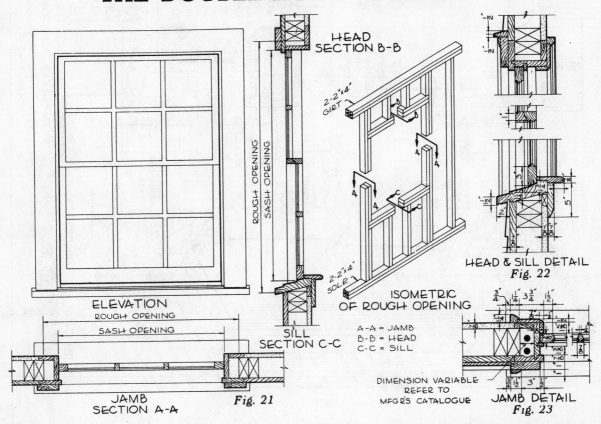

ELEVATION
ROUGH OPENING
SASH OPENING

JAMB SECTION A-A   Fig. 21

HEAD SECTION B-B

SILL SECTION C-C

ISOMETRIC OF ROUGH OPENING

A-A = JAMB
B-B = HEAD
C-C = SILL

HEAD & SILL DETAIL
Fig. 22

DIMENSION VARIABLE REFER TO MFG'R'S CATALOGUE

JAMB DETAIL
Fig. 23

Objective

To learn the construction and material sizes employed in drawing a double-hung stock window for a frame wall and a brick wall.

Procedure

1. Select the rough opening size from manufacturer's data (refer to table of stock widths and heights for double-hung windows) and draw the double 2- x 4-in. studs shown in section *A-A*, called the *jamb*, and the double 2 x 4's shown in sections *B-B* and *C-C* called the *head* and *sill* (Fig. 21).

2. Draw the width and height of the sash, dimensions of which can also be obtained from the manufacturer's specifications.

3. The 7/8-in. sheathing and plaster, the trim, may next be drawn including inside and outside casing. For dimensions of trim refer to Fig. 22, Head and Sill Detail, and to Fig. 23, Jamb Detail.

4. From sections *A-A*, *B-B*, and *C-C*, Fig. 21, project and complete the exterior elevation of the window.

5. Draw the exterior elevation of the double-hung window in the frame wall and in the brick wall as represented on ¼-in. scale drawings with their plan symbols at a scale of ½ in. = 1 ft. (Plate 7).

6. In drawing the details of the double-hung window in the brick wall (Plate 7), the procedure is somewhat different from the frame detail. The thickness of the wall into which the window is to be drawn must be given the first consideration. The stone sill and wall in the sill section are drawn first, then the wood sill, stool, furring strips, and plaster.

7. The jamb section of the window for the brick wall is similar to the frame construction with the exception that a back lining is used. This lining boxes in the sash weights and prevents particles of mortar from falling into the sash-weight box when the brick wall is erected. Steel angles are employed in the head section spanning the brick opening used to support the brickwork above. Next draw the top rail, side rail, and bottom rail.

8. In order better to visualize and understand the double-hung window in the brick wall, draw the isometric of the window from the sections shown on Plate 7. Use scale 1½ in. = 1 ft.

Test Problems

1. Draw the jamb section of a double-hung window for a brick wall and a frame wall. Use scale of 1½ in. = 1 ft. Point out the differences.

2. To a scale of ½ full size, draw the meeting rail and muntin of a double-hung window.

[25]

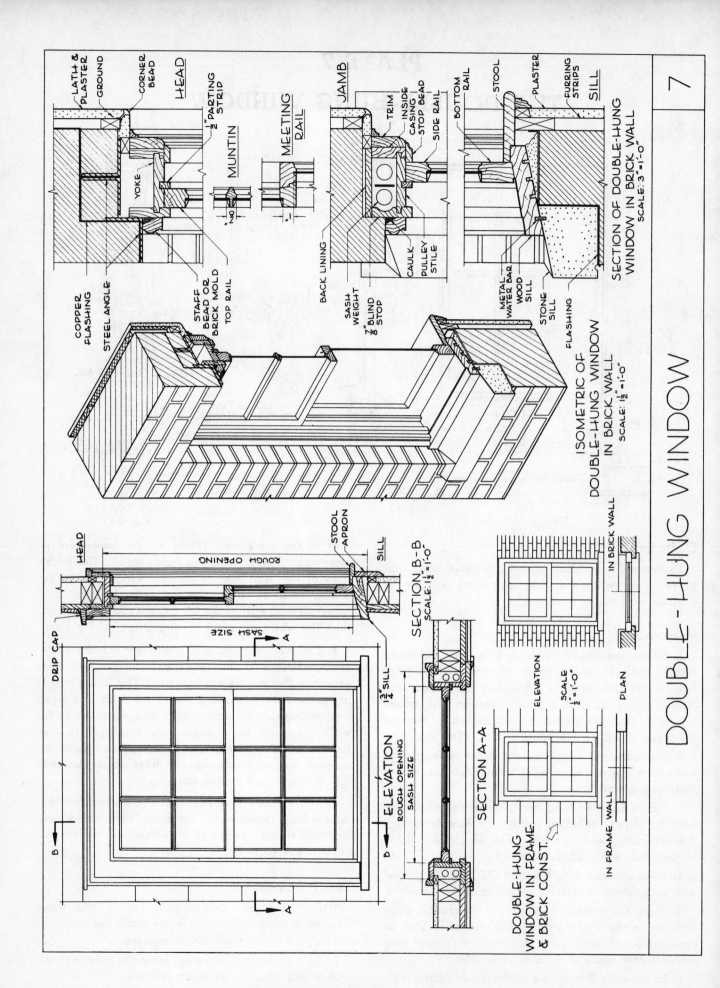

HEAD

LATH & PLASTER
GROUND
CORNER BEAD
½" PARTING STRIP
MUNTIN
YOKE

MEETING RAIL

JAMB

TRIM
INSIDE CASING
STOP BEAD
SIDE RAIL
BACK LINING
SASH WEIGHT
⅞" BLIND STOP
CAULK
PULLEY STILE

SILL

STOOL
PLASTER
FURRING STRIPS
BOTTOM RAIL
METAL WATER BAR
WOOD SILL
STONE SILL
FLASHING

SECTION OF DOUBLE-HUNG WINDOW IN BRICK WALL
SCALE: 3"=1'-0"

COPPER FLASHING
STEEL ANGLE
STAFF BEAD OR BRICK MOLD
TOP RAIL

ISOMETRIC OF DOUBLE-HUNG WINDOW IN BRICK WALL
SCALE: 1½"=1'-0"

HEAD
DRIP CAP
ROUGH OPENING
SASH SIZE
STOOL
APRON
SILL

SECTION B-B
SCALE: 1½"=1'-0"

1¾" SILL

ELEVATION
ROUGH OPENING
SASH SIZE

B
A
A
B

SECTION A-A

DOUBLE-HUNG WINDOW IN FRAME & BRICK CONST.

IN BRICK WALL

ELEVATION

SCALE
1½"=1'-0"

PLAN

IN FRAME WALL

DOUBLE-HUNG WINDOW

7

The Door

THERE IS A CORRECT ENTRANCE DOOR FOR EACH TYPE OF HOUSE

The door, like the window, plays an important role in architectural design. The character of the entire house is exemplified by an entrance door of correct design. A Tudor door, for instance, should not be used on a colonial-type house, nor a colonial door on a ranch-type home. The selection of the proper type of entrance door is perhaps a more difficult task than the selection of windows. Fortunately the student is again aided by the manufacturers, who list dozens of different stock door treatments in their catalogues.

Not only are entrance doors predesigned and stocked at the various mills, but also a wide variety of interior doors, special closet doors, and garage doors are available.

Many new and interesting developments have appeared in the last few years. Among these are new lightweight built-up doors for interior use. Such a door consists of a honeycomb, cellular center, with plywood glued to each side (Fig. 23a).

Also a new type of sliding door, which comes in two overlapping sections, is popular for use in closets. No valuable floor space is wasted as with a conventional swinging door. Special wall width is not required either, since the sections overlap, and do not disappear in the wall.

Garage doors have also shown a marked improvement in design. The trend today is toward a horizontally sectioned door with hinges between each two

sections. The action is overhead, with the door raised either manually or by automatic means.

The materials most used for wood doors are Douglas fir and Ponderoso pine. These western woods are cut from the heartwood of big trees. Each piece of wood is select quality, straight grained, and free from excessive sap. In the honeycomb type of door, the interior structure is made of special fiber material or wood. The outside layer may be of any type of veneer desired.

Metal doors are not used extensively in residential structures, although many types and styles are found in public buildings and in commercial and industrial uses. A metal-clad wood door, however, is used where a fireproof door is called for. Such a door is called a "kalamein" door, and is used as a fireproof entrance door between the house and an adjacent garage.

All-glass doors are available for residential use, but are not used in small homes of conventional design.

What the Student Does

Here again, as with the window, the student does not design the door. He selects it from the various trade catalogues. A standard stock frame is likewise ordered to fit the over-all size of the door. The task for the student then is to show the properly framed rough opening in the wall. The views in Fig. 23b show how the door, frame, and rough opening are related.

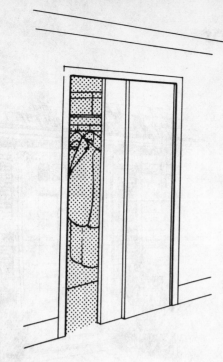

SLIDING OVERLAPPING
CLOSET DOORS

HONEYCOMB DOOR HAVING
LIGHTWEIGHT AND GREAT
STRENGTH

Fig. 23a

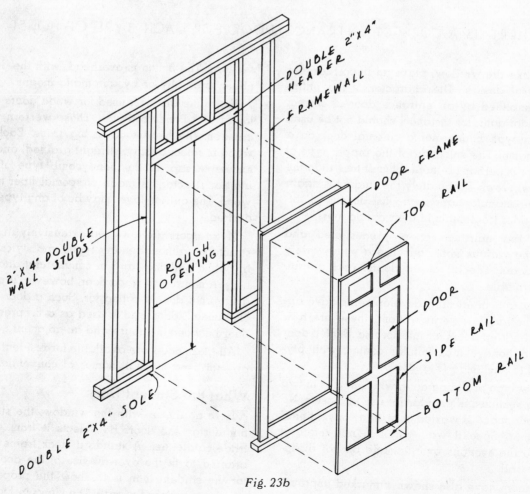

DOUBLE 2"x4"
HEADER

FRAMEWALL

DOOR FRAME

TOP RAIL

2"x4" DOUBLE
WALL STUDS

ROUGH OPENING

DOOR

SIDE RAIL

BOTTOM RAIL

DOUBLE 2"x4" SOLE

Fig. 23b

The frame is usually ⅛ in. larger than the door size, and the rough opening is made about ½ in. larger all around than the frame. This clearance permits adjustment of the frame to align it to a perfectly vertical position. Note the similarity in Fig. 23b between the rough opening framing for the door and the window. An interior door is framed in a similar manner.

The Various Sections

In order to show the construction of the framing members, door frame, and door, and how the parts fit together, sections are viewed at A-A, B-B, and C-C (Fig. 23c). This method is similar to the method used in detailing the three window sections.

Section A-A shows the construction through the head of the framing. Section B-B shows the jamb construction, and C-C shows the sill construction.

The drawing at the right is minus the frame and door, as it is intended to show just where, on the rough opening, the completed sections are taken.

Interior doors are framed exactly the same as exterior doors, except for the sill section.

All frame structures, regardless of the exterior treatment, have their door openings framed in the same way. Where brick veneer is used, it is necessary to use a deeper door frame to allow for the extra wall thickness.

The rough opening in masonry walls, such as solid brick or concrete block, is measured from the bare block. In masonry construction a lintel must be used across the opening to support the material above.

A lintel is generally an angle iron, which bears on each end for a length of 4 in. The angle iron forms a shelf on which the brick can be placed above the opening. Common sizes of lintel angles are 3 x 3 in., and 3 x 4 in., by $\frac{5}{16}$ in. thick, for the brick-veneer construction, and two 3- x 4-in. angles used back to back for concrete-block construction.

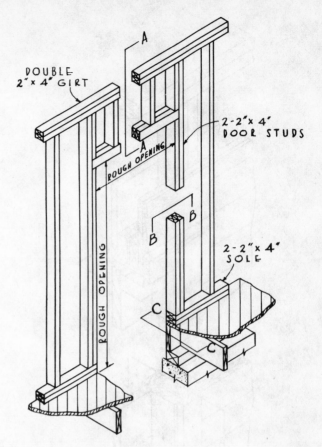

THIS DRAWING SHOWS WHERE TYPICAL DOOR SECTIONS ARE DRAWN.

Fig. 23c

The Exterior Door Sections

On page 30 are shown the three typical door sections for an entrance door in wood-frame construction.

The pictorial at the left shows a cutaway of the head, jamb, and sill sections. At the right each section is separately shown in detail. Study the sections and compare each part with the pictorial.

Questions and Answers Relating to Plate 8

Before beginning to draw Plate 8, the construction of the door, study the following questions and answers carefully.

1. *Do you think an entrance door of this design would be suitable for a ranch-type home? Why?*

   No. This door has a classical appearance, typical of the dignity of a southern colonial home.

2. *Are the two upper rectangles in the door glass lights or wood panels? How can you tell?*

They are glass lights. We can tell this because in the sectional view they are not shown with a wood symbol. Two lines, close together, is the symbol used for glass. Some draftsmen fill in the space with solid black.

3. *What are the width, height, and thickness of the door?*

   3 ft. 0 in., 7 ft. 0 in., 1¾ in.

4. *In the left vertical section, why does the manufacturer show 2 rough opening dimensions?*

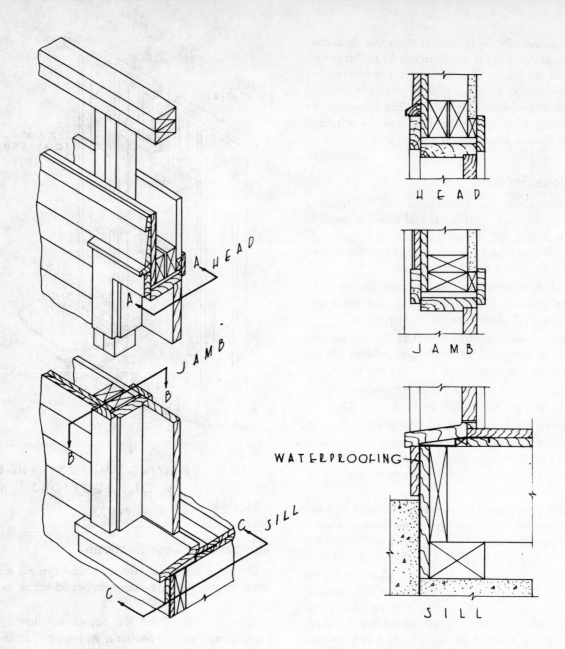

H E A D

J A M B

WATERPROOFING

S I L L

To allow for 2 available stock door heights.

5. *What are side lights?*

Glass panels flanking the door to permit light to entrance hall.

6. *Why are the side lights of different design?*

The manufacturer wishes to show different designs available.

7. *Are the panels directly below the side lights glass or wood? How are they constructed?*

Wood, as shown in the section of the solid brick construction. Note panel is double, the side light rests on a sill above the panels.

8. *In the plan section, directly below the elevation, why is the left 10-in. panel shown differently from the right 10-in. panel?*

The left panel shows glass; therefore it is a section taken through the side light, whereas the right panel shows a section taken through the wood panel below the side light.

9. *Does the door, as shown, open in, or out?*

The door opens in. The door stops along the jamb would prevent it from opening out. Although inward-opening doors are permissible in residential construction, they cannot be used in public buildings, because of fire regulations.

10. *Why is one-half the door shown set in wood fram-*

ing with wood siding, and the other half in brick-veneer wall?

The manufacturer wishes to show that the door is adaptable to both types of construction.

11. The sectional details and plan at the right side of the drawing show the door set in what type of wall construction?

Solid brick.

12. What is the purpose of the blocking shown in the plan section at the right of the drawing?

To act as nailing base for trim.

13. In the frame section at the left, is the double 2- x 4-in. header above the transom shown correctly?

No. It is better practice to place the 2 x 4's on their 2-in. side.

14. What type of foundation sill construction is shown in the frame and in the brick-veneer sections?

Box sill.

Note: Have you been able to "read" Plate 8 successfully? Reading a drawing is known as blueprint reading—a most important part of your training.

GARAGE DOOR (8'-0" WIDE 7'-0" HIGH)

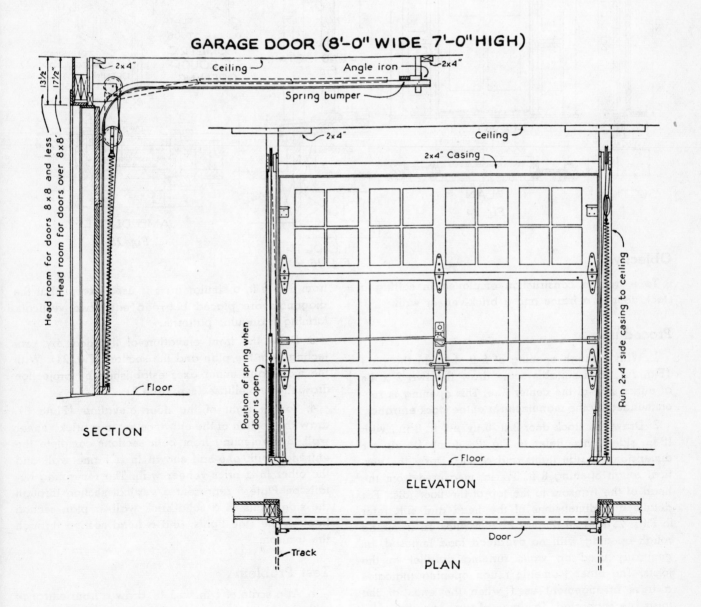

PLATE 8
MAIN ENTRANCE DOOR

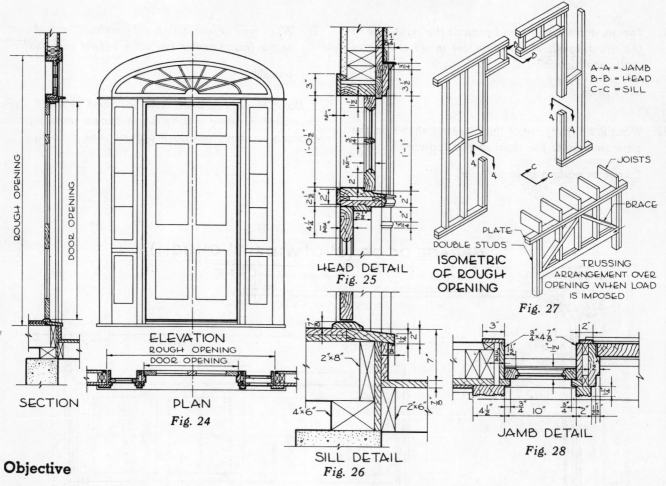

ELEVATION
ROUGH OPENING
DOOR OPENING

SECTION

PLAN
Fig. 24

HEAD DETAIL
Fig. 25

ISOMETRIC
OF ROUGH
OPENING

A-A = JAMB
B-B = HEAD
C-C = SILL

JOISTS

BRACE

PLATE
DOUBLE STUDS

TRUSSING
ARRANGEMENT OVER
OPENING WHEN LOAD
IS IMPOSED

Fig. 27

SILL DETAIL
Fig. 26

JAMB DETAIL
Fig. 28

Objective

To learn the construction employed in setting a stock door in a frame and a brick-veneer wall.

Procedure

1. With a rough opening of 5 ft. 4 in. in the plan (Fig. 24), to a suitable scale draw the two 2 x 4's at either side of the center line. This opening is recommended by the manufacturer of the stock entrance.

2. Draw the stock door 3 ft. 0 in. x 6 ft. 8 in., with 10-in. side lights. Refer to Fig. 28, Jamb Detail, for dimensions of side lights and casing. Draw the vertical rough opening 8 ft. 3¼ in. measured from the head of the transom to the top of the floor joist. For details and dimensions of the head and sill, refer to Figs. 25 and 26. Figure 27 illustrates an isometric rough opening with no overhead load imposed, as generally used on walls running parallel to the joists. The other isometric rough opening indicates a truss arrangement used when the ends of the joists are supported. This type of truss is suitable for the weight over small openings. For openings ranging

from 3 to 6 ft. a similar truss is used except that the diagonals are placed between each two verticals, forming triangular patterns.

3. Draw the front elevation of the door by projecting from the plan and the section (Fig. 24). With the major and minor axes established by projection draw the semiellipse (see Plate 3).

4. To the right of the door elevation (Plate 8), draw the section of the entrance set in a brick-veneer wall. By projecting from both sections complete the entrance with one-half shown in a frame wall and the other in a brick-veneer wall. The remaining details on Plate 8 represent a vertical section through the side lights in a solid-brick wall, a plan section through the side lights, and a head section through the transom.

Test Problem

1. At a scale of 1 in. = 1 ft., draw a front entrance without side lights in a brick-veneer wall with frame backing.

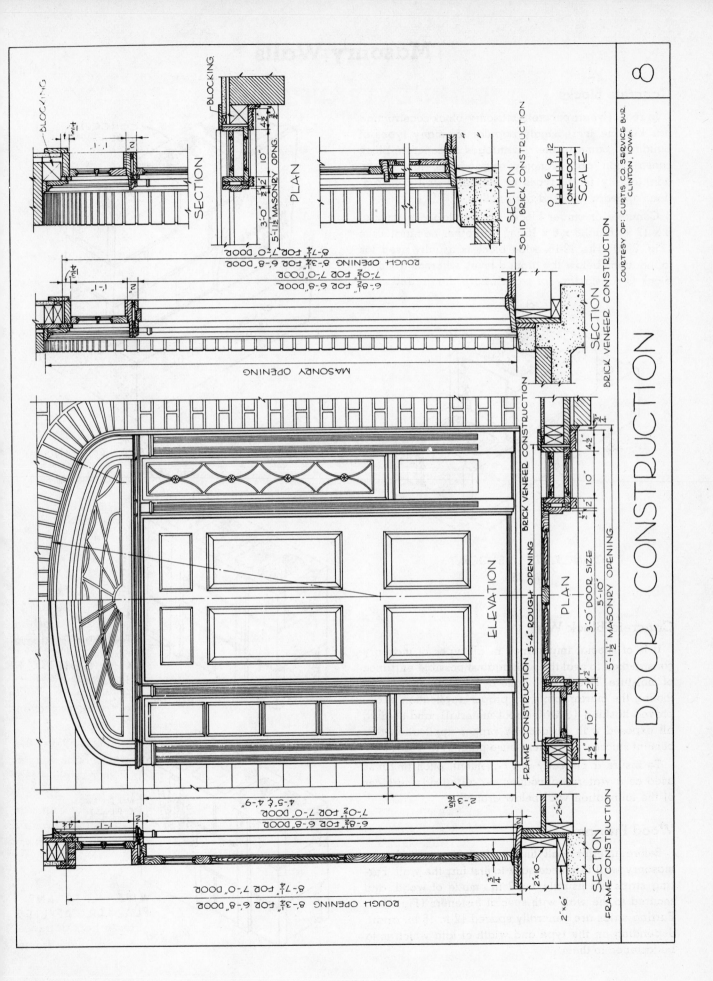

DOOR CONSTRUCTION

BLOCKING

SECTION

BLOCKING

PLAN

3'-0"
5'-11½" MASONRY OPENG.

SECTION
SOLID BRICK CONSTRUCTION

COURTESY OF: CURTIS CO. SERVICE BUR.
CLINTON, IOWA.

8

SCALE
ONE FOOT
0 3 6 9 12

ROUGH OPENING 8'-7¾" FOR 7'-0" DOOR
8'-7¾" FOR 7'-0" DOOR
7'-0¼" FOR 7'-0" DOOR
6'-8¼" FOR 6'-8" DOOR

MASONRY OPENING

SECTION
BRICK VENEER CONSTRUCTION

ELEVATION

BRICK VENEER CONSTRUCTION 5'-4" ROUGH OPENING

PLAN

3'-0" DOOR SIZE
5'-10"
5'-11½" MASONRY OPENING

FRAME CONSTRUCTION 5'-4" ROUGH OPENING

6'-8¼" FOR 6'-8" DOOR
7'-0¼" FOR 7'-0" DOOR
4'-5¾" 4'-9"
2'-3"

ROUGH OPENING 8'-7¾" FOR 6'-8" DOOR
8'-7¾" FOR 7'-0" DOOR

SECTION
FRAME CONSTRUCTION

2'x6"
2'x10"
2'-6"

Masonry Walls

Concrete Blocks

In recent years concrete-masonry-block construction has become increasingly popular for many types of buildings. Some of the advantages of concrete-block construction are economy, ruggedness, fire safety, adaptability to all types of masonry wall construction, appearance, and availability.

Concrete or cinder blocks are available in sizes of 8 x 12 x 16 in., 8 x 8 x 16 in., and other nominal sizes (Fig. 28a). The 12-in. wide block is usually used for foundations below the ground level, whereas the 8-in. block is satisfactory for walls above the ground.

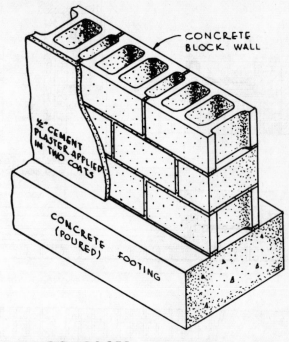

CONCRETE BLOCK WALL
ON POURED CONCRETE FOOTING
Fig. 28b

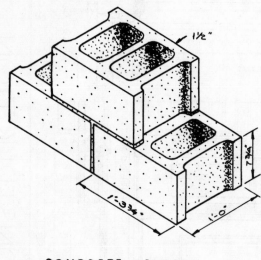

CONCRETE BLOCKS
Fig. 28a

Concrete-Block Wall

It is of special importance in all types of masonry construction to seal the wall against possible entrance of moisture. This can be done by carefully filling and tooling the mortar joints, by proper application of approved flashing (a waterproof material), and sealing all exposed wall surfaces by proper application of a cement stucco or a cement-base paint (Fig. 28b).

To insure a perfectly dry basement, pitch or tar is used as a waterproof coating on all outside surfaces of the foundation wall below ground.

Wood Furring

Before interior wall finishes can be applied to a masonry wall it is necessary to first furr the wall. Furring strips are usually 1 x 2 in., made of wood, and secured to the wall with special fasteners (Fig. 28c). Furring strips are generally spaced 12 to 16 in. apart, depending on the type and width of lath which is to be fastened to them.

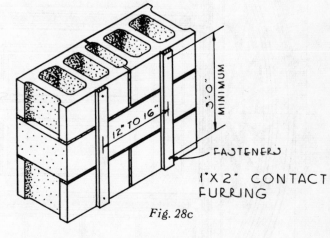

1" X 2" CONTACT FURRING
Fig. 28c

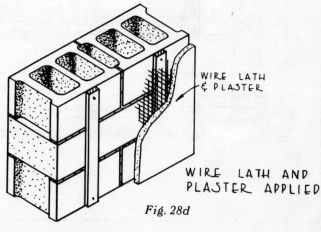

WIRE LATH AND PLASTER APPLIED
Fig. 28d

When wire lath or rock lath is applied to the furring strips, the 1-in. space between the lath and the wall may be used to accommodate insulation (Fig. 28d).

The term "contact furring" implies that the furring strips are fastened to the wall. Sometimes, however, an entire wall may be supported by furring strips not in contact with the wall to provide space for plumbing, heating, or electric conduits. In this case furring strips may be as large as 2- x 3-in. or 2- x 4-in. studs.

For basement walls below grade it is sometimes desirable to add 1- x 2-in. cross-furring strips on which the lath or other finish material is applied (Fig 28e).

The extra space between the wall and the finish material will allow moisture, if any, to dry out more readily.

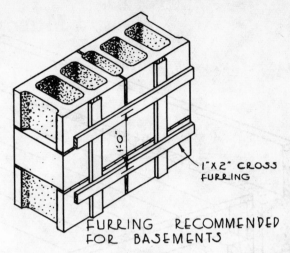

FURRING RECOMMENDED FOR BASEMENTS

Fig. 28e

Concrete Floor Slabs

In good construction, concrete floor slabs are poured on cinder or gravel fill, wetted, and well tamped. A layer of roofing felt or waterproofed fabric, applied to the top of the fill and mopped with tar, provides a moisture barrier between ground and slab (Fig. 28f).

Expansion and Contraction

A variation in temperature will cause masonry walls and floor slabs to expand and contract; consequently expansion joints are required to accommodate the resulting change in dimensions. Built-up stresses in the wall are likely to cause cracking around openings, or where walls abut, or where story heights change, unless adequate provision is made for proper bonding of walls. A steel reinforced belt course is sometimes used for this purpose extending around the building, especially in long walls.

Where the concrete floor slab meets the foundation wall a tar joint is used to prevent seepage of moisture and provide for expansion (Fig. 28g).

Another method of making a tight joint is to force beveled siding, well oiled or soaped, between the floor slab and the wall.

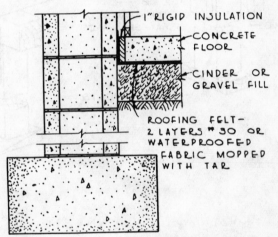

SECTION OF FOUNDATION WITH CONCRETE FLOOR ON CINDER FILL

Fig. 28f

Form Work for Concrete Slab

Form work required to cast reinforced concrete slabs not on the ground is constructed as shown in Fig. 28h. The 2- x 8-in. plank forms the edge of the slab.

A mesh of steel reinforcing bars is set 1 in. above the platform before the concrete is poured. The entire floor consists of several such units bonded together by reinforcing rods.

Figure 28i shows the concrete slab section after the forms have been removed.

Wood Flooring on Concrete Slab

Wood sleepers are embedded in the concrete with

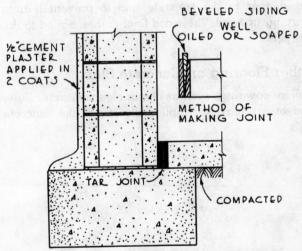

SECTION OF FOUNDATION SHOWING TAR JOINT BETWEEN FOUNDATION FLOOR & BASEMENT WALL

Fig. 28g

[35]

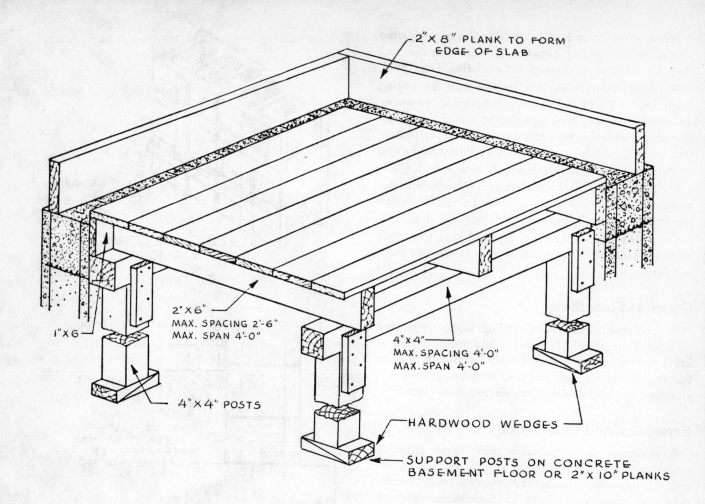

2" X 8" PLANK TO FORM
EDGE OF SLAB

2" X 6"
MAX. SPACING 2'-6"
MAX. SPAN 4'-0"

1" X 6

4" X 4"
MAX. SPACING 4'-0"
MAX. SPAN 4'-0"

4" X 4" POSTS

HARDWOOD WEDGES

SUPPORT POSTS ON CONCRETE
BASEMENT FLOOR OR 2" X 10" PLANKS

Fig. 28h

their upper surfaces projecting slightly above the slab (Fig. 28j). One side of each sleeper is beveled so that the base is wider than the top. This serves to anchor the sleeper to the concrete and to prevent it from warping upward. The wood floor is then nailed to the sleepers.

Other Flooring on Concrete Slab

Floor coverings such as tile, linoleum, marble, slate, and others may be applied directly to the concrete slab.

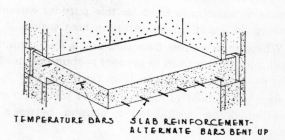

TEMPERATURE BARS   SLAB REINFORCEMENT—
ALTERNATE BARS BENT UP

Fig. 28i

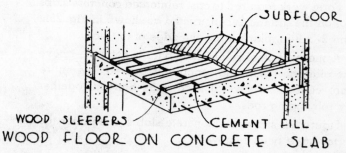

SUBFLOOR

WOOD SLEEPERS   CEMENT FILL
WOOD FLOOR ON CONCRETE SLAB

Fig. 28j

[36]

Complete Veneer Section with Concrete-Block Backing

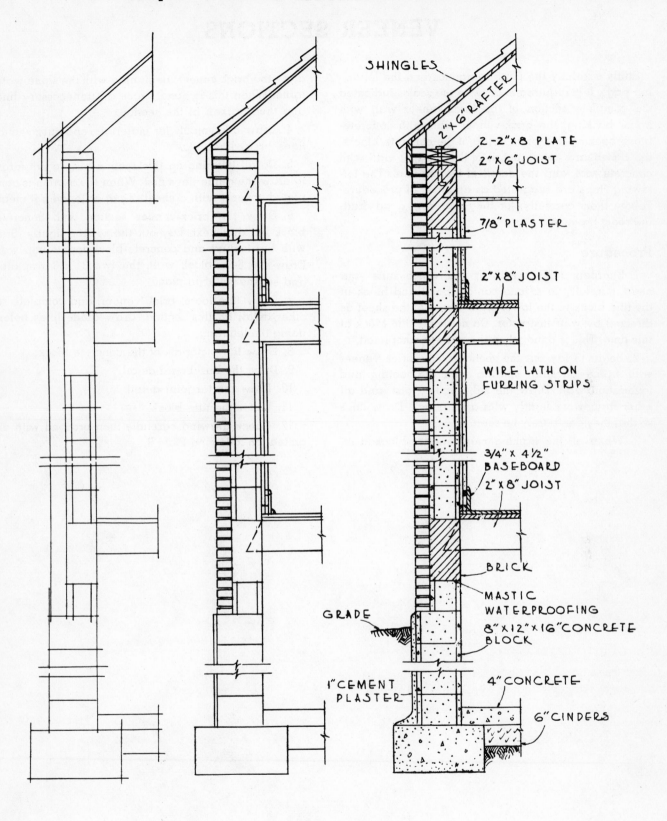

SHINGLES

2"X6"RAFTER

2-2"X8 PLATE

2"X6"JOIST

7/8"PLASTER

2"X8"JOIST

WIRE LATH ON FURRING STRIPS

3/4" X 4½" BASEBOARD

2"X8"JOIST

BRICK

MASTIC WATERPROOFING

8"X12"X16"CONCRETE BLOCK

GRADE

4"CONCRETE

1"CEMENT PLASTER

6"CINDERS

The above represents the three steps in drawing the complete brick-veneer wall section with concrete-block backing. Note the use of brick where joists enter wall.

1. Lightly block in the structural members.
2. Erase unnecessary lines and darken in outline.
3. Indicate sectioned material by its symbols. Complete all lettering. Draw guide lines before lettering.

PLATE 9
VENEER SECTIONS

Study carefully the plate reproduced on the following page. It is required to draw to the scales indicated the complete section of the brick-veneer wall with frame backing, the brick-veneer wall with concrete-block backing, the brick detail of the concrete blocks, the baseboard detail, detail of the parapet wall with concrete roof, and the detail of the tar joint. The following steps are suggested as an order of procedure. Follow them carefully, for they represent good drafting room practice.

Procedure

1. Sharpen a 2H pencil, or one which suits your need, carefully to a long conical point and block in the title block in the lower right corner of the sheet as directed by your instructor. Do not letter title block at this time. This is done when the plate is completed.

2. Begin to lay out the section of the brick veneer with frame backing, starting with the footing and foundation wall. Draw the sill, header, joist, and all other framework lightly with a 2H pencil. Draw lines so that they can barely be seen.

3. When all the framing members are blocked in, draw the brick veneer, beginning with the stone water table. When this is done, erase all unnecessary lines and then darken in the section.

4. Draw all symbols for materials, end cuts, section lines, break lines, etc.

5. Do all lettering on this section but do not forget to draw the guide lines first. When the section is completed cover it with a sheet of paper to keep it clean.

6. Draw the brick-veneer section with concrete-block backing next. Lay out the section lightly. Start with the footing and concrete-block foundation wall. Draw the 8-in. block wall, the two 2- x 8-in. plates, and set the rafter in place.

7. Draw the floors, brick veneer, and complete all other detail on this section. Draw guide lines before doing the lettering.

8. Draw the pictorials of the concrete blocks.

9. Draw the baseboard detail.

10. Draw the tar joint detail.

11. Letter the title block.

12. Check drawing carefully then proceed with examination following Plate 9.

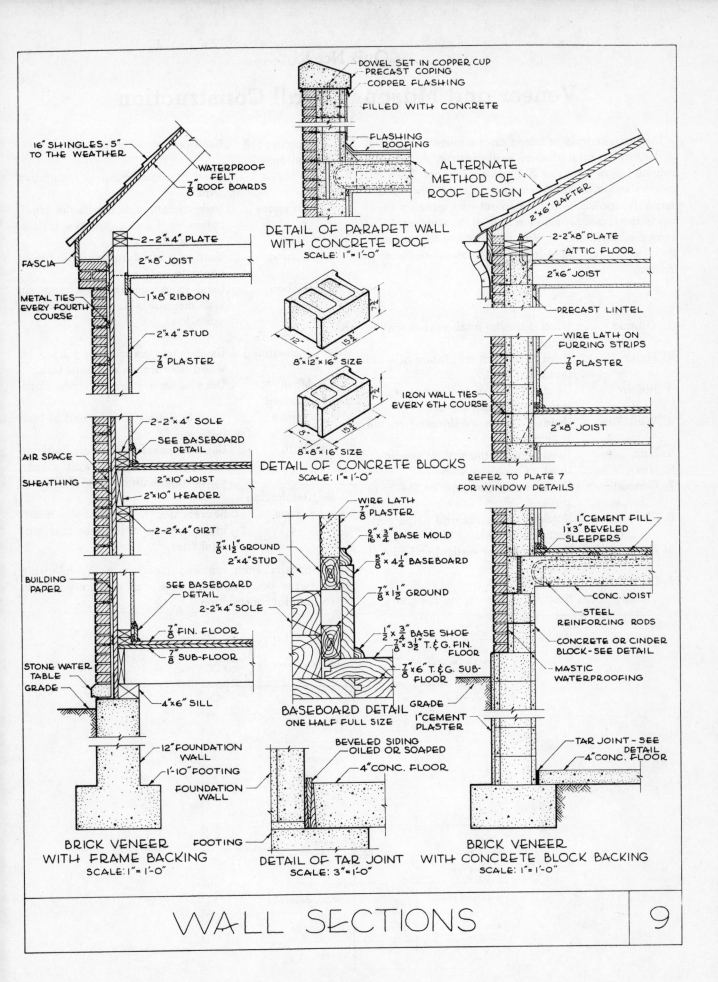

DOWEL SET IN COPPER CUP
PRECAST COPING
COPPER FLASHING
FILLED WITH CONCRETE
FLASHING
ROOFING

ALTERNATE METHOD OF ROOF DESIGN

DETAIL OF PARAPET WALL WITH CONCRETE ROOF
SCALE: 1"=1'-0"

2"x6" RAFTER

16" SHINGLES-5" TO THE WEATHER
WATERPROOF FELT
⅞" ROOF BOARDS

FASCIA
2-2"x4" PLATE
2"x8" JOIST
1"x8" RIBBON
2"x4" STUD
⅞" PLASTER

METAL TIES EVERY FOURTH COURSE

2-2"x8" PLATE
ATTIC FLOOR
2"x6" JOIST
PRECAST LINTEL

7¼
12
15⅝
8"x12"x16" SIZE

WIRE LATH ON FURRING STRIPS
⅞" PLASTER

IRON WALL TIES EVERY 6TH COURSE

2"x8" JOIST

AIR SPACE
SHEATHING

2-2"x4" SOLE
SEE BASEBOARD DETAIL
2"x10" JOIST
2"x10" HEADER
2-2"x4" GIRT

7¼
15⅝
8"
8"x8"x16" SIZE

DETAIL OF CONCRETE BLOCKS
SCALE: 1"=1'-0"

REFER TO PLATE 7 FOR WINDOW DETAILS

WIRE LATH
⅞" PLASTER
9/16" x ¾" BASE MOLD
⅝" x 4¼" BASEBOARD
⅞" x 1½" GROUND
½" x ¾" BASE SHOE
⅞" x 3½" T.&G. FIN. FLOOR
⅞" x 6" T.&G. SUB-FLOOR

⅞" x 1½" GROUND
2"x4" STUD

BUILDING PAPER

SEE BASEBOARD DETAIL
2-2"x4" SOLE
⅞" FIN. FLOOR
⅞" SUB-FLOOR

1" CEMENT FILL
1"x3" BEVELED SLEEPERS

CONC. JOIST
STEEL REINFORCING RODS
CONCRETE OR CINDER BLOCK-SEE DETAIL
MASTIC WATERPROOFING

STONE WATER TABLE
GRADE
4"x6" SILL

BASEBOARD DETAIL
ONE HALF FULL SIZE

GRADE
1" CEMENT PLASTER

12" FOUNDATION WALL
1'-10" FOOTING
FOUNDATION WALL

BEVELED SIDING OILED OR SOAPED
4" CONC. FLOOR

TAR JOINT - SEE DETAIL
4" CONC. FLOOR

BRICK VENEER WITH FRAME BACKING
SCALE: 1"=1'-0"

FOOTING

DETAIL OF TAR JOINT
SCALE: 3"=1'-0"

BRICK VENEER WITH CONCRETE BLOCK BACKING
SCALE: 1"=1'-0"

WALL SECTIONS — 9

Quiz No. 1

Veneer and Masonry Wall Construction

This examination is based on the material covered under veneer and masonry wall construction. The left column below contains 20 numbered words. The right column contains 20 statements. Select the word that correctly applies to the statement and write its number in the space provided in front of the statement. For example, word No. 4, Wall ties, applies to statement No. 1 which is: "Used to anchor brick-veneer wall to framing."

1. Ground ....Used to anchor brick-veneer wall to framing.
2. Facia ....Used to prevent infiltration of wind through a wall.
3. Rafter ....Used to achieve better bracing in frame-wall construction.
4. Wall Ties ......Used to fasten the framing to the foundation.
5. Lath ....Used to allow the wall to breathe.
6. Girt ....Used as a plaster stop.
7. Concrete ....Used to cap the tops of the wall blocks ....studs.
8. Sleeper ....Notched into studs and helps support ceiling joists.
9. Anchor bolts ..Used to enclose vertical end cuts of rafters.
10. Expansion joint ....Notched and bears on the plate.

11. Roofing felt ....Used as a support for plaster.
12. Building paper ....Used in construction of foundation walls.
13. Air space ....Used in conjunction with the application of interior finishes to masonry walls.
14. Furring ....Used as a moisture barrier between concrete slab and fill.
15. Ribbon ....Used to accommodate change in slab dimension due to temperature variation.
16. Diagonal sheathing ....Used to act as a nailing base for wood flooring on concrete slab.
17. Mastic ....Used to strengthen concrete slabs.
18. Crossed lines ....Used to denote the cut end of lumber.
19. Earth ....Used to prevent moisture leakage at top of foundation wall in masonry construction.
20. Reinforcing rods ....Represented by a symbol consisting of groups of three or four parallel lines.

Opposite each building member in the following list, write down its nominal size as generally used in residential construction.

BUILDING MEMBER	NOMINAL SIZE	BUILDING MEMBER	NOMINAL SIZE
COMMON BRICK		SOLE	
STUD		PLATE	
SILL		SUB-FLOOR	
HEADER		CONCRETE BLOCK	
JOIST		ANCHOR BOLTS	
RAFTER		FIRE STOP	
FURRING STRIP		PLASTER	
SHEATHING BOARD		CONC. FOUNDATION WALL	
RIBBON		CROSS FURRING	
GIRT		SLEEPER	

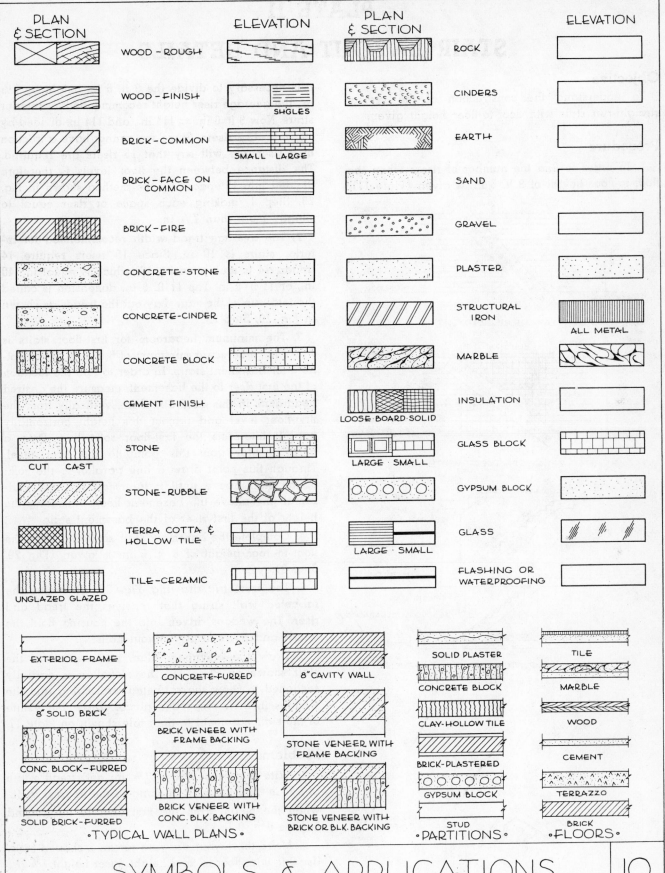

PLAN & SECTION		ELEVATION	PLAN & SECTION		ELEVATION
WOOD – ROUGH			ROCK		
WOOD – FINISH		SHGLES	CINDERS		
BRICK – COMMON		SMALL LARGE	EARTH		
BRICK – FACE ON COMMON			SAND		
BRICK – FIRE			GRAVEL		
CONCRETE – STONE			PLASTER		
CONCRETE – CINDER			STRUCTURAL IRON		ALL METAL
CONCRETE BLOCK			MARBLE		
CEMENT FINISH			INSULATION	LOOSE·BOARD·SOLID	
STONE	CUT CAST		GLASS BLOCK	LARGE · SMALL	
STONE – RUBBLE			GYPSUM BLOCK		
TERRA COTTA & HOLLOW TILE			GLASS	LARGE · SMALL	
TILE – CERAMIC	UNGLAZED GLAZED		FLASHING OR WATERPROOFING		

·TYPICAL WALL PLANS·

EXTERIOR FRAME

8" SOLID BRICK

CONC. BLOCK – FURRED

SOLID BRICK – FURRED

CONCRETE – FURRED

BRICK VENEER WITH FRAME BACKING

BRICK VENEER WITH CONC. BLK. BACKING

8" CAVITY WALL

STONE VENEER WITH FRAME BACKING

STONE VENEER WITH BRICK OR BLK. BACKING

·PARTITIONS·

SOLID PLASTER

CONCRETE BLOCK

CLAY-HOLLOW TILE

BRICK-PLASTERED

GYPSUM BLOCK

STUD

·FLOORS·

TILE

MARBLE

WOOD

CEMENT

TERRAZZO

BRICK

SYMBOLS & APPLICATIONS

10

PLATE 11
STAIR LAYOUT AND DETAILS

Objective

To understand the construction of the typical straight-run stair with floor-to-floor height given.

Procedure

1. In order to find the number of risers when the floor-to-floor height of 9 ft. 6 in. is given (Plate 11),

STEP 1. LAY OFF RISER HEIGHT.

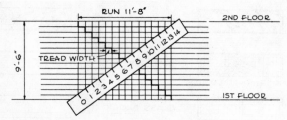

STEP 2. LAY OFF TREAD WIDTH

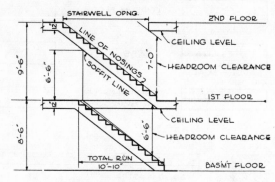

STEP 3. COMPLETE LAYOUT TO BASEMENT
Fig. 29

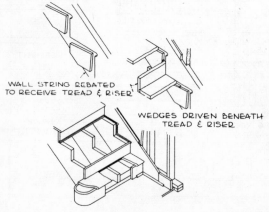

WALL STRING REBATED TO RECEIVE TREAD & RISER

WEDGES DRIVEN BENEATH TREAD & RISER

Fig. 30

it is necessary to divide the 9 ft. 6 in. height by 7½ in., the average riser height recommended for interior stairs. Now 9 ft. 6 in. = 114 in., and 114 in. divided by 7.5 in. = 15.2 risers. Since we cannot have a fraction of a riser, we will say that 15 risers are required. The distance between the floor levels is therefore divided into 15 spaces by the method shown in Fig. 29, Step 1, making each space or riser equal to slightly more than 7½ in.

2. The average tread width recommended for interior stairs is 10 in. Since 15 risers require 14 treads, 14 is multiplied by 10, which is equal to 140 in., or 11 ft. 8 in. The 11 ft. 8 in. dimension is called the *total run* of the stair. Lay out the treads as shown in Fig. 29, Step 2.

3. The minimum headroom for first-floor stairs is 7 ft. 0 in., whereas a minimum of 6 ft. 6 in. is acceptable for basement stairs. In order to find the location of the first riser to the basement, measure the desired headroom, in this case 6 ft. 6 in., vertically from the first-floor level and project this height horizontally until it intersects the first-floor soffit line. Drop a perpendicular from this point to the floor level. Through this point draw a line parallel to the soffit of the stair above until it intersects the first horizontal line above the basement floor, indicating the height of the first riser of the basement stair.

4. Complete the basement stair similarly when the floor-to-floor height of 8 ft. 6 in. is given (Fig. 29, Step 3).

5. The isometric drawing Fig. 30, illustrates the rabbeted wall string that receives the tread and riser. The wedges driven into the housing hold the treads and risers firmly without nails.

6. Draw the elevation, plan, and section of the stair shown on Plate 11. The elevation is partially sectioned to show the rabbeted wall string and the wedges in their respective places. Draw the volute of the stair easement to the scale shown on Plate 11.

Problems

1. With a riser height of 7⅝ in. and tread width of 9¾ in. find the well opening to the nearest ½ in. when the height from the first floor to the second floor is 9 ft. 0 in.

2. Make the layout drawing for an L-shaped stair. Use 9 ft. 0 in. floor-to-floor height. Riser height 7¾ in., tread width 9½ in.

3. Draw a plan, elevation, and section of an L-shaped stair.

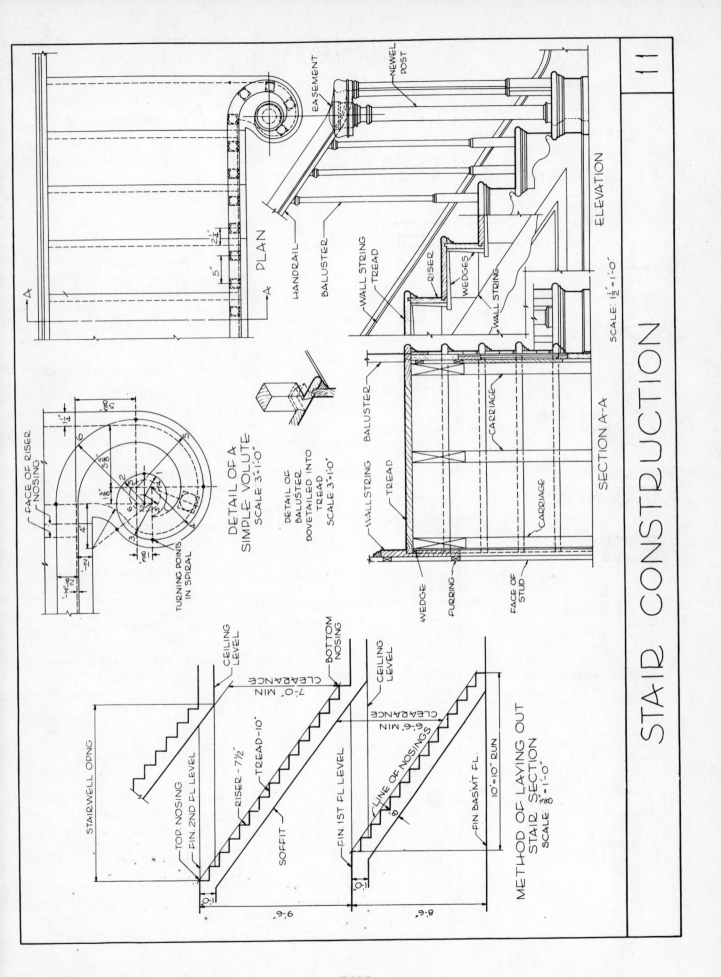

STAIR CONSTRUCTION

PLAN

EASEMENT

NEWEL POST

HANDRAIL

BALUSTER

WALL STRING

TREAD

RISER

WEDGES

WALL STRING

WALL STRING

ELEVATION

SCALE: $1\frac{1}{2}$"=1'-0"

FACE OF RISER

NOSING

TURNING POINTS IN SPIRAL

DETAIL OF A SIMPLE VOLUTE
SCALE: 3"=1'-0"

DETAIL OF BALUSTER DOVETAILED INTO TREAD
SCALE: 3"=1'-0"

BALUSTER

WALL STRING

TREAD

CARRIAGE

CARRIAGE

WEDGE

FURRING

FACE OF STUD

SECTION A-A

STAIRWELL OPNG

CEILING LEVEL

BOTTOM NOSING

CEILING LEVEL

7'-0" MIN CLEARANCE

TOP. NOSING

FIN. 2ND FL. LEVEL

RISER – 7½"

TREAD – 10"

SOFFIT

6'-6" MIN CLEARANCE

LINE OF NOSINGS

FIN 1ST FL LEVEL

FIN BASM'T FL.

10'=10" RUN

METHOD OF LAYING OUT STAIR SECTION
SCALE: $\frac{3}{8}$"=1'-0"

11

[43]

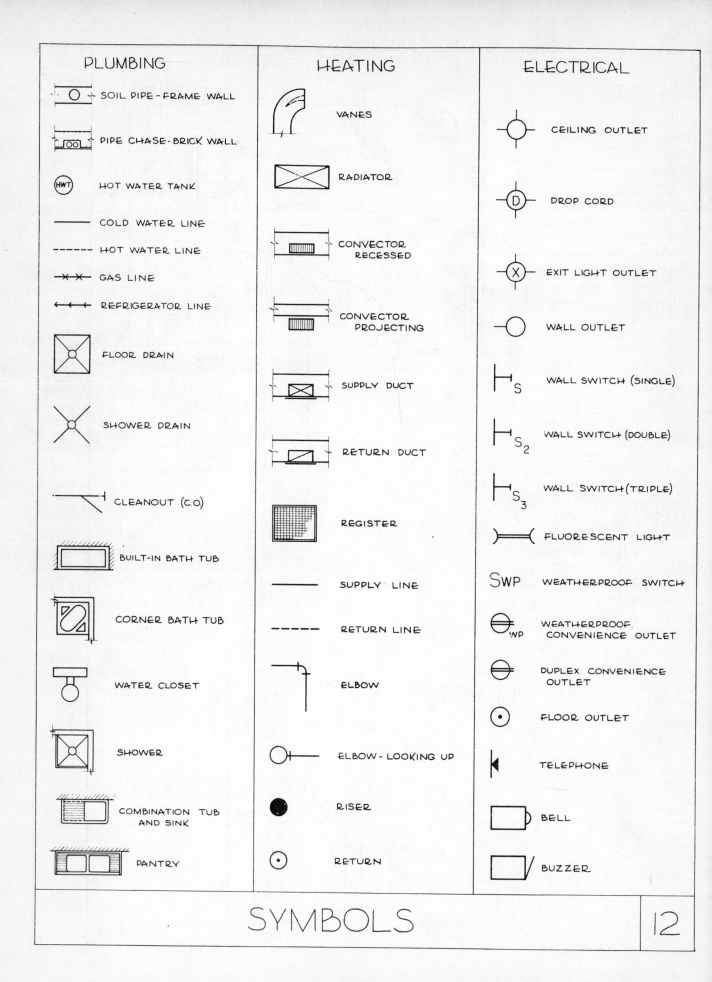

PLUMBING

SOIL PIPE - FRAME WALL

PIPE CHASE - BRICK WALL

(HWT) HOT WATER TANK

COLD WATER LINE

HOT WATER LINE

GAS LINE

REFRIGERATOR LINE

FLOOR DRAIN

SHOWER DRAIN

CLEANOUT (C.O)

BUILT-IN BATH TUB

CORNER BATH TUB

WATER CLOSET

SHOWER

COMBINATION TUB AND SINK

PANTRY

HEATING

VANES

RADIATOR

CONVECTOR RECESSED

CONVECTOR PROJECTING

SUPPLY DUCT

RETURN DUCT

REGISTER

SUPPLY LINE

RETURN LINE

ELBOW

ELBOW - LOOKING UP

RISER

RETURN

ELECTRICAL

CEILING OUTLET

DROP CORD

EXIT LIGHT OUTLET

WALL OUTLET

S WALL SWITCH (SINGLE)

S_2 WALL SWITCH (DOUBLE)

S_3 WALL SWITCH (TRIPLE)

FLUORESCENT LIGHT

SWP WEATHERPROOF SWITCH

WP WEATHERPROOF CONVENIENCE OUTLET

DUPLEX CONVENIENCE OUTLET

FLOOR OUTLET

TELEPHONE

BELL

BUZZER

SYMBOLS

12

The Fireplace and Chimney

In most homes the fireplace is still an important feature and must be designed with care by a competent architect, draftsman, or builder. The shape and proportions should be such as to reflect the heat and still prevent smoke and gases from escaping into the room. This result is accomplished by proper sloping of the sides and back of the fireplace and by having a smoke chamber, flue, throat, and damper of proper proportions.

The sides and back of the fireplace are generally lined with one 4-in. layer of firebrick having fireclay joints. Brick and mortar should not be used as a lining, since mortar does not resist heat very well. The back of the fireplace should slope forward and form the throat, which should be from 2½ to 4 in. in depth and of the same width as the fireplace opening.

The area of the throat should not be less than that of the flue. The throat should be between 2 and 4 in. above the top of the fireplace opening and as near to the front of the fireplace as possible. The purpose of the smoke shelf is to prevent the air from rushing down and forcing smoke into the room. A hinged cast-iron damper of standard design is installed in the throat and used to regulate the draft as desired.

The hearth, extending about 1 ft. 8 in. in front of the fireplace opening, and constructed of brick or concrete, is used to catch burning embers that may fall out of the fire. The hearth may be finished in tile, brick, marble, or stone and is laid flush with the finished floor around it. No woodwork should be placed within 8 in. of the sides and top of the fireplace opening.

Chimneys are generally constructed of brick, although other materials such as rubble or cut stone may be used. When the walls of the chimney around the flue are 4 in. thick, a terra-cotta flue lining should be used, to prevent the heat and the hot gases from disintegrating the mortar in the brick joints and thereby causing the gases to seep into the rooms. If no flue lining is used in the chimney, the walls should be at least 8 in. thick.

It is desirable to design a house so that the chimney is located inside the building, so as to take advantage of the warmth it radiates into the rooms. The tops of the chimneys are carried a short distance above the highest point of the roof, so that the roof will not interfere with the draft. Every chimney should rest on a concrete footing so as to eliminate any possibility of settling or causing other damage.

Framing around the fireplace, hearth, and chimney must be given careful attention, since no wooden construction or other inflammable material must come in contact with the brickwork. The minimum distances that such framing members must be kept away from the chimney will be discussed in later pages.

The fireplace and chimney details on a typical set of architect's plans consist of three drawings: the elevation, a sectional plan, and a side vertical section (Plate 13). The elevation shows the opening of the fireplace, the fireproof material around the opening, and the general design of the mantel. The smoke chamber and flue are generally shown in dotted line. The sectional plan, projected and drawn directly below the elevation, is a horizontal cut through the opening of the fireplace. On this plan are shown the flue for the furnace, the firebrick lining, the hearth, and the framing around the brickwork. The side vertical section is taken through the center of the fireplace opening. It shows the construction of the hearth, the ashpit with cleanout door, and the location of the throat and damper, and gives the necessary working dimensions to the builder.

Fireplace and Chimney in the Small House

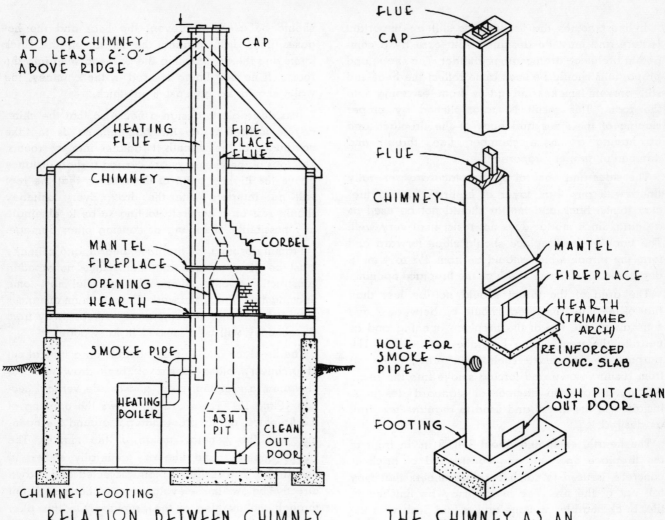

TOP OF CHIMNEY AT LEAST 2'-0" ABOVE RIDGE

CAP

HEATING FLUE

FIRE PLACE FLUE

CHIMNEY

MANTEL
FIREPLACE
OPENING
HEARTH

CORBEL

SMOKE PIPE

HEATING BOILER

ASH PIT

CLEAN OUT DOOR

CHIMNEY FOOTING

RELATION BETWEEN CHIMNEY STRUCTURE AND HOUSE STRUCTURE

FLUE
CAP

FLUE

CHIMNEY

MANTEL

FIREPLACE

HEARTH (TRIMMER ARCH)

REINFORCED CONC. SLAB

HOLE FOR SMOKE PIPE

ASH PIT CLEAN OUT DOOR

FOOTING

THE CHIMNEY AS AN INDEPENDENT STRUCTURE

In small-house construction, economy dictates the use of only one chimney. Therefore, if a fireplace is desired, it must use the same chimney that is provided for the heating plant. Thus the chimney must contain a separate flue, or smoke passage, for each fireplace or heater that is connected to it. In this way the fireplace, boiler, or furnace may operate as an independent unit, with its own draft regulation. These considerations, plus the fact that the chimney must be structurally independent of the house framing, require that a chimney be carefully designed and constructed.

Fireplace Construction

The face of the fireplace may be constructed of brick, stone, marble, or tile. Note that a steel angle iron, called a lintel, is used to support the stonework over the opening (Fig. 30a). The opening of an average residential fireplace is 3 ft. 0 in. wide by 2 ft. 6 in. high. The mantel may be made of stone, brick, marble,

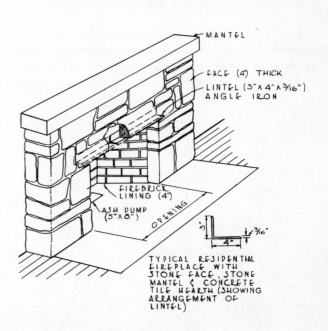

MANTEL

FACE (4") THICK

LINTEL (3"x 4"x 3/16") ANGLE IRON

FIREBRICK LINING (4")

ASH DUMP (5"x 8")

OPENING

TYPICAL RESIDENTIAL FIREPLACE WITH STONE FACE, STONE MANTEL & CONCRETE TILE HEARTH (SHOWING ARRANGEMENT OF LINTEL)

Fig. 30a

concrete, or wood. If wood trim is used around the face, it must not be closer to the opening than 8 in. on the sides and 12 in. along the top. The hearth is concrete, slate, tile, stone, or brick. Ashes may be dumped into the ashpit below, through a hole in the hearth, which is covered by a pivoted iron door.

If we cut the fireplace horizontally, we can see the shape of the firebrick lining, flue, and chimney. If a horizontal cut is taken through the fireplace, the fire-brick lining, the flue, and chimney can be seen (Fig. 30b).

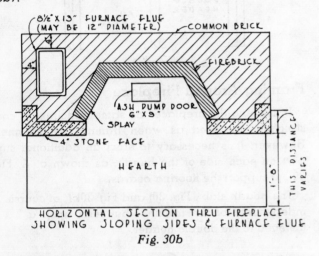

HORIZONTAL SECTION THRU FIREPLACE SHOWING SLOPING SIDES & FURNACE FLUE

Fig. 30b

A vertical section reveals that the rear wall, as well as the side walls, are sloped (Fig. 30c). The sloping walls act as heat-reflecting surfaces to direct the heat into the room.

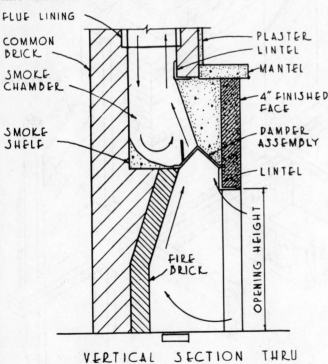

VERTICAL SECTION THRU FIREPLACE SHOWING SLOP-ING BACK DAMPER & PATH OF AIR

Fig. 30c

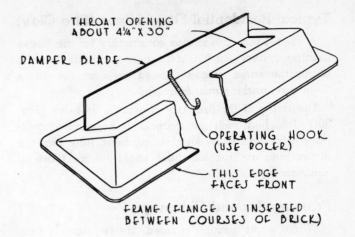

PICTORIAL VIEW OF DAMPER ASSEMBLY

Fig. 30d

The damper assembly, a standard manufactured item, consists of a metal frame and swinging blade, which may be adjusted to regulate the amount of draft (Fig. 30d). The entire assembly is set in place before the face material is added. Note how the smoke shelf and the open damper blade prevent cold air from blowing down the chimney flue and into the room. Improperly designed fireplaces allow smoke to blow back through the opening into the room, making it impossible to create a positive draft.

The flue size and the damper size are dependent upon the size of the fireplace opening. For the average residential fireplace, with a 2 ft. 6 in. x 3 ft. 0 in. opening, a 12-in. diameter round flue, or a 13- x 13-in. rectangular flue is generally required.

In order that flues may operate more efficiently, a flue lining with glazed inner surface prevents any soot deposits forming while the chimney is in operation (Fig. 30e).

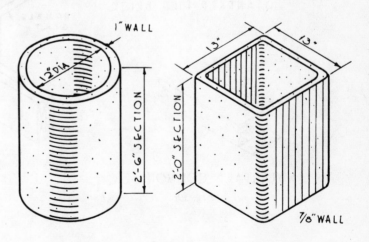

TYPICAL RESIDENTIAL FLUE LININGS MADE FROM FIRE CLAY

Fig. 30e

Typical Residential Flue Linings (Fire Clay)

A 13- x 13-in. flue is also satisfactory for the house heating system. An 8½- x 18-in. rectangular flue has about the same cross-sectioned area as the 13- x 13-in. size, and is sometimes used.

The lining of the fireplace is usually firebrick (Fig. 30f). This heat-resistant material is superior to ordinary brick and stone for resisting heat. Note that the dimensions of firebrick differ slightly from those of common brick.

Framing Around Chimney

When wood framing is used, fire regulations prohibit anchoring wooden members in the masonry work of the chimney. Consequently openings around chimneys must be framed in much the same way that stair openings are framed. Figure 30g and Fig. 30h are typical examples of framing around chimney and fireplace.

In the plan and pictorial views, the chimney is framed by a pair of double trimmers (two joints nailed together), which rest directly on the double girt.

A double header, carried by the trimmers, supports the regular floor joist. The 1⅝-in. space between the framed opening and the chimney is filled with incombustible material, such as asbestos or magnesia cement.

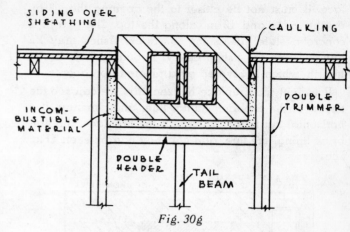
Fig. 30g

Framing Around Fireplace

In framing the fireplace, the same principles of construction are used as when framing the chimney. However, it is necessary to erect an additional support on each side of the hearth, as shown at A, Fig. 30i, to support the flooring boards.

The hearth slab (Fig. 30j and Fig. 30k), of course, is independent of the framing, but rests upon a 2 x 4 fastened to the double header.

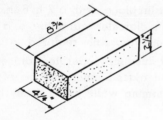

STANDARD FIRE BRICK

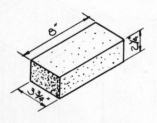

STANDARD COMMON BRICK
Fig. 30f

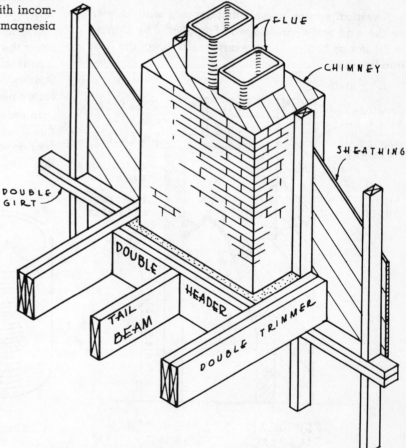

FRAMING THE CHIMNEY
Fig. 30h

[48]

Sometimes the hearth slab extends to the back of the chimney. In this case the slab must contain openings sufficiently large to receive the flue and ash-dump door frame.

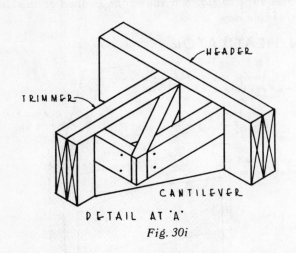

DETAIL AT 'A'
Fig. 30i

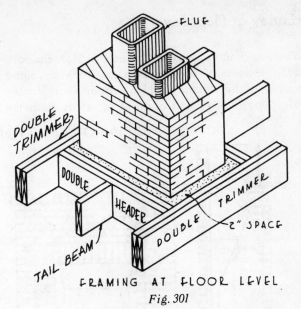

FRAMING AT FLOOR LEVEL
Fig. 30l

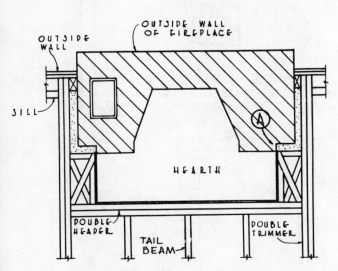

FRAMING THE FIREPLACE
Fig. 30j

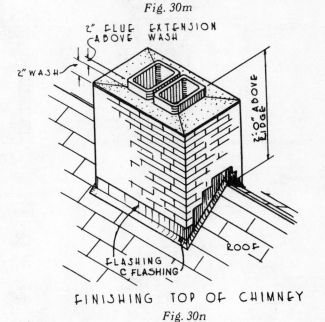

FRAMING AT ROOF
Fig. 30m

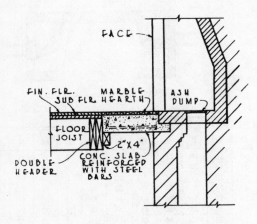

SUPPORTING THE HEARTH SLAB
Fig. 30k

FINISHING TOP OF CHIMNEY
Fig. 30n

[49]

Chimney at Floor Level

Where a chimney passes through a floor, the joist framing consists of double trimmers, running along two sides of the chimney, which support short double headers, parallel to and about 2 in. away from the front and back of the chimney (Fig. 30 l). The 2-in. space is filled with incombustible material.

Similar arrangement is used where a chimney passes through a roof (Fig. 30m).

The view in Fig. 30n shows the method of finishing top of chimney.

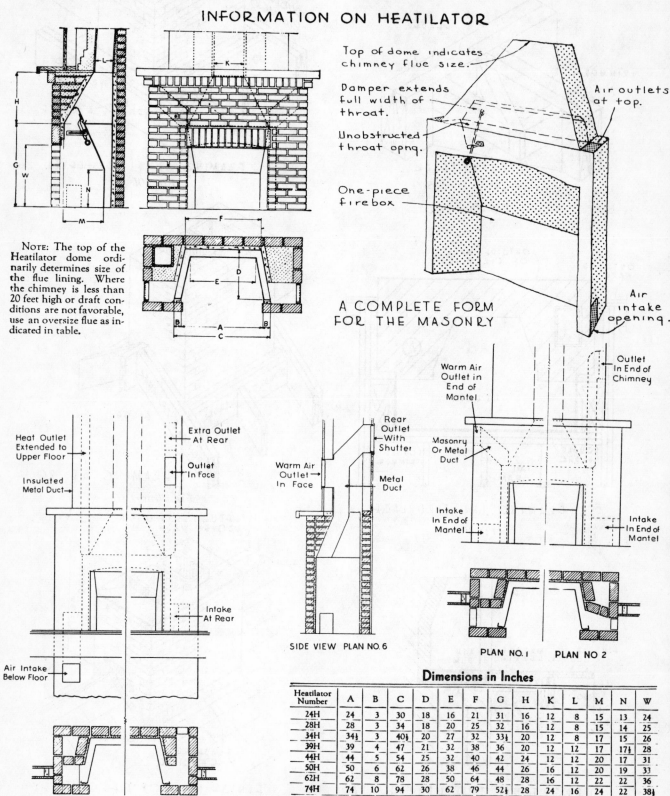

NOTE: The top of the Heatilator dome ordinarily determines size of the flue lining. Where the chimney is less than 20 feet high or draft conditions are not favorable, use an oversize flue as indicated in table.

INFORMATION ON HEATILATOR

Top of dome indicates chimney flue size.

Damper extends full width of throat.

Unobstructed throat opng.

One-piece firebox

Air outlets at top.

Air intake opening.

A COMPLETE FORM FOR THE MASONRY

Heat Outlet Extended to Upper Floor

Insulated Metal Duct

Extra Outlet At Rear

Outlet In Face

Intake At Rear

Air Intake Below Floor

Warm Air Outlet In Face

Rear Outlet With Shutter

Metal Duct

SIDE VIEW PLAN NO. 6

Warm Air Outlet in End of Mantel

Outlet In End of Chimney

Masonry Or Metal Duct

Intake In End of Mantel

Intake In End of Mantel

PLAN NO. 1   PLAN NO 2

PLAN NO. 5   PLAN NO. 6

Dimensions in Inches

Heatilator Number	A	B	C	D	E	F	G	H	K	L	M	N	W
24H	24	3	30	18	16	21	31	16	12	8	15	13	24
28H	28	3	34	18	20	25	32	16	12	8	15	14	25
34H	34½	3	40½	20	27	32	33½	20	12	8	17	15	26
39H	39	4	47	21	32	38	36	20	12	12	17	17½	28
44H	44	5	54	25	32	40	42	24	12	12	20	17	31
50H	50	6	62	26	38	46	44	26	16	12	20	19	33
62H	62	8	78	28	50	64	48	28	16	14	22	22	36
74H	74	10	94	30	62	79	52½	28	24	16	24	22	38½

NOTE: For arched opening height, add the following to dimensions "W" shown above: 24H—⅞", 28H—1¼", 34H—1¼", 39H—1½", 44H—2⅜", 50H—2⅝", 62H—3⅛", 74H—4⅞". Arched openings are slightly lower at sides than dimension "W".

PLATE 13
FIREPLACE CONSTRUCTION

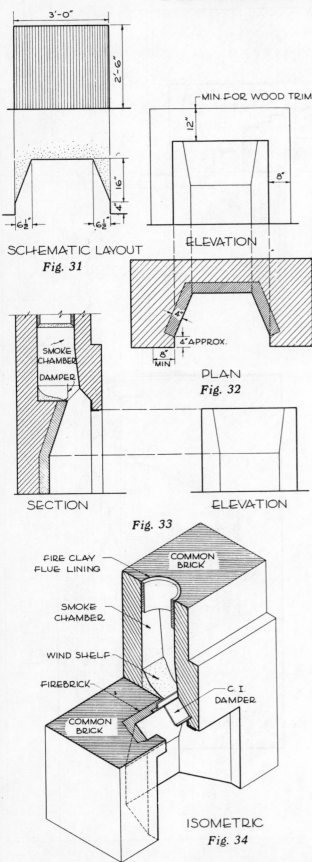

SCHEMATIC LAYOUT
Fig. 31

MIN. FOR WOOD TRIM

ELEVATION

PLAN
Fig. 32

SMOKE CHAMBER

DAMPER

SECTION

ELEVATION

Fig. 33

FIRE CLAY FLUE LINING

COMMON BRICK

SMOKE CHAMBER

WIND SHELF

FIREBRICK

COMMON BRICK

C. I. DAMPER

ISOMETRIC
Fig. 34

Objective

To study the details and structural features of the fireplace and the method employed in developing the drawing.

Procedure

1. In preparing Plate 13, begin by drawing the elevation opening of the fireplace, 2 ft. 6 in. x 3 ft. 0 in., the average opening for medium-sized fireplaces. Next draw the plan directly below the elevation with a 1 ft. 8 in. depth (Fig. 31).

2. The line representing the minimum distance of wood trim may next be drawn around the elevation opening, 8 in. on the sides and 12 in. on the top. Draw the 4-in. firebrick lining in plan and the 8-in. thickness of common brick behind the firebrick (Fig. 32). Before the extremities of the brickwork of the fireplace can be found, determine the size of the flue from the floor below and maintain the minimum thickness of brickwork around the flue (Plate 13).

3. The elevation section may next be projected from the front elevation, including the firebrick back lining with its forward slope. The throat with standard damper of proper proportion to the flue may then be drawn (Fig. 33). The isometric, Fig. 34, will serve as the visual aid in preparing the drawings.

4. The 6-in. reinforced-concrete slab of the hearth, with its marble slab flush with the floor, may next be drawn 20 in. from the face of the fireplace opening. The details of the mantel in section and the framing around the fireplace in plan may then be drawn. The section also shows the ash trap and the corbeled brickwork to the ashpit with the cleanout door (Plate 13).

5. Complete the fireplace (Plate 13), giving all dimensions and specifications required for its construction.

Test Questions

1. What fireproof materials may be used around the fireplace opening?

2. How close can wood trim be brought to the fireplace opening?

3. What is the depth of the fireplace when the opening is 2 ft. 6 in. x 2 ft. 10 in.?

4. Determine the area of the flue when the fireplace opening is 2 ft. 6 in. x 2 ft. 10 in.

5. Where should the flue be located with reference to the fireplace opening?

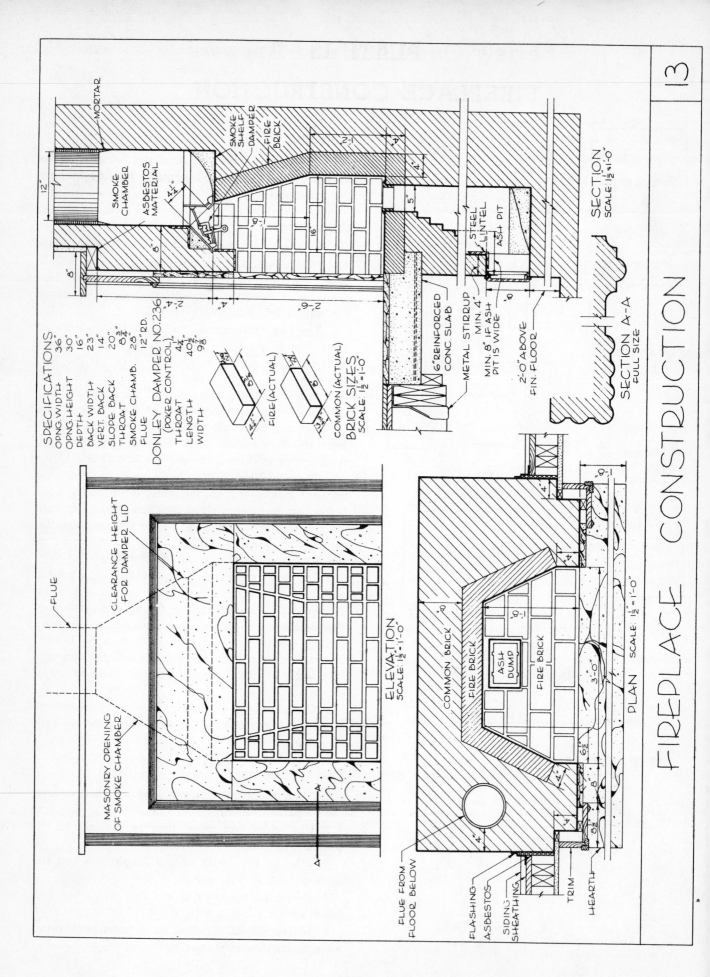

13

SPECIFICATIONS

OPNG. WIDTH	36"
OPNG. HEIGHT	30"
DEPTH	16"
BACK WIDTH	23"
VERT. BACK	14"
SLOPE BACK	20"
THROAT	$8\frac{3}{4}$"
SMOKE CHAMB.	28"
FLUE	12" RD.

DONLEY DAMPER NO.236
(POKER CONTROL)

THROAT	$4\frac{1}{4}$"
LENGTH	$40\frac{1}{2}$"
WIDTH	$9\frac{7}{8}$"

FIRE (ACTUAL)

COMMON (ACTUAL)

BRICK SIZES
SCALE 1½"=1'-0"

SECTION
SCALE 1½"=1'-0"

SECTION A-A
FULL SIZE

FLUE

CLEARANCE HEIGHT
FOR DAMPER LID

MASONRY OPENING
OF SMOKE CHAMBER

ELEVATION
SCALE 1½"=1'-0"

FLUE FROM
FLOOR BELOW

COMMON BRICK

FIRE BRICK

ASH
DUMP

FIRE BRICK

FLASHING

ASBESTOS

SIDING

SHEATHING

TRIM

HEARTH

PLAN SCALE 1½"=1'-0"

FIREPLACE CONSTRUCTION

Review Questions and Answers
Plates 1 to 13

1. *To achieve good single-stroke lettering, what three factors must be considered?*

The instrument with which the letter is to be made, usually a soft pencil; the form and shape of the letter; and the "how to do it," which entails rapid strokes having a definite beginning and end and confined between the guide lines.

2. *When lettering is traced in ink, are pencil guide lines necessary?*

Pencil guide lines are always necessary for lettering, whether the lettering is done in pencil or in ink. The guide lines help to prevent irregularities in the letters and words.

3. *What is the difference between upper-case and lower-case letters?*

Upper-case letters are capitalized, whereas lower-case letters are not capitalized.

4. *Should fractions occupy the same space between guide lines as regular figures?*

Fractions, as a rule, extend above and below the guide lines, in order to prevent the crowding of the numerals between the guide lines.

5. *Should letters and figures be spaced equally or should they have an equal area between them?*

Letters and figures should be spaced so that there is an equal area of space between them. It is hardly possible to measure the equal area between letters and words, but the eye can be trained to recognize equal and unequal areas.

6. *Which is the better practice, to letter directly or to sketch the words lightly to achieve good spacing?*

When a given number of letters or words are to be spaced in a given block or space, it is advisable first to sketch in the letters lightly to see if all letters and words fit into the assigned space. Of course this procedure is not necessary when letters and words are not intended for a given space.

7. *Of the following grades of pencils, which is the best to use for architectural lettering? 3B, F, 4H, 7H.*

The best grades of pencils for architectural lettering in the group shown are the F and 4H or any pencil between these grades. The 3B is too soft and is used for sketching and rendering. The 7H is too hard. The grade of drawing paper often determines the grade of hardness of the pencil to be used.

8. *What is a cylindrical helix?*

A cylindrical helix is generated by a point moving around and along the surface of a cylinder with a uniform velocity in both directions. The curve of the handrail on a circular stair can be called a cylindrical helix.

9. *What two instruments may be used in dividing the space between two given lines into any number of equal parts?*

The scale rule and the dividers. The scale-rule method is by far the more accurate and rapid. By using the dividers the space can be divided by trial and error.

10. *Is a perpendicular line always vertical?*

No. It can be said that the ground level is perpendicular to the side of the building, but it is not vertical to the side of the building.

11. *What is meant by parallel lines?*

When two lines are drawn parallel to each other, they are an equal distance apart at any given point. The rails of a railroad track are said to be parallel to each other.

12. *Are isometric and perspective drawing the same thing?*

No. In isometric drawing the lines will not converge, whereas in perspective drawing lines will converge to a point called the *vanishing point*.

13. *What is meant by nonisometric lines?*

Nonisometric lines are oblique to the isometric axes and therefore cannot be measured directly.

14. *Can dimensions be laid off directly on an iso-metric drawing?*

Yes. However, isometric drawing must not be confused with isometric projection. The isometric drawing is about 22.5 per cent larger than the isometric projection.

15. *Of what material are footings generally made?*

Footings are generally made of concrete. In a 1-3-5 concrete mix, there are 1 part of cement, 3 parts of sand, and 5 parts of crushed rock or gravel.

16. *What is meant by frost line?*

The frost line is the depth that frost can penetrate into the ground. It lies deeper at zero weather than at, say 50°F.

17. *Why should excavations for footings be carried below the frost line?*

Footings are the bearings of the house or structure. They must be carried below the frost line so that any moisture that may seep into the concrete cannot freeze and crack the footing. Building codes specify the minimum depths of footings for various localities.

18. *What footing depth is required by the building code in New York?*

The footing depth in New York is required to be a minimum of 4 ft.

19. *If an 8-in. foundation wall is used on light construction, how wide should its footing be?*

The footing should protrude on either side of the foundation wall a minimum of half the thickness of the foundation wall but never less than 6 in. On an 8-in. foundation wall, therefore, the total footing width will be 20 in.

20. *How deep would the footing be if a 16-in. foundation wall were used?*

On light construction the depth of a footing should be the thickness of the wall but never less than 12 in. The depth of the footing is therefore 16 in.

21. *Is a sole or sole plate used in box-sill construction?*

Yes. It is the 2 x 4 or sometimes a double 2 x 4 laid on top of the subflooring wherever outside walls and partition walls are located.

22. *In solid-sill construction, what is the member often omitted by careless builders?*

The header. This member acts as a fire stop and prevents a fluelike action between the walls in case of fire. Headers also help to solidify the building and keep the joists in perfect alignment.

23. *What is the purpose of anchor bolts?*

Anchor bolts are used to tie the framing of the building to the concrete foundation wall. They are imbedded in the wall with their top ends exposed when the concrete is poured. The wood sill is then securely bolted to the foundation wall.

24. *Why is the sill normally set back from the outside face of the foundation wall?*

The sill is generally set back 1 in. or ⅞ in. from the outside face of the wall. This is done so that the 1-in. or ⅞-in. sheathing will be flush with the face of the concrete wall.

25. *What may be done to add strength to footings?*

Footings are generally reinforced by ¾-in. diameter reinforcing rods, laid before the concrete is poured.

26. *List the structural members used in box-sill construction, starting with the member directly on top of the foundation wall.*

The structural members used in the box-sill construction are the sill, header, joist, subfloor, sole, and stud.

27. *What advantage has the solid sill over the box sill?*

In the solid-sill construction, the studs rest directly on the sill, making for a smaller shrinkage factor.

28. *Why is a wider foundation wall required in brick-veneer construction than in frame construction?*

The foundation wall for a brick-veneer construction with frame backing is generally wider than the wall for a frame structure, because a bearing space must be provided for the 4-in. layer of brick.

29. *In brick-veneer construction, why is a space allowed between the framing and the brickwork?*

The space between the framing and the brickwork acts as an insulator and allows any moisture that may seep through the brickwork to dry.

30. *What is meant by furring?*

By furring is meant the leveling up or building out of a wall or ceiling by wood strips. If the concrete walls in a cellar were to be finished off with plywood panels, it would first be necessary to fasten furring strips to the concrete before the plywood could be nailed fast.

31. *Name two types of lath used in connection with plastering.*

Two types of lath used in connection with plastering are rock lath and metal lath. Rock lath is a form of plaster gypsum composition bored with holes so that the finished plaster coat can find a grip on its surface. Metal lath is a specially prepared lath made of sheet metal pierced in various ways to permit plaster to bind itself with the metal lath.

32. *What is a fire cut and what is its purpose?*

Floor joists that are supported by masonry walls are cut at an angle at their top ends, so that the joists can fall out of their bearing sockets if in case of fire they were to burn through. Joists that are not fire cut at their ends might endanger life and property in case of fire.

33. *What is the minimum bearing surface of floor joists in solid-brick walls?*

Most building codes require a 4-in. minimum bearing surface of floor joists in masonry walls.

34. *What is meant by a party wall?*

A party wall must not be confused with a partition wall. A partition wall separates two rooms of an apartment, whereas a party wall separates adjoining apartments or buildings.

35. *What is the purpose of a step arrangement between the concrete foundation wall and the brickwork in solid-brick construction?*

A step arrangement is generally required on a concrete wall when the concrete wall is in line with the grade level, to prevent moisture from seeping into the interior.

36. *What is the difference between a girt and a plate?*

The girt, a 2 x 4 double 2 x 4 rests on the top ends of wall studs, which in turn support the ceiling joists, whereas the plate consists of the 2 x 4's upon which the bottoms of the vertical wall studs rest.

37. *In balloon framing, one continuous stud is used from sill to plate. How should second-floor joists be supported in this type of framing?*

The second-floor joists are nailed to the sides of the studs and are supported by a ribbon which is notched into the studs. (Refer to Plate 9, section on brick veneer with frame backing.)

38. *What are grounds?*

Grounds are strips of wood of the thickness of the plaster, secured to the framing. They aid the plasterer and serve as nailing strips for securing the wood finish.

39. *What is the purpose of a water table?*

A water table is a special molding usually placed above the skirting to throw off water.

40. *What three portions of a window do manufacturers most often refer to in the description of their products?*

The manufacturer most often refers to the sash opening, the rough opening, and/or the masonry opening of the window.

41. *In what order should the draftsman proceed when laying out a plan, elevation, and section of a window?*

The draftsman must first find the sash opening of the window from the manufacturer's specifications, both in plan and elevation, then the rough opening. After the details of the inside and outside casing are drawn, the elevation of the window can be projected from the plan and elevation section.

42. *List five different manufacturers of windows.*

Pella, Anderson, Fenestra, Ceco, Curtis.

43. *What must be done to the framework over large openings to resist the additional load placed upon it?*

Over large openings the framework must be

trussed, especially when floor joists are to be supported.

44. *What purpose do side lights serve in entrance doors?*

Side lights on entrance doors are intended to admit light into the entry or hall.

45. *What material other than framework may be used as a backing for brick-veneer?*

Cinder blocks or concrete blocks may be used as a backing for brick-veneer walls. They are considered better than frame backing because they are not subject to shrinkage.

46. *What is the actual size of an 8- x 16-in. concrete block?*

The actual size is 8 x 7¾ x 15¾ in.

47. *Name three types of masonry blocks in use today.*

Concrete blocks, concrete tile, gypsum blocks.

48. *List three methods of supporting masonry over openings?*

Masonry over openings may be supported by angle irons, precast concrete lintels, and stone lintels.

49. *Name two types of floor finishes other than wood.*

Terrazzo and flagstone.

50. *What is the purpose of sleepers and why are they beveled?*

Sleepers are beveled wooden members embedded in concrete. They act as nailing bases for the finished wood floor. The bevel prevents the sleeper from working out of position.

51. *Which is considered better building practice, to lay a basement floor on the top of a footing or level with the top of the footing?*

It is always considered better practice to lay the concrete basement floor on the projection of the footing, because in this position the floor and the footing will be bound in a solid mass, and the floor will not be so liable to crack.

52. *Why is it considered better practice to nail the base shoe to the finished floor than to the baseboard?*

If shrinkage occurs, the shoe mold will cover it.

A still better method, not always feasible, is to nail the shoe diagonally into the subfloor. This method takes care of any movement of floor or baseboard, either horizontally or vertically.

53. *What is a parapet wall?*

A parapet wall is a wall projecting above the roof. Parapet walls are generally capped by stone, tile, or copper copings.

54. *Is the use of shingles permitted in flat roof construction?*

Wood shingles should not be used on a roof with a pitch of less than ¼.

55. *What geometric principle previously learned is applied in stair layout?*

The geometric principle applied in stair layout is to divide the space between two given lines into any number of equal parts. This principle is used in laying out the treads of a stair when the floor-to-floor height is known.

56. *How many risers would be required for a stair if the distance from finished floor to finished floor were 9 ft. 8 in. and a 7½-in. riser were desired?*

9 ft. 8 in. floor-to-floor height = 116 in.
116 ÷ 7.5 = 15.4 in., or 15 risers.

57. *What is the difference between an open-string and a closed-string stair?*

When the stair stringers are rebated to receive the ends of treads, the stair is called a closed-string stair. When treads rest on the stringers, the stair is called an open-string stair.

58. *Of what material are flue linings usually made?*

Flue linings are generally of terra cotta, either cylindrical or rectangular in shape.

59. *Why are the sides and back of a fireplace sloped?*

The purpose of sloped sides and back in the fireplace is to reflect the heat into the room.

60. *What is the minimum thickness of the chimney when used on an outside wall?*

The thickness of the chimney used on an outside wall should be 8 in.

Architectural Drafting Examination No. 1

True or False (T F) and Multiple Choice

In answering the following questions, write the number of each question, followed by the letter that is most nearly correct.

T F 1. A circle contains 380 deg.

T F 2. The sum of all the angles of a triangle totals 180 deg.

T F 3. A cornice is formed by the intersection of the rafter and the ceiling joist.

T F 4. The brickwork in brick-veneer construction is used to support the roof rafters.

T F 5. A solid sill may be used in brick-veneer construction.

T F 6. Wall ties are used to strengthen mortar joints in brickwork.

T F 7. Rafters are structural members that support the roof.

T F 8. Joists must be beveled at the rafter slope to permit nailing of roof boards to rafters.

T F 9. A double thickness of shingles is usually required in the starting row of a roof.

T F 10. The rafter span is figured along the slope of the rafter from one end to the other.

T F 11. The clear span of a joist is taken from inside face of one support to the inside face of the next support.

12. (Multiple Choice) Of the following terms, select three that are parts of cornice construction: (a) girt, (b) sole, (c) fascia, (d) tread, (e) carriage, (f) plancher, (g) frieze.

T F 13. Beveled siding may be used on roofs in frame construction.

14. (Multiple Choice) Of the following terms select those which do not pertain to window construction: (a) stool, (b) ridge pole, (c) firestop, (d) apron, (e) lites, (f) jamb, (g) mullion, (h) plinth block, (i) rough opening, (j) sleepers.

15. (Multiple Choice) Of the following manufacturers names select those which are concerned with the manufacture of windows: (a) Pella, (b) Curtis, (c) Johns Manville, (d) Barrett, (e) Portland Cement, (f) Anderson, (g) Pittsburgh-Corning, (h) Ceco, (i) Ruberoid, (j) Truscon.

T F 16. The same symbol is used for sand, cement, and plaster in both plan and section.

T F 17. The same symbol is used for both rough-cut and finished lumber.

T F 18. According to the 1946 Building Code of New York City, the minimum tread width for interior residential stairs is 9½ in. and the maximum riser height is 7¾ in.

T F 19. That combination of tread and riser which is most often used is 7½-in. riser and 10-in. tread.

T F 20. According to the building code in Question 18, the proportion of the tread and riser is determined by the product of the two, which must be between 70 and 75.

21. (Multiple Choice) The minimum headroom clearance between a basement stair and a stair above is (a) 6 ft. 0 in., (b) 7 ft. 0 in., (c) 6 ft. 6 in., (d) 6 ft. 3 in., (e) 7 ft. 6 in.

T F 22. The run of a stair is the horizontal distance from the face of the first riser to the face of the last riser.

T F 23. The member that directly supports the tread and riser is known as the stringer.

T F 24. The opening in a floor to permit the use of a stair is known as the total run.

T F 25. A well-designed stair is one in which the wall string is rabbeted to receive the tread and riser.

T F 26. The flue area should be one-tenth to one-twelfth the area of the finished fireplace opening.

T F 27. The throat area of a damper should always be more than the flue area.

28. (Multiple Choice) Wood trim should always be kept away from the fireplace opening a minimum of ...... in. at the side and ...... in. at the top. (a) 14, (b) 8, (c) 10, (d) 24, (e) 12, (f) 6, (g) 4.

PART II
STANDARD DETAILS FOR HOUSE CONSTRUCTION

This part consists of a compilation of the various standard details of house construction used all over the country. The student may be familiar with some of the details, since they have been previously discussed. Repeating them here will serve as a review. Study this part with care, since there will be a future need for much of the information it contains.

Footing with Drain Tile

The sketch in Fig. 35a shows how drain tile may be used at the base of a footing to drain away excess water from wet locations. The joints are left open to allow the water to drain into the tile conduit. A cesspool usually is used to receive the runoff.

Lally-Column Footing

A lally column is used in the basement for supporting a girder (Fig. 35b). The girder runs the full length or width of the basement and supports the floor joists. Usually one lally column, or post, is required every 8 ft. 0 in. of girder span. Since the column or post carries considerable weight from the floor above, it must rest on a footing so that the load will be distributed over a large area.

Girder Set in Wall

The girder, whether it is steel or wood, is usually set in a girder box formed when the foundation is poured (Fig. 35c). If concrete blocks are used, a block is left out and the box is formed with brick. At least 4 in. of bearing should be allowed, plus 1 in. for clearance.

The Recessed Sill

Sometimes it is required to have the floor line close to the ground. To accomplish this, the floor joists may bear on a ledge formed in the foundation, rather than on the sill (Fig. 35d). The sill is set in fresh mortar, with its top level with the joists.

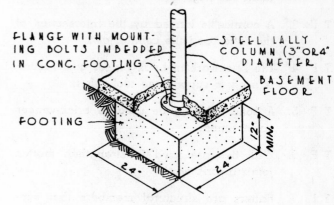

FOOTING FOR LALLY COLUMN
Fig. 35b

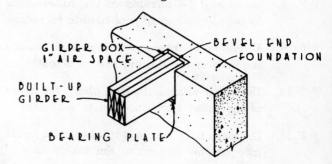

WOOD GIRDER SET IN WALL
Fig. 35c

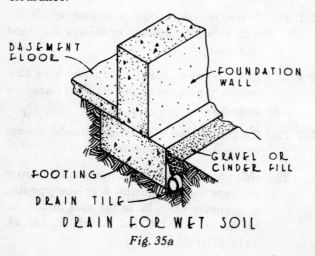

DRAIN FOR WET SOIL
Fig. 35a

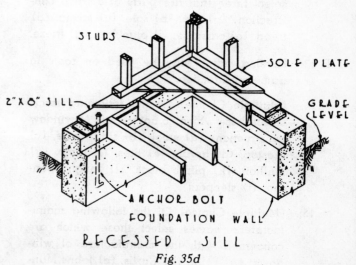

RECESSED SILL
Fig. 35d

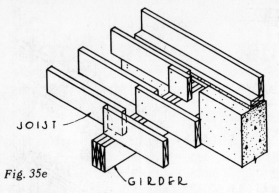

JOIST

GIRDER

Fig. 35e

FRAMING JOISTS ON TOP
OF GIRDER

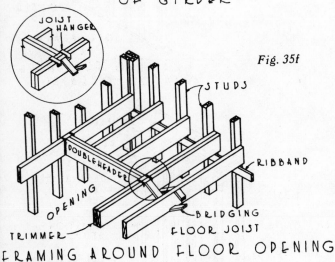

JOIST HANGER

Fig. 35f

STUDS

DOUBLE HEADER

RIBBAND

OPENING

TRIMMER

BRIDGING

FLOOR JOIST

FRAMING AROUND FLOOR OPENING

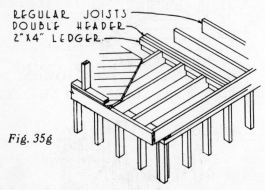

REGULAR JOISTS
DOUBLE HEADER
2"X4" LEDGER

Fig. 35g

FRAMING OF SECOND STORY
OVERHANG

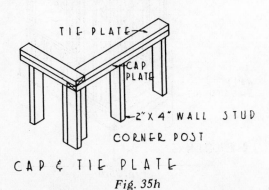

TIE PLATE

CAP PLATE

2"X4" WALL STUD

CORNER POST

CAP & TIE PLATE

Fig. 35h

Framing Joist on Top of Girder

Joists should lap the full width of the girder and be nailed with three 16d (sixteen-penny) nails (Fig. 35e).

In good construction, wood sills on masonry are creosoted to prevent decay of the wood. Many times copper shields are placed on top of the foundation wall before the sill is set. The copper shield helps to prevent decay caused by termites.

Framing Around Floor Openings

Where extra loads are placed on joists, double headers and trimmers should be accurately fitted and securely nailed in place. Trimmers and headers around chimneys and hearths should be set 2 in. from the face of the masonry; the 2-in. space is then filled with incombustible material (Fig. 35f).

Framing Second-Story Overhang

In some types of colonial architecture, the second floor is overhung by a distance of 10 or 12 in. The framing for such a condition is shown in Fig. 35g.

A 2- x 4-in. ledger is securely nailed to the double header to receive notches in cantilever joists used to support the overhang.

Note that in this example the overhang runs parallel with the regular joists. If the overhang ran perpendicular to the joists, there would be no problem at all, as the regular joists would be continued the amount of the overhang, and finished off with a header.

Cap and Tie Plate

Cap and tie plates should be used on all exterior walls, and the corners lapped and nailed with three 16d nails as shown in Fig. 35h.

Framing Partition Door

Interior door frames or jambs should be set plumb and square by use of wedges (Fig. 35i). Low-grade shingles are often used for this purpose. It is important to place wedges behind the jamb where the hinges are going to be placed. If this is not done, the hinge screws are fastened only to the jamb, which does not offer enough thickness to support a heavy door permanently.

Corner Posts and Partition Starters

A single 4- x 4-in. post is not a satisfactory member for a corner post. The reason is not because of insufficient strength, but because it offers no nailing edge for the lath. Consequently some arrangement similar to the method shown at the left must be used. Note that 2- x 4-in. blocks are used between the double 2- x 4-in. corner studs (Fig. 35j).

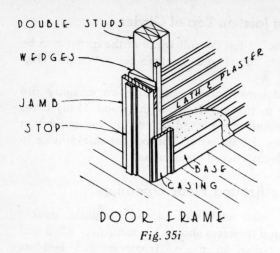

DOOR FRAME

Fig. 35i

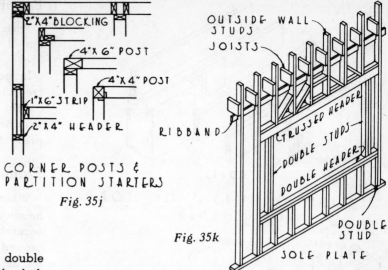

CORNER POSTS & PARTITION STARTERS

Fig. 35j

FRAMING FOR WIDE WINDOW OPENINGS

Fig. 35k

When a partition begins opposite a stud, double studs are used so that again a nailing edge for lath is formed.

When a partition starts between two studs, 2- x 4-in. headers are placed between them, and a 1- x 6-in. vertical lathing strip forms the nailing corner with the first partition stud.

Framing For Wide Windows

Conventional windows are framed as previously discussed. However, when a large picture window is used, care must be exercised in framing the header, as considerable weight of the structure above has to be carried by the long-span header. Consequently, some form of truss is recommended, as shown in Fig. 35k.

Proper framing in such cases assures crackfree walls. Any window over 4 ft. 0 in. wide may be classed as a wide window, and should be framed as shown.

Framing For Non-bearing Partitions

Double joists with solid 2- x 4-in. bridging 18 in. on centers should be used under nonbearing partitions, because of the additional weight of the partition itself (Fig. 35l). If the span of the joists is more than 10 ft. 0 in., triple joists should be used.

Note how the 1- x 6-in. board is used as a lathing board to form the proper nailing corner where ceiling meets partition.

Corner Bracing

Corner bracing is employed when horizontal sheathing is used in place of diagonal sheathing.

The 2- x 4-in. corner braces may be set flat, as shown in Fig. 35m, or may be turned edgewise and let into the studs. The diagonal brace would then be one continuous piece.

This latter method is better where insulation is to be used, since the braces do not block the stud space.

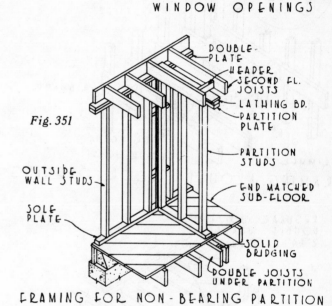

Fig. 35l

FRAMING FOR NON-BEARING PARTITION

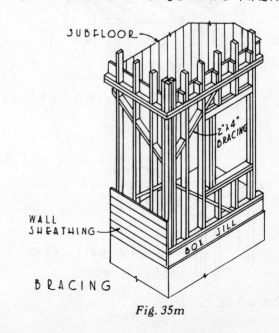

BRACING

Fig. 35m

Room Dormer Framing

Double rafters should be used at each side of a dormer (Fig. 35n), and all rafters should have at least 2½ in. bearing on the cap plate. Rafters should be toenailed on each side with 10d nails.

Note the nailing strip along the double rafter, to receive the roofing boards. Also note how the gable studs are cut to receive the end rafters.

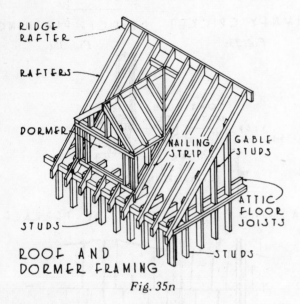

ROOF AND DORMER FRAMING

Fig. 35n

Dormer Flashing

Just as important as dormer framing is dormer flashing (Fig. 35o). Galvanized iron or copper flashing or "copper shingles" are overlapped as shown in the illustration.

DORMER FLASHING

Fig. 35o

Shingled Ridge Cap

The row of alternately lapped shingles along the top of the roof is known as the ridge cap (Fig. 35p). To prevent leakage at this most important point, continuous flashing must be used.

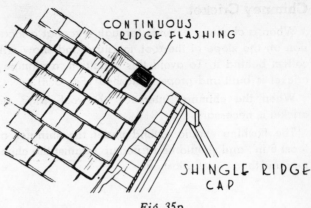

SHINGLE RIDGE CAP

Fig. 35p

Hip Flashing

The method of flashing and alternate overlap of shingles is similar to that described for the ridge cap. Galvanized iron or copper is used for the best results (Fig. 35q).

FLASHING AT HIP

Fig. 35q

Valley Flashing

Roof valleys that are not properly flashed are the source of many hard-to-find leaks. Galvanized iron and copper are the materials best suited for valley flashing (Fig. 35r).

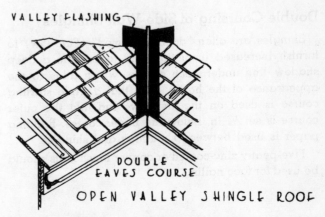

OPEN VALLEY SHINGLE ROOF

Fig. 35r

Chimney Cricket

When a chimney extends through a roof at a location on the slope of the roof, moisture and snow will collect behind it. To avoid this condition, a chimney cricket is built and properly flashed (Fig. 35s).

When the chimney intersects the roof ridge, no cricket is necessary.

The flashing should extend under the shingles at least 6 in., and should be turned up against the chimney and then counterflashed.

Drip Cap Flashing

The caps of windows and doors should be carefully flashed to prevent water leakage. The flashing material should extend up behind the siding about 5 in., then fit snugly over the cap moulding. If galvanized, caps should be painted before siding is put in place (Fig. 35t).

Flashing of Stoop or Terrace

To prevent troublesome moisture leakage between a concrete stoop or apron, a continuous strip of metal flashing should be placed in the wet concrete, running the full length of the joint (Fig. 35u).

The continuous flashing strip should extend about 8 in. under the siding.

Shingled Corner Detail

Figure 35v shows two methods of shingling an outside corner. In the extreme left corner, two corner boards are nailed directly to the sheathing, and the shingles are fitted snugly against them. At the right corner, alternate shingles are "laced" or lapped to resemble the ridge cap.

A 2- x 2-in. single inside strip is used on inside corners.

Double Coursing of Side-Wall Shingles

Shingles are often "double coursed" (Fig. 35w) to furnish increased insulation and to provide a deep shadow line under each course, which adds to the appearance of the house. Note that a triple starting course is used on the first row, and that the outer course is set ½ in. below the under course. Building paper is used between sheathing and shingles.

Five-penny zinc-coated or copper finish nails should be used for face nailing.

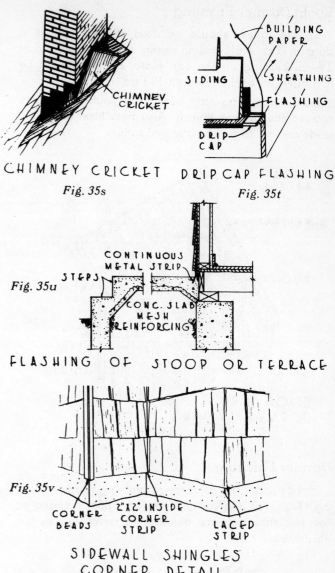

CHIMNEY CRICKET
Fig. 35s

DRIP CAP FLASHING
Fig. 35t

BUILDING PAPER
SIDING
SHEATHING
FLASHING
DRIP CAP

CONTINUOUS METAL STRIP
STEPS
CONC. SLAB
MESH REINFORCING
Fig. 35u

FLASHING OF STOOP OR TERRACE

CORNER BEADS
2"x2" INSIDE CORNER STRIP
LACED STRIP
Fig. 35v

SIDEWALL SHINGLES CORNER DETAIL

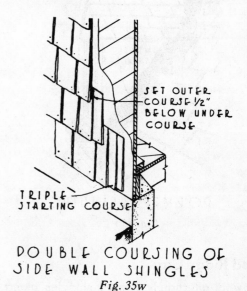

SET OUTER COURSE ½" BELOW UNDER COURSE
TRIPLE STARTING COURSE

DOUBLE COURSING OF SIDE WALL SHINGLES
Fig. 35w

Proper Setting of Wood Gutters

Wood gutters, when made of thoroughly seasoned kiln-dried Douglas fir, or equal, will last the life of the house. The gutter must be wide enough to carry the water away as fast as it drains from the roof, and it must also be set at the proper height in regard to the roof line so that snow may slide over it in the winter (Fig. 35x).

Note particularly that the back of the gutter does not rest against the frieze board, but is separated from it by blocks of wood nailed at intervals of about 3 ft. 0 in., this allows for overflow and air circulation, and prevents rotting.

Wood gutters should be painted inside and out before installation, and regularly thereafter, at intervals of about two years.

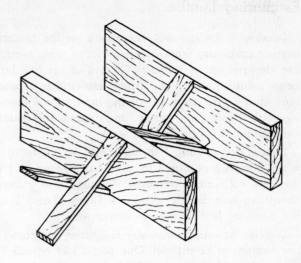

WOOD CROSS BRIDGES

Fig. 35y

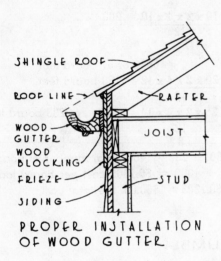

PROPER INSTALLATION OF WOOD GUTTER

Fig. 35x

Cross Bridging

Cross bridging is a term applied to the diagonal braces nailed between the floor joists. Their purpose is to stiffen the joists and prevent them from trying to buckle sideways when a heavy load is placed upon them (Fig. 35y).

Bridging members are placed every 8 ft. along the span of the joist. If a span is greater than 8 ft. 0 in. but less than 16 ft. 0 in., the bridging members are centered on the span.

The usual size of wood bridging is 1 x 3 in. There is also available a stamped steel cross bridge that is made to exact size, and requires less labor to install.

Steel Girders

The use of steel girders in small-home construction has been increasing in recent years in order to satisfy the desire for more clear space in the basement. A single 8-in. steel girder, spanning the full width of the basement from wall to wall, is often the only additional support needed for the floor joists to rest upon (Fig. 35z).

Where spans are longer, lally columns should be used on 8 ft. to 10 ft. centers. An 18 ft. 0 in. span on a single beam without lally columns would require a 10-in. deep beam, while the same span could be served by a 6-in. deep beam if a lally column were used to support the beam at mid-span.

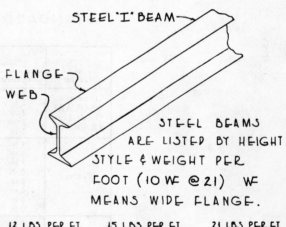

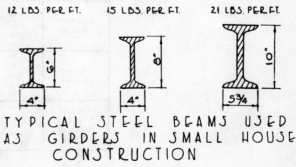

TYPICAL STEEL BEAMS USED AS GIRDERS IN SMALL HOUSE CONSTRUCTION

Fig. 35z

Estimating Lumber

Lumber is the general expression for the material used in carpentry work. Pieces of large cross sections are designated as *timbers*. Grades of lumber have been established by the trade association. Spruce, pine, and fir are used for framing lumber and sheathing; oak, white pine, maple, and cypress are usually used for flooring and finished work.

Boards are usually 1 in. thick and from 2 to 10 in. wide. Boards less than 1 in. thick are figured as 1 in. thick for estimating purposes. *Tongued and grooved* sheathing boards are called 1 x 4, 1 x 6, and 1 x 8, but measure less than these dimensions.

Lumber for *rough carpentry* is figured according to the number of board feet. One board foot equals 144 sq. in. of wood surface 1 in. thick.

By writing the standard dimensions of lumber over 12 ft. in the form of a fraction, the number of board feet of lumber is determined. For instance, 2 x 8 in. floor joist, 14 ft. long, would equal

$$\frac{2 \times 8 \times 14}{12} = \frac{56}{3} = 18\frac{2}{3} \text{ board feet.}$$

For several pieces, the amount of board feet in one piece is multiplied by the number of pieces involved.

When it is necessary to find the cost per board foot when the cost per thousand board feet is known, divide the cost by 1000. Similarly, when the cost per 100 board feet is known, divide by 100 to get the cost per board foot.

Problem: Find the cost of 40 pieces of 2 x 4 in. x 18 ft. at $150.00 per thousand.

Solution: $\dfrac{40 \times 2 \times 4 \times 18}{12} = 480$ board feet.

$150.00 \div 1000 = \$0.15$, the cost per board foot.

480 board feet $\times \$0.15 = \$72.00$, the cost of 480 board feet.

Problem: Find the cost of the following lumber.

    10 pc. of 2 x 4 in. x 10 ft.
    20 pc. of 2 x 4 in. x 12 ft.
    25 pc. of 2 x 4 in. x 14 ft.

When the cost of 2 x 4's is at $130.50 per thousand board feet.

Solution: $\dfrac{10 \times 2 \times 4 \times 10}{12} = \dfrac{200}{3}$

$$= 66\frac{2}{3} \text{ or } 67 \text{ board feet.}$$

$$\frac{20 \times 2 \times 4 \times 12}{12} = 160 \text{ board feet.}$$

$$\frac{25 \times 2 \times 4 \times 14}{12} = 233\frac{1}{3}, \text{ or } 233 \text{ board feet.}$$

$67 + 160 + 233 = 460$, total number of board feet.
$\$130.50 \div 1000 = \$0.1305$ cost per board foot.
$460 \times \$0.1305 = \$60.03$, the total cost.

STANDARD SIZES OF LUMBER

Type of Lumber	Nominal Size		Actual Size S4S At Comm. Dry Shp. Wt.	
	Thickness	Width	Thickness	Width
Dimension **4-SQUARE** Guide-Line **FRAMING**	2 in.	4 in.	1⅝ in.	3⅝ in.
	2 in.	6 in.	1⅝ in.	5⅝ in.
	2 in.	8 in.	1⅝ in.	7½ in.
	2 in.	10 in.	1⅝ in.	9½ in.
	2 in.	12 in.	1⅝ in.	11½ in.
Timbers	4 in.	6 in.	3⅝ in.	5½ in.
	4 in.	8 in.	3⅝ in.	7½ in.
	4 in.	10 in.	3⅝ in.	9½ in.
	6 in.	6 in.	5½ in.	5½ in.
	6 in.	8 in.	5½ in.	7½ in.
	6 in.	10 in.	5½ in.	9½ in.
	8 in.	8 in.	7½ in.	7½ in.
	8 in.	10 in.	7½ in.	9½ in.
Common Boards	1 in.	4 in.	²⁵⁄₃₂ in.	3⅝ in.
	1 in.	6 in.	²⁵⁄₃₂ in.	5⅝ in.
	1 in.	8 in.	²⁵⁄₃₂ in.	7½ in.
	1 in.	10 in.	²⁵⁄₃₂ in.	9½ in.
	1 in.	12 in.	²⁵⁄₃₂ in.	11½ in.
Shiplap Boards	1 in.	4 in.	²⁵⁄₃₂ in.	3⅛ in. face
	1 in.	6 in.	²⁵⁄₃₂ in.	5⅛ in. face
	1 in.	8 in.	²⁵⁄₃₂ in.	7⅛ in. face
	1 in.	10 in.	²⁵⁄₃₂ in.	9⅛ in. face
	1 in.	12 in.	²⁵⁄₃₂ in.	11⅛ in. face
Tongued and Grooved Boards	1 in.	4 in.	²⁵⁄₃₂ in.	3¼ in. face
	1 in.	6 in.	²⁵⁄₃₂ in.	5¼ in. face
	1 in.	8 in.	²⁵⁄₃₂ in.	7¼ in. face
	1 in.	10 in.	²⁵⁄₃₂ in.	9¼ in. face
	1 in.	12 in.	²⁵⁄₃₂ in.	11¼ in. face

PART III
PLANNING THE HOUSE

Selecting the Site and Lot

Before the actual planning of a new house is begun, some thought must be given to the selection of a suitable site. The word *site* must not be confused with the word *lot*. Whereas lot refers to the actual plot of ground on which the house is to be built, site pertains to the locality wherein the lot is situated.

Public Utilities

Perhaps one of the most important considerations in selecting a site is the availability of public utilities. These include water supply, sewage disposal, gas, and/or electricity. In the residential development of a town or city, contractors and builders usually buy up a site and proceed to develop it by dividing it into plots and erecting houses. Usually this is done with the cooperation of the city and the public utilities, who in turn install adequate facilities for water, sewage, street lights, gas mains etc.

When the fringe areas surrounding already developed sites are bought up by realty corporations, and opened for development, the public utilities are often not available at the time the property is bought. Under such conditions a prospective buyer might sign a contract with the builder which says that when public services are installed, his property may be assessed for his prorata share of the cost. Such assessment clauses should be carefully read and understood before signing any contract.

Convenience

Convenience to schools, churches, transportation, shopping, etc., is another important consideration, but this convenience often must be compromised to gain other objectives, such as location in the more desirable residential areas.

Zoning Regulations

Most municipalities are planned with certain areas zoned to meet the needs of industrial, commercial, civic, and residential requirements, and a prospective buyer should inform himself regarding the location of the various zones (Fig. 36a). Many times a homeowner learns that the house on the opposite corner of his block is being torn down to make way for a filling station. Protesting such a development, he and other neighbors file objections at the town hall, only to learn that the property in question is located in a business zone, the dividing line of which runs along

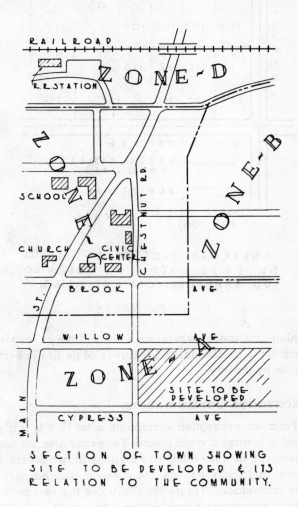

SECTION OF TOWN SHOWING SITE TO BE DEVELOPED & ITS RELATION TO THE COMMUNITY.

Fig. 36a

the center of his own block! It is wise to choose a site well within the zone limits, as many times these boundaries are moved to accommodate the normal growth of the business center of a town.

Of the two residential zones shown on the map (Fig. 36a), zone A is the more desirable, because it is located a safe distance from zone D, which represents an industrial zone, adjacent to the railroad. Consequently, the frontage of any lots in zone E might be restricted to a minimum of 60 ft., while those in zone A would require a frontage of 100 ft. Zone C is reserved for commercial and business interests.

Division of Site Into Lots

The enlarged view of the proposed site shows how the area is divided into lots. Some lots are larger and more desirable than others, but each must conform to the minimum frontage restrictions set up by the city

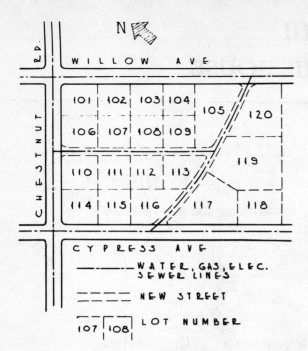

ENLARGED SECTION OF SITE TO
BE DEVELOPED — SHOWING
THE NUMBERED LOTS & UTILITIES.

Fig. 36b

zoning ordinance, where such an ordinance exists. Each lot is numbered, and a survey of its size is kept on file by the city.

Excavation Considerations

From an excavation standpoint, a lot that is fairly level is always a good choice. The excavation for the basement, in a level lot, may be done in two different ways, and oddly enough, the cheaper way has definite advantages. Figure 36c illustrates the two methods of excavating a level lot for a basement.

Sometimes the lots on one side of the street are

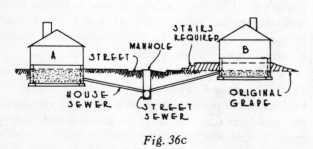

Fig. 36c

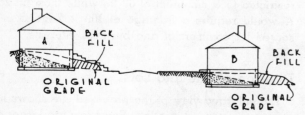

Fig. 36d

higher in elevation than those opposite. Is it better to build on the high land, or on the low land? The illustration (Fig. 36d) shows some important considerations. Excavation and backfilling costs will be about the same, but house A (Fig. 36d) requires several steps to reach first-floor level from street level. On the other hand, soil drainage into the street gutters is more favorable with house A. The lower part of the back yard of house B may become flooded if there is not adequate drainage at this point. House A has the added advantage that a garage may be built under the first floor without much difficulty. Of the four types of lots discussed so far, perhaps the best all around choice and method of excavation is that shown with house B (Fig. 36c).

Shade Trees

A lot containing trees and bushes may look like a jungle when it is purchased, and the cost of clearing the lot may add a little more to the budget, but if judgment is used in selecting the proper trees, the owner may have a made-to-order plot that will furnish the proper setting for his home. It takes years to grow a sizable shade tree, and any owner would be fortunate to be able to buy a lot with full-grown trees on it (Fig. 36e).

Lot Survey

A plan showing the dimensions and elevations of a

SHADE TREES ARE A VALUABLE
ASSET TO ANY LOT.

Fig. 36e

plot of ground, as established by a surveyor, and kept on record at the local courthouse, is called a lot survey.

It is the only legal document that shows the undisputed boundaries of a given lot. It usually forms a part of the deed, and any home owner is entitled to obtain a photostat of the original lot survey as filed with the city. The lot survey plan shows the outlines of the house, and consequently resembles what is called a "plot plan." The two plans should not be confused. The latter plan is not a legal document, and is actually drawn from the information appearing on the lot survey plan. The plot plan includes such things as walks, driveway, trees, gardens, etc., and is made by the draftsman.

Study carefully the lot survey shown in Fig. 36f. It represents the survey of Plot No. 119, Fig. 36b.

The following explanation will help to understand the figure.

EL. 206.06 means that the point so marked is 206.06 ft. above sea level.

90.92 means that the boundary is 90.92 ft. in length between the dots.

S35°10'E means that the line proceeds in a direction reckoned from south, turned 35 deg. 10 min. eastward. All directions are reckoned either from north or south, whichever yields the least angle.

The New House: Preliminary Considerations

In past years not much thought was given to the actual planning of a house for the specific needs of the family that was going to live in it. A house was bought, and the family fitted themselves to it. Today the trend is to fit the house to the family. A man probably buys but one house in a lifetime, so is it not logical for him to want a house that will meet his family's needs for as long as he lives in it? Following is a discussion of three important preliminary considerations: size, shape, and style.

Size

Acquiring a new postwar home has resolved itself into three classifications: Buying from a large-scale building organization on a mass-planned site, buying from a small contractor on a site of the owner's choice, or building the home oneself, in any desired location.

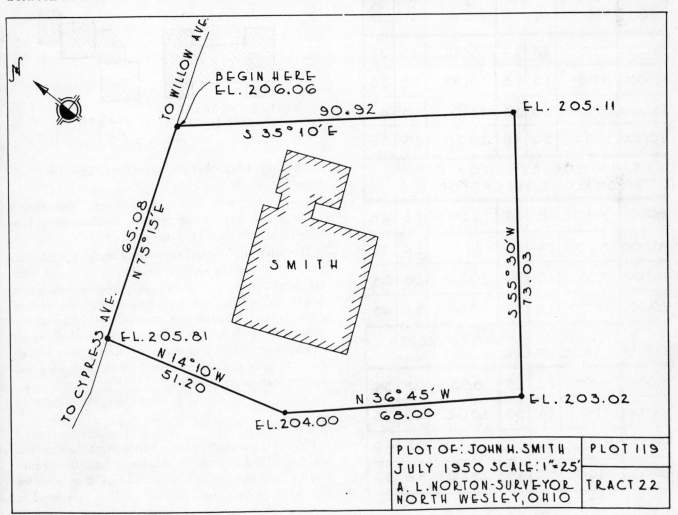

Fig. 36f

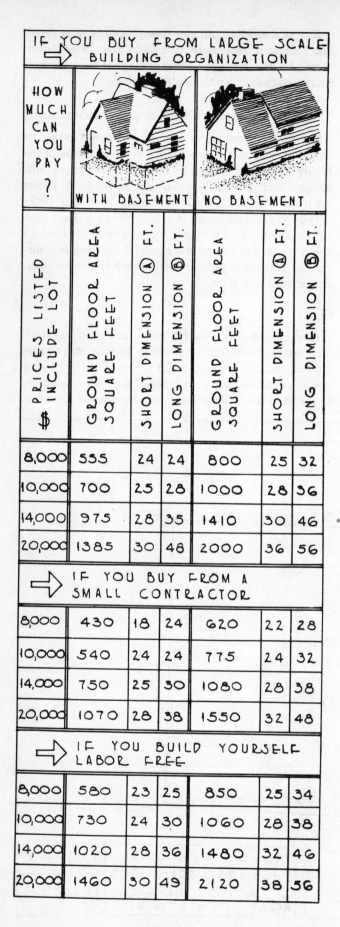

	WITH BASEMENT			NO BASEMENT		
PRICES LISTED INCLUDE LOT $	GROUND FLOOR AREA SQUARE FEET	SHORT DIMENSION (A) FT.	LONG DIMENSION (B) FT.	GROUND FLOOR AREA SQUARE FEET	SHORT DIMENSION (A) FT.	LONG DIMENSION (B) FT.
IF YOU BUY FROM LARGE SCALE BUILDING ORGANIZATION						
8,000	555	24	24	800	25	32
10,000	700	25	28	1000	28	36
14,000	975	28	35	1410	30	46
20,000	1385	30	48	2000	36	56
IF YOU BUY FROM A SMALL CONTRACTOR						
8,000	430	18	24	620	22	28
10,000	540	24	24	775	24	32
14,000	750	25	30	1080	28	38
20,000	1070	28	38	1550	32	48
IF YOU BUILD YOURSELF LABOR FREE						
8,000	580	23	25	850	25	34
10,000	730	24	30	1060	28	38
14,000	1020	28	36	1480	32	46
20,000	1460	30	49	2120	38	56

HOW MUCH CAN YOU PAY?

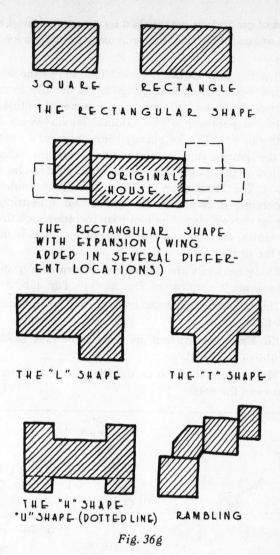

SQUARE   RECTANGLE

THE RECTANGULAR SHAPE

ORIGINAL HOUSE

THE RECTANGULAR SHAPE WITH EXPANSION (WING ADDED IN SEVERAL DIFFERENT LOCATIONS)

THE "L" SHAPE   THE "T" SHAPE

THE "H" SHAPE
"U" SHAPE (DOTTED LINE)   RAMBLING

Fig. 36g

Each method has obvious advantages and disadvantages.

The owner who wants a relatively inexpensive house may have to compromise location, neighborhood, and individuality of design.

The table at the right represents some typical comparisons of various sized homes listed with and without basements, and under the three classifications mentioned above. Costs have been compiled based on price levels of labor and materials existing at the time of this writing. It is apparent that the basementless house provides a means of obtaining greater first-floor area, for a given cost, and for this reason is becoming extremely popular.

Shape

Since it is useless to plan a house that is larger than we can afford to build, it is wise to limit the square feet of floor area to match our budget, then plan for our needs within such limits. The data presented in the previous table are primarily for houses of rectangular shape, with simple roof structure. Too much deviation from these conditions will result in higher costs. Remember this: As a house becomes less square in shape (Fig. 36g), it costs more to build and own, any way you look at it. For instance, here are just a few items of increased cost when building a rambling-type house: excavation, foundation, roof, exterior finish, heating, and electric wiring.

Style

There has been a trend to break away from conventional architectural exteriors which are supposed to be copies of colonial, Georgian, Dutch, English, and other treatments, and adopt a contemporary design based upon common sense and function. Why imitate a house today that was designed by colonists in 1765? We do not live as they lived, after all; their house was functional for their needs, but certainly not for ours.

Suppose, for example, we decided to build a colonial-type house. If it is to be authentically styled it should contain a swinging caldron in a large fireplace, for cooking. But who wants to cook in such a manner?

Therefore we install a modern kitchen! Further, authentic design calls for small windows, made up of several small lights. In early times there existed a high tariff on glass, and consequently window lights were kept to a minimum in size. But small lights are not functional, they hinder our view and are difficult to clean, and if the sash is made of wood it is costly to paint. Therefore we again violate authenticity by utilizing large windows and open glazing! Likewise, wooden roof shingles are not fireproof, so we use composition shingles. What we are trying to show here is that our colonial house is becoming less and less colonial and more and more modern. The questions arise: How far should we go in being authentic? Does a colonial house furnish the proper setting for a streamlined automobile?

When our house has finally been equipped for modern living, what have we really? At best, it is an irreconcilable mixture of old and new. It may take the name of "modern colonial," but that is a misnomer, for anything that is modern cannot at the same time be colonial.

We are therefore going to stress the planning of small homes without regard to such architectural designations as colonial, Cape Cod, Georgian, etc. Rather, we will try to make the best use of shapes and materials to design a suitable home planned for a specific family. When our house has been completed, if one should ask, "What type of architecture is it?" the answer should be simply, "It is contemporary," which means that the structure is designed for today's living, to suit the needs of the occupants. If our house should happen to have a gambrel roof, it will not be because we are trying to imitate a Dutch colonial, but because the gambrel roof is extremely functional

—it offers the most second-floor headroom of any of the pitched roofs. If the roof is flat, it is not because we want to create a modern look, but because, for the specific case at hand, we wish to live under a roof, not in it.

MANSARD (OBSOLETE)

GAMBREL ROOF

HIP ROOF

GABLE ROOF

FLAT SLOPE ROOF

Problems: Size, Shape, and Style

1. How much would you expect to pay for a 1½-story house, without basement, with a ground floor area of 900 square feet? Assume house will be bought from a large-scale builder. (Use table, page 68.)

   Answer: _____

2. If the same house were built by a small contractor, how much would it cost?

   Answer: _____

3. Calculate the floor area of the house shown in the accompanying sketch. Figure area of parts A and B separately, then add.

   Answer: _____

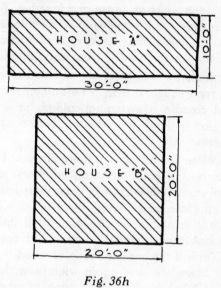

4. How much would it cost to build a 1½-story house with full basement, if the size of the house is about 29 ft. 0 in. x 35 ft. 0 in., and labor is furnished by the owner?

   Answer: _____

5. The dimensions shown in the table on page 68 are merely suggested dimensions. Other dimensions may be substituted, provided the area remains the same. According to the table, $8000 would buy a 22 ft. 0 in. x 28 ft. 0 in. basementless house from a small contractor. What should the short dimension be if the longer dimension is made 31 ft. 0 in.?

   Answer: _____

6. Approximately how many square feet of floor area would be planned with a budget of $12,000 if a house is to be 1½ story, basementless?

   Answer: _____

7. What might be a suitable length and width for the house in problem 6?

   Answer: _____

8. Examine the two house shapes shown in Fig.

36h. House A is rectangular, house B is square. The total wall perimeter, or length, of each house is the same, namely 80 ft. (30 + 10 + 30 + 10 and 20 + 20 + 20 + 20); consequently we might expect to pay the same for the walls of each house as they both contain the same amount of material. But house B contains 33⅓ per cent more floor area than house A (20 × 20 = 400, 30 × 10 = 300). Can you see why a square or nearly square house shape is so often used?

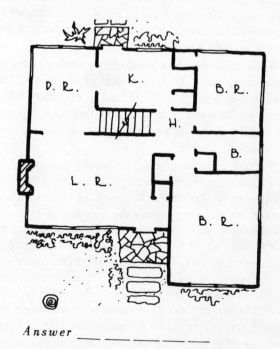

Fig. 36h

9. In the space below each of the house plans shown, write the name of the basic shape that it represents. See page 68.

Answer _____

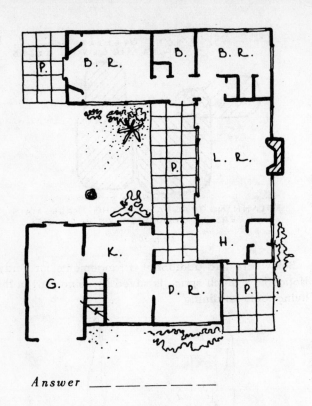

Answer _____

Answer _____

10. In the space below each sketch, identify the type of roof. Where more than one type is used on the same house, list each type that is found. (See page 69.)

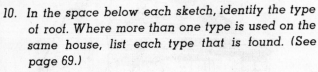

Answer _____

Answer _____

Answer _____

Answer _____

Answer _____

[71]

The Technique of Over-All Planning

A common error in home planning is to start with a determined conception of a favorite room; say a "dream" living room, and then add other rooms around it. Such a plan proceeds in a haphazard manner, without regard to shape or cost. By the time we have added everyone's favorite room, a two-car garage, a rumpus room, a den, a super kitchen and laundry, we have no defined shape, and what is worse, we have a monstrosity!

Obviously our planning has been started in the wrong direction. Instead of planning from the inside out, we shall endeavor to plan from the outside in (over-all planning). Then we will attempt to reconcile the space we need to live in with the money we can afford to spend, and then plan that space so that it serves our needs functionally and economically.

We Eat, We Live, We Sleep

No matter how young, or old, or how small, or large a family may be, there are three basic functions that must be provided for, namely, eating, living, and sleeping. The planner must provide sufficient area properly located in regard to its purpose.

A good beginning, then, is to examine some samples of good planning to discover how the architects have grouped the eating, living, and sleeping areas.

In Fig. 36i is a pictorial view of a contemporary house designed by Paul R. Williams, A.I.A. In Fig. 36j appears the floor plan. If we encircle the eating, living, and sleeping areas as shown in Fig. 36j, we have an elementary planning diagram.

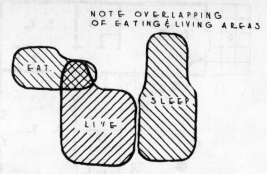

PLANNING DIAGRAM OF THE THREE MAIN
AREAS FOR HOUSE SHOWN IN FIG. 36j

Fig. 36k

Below are two additional arrangements for study. Notice how much space is saved by using part of the living room for dining.

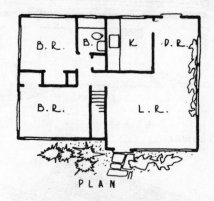

PLAN

PLANNING DIAGRAM

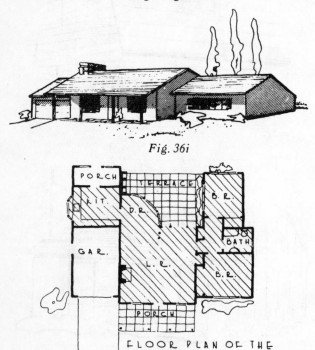

Fig. 36i

FLOOR PLAN OF THE
ABOVE HOUSE

Fig. 36j

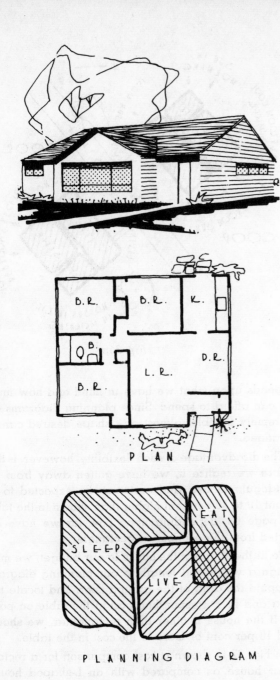

PLAN

PLANNING DIAGRAM

2. When planning with a limited budget, it is necessary to hold eating and living areas to a minimum. To accomplish this a dining alcove is often added at one end of the living area, and the kitchen becomes merely a food preparation center, occupying a minimum of floor area.

Another important consideration is the arrangement of the living area so that it has access to a view, if possible. If the front does not offer a pleasing view, perhaps the rear yard can contain a patio or garden.

If there are small children, it is wise to have a play area that may be supervised from the kitchen window.

In allotting space for the three main areas, keep in mind that the sleeping area includes bathroom and closets; the living area includes front entrance, stairs, closets, den or library where the budget will permit, and a part of the eating area when desired. The eating area includes the laundry as well as the kitchen in a single-story structure without a basement.

In addition to what we have discussed so far, there remains the matter of orientation.

Orientation

In regard to a plan or layout, orientation refers to the direction in which a given wall faces. Every plan should contain an orientation symbol which gives the direction of north, south, east, and west. Usually only the north position is labeled. See Survey Plan, page 67.

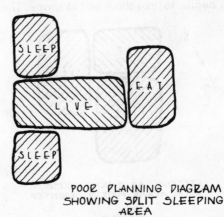

POOR PLANNING DIAGRAM
SHOWING SPLIT SLEEPING
AREA

Fig. 361

GOOD PLANNING DIAGRAM
SHOWING SEPARATELY GROUPED
AREAS

Fig. 36m

Grouping the Three Main Areas

The success of the planning of a new house depends upon the proper placing or grouping of the various areas. The examples of good planning presented on the previous page bring to light two important considerations:

1. Each area should be grouped by itself, and not split into separate parts. For example, Fig. 361 shows that the sleeping quarters have been divided into two separate areas. Such an arrangement calls for two bathrooms, and leads to undesirable closet location. It is far better to keep the bedrooms and bathroom as an integrated unit, together with all the necessary clothes closets and linen closets. The second diagram, Fig. 36m, shows how the planning diagram should look. Such a diagram lends itself to a U-shaped house.

A house is definitely more livable when the various areas are properly oriented. A kitchen that has an east exposure is bright and cheerful during the breakfast and morning hours, whereas a kitchen with a northern exposure is cold and lacks brightness.

Living areas are more enjoyable when they receive the afternoon sun; consequently a south or southwest exposure is preferable.

Bedrooms that face north are cooler in the summer. Naturally they are more difficult to heat in the winter, but with today's modern heating systems, this is no problem.

In Fig. 36n is shown a planning diagram consisting of three given areas, placed without regard to orientation, and in Fig. 36o are shown the same areas properly oriented.

In Fig. 36p is shown the answer to the common problem: What happens when identical houses are built on opposite sides of the street? Obviously, the house on the north side of the street is far more desirable. Good planning calls for placing the areas differently on opposite sides of a street. This is easily accomplished when working with planning diagrams, and with a little practice the student will gain facility in the proper placing of the three main areas.

Fitting the Shape of the House to the Budget

When the areas have been grouped satisfactorily, the house begins to take some sort of shape. The shape

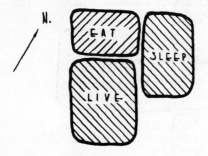

RECTANGULAR SHAPE HOUSE
WITH AREAS POORLY ORIENTED

Fig. 36n

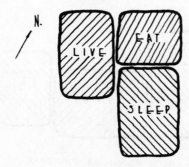

SAME HOUSE AS ABOVE, BUT WITH
CORRECT ORIENTATION

Fig. 36o

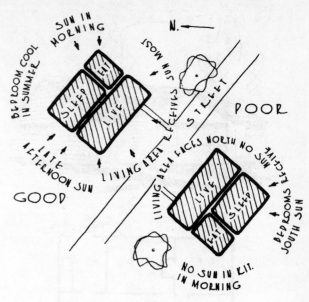

Fig. 36p

depends upon what we have in mind and how much we can afford to spend. Since planning diagrams are extremely flexible, almost any shape desired can be arranged.

The disadvantage of such flexibility, however, is that before we realize it, we have gotten away from the rectangular house, and costs can be expected to be about 10 to 50 per cent higher than shown in the table on page 68, depending upon how far we have departed from the economical rectangle.

To fit the shape of the house to our budget, we must assign a width and length to our planning diagram, compute the area of the ground floor, and locate this area and its corresponding cost in the table on page 68. If the house is other than rectangular, we should add 10 per cent or more to the cost in the table.

In Fig. 37 is shown a cost comparison for a rectangular house as compared with an L-shaped house, both with the same relative size areas.

An H- or U-shaped house may cost 20 to 25 per cent more, and a rambling house 50 per cent more than the same area built to a rectangular shape.

The above prices are based on houses with no basement. The increased cost of the L shape results from more complicated roof construction, plus slightly more exterior wall because of increased perimeter.

Problem: The following relative space requirements are needed for a certain family of four:

The living and eating areas are to overlap for a dining alcove. Arrange these areas for a properly planned rectangular house, and show approximate over-all dimensions to conform to a $17,000 budget. Assume full basement. Note orientation given. You may show sleeping area L-shaped to occupy a corner

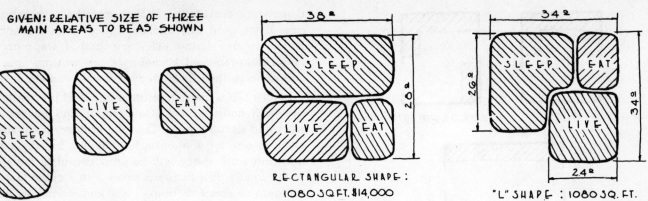

GIVEN: RELATIVE SIZE OF THREE
MAIN AREAS TO BE AS SHOWN

RECTANGULAR SHAPE:
1080 SQ.FT. $14,000

Fig. 37

"L" SHAPE : 1080 SQ. FT.
14000+10% =$15,400

if you wish, as was done on page 74. Draw a planning diagram within the lot space provided below, freehand. Draw areas proportional to relative size as given. Remember to leave sufficient space between lot line and your diagram.

The Technique of Room Planning

After the main areas have been arranged and properly oriented for a given location, and the exterior dimensions have been approximated so that the floor area conforms to the budget, we are ready to plan the rooms. If, during this next planning stage, our rooms prove to be too small, we must either increase the budget, omit certain rooms, or combine certain areas to the best possible advantage. Therefore it is of extreme importance to plan a room for maximum utility in minimum space.

The Kitchen

The kitchen is, beyond a doubt, the most important

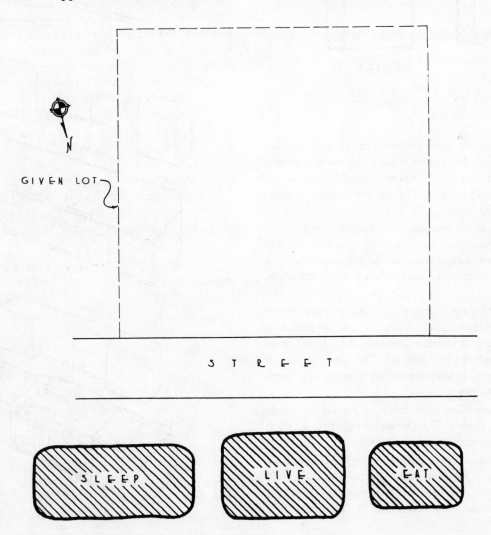

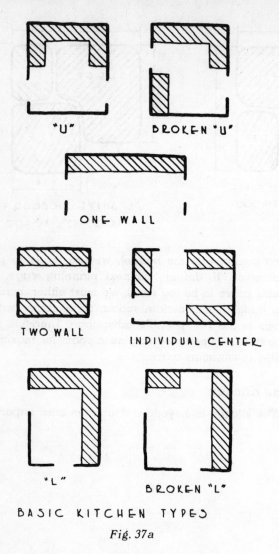

BASIC KITCHEN TYPES

Fig. 37a

these work centers the kitchen must be of a certain size. If we plan any kitchen smaller than the minimum, we are losing efficiency, and if we plan a larger-than-required kitchen, we are wasting space. Our concern then, is to study the work centers.

Figure 37b is the refrigeration and food-preparation center. It consists of the refrigerator and necessary work and storage space. The refrigerator will not vary much in size for different sized families, but the storage and work space will be proportional to the size of the family. If a family is small, 5 to 7 cubic feet of refrigerator space is ample, but larger families can use up to 12 cubic feet of refrigerator space. The width of the latter refrigerator is only 6 in. more than the former, but the cabinet and worktable length might be doubled for the larger family.

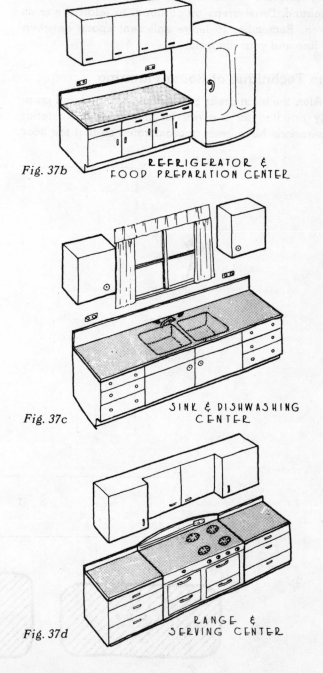

Fig. 37b REFRIGERATOR & FOOD PREPARATION CENTER

Fig. 37c SINK & DISHWASHING CENTER

Fig. 37d RANGE & SERVING CENTER

room in the house. It is the center of much activity during the day, for the entire family. In recent years, architects, planners, and housewives alike have become increasingly aware of what constitutes a well-planned kitchen.

Manufacturers of kitchen equipment have done their share in giving us space-saving and efficient fixtures, and have been responsible for much of our education through their advertising and valuable literature.

Certain nationally circulated magazines have undertaken independent research in economical kitchen planning, and have brought their findings to thousands of interested readers. Therefore it is not without considerable understanding that we approach this important subject.

First, let us examine what may be called the basic kitchen types. Figure 37a shows seven types, each suitable for a workable kitchen layout.

Each shaded area represents the space occupied by the work centers. A given family requires the correct size work centers for food preparation and storage, washing, cleaning, and cooking; to accommodate

Figure 37c shows the sink and dish-washing center; here again, a shorter cabinet with less storage space may be selected by the small family.

The range and serving center is shown in Fig. 37d, and this likewise may be varied to suit the size of the family. Most planners have a good idea of how much kitchen they need, and will find little difficulty in arranging the three work centers within the shaded areas shown on page 75.

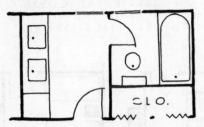

TOILET, BATH AND LAVATORY THAT CAN BE USED BY TWO OR THREE PEOPLE AT THE SAME TIME.

Fig. 37e

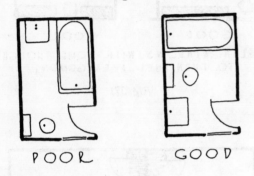

POOR   GOOD

(DOOR OPENS ON TOILET)

Fig. 37f

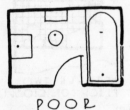

POOR   GOOD

(DOOR OPENS AGAINST TUB)

Fig. 37g

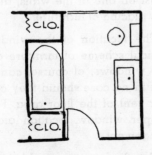

TUB BETWEEN TWO CLOSETS

Fig. 37h

The Bathroom

The bathroom of today is designed so that it serves adequately the needs of an entire family, instead of one person. As shown in Fig. 37e, there has been added to the conventional bathroom, an outer lavatory with two washbasins and a linen closet. Thus while one person has the privacy of the bathroom, two others may make use of the lavatories. This arrangement is especially adaptable to a family with school-age children.

If the budget will not permit such a layout, perhaps a small lavatory, equipped with a toilet, can be added near the kitchen.

In regard to bathroom fixtures, the manufacturers have again done a splendid job in educating the public. Individual units are available to suit any budget, and before one attempts actually to plan this important room, he should certainly see what is being offered, by obtaining the valuable information available from the various manufacturers.

Once the fixtures have been selected, they should be arranged with considerable thought as to their location relative to walls, doors, windows, and to economical plumbing. It is not generally desirable to place the bathtub under a window. A toilet should not be placed so that it is in full view through the open bathroom door. A lavatory should not be so close to the wall that there is no elbow room.

In Figs. 37f, 37g, 37h are shown some good and poor examples of bathroom planning.

The Dining Space

The high cost of a separate dining room and the desire for more open space and fewer partitions have led to the functional arrangement of combining the living room and dining area. Dining privacy can be had by a folding "accordion" partition which may be extended to form a closed room, or folded out of sight.

Windows 4 feet above the floor, and built-in cabinets allow the most efficient use of the floor area.

In planning dining alcoves and breakfast nooks, the planner should not be so anxious to save space that he overlooks the required dimensions of chairs, tables, and occupants. Figure 37i shows a compact but well-planned dining alcove.

The Living Room

Today's living room offers unlimited opportunity for the home designer. Here may be found a chance for expression of every family's whim, from fireplace or built-in television set to small-scale hothouse and solarium. Multiple doors may be thrown open to "bring inside" a vine-covered patio or barbecue pit. Spacious glass areas may overlook a private garden or natural view.

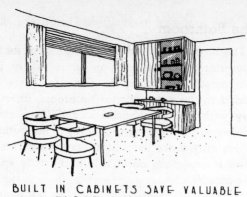

Fig. 37i   BUILT IN CABINETS SAVE VALUABLE FLOOR SPACE

ALLOW SUFFICIENT CLOSET SPACE IN BEDROOMS. SLIDING DOORS ARE SPACE SAVING

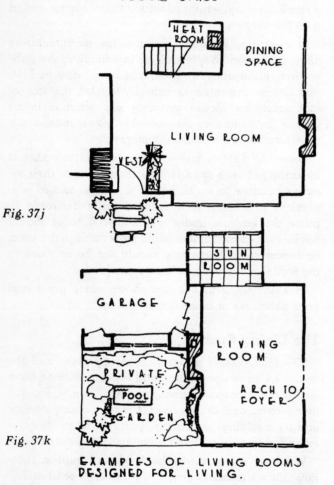

Fig. 37j

Fig. 37k

EXAMPLES OF LIVING ROOMS DESIGNED FOR LIVING.

GOOD   POOR

(PLAN WINDOWS WITH SOME THOUGHT TO FURNITURE ARRANGEMENT)

Fig. 37l

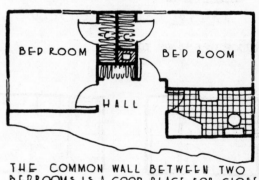

THE COMMON WALL BETWEEN TWO BEDROOMS IS A GOOD PLACE FOR CLOSETS

Fig. 37m

Such a living room will surely live up to its name, and is one of the joys of planning a contemporary house.

Figure 37j shows a combination living-dining space, with fireplace, spacious glass area, and clever vestibule, formed by living plants instead of a partition.

In Fig. 37k is shown a living room overlooking a private garden, and with a connecting sunroom.

The Bedroom

The bedroom has undergone two basic changes in recent years. Sliding closet doors have become popular, because of their space saving and attractive appearance; and the usual bedroom window has grown wider and shorter, with its sill located about 4 feet from the floor. The high location of the windows, at least on one of the walls, allows increased space for the placing of furniture.

The location of the windows should follow some logical scheme of furniture arrangement. The size of the windows, of course, can be as large as desired, but in no case should they contain less glass than 15 per cent of the floor area. Figure 37l shows how the proper window location aids in good furniture arrangement.

Two bedrooms are seldom placed side by side without taking advantage of using the common wall between them as a closet wall. Figure 37m shows how a chimney, a hall linen closet, and two bedroom closets are fitted compactly together. Many times it works out well to plan a bathroom between two bedrooms, with one entrance through the master bedroom, and another through the hall.

The master bedroom should, in general, have its own bathroom, or be favorably located in respect to the main bathroom. When there is to be an expansion attic above, it is wise to provide for sufficient plumbing to serve a bathroom in the expansion space, especially if the upstairs is to be used for bedrooms.

The Laundry

In the basementless house, the kitchen usually serves as the laundry, unless the budget will permit a separate room. Consequently sufficient space must be allowed for a standard washing machine, and the sink should be of the dual-basin type, with one deep basin. Cabinet space should be provided for storage of the ironing board and iron.

Planning an adequate laundry space is no problem when the house has a basement. A well-planned basement laundry is shown in Fig. 37n. If the owner cannot afford the fixtures at the time the house is built, the plumbing and electricity should be provided for, so that future connections may be made at any time.

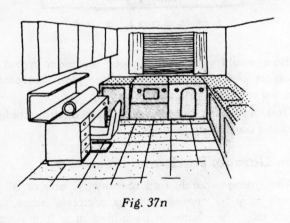

Fig. 37n

The Utility Room

The term *utility room* appeared at the time basementless houses became popular. Some utility rooms housed the heating plant, laundry, and storage space. In our work the utility room in basementless houses will be a room designed mainly to accommodate the heater and domestic hot-water equipment. It will also act as a logical center for electric switch, meter, and fuse boxes.

In planning the utility room, allow sufficient space around the heating or conditioning unit for installation, repair, and maintenance. Be sure there is plenty of illumination, adequate ventilation, and shelf space.

It is usually more desirable to locate the heating unit in the basement, in which case the utility room on

the first floor can be omitted. Figure 37o shows how the modern heating unit actually becomes a piece of basement furniture.

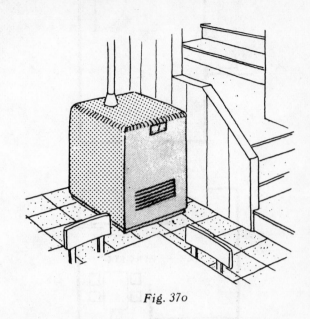

Fig. 37o

Planning Exercise

In the four kitchen plans given below, name the basic type (see page 76) and shade in the areas best suited for work centers, labeling each work center. Use abbreviations as follows: W for washing and cleaning, C for cooking, and R for refrigerator.

Sample Problem

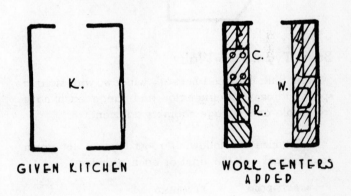

GIVEN KITCHEN   WORK CENTERS ADDED

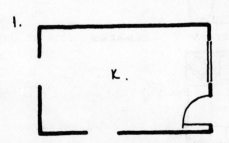

1.

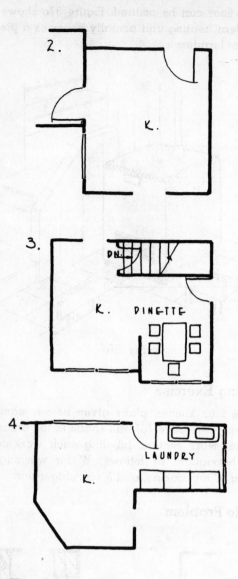

2.

3. DN. K. DINETTE

4. LAUNDRY K.

Basic Type: Two-Wall

Note: Sink is placed beneath window, with storage space adjacent. Refrigerator and range each have worktable and storage cabinets adjacent.

1. Criticize the following room layouts. Jot down your remarks at the right of each drawing.

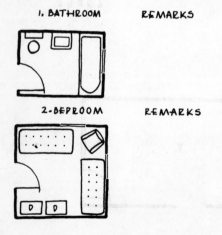

1. BATHROOM   REMARKS

2. BEDROOM   REMARKS

2. The second floor of a 2-story house has been planned with four bedrooms, hall, and bathroom. Criticize the layout in respect to the following:

Bedroom doors ....

Hall ....

Closet arrangement ....

Bathroom ....

Windows ....

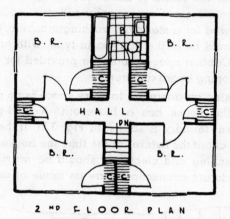

2 ND FLOOR PLAN

How would you improve upon the room layout of Problem 2? Redraw the second-floor plan incorporating the revisions you recommend.

You may sketch freehand or use a straightedge. Tracing paper may be used.

The Garage, Porch, and Breezeway

The garage, porch, and breezeway, one or all of which may be necessary for a complete home, are items that often have to be added at a future date when the budget is limited. If this is the case, careful provision for the future additions should be made at the time the house is planned. The following discussion is intended to guide the student in the planning of garages, breezeways, and porches, whether they are added later or built as a part of the original house.

The Garage

A detached garage, standing alone a short distance from the house, does not improve the appearance of the house. Furthermore, it is inconvenient to walk between the garage and the house in bad weather. Also, the additional length of driveway required increases the total cost of the house, and heating the garage is out of the question. Consequently, the wise choice is to plan for an attached garage.

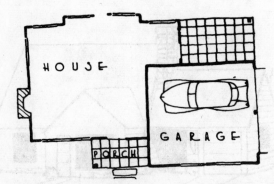

Fig. 37p

ATTACHED GARAGE MAKES HOUSE APPEAR
LARGER.

Fig. 37q

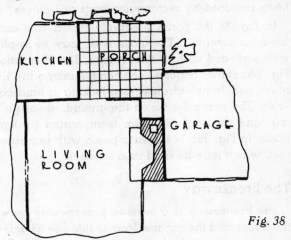

Fig. 37r

The sketch in Fig 37p shows how a garage aids in making the house appear longer. The doors face the side of the lot, and the windows are styled to complement the living-room window.

A two-car garage will measure about 20 ft. 0 in. x 20 ft. 0 in., and the plan view (Fig. 37q) shows the considerable area required in relation to the house area. When adding a garage to your preliminary sketches, do not underestimate its relative size.

The portecochere of years gone by has appeared again as a carport, in an attempt to provide a compromise means of shelter for the family car. The carport, however, should not be considered a garage,

and it is far wiser to plan a closed garage (see Fig. 37p). A carport provides shelter for a car, but it does not afford satisfactory protection in cold or rainy weather.

The Porch

Unlike the garage, which has been recognized for many years as a necessary part of the average home, the porch has had alternate periods of acceptance and rejection. Thirty years ago the desirable home had a spacious front porch, with numerous railings, and posts that supported the separate roof. Later the size of the porch was cut in half and moved to one corner

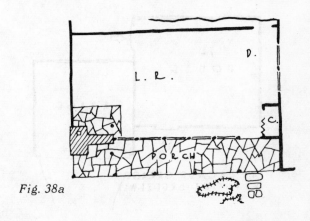

Fig. 38

PORCH BUILT INTO A CORNER OF
THE HOUSE

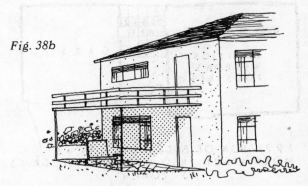

Fig. 38a

Fig. 38b

RIDGE OF PORCH USED AS SUN DECK

[81]

of the house, and a few years later, the porch disappeared altogether from the front of the house, only to appear at the rear. But now the porch or patio has come into popular use, as a necessary part of outdoor living.

The porch roof may or may not be a separate roof, and is often an extension of the main roof. Sometimes the porch occupies one corner of a house in the space normally occupied by a bedroom. In this case, it may be glazed for winter use and screened as an outdoor sleeping porch in warm weather. Railings have given way to horizontal bars, flower boxes, or just plain open spaces. The old-fashioned round pillars have been replaced by rectangular posts or trellises.

In Fig. 38 the porch is entirely closed, and can be used for sleeping. The glass sash may be replaced with screened sash in the summer. The illustration in Fig. 38a shows a stone-floor porch flanking the living room and front entrance, overlooking a landscaped lawn. The porch floor is on the ground, needs no railing, and the roof extension is supported by square posts. In Fig. 38b is shown a porch with separate flat roof, which may be used as a sundeck.

The Breezeway

The breezeway is a covered passageway between the house and the garage. It came into use as a device to have an attached, yet separate, garage. Sometimes, when the house is small in comparison with the size of the garage, an entire wall is rendered windowless because of the attached garage. This disadvantage is overcome by moving the garage away from the house, and connecting it with a breezeway.

The plan in Fig. 38c shows how the use of the breezeway furnishes a shelter in going from house to garage, serves as a porch for outdoor eating, and gives the house additional length, thus enhancing its appearance.

A breezeway and garage combination is shown in Fig. 38d, constructed as an integral wing to the house. Figure 38e shows the partial floor plan of the same house, showing the relative size of breezeway and single garage.

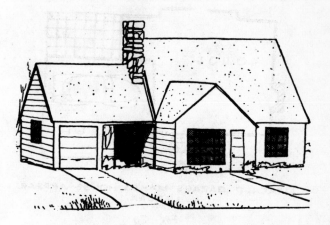

BREEZEWAY AND SINGLE-CAR GARAGE UNDER A COMMON ROOF

Fig. 38d

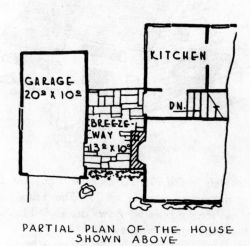

PARTIAL PLAN OF THE HOUSE SHOWN ABOVE

Fig. 38e

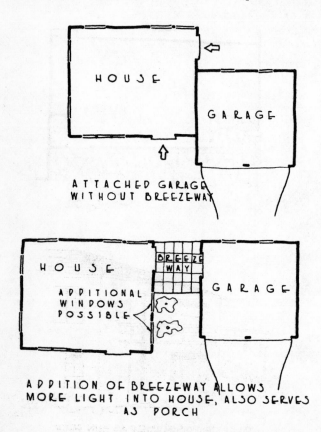

ATTACHED GARAGE WITHOUT BREEZEWAY

ADDITION OF BREEZEWAY ALLOWS MORE LIGHT INTO HOUSE, ALSO SERVES AS PORCH

Fig. 38c

Typical Planning Problems

We are now ready to put to use the facts we have learned in Part III and plan a house for a given set of conditions. Study carefully the following problems, for they represent a logical method of procedure.

Problem No. 1

A certain family of three require two bedrooms, living room, kitchen, and dining room on one floor. The relative sizes, but not necessarily the actual shapes, of the three main areas are as shown in Fig. 38f. Sketch, freehand, a planning diagram for a rectangular house (Fig. 38f), placing each area so that it has a desirable exposure in relation to the compass points given, as well as in relation to the given plot.

Additional Information

It is desired to have a full basement, and an expansion attic that can later be used for two additional rooms with complete bathroom. The budget has been set at about $17,000 maximum, and the house will be built to order by a local contractor.

Determine the approximate outside dimensions and size the various rooms. Allow ample closet space, and provide space for basement stairs as well as full stairway to attic.

Solution

Referring to the chart on page 68, for a house with basement built by a small contractor, we find that $17,000 will buy about 900 square feet of floor area. We arrive at this figure by observing that $14,000 will buy 540 square feet, so $17,000 will buy 17,000 ÷ 10,000, or 1.7 times as much, and 1.7 × 540 = 918 feet.

Suitable over-all dimensions of the house would be 30 ft. 0 in. x 30 ft. 0 in., or 28 ft. 6 in. x 32 ft. 0 in., 24 ft. 0 in. x 38 ft. 0 in., or any other combination of length that will yield approximately 900 square feet of area when the length is multiplied by the width. We shall try 28 ft. 0 in. x 32 ft. 0 in. and see how it works out.

Step 3

Figure 38g shows a sketch of the room layout with its approximate dimensions. Note how the size of the room dimensions are lettered in order to save space; thus in the living room, 13 ft. 4 in. is shown 13^4, and 15 ft. 0 in. is shown 15^0. Abbreviations are used to label the rooms as follows:

BR .... Bedroom
B .... Bath
K .... Kitchen

STEP 1: RELATIVE SIZE OF THREE MAIN AREAS GIVEN

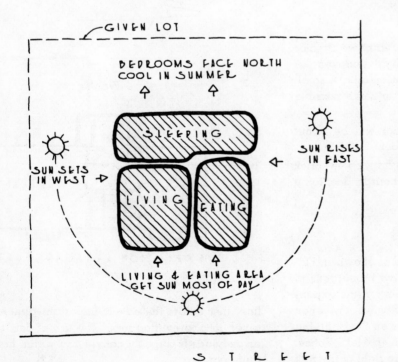

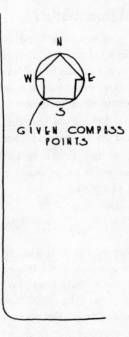

GIVEN COMPASS POINTS

STEP 2: PROPER ORIENTATION (EXPOSURE) AND ARRANGEMENT OF THE THREE MAIN AREAS

Fig. 38f

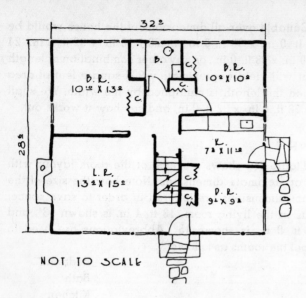

NOT TO SCALE

Fig. 38g

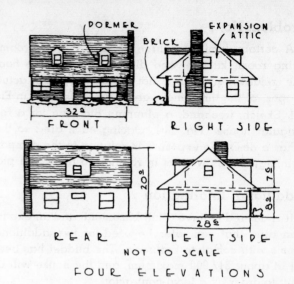

NOT TO SCALE

FOUR ELEVATIONS

Fig. 38h

DR .... Dining room
LR .... Living room

Also the following might be used:

H .... Hall
P .... Porch or patio
L .... Lavatory
DA .... Dining alcove
U .... Up (stairs)
D .... Down (stairs)
LC .... Linen closet
C .... Closet

Additional Information

A simple gable roof will be used, with two dormer windows facing front, to provide light and ventilation to the future rooms in the expansion attic. A small dormer window will also face rear, to serve possible future bathroom in attic space.

The ceiling height on the first floor will be about 8 ft. 0 in., and on the second floor, about 7 ft. 6 in.

The front of the house is to be finished in brick veneer, other walls to be wood clapboards. Roof to be composition shingles.

Step 4

Sketch roughly the four elevations as shown in Fig. 38h. Always keep in mind the relative proportions of the various parts. Note how the ceiling of the expansion attic follows the roof line. Remember, when viewed from the front, the chimney is on the right, but in the rear elevation it appears on the left. Notice, also, how the chimney appears to the right of the roof ridge in the left elevation, and to the left of the ridge when viewed from the right side.

Note that the tops of all doors and windows are in

PICTORIAL OF COMPLETED HOUSE

Fig. 38i

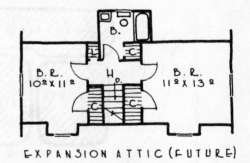

EXPANSION ATTIC (FUTURE)

Fig. 38j

line, just below the eaves. Important dimensions are given in abbreviated form. The use of dots to replace arrowheads is a recent convention which has become quite popular.

In Fig. 38i is a pictorial of the house we have planned, and in Fig. 38j a possible future expansion plan of the attic.

SOLUTION

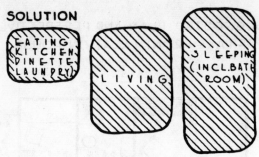

Fig. 38k

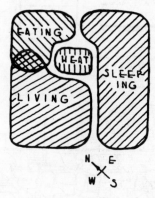

Fig. 38l

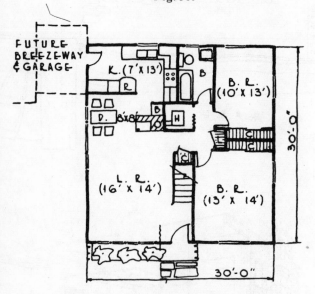

Fig. 38m

Fig. 38n

Problem No. 2

To plan a house to satisfy the following conditions:

Family .... { 2 adults
                                              2 boys, ages
                                              6 and 9

Type preference .... { Single-story
                                              Expansion attic
                                              No basement

Builder .... Local, small
Budget $12,000

Step 1

Sketch relative size of three areas, from a consideration of the given family (Fig. 38k).

First floor to include combination living-dining space, kitchen-laundry, two bedrooms, bathroom, and space for heating unit. Future provision for breezeway and one-car garage.

Plot is to be No. 108, as shown on page 68, with a frontage of 70 ft. and a depth of 100 ft. Front faces southwest.

Shape of house to be rectangular. Regular stairway up to attic and down to basement. Fireplace in living room desired.

Step 2

From chart, page 68, $12,000 will buy about 900 sq. ft. of area (30 x 60 say). Arrange areas for proper exposure (Fig. 38l).

Step 3

Sketch room layout showing approximate room sizes (Fig. 38m).

Step 4

Suggested exterior (Fig. 38n).

Problem No. 3

Plan a minimum lake-front vacation house for a family of two adults and two boys. This house is to be used in the summer and fall only. A fireplace must be provided as well as sleeping capacity for one additional person. The budget is extremely limited, about $4000. Consequently the interior dimensions will be held to 24 ft. 0 in. x 24 ft. 0 in. The living room is to be used for guest sleeping, as well as for eating of all meals.

The construction will be as follows:

Basement: none

Floor: 4 in. concrete on cinders

Roof: flat sloping, wood with tarred roofing

Walls: studs-plywood veneer, Masonite interior

Windows: stock wood sash, hinged

Picture window: built-up, single-glazed; three vent lights

Chimney: rubble

Closet curtains: accordion type, Modernfold

Front door: wood stock

The approximate allocation of space will be as shown in Fig. 38o.

The bathroom shall consist of a toilet, lavatory, and shower stall. Direct access from each of the two bedrooms must be planned. Also, a door opening out onto a stone step shall be provided.

The master bedroom will accommodate two single beds, a vanity, and chest of drawers. The small bed-

Fig. 38o

room will contain a double-deck bunk bed and two chests of drawers.

The multi-use living-dining room will have large picture window formed with 16 separate glass lights, two to be for ventilation.

Roof will have generous overhang on all sides, with 3 ft. 0 in. overhang in front.

Kitchen will be a compact purchased unit, containing electric range, sink, and refrigerator, together with storage space. Sketch of this unit is shown in Fig. 38p.

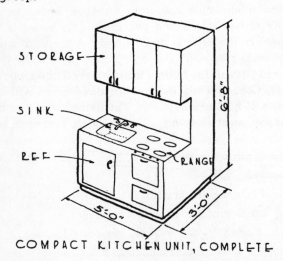

COMPACT KITCHEN UNIT, COMPLETE

Fig. 38p

SUGGESTED PLAN AND PERSPECTIVE OF LAKE-FRONT VACATION HOUSE

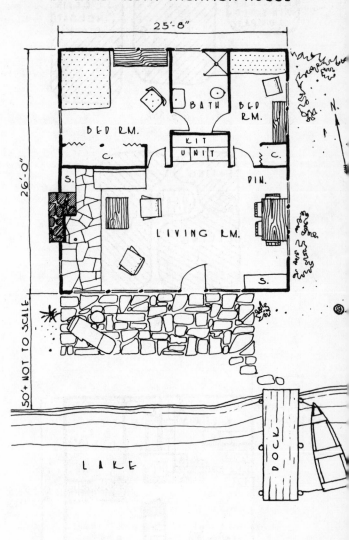

PART IV
STARTING THE HOUSE PLANS

Before the draftsman is required to draw the plans and elevations or the working drawings of the house, the owner and architect have generally reached certain conclusions as to its general design or style, the kind of material to be used, the size, and the approximate cost.

Following is a sample outline the architect might submit to the draftsman for further development.

Design for One-Story Frame House with Basement

ROOMS

1. Living room with fireplace; den adjacent to living room
2. Dining room
3. Three bedrooms with closets
4. Bathroom
5. Kitchen and lavatory
6. Basement—partially excavated
7. Ceiling height—8 ft. 0 in. throughout
8. Attached garage
9. Heating—one-pipe hot-water system

TYPE OF CONSTRUCTION

1. Concrete footings and foundation—box-sill construction
2. Double-hung standard windows—6 lights for each frame—picture window in living room
3. Suitable entrance door—style to conform with general design of building
4. Colonial siding—10 in. to weather
5. Gable roof—asphalt shingles—attic unfinished.

In many instances the architect will submit to the draftsman a freehand sketch of the plan showing the arrangement of rooms and indicating the approximate size of each room. From this sketch the draftsman will prepare a preliminary drawing to a ⅛-in. scale. Of course certain considerations and adjustments must be made, insofar as the arrangement and general dimensions of rooms are concerned, because the scale drawing will never quite work out like the preliminary rough sketch. When a suitable arrangement of rooms and good circulation are obtained, the draftsman will lay out the ¼-in. scale drawing of the first-floor plan, as in Plate 16.

It might be well to repeat here that this text does not primarily concern itself with room arrangements and interior design but rather with teaching the beginning draftsman how to prepare the working plans and details when a room arrangement has

been decided upon. There are many good books on planning the home, and the architectural draftsman should be familiar with this subject. In determining the size of a room, the draftsman must know something of the size and type of furniture that is to go into it. This information in turn necessitates a knowledge of the likes and dislikes of the owner, who is influenced either by his tastes or his pocketbook. Here it is enough to say that a well-planned home will satisfy the habits and mode of living of the family that is to occupy it.

The plans of the house must not be developed too far before the elevations are blocked in. It is customary to develop the plan and the elevation together, because this method saves considerable time and minimizes the possibility of mistakes. A vertical temporary wall section should be drawn alongside the elevation, extending from the footing to the cornice and including a window section. This temporary wall need not be drawn in detail but should be complete enough to aid in the construction of the elevation.

Plate 14 illustrates a layout such as the draftsman might prepare from the information given by the architect. It is by no means complete, but it serves as a basis for further study. The rooms are located so as to provide good circulation. Windows and doors are shown in their proper places to provide light, air, and the placement of furniture. Elevations, projected from the plan, are studied for good proportions and appearance. Details through the sill and cornice suggest the construction that might be used.

Another basic layout, or second stage, like that suggested on Plate 15, will show the owner the possibility of a larger house with the addition of a basement, dining room, and attached garage. Here again, the draftsman will give the names of the rooms and the sizes without making a working drawing with the dimensions needed by the builder.

The final stage, Plate 16, represents a working plan, completely dimensioned, with window and door schedules, as required by the builder. It is this final stage that will be developed and carried through to make a complete set of working drawings.

The student is here reminded not to begin with Plate 16, the final stage, but first to draw Plates 14 and 15 so as to give himself a general conception of a plan and elevation and to learn the procedure in their development.

PLATE 14

THE BASIC LAYOUT—FIRST STAGE

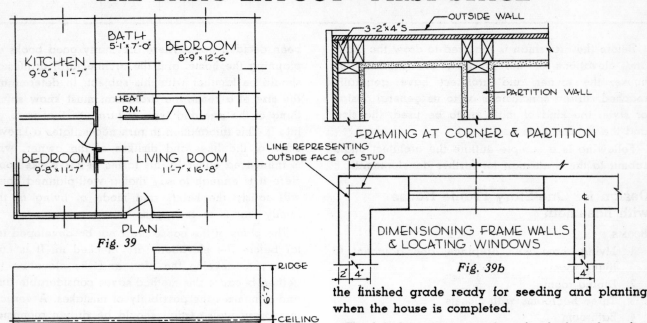

PLAN
Fig. 39

ELEVATION

Fig. 39a   SCALE: $\frac{1}{4}'' = 1'-0''$

FRAMING AT CORNER & PARTITION

DIMENSIONING FRAME WALLS & LOCATING WINDOWS
Fig. 39b

Objective

To draw a simple floor plan and the elevations in the proper sequence when room dimensions are given.

Procedure

1. Block in the outline of the plan and draw the center line of all wall partitions with a light continuous single line, using for dimensions the sizes of the rooms given (Fig. 39).

2. With dividers step off the thickness of outside walls, which is 6 in., and of partition walls, 4 in.

3. Locate all openings such as windows and doors by center lines and draw their widths to 3 ft. 0 in. The main door is 3 ft. 0 in. wide; the bedroom and bathroom doors are 2 ft. 8 in. and 2 ft. 0 in., respectively. The bathroom window is 2 ft. 6 in. wide. *Note:* All window widths represent the rough opening and not the sash opening.

Next indicate the direction of swing for all doors.

4. In preparing the elevations, draw a horizontal line for the finished floor level, 1 ft. 9 in. above the grade level (Fig. 39a). The grade level in this case is

the finished grade ready for seeding and planting when the house is completed.

The 1 ft. 9 in. dimension from finished grade to finished floor level determines many important features of the house and must therefore be given careful consideration. For example, the number of steps to the front entrance is affected by this dimension. If the house is to have cellar windows above grade, this requirement will of necessity bring the floor level higher and add to the number of steps to the front entrance, thus affecting the general appearance and design of the house. If the cellar windows are to be below grade, areaways must be provided to admit light and air. All these points should be decided upon by the architect or owner before the draftsman decides to go any further.

5. The ceiling level, 8 ft. 0 in. from the finished floor, and the ridge level, 6 ft. 7 in. measured from the ceiling, may next be drawn. Project the window and door openings from the plan and establish the height of the windows, 7 ft. 0 in. from the finished floor level to the top of the window sash. The conventions shown in Fig. 39b are aids for dimensioning outside walls, partitions and windows.

6. Complete the side elevations by projecting from the plan. Project from the plan and draw the chimney, extended 2 ft. 4 in. above the ridge.

7. Draw the suggested arrangement of the cornice and sill details on Plate 14.

Problem

Lay out the second stage, Plate 15, similarly to Plate 14. Show footings and foundation walls by dotted lines and give all important dimensions.

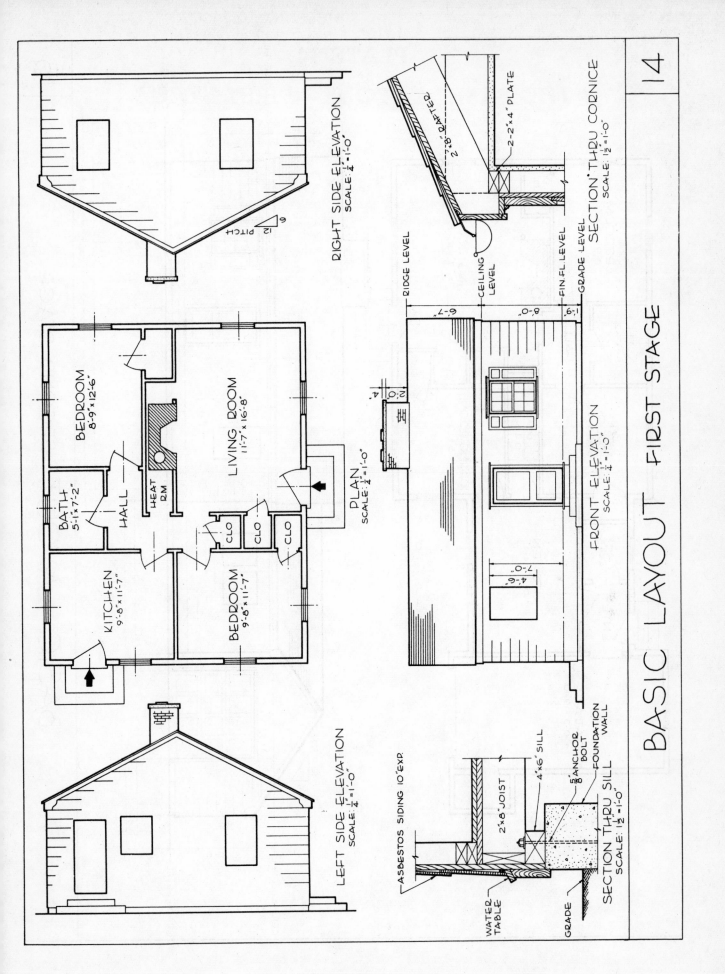

RIGHT SIDE ELEVATION
SCALE: 1/4"=1'-0"

6
12 PITCH

SECTION THRU CORNICE
SCALE: 1 1/2"=1'-0"

2"×8" RAFTER

2-2"×4" PLATE

RIDGE LEVEL

CEILING LEVEL

FIN. FL. LEVEL

GRADE LEVEL

9'-7"

8'-0"

1'-6"

BEDROOM
8'-9"×12'-6"

LIVING ROOM
11'-7"×16'-8"

BATH
5'-1"×7'-2"

HALL

HEAT RM.

CLO

CLO

CLO

KITCHEN
9'-8"×11'-7"

BEDROOM
9'-8"×11'-7"

PLAN
SCALE: 1/4"=1'-0"

FRONT ELEVATION
SCALE: 1/4"=1'-0"

2'-0"

7'-0"

4'-6"

LEFT SIDE ELEVATION
SCALE: 1/4"=1'-0"

ASBESTOS SIDING 10"EXP.

WATER TABLE

GRADE

2"×8" JOIST

4"×6" SILL

5/8" ANCHOR BOLT

FOUNDATION WALL

SECTION THRU SILL
SCALE: 1 1/2"=1'-0"

BASIC LAYOUT   FIRST STAGE

14

[89]

BASIC LAYOUT SECOND STAGE

PLAN
SCALE: ¼" = 1'-0"

FRONT ELEVATION
SCALE: ¼" = 1'-0"

GARAGE
10'-3" x 19'-10"

CLO.

ENTRY

LAV.
4'-4" x 5'-2"

KITCHEN
10'-2" x 14'-1"

DINING ROOM
9'-8" x 10'-1"

CLO.

CLO.

DOWN
13 RISERS

LIN.

HALL

BATH
5'-1" x 7'-2"

BEDROOM
9'-8" x 9'-9"

BEDROOM
8'-9" x 12'-6"

CLO.

LIVING ROOM
11'-7" x 16'-8"

RIDGE LEVEL

CEILING LEVEL

FIN FL LEVEL

GRADE LEVEL

6'-7"

8'-0"

1'-6"

7'-3"

9'-0"

12

2'-0"

2'-2"

12 PITCH

9

CEILING LEVEL

GRADE LEVEL

6'-6"

4'-0"

12

15

PLATE 16

THE COMPLETE SET OF WORKING DRAWINGS— FINAL STAGE

The First-Floor Plan

In preparing the first-floor plan, Plate 16, block in the outline of the building with a light continuous line, disregarding door and window openings for the moment. Next draw the center line for all wall partitions. The outside-wall thickness, which is 6 in., may then be laid off with the dividers, and then the thickness of partitions, which is 4 in., may be drawn. Door and window openings are located by center lines and their widths are determined. In order to draw the door and window openings on the ¼-in. scale drawing, the draftsman must know the type and size of the windows to be used. The type of window selected is generally one that will conform to the design or the appearance of the building. The sizes of windows for the various rooms must meet requirements for light and air. The light requirements for a room call for a minimum glass area equal to 10 per cent of the floor area. The requirements for air are that the windows can be opened to a minimum area equal to 5 per cent of the floor area. (Refer to manufacturer's data for sash and rough openings for windows.)

The widths of windows and doors on the plan are those of the rough opening. The draftsman may show sash openings or the actual width of doors, provided he understands the framing around the opening and allows for close conditions such as those shown for the door leading into the master bedroom. The direction of swing for doors should next be studied for easy access and circulation. Fixtures in the kitchen, such as stove, sink, refrigerator, and cabinets, and all bathroom fixtures are then indicated. Before the stair to the basement is drawn, a preliminary layout, similar to the method shown on Plate 11 and Fig. 29, is made to determine the number of risers and treads, the headroom, and the well opening. The fireplace should show the over-all length and width of the brickwork, the flue from the cellar, and the outline representing the hearth.

The next step, and perhaps the most important to the builder, is to provide the working dimensions on the plan. Incorrect dimensions cause the builder much delay and additional expense. The most common mistake is the failure of cumulative dimensions to check with over-all dimensions. A simple rule is to dimension the plan around the outside, beginning at one corner of the building from the outside face of the stud to the center line of the window or door opening. These dimensions will become cumulative and should be checked with an over-all dimension. Inside dimensions, locating partitions and doors, are then drawn and should line up both vertically and horizontally whenever possible.

After the plan has been dimensioned and carefully checked, the names of the rooms may be neatly lettered in with the single-stroke architectural-style letter. The type of finished floor, and the directional arrows with the size and spacing of the joists overhead may then be indicated. Many draftsmen prefer placing the door and window sizes directly on the plan instead of using the door and window schedule. This method is not always advisable, however, since the consequent crowding of dimensions and figures may cause unnecessary delay and errors in building.

Partition Walls

Note that an interior or partition wall differs from an outside wall in that it rarely rests on a solid wall. Partitions may be either bearing or nonbearing and may run in the direction of joists or at right angles to joists. When the partition runs in the direction of the joists, its weight and whatever other weight it supports may rest only on one or two joists. In this case additional supporting strength must be provided. Computations show that the average weight of a partition is three times the weight that the average single joist can carry. At least two joists should be placed under nonbearing partitions running parallel to the joists, or at least three joists when the partition is more than 9 ft. high.

When partitions run at right angles to the joists, no extra support is required. If two partitions are close together, as in closets running parallel to each other near the center of the span, greater support is necessary. In this case, joists should be spaced 12 in. on center instead of the usual 16 in.

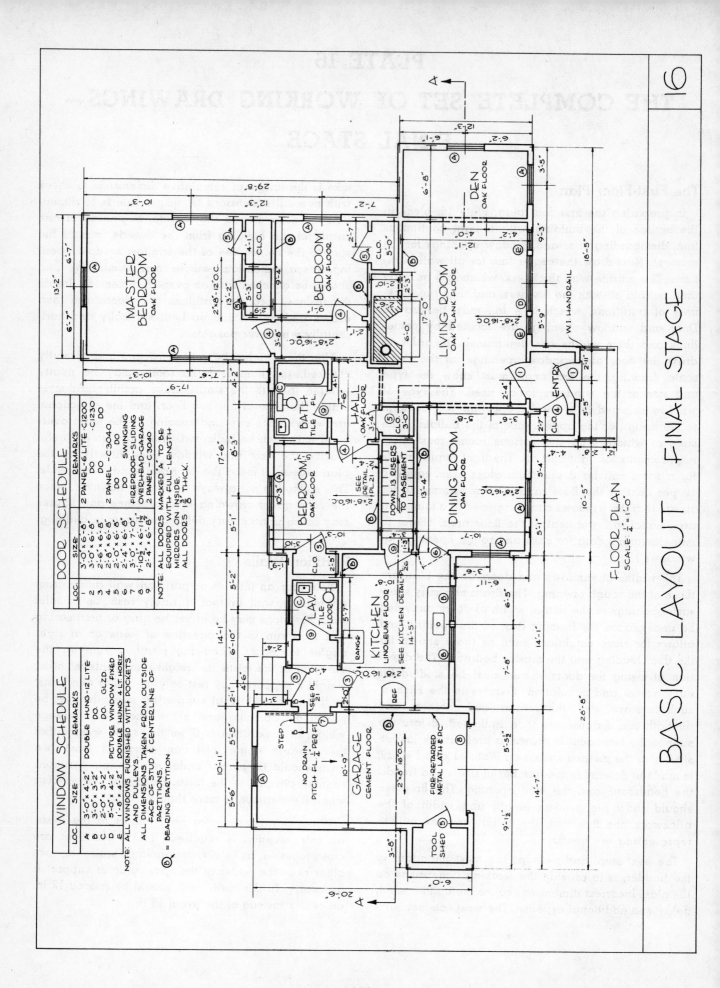

PLATE 16

THE COMPLETE SET OF WORKING DRAWINGS—
FINAL STAGE

16

BASIC LAYOUT — FINAL STAGE

FLOOR PLAN
SCALE: ¼" = 1'-0"

DOOR SCHEDULE

LOC.	SIZE	REMARKS
1	3'-0" x 6'-8"	2 PANEL-6 LITE -C1200
2	3'-0" x 3'-2"	DO -C1230
3	2'-6" x 6'-8"	DO
4	2'-6" x 6'-8"	2 PANEL - C3040
5	2'-0" x 6'-8"	DO
6	2'-4" x 6'-8"	DO SWINGING
7	3'-0" x 7'-0"	FIREPROOF-SLIDING
8	7'-0" x 6'-1½"	OVERHEAD-GARAGE
9	2'-4" x 6'-8"	2 PANEL - C3040

NOTE: ALL DOORS MARKED "A" TO BE EQUIPPED WITH FULL-LENGTH MIRRORS ON INSIDE. ALL DOORS 1⅜" THICK.

WINDOW SCHEDULE

LOC.	SIZE	REMARKS
A	3'-0" x 4'-2"	DOUBLE HUNG-12 LITE
B	3'-0" x 3'-2"	DO
C	2'-0" x 3'-2"	DO GLZD.
D	5'-0" x 4'-2"	PICTURE WINDOW FIXED
E	1'-6" x 4'-2"	DOUBLE HUNG 4 LT HORIZ.

NOTE: ALL WINDOWS FURNISHED WITH POCKETS AND PULLEYS. ALL DIMENSIONS TAKEN FROM OUTSIDE FACE OF STUD & CENTERLINE OF PARTITIONS.

Ⓐ = BEARING PARTITION

PLATE 17
THE BASEMENT PLAN

In preparing the basement plan, a sheet of tracing paper may be fastened directly over the finished first-floor plan. Trace a continuous line around the outside of the plan, ⅞ in. inside of the outer line of the first-floor plan. The ⅞-in. space is the allowance for siding or shingles. The sheathing line will then be flush with the outside face of the foundation wall. Step off the thickness of the foundation wall, 12 in., and draw this line similarly around the building. Next draw the footing, 6 in. on either side of the foundation wall, in dotted lines. It can be seen that the main portion of the building, directly below the living room, dining room, bath, and the two smaller bedrooms, is the excavated portion of the building or the basement. Other areas are excavated to a minimum of 18 to 24 in. below the bottoms of the joists overhead. Foundation walls with footings are therefore required between excavated and unexcavated parts of the plan, not only to support the girder and joists but also to act as retaining walls for the unexcavated earth. Openings 2 ft. wide should be provided for access to unexcavated areas. Twelve-inch vent openings are left in the foundation walls of unexcavated areas for air circulation and for drying out any moisture that may seep in.

It has been pointed out before that the draftsman is hardly able to complete a plan in its entirety without some preconceived knowledge of the elevations and details. For example, it would hardly be possible to know whether the basement windows require areaways unless the difference in height between the top of the foundation wall and the finished grade line is known. On our plan, the basement windows are partially below grade and therefore require areaways. Since the areaways are only 1 ft.

6 in. below grade, 6-in. walls are satisfactory. The detail drawing of the basement window on Plate 17 clearly indicates the 4- x 6-in. sill that spans the opening of the basement window.

The outline of the chimney can next be traced from the first-floor plan and located by dimensions from the inner faces of the foundation walls.

It will be seen that the spans from wall to wall in the basement proper are too long for ordinary joists and hence require an intermediate support, namely, a girder. An 8-in. steel I beam, weighing 25.5 lb. per linear foot, is found to be satisfactory, provided it is supported intermittently by 4-in. lally columns set on 24-in. concrete footings. To make the top of the girder level with the foundation wall to receive the joists, it is necessary to notch the foundation wall at both ends of the girder as shown on the girder detail. A minimum bearing surface of 4 in. is required.

Where large openings occur in the plan such as for the garage doors, no foundation wall and footing is required. The floor level of the garage must be a minimum of 12 in. below the finished first-floor level, according to the New York City Building Code, as can be seen by the step from the kitchen entry to the garage on the first-floor plan. The construction of the garage floor, 1-in. cement finish on 4-in. cinder concrete on 12-in. cinder fill, should be indicated.

Dimensioning the basement plan is similar to the procedure followed in the first-floor plan, except that dimensions are taken from one outside face to the other outside face of the concrete wall, or from the inside face to the inside face of the concrete wall for interior dimensions. Dimensions for windows or vents are those of the rough openings, that is, from face of masonry to face of masonry.

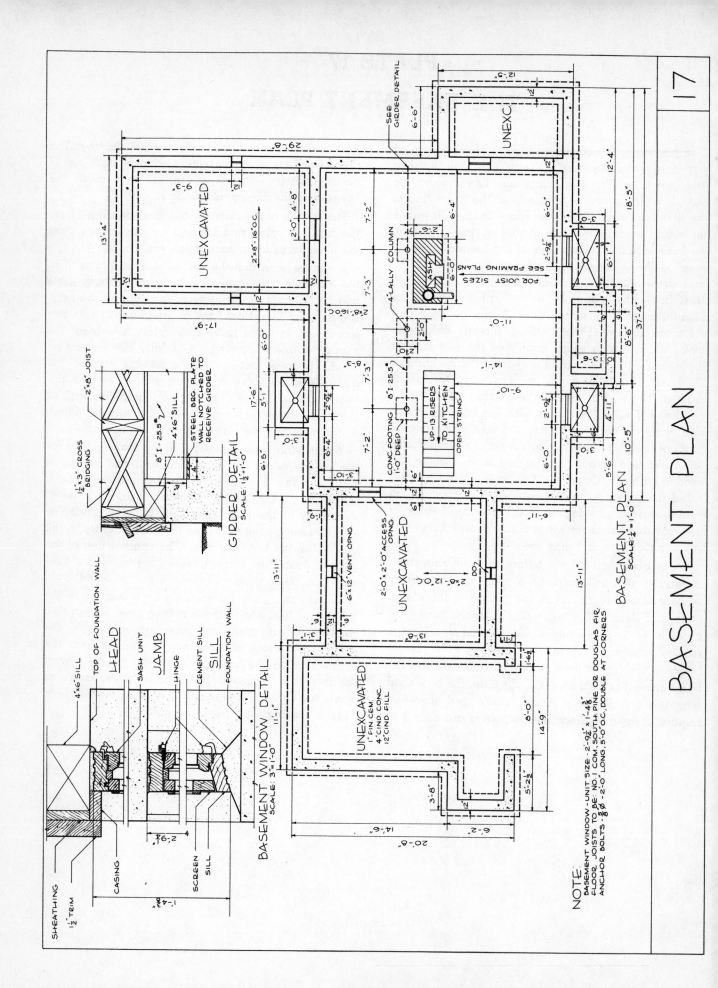

BASEMENT PLAN

17

PLATES 18 AND 19

THE ELEVATIONS

In preparing the elevations, begin by drawing the ground or grade line at a convenient place on the paper. The finished first floor, 1 ft. 9 in. above the grade line, may next be drawn; then the ceiling level, 8 ft. 0 in. above the first floor, and the ridge, 6 ft. 7 in. above the ceiling level. The *ceiling level* is the top of the double 2- x 4-in. plate or the underside of the ceiling beams.

Next, to the right of the proposed elevation, draw a section through the building from which can be projected not only the grade, floor, and ceiling and ridge levels but also the cornice lines, water table, basement floor level, and the areaways. Windows, doors, and vertical ends of the elevation may be projected and traced from the first-floor plan. A great deal of time can be saved if the front and side elevations are developed together. This procedure is not always feasible, however, especially when the elevation has a long frontage. The student should have at hand all drawings previously made, including plans and sketches, for reference to dimensions and details. The heights of windows from the finished floor level are 2 ft. 10 in., 2 ft. 6 in., and 3 ft. 10 in. The minimum head height of windows measured from the finished floor should be 7 ft. 0 in.

After the windows are blocked in, the details such as muntins, meeting rail, and trim around the outside of the window may be drawn. Then the cornice details are projected from the section to the elevation.

Footings and foundation walls below grade, including areaways, are drawn in dotted lines. The siding lines may then be indicated, their size and type being dictated by the specifications or the desire to obtain certain architectural effects. The ends of the siding boards at the corners may be mitered or may butt against corner boards. This choice also is left to the discretion of the designer or draftsman. Although mitered corners have a more pleasing effect, there is more work attached to this type of construction than if corner boards are used.

The chimney, a minimum distance of 2 ft. 0 in. above the highest portion of the roof, may next be projected from the plan.

In preparing the rear elevation it is best to fasten the tracing paper over the first-floor plan laid upside down. Vertical ends, windows, and doors can then be projected from the plan, and the heights can be stepped off from the front elevation.

The vertical ends of the side elevations, Plate 19, may similarly be projected from the plan, and the heights can be carried with the T square from the completed front elevation and placed alongside the drawing paper. The details on Plate 19 will help the student better to visualize the cornice arrangement, water table, and cornice return required on the elevations. The beginning draftsman will find that the elevations at this stage, although complete in general appearance, will require minor changes and corrections later on when roof pitches and framing plans are studied.

It is common practice, even for architects and experienced draftsmen, to make slight changes in completed drawings after other drawings and details are made.

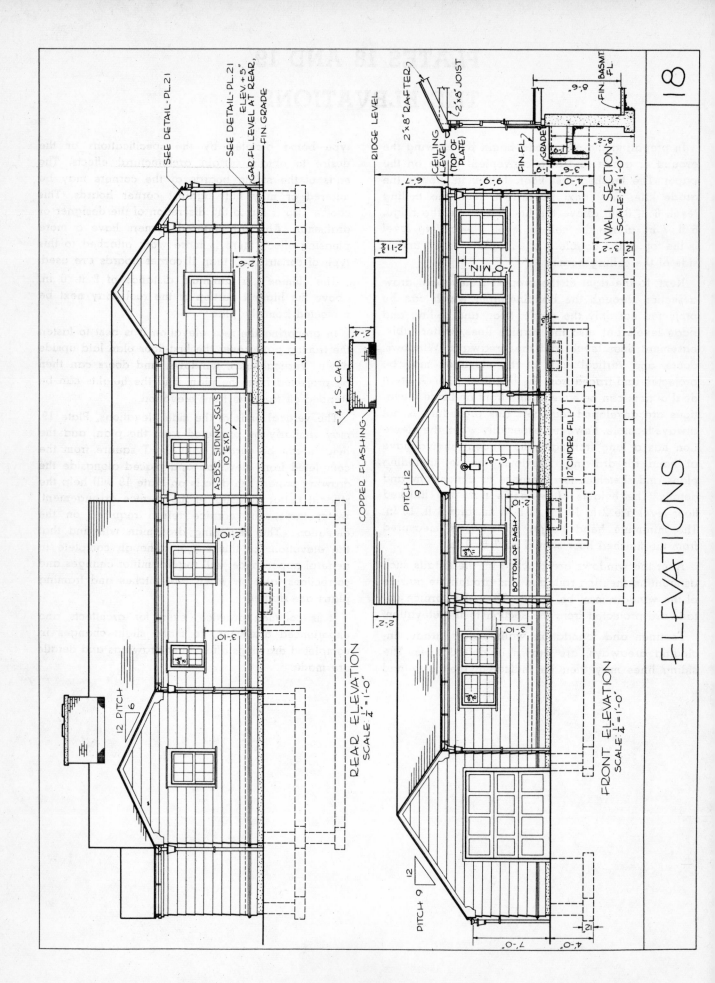

PLATES 18 AND 19

THE ELEVATIONS

ELEVATIONS

REAR ELEVATION
SCALE: ¼" = 1'-0"

FRONT ELEVATION
SCALE: ¼" = 1'-0"

WALL SECTION
SCALE: ¼" = 1'-0"

SEE DETAIL-PL.21

SEE DETAIL-PL.21

ELEV.+5"
(GAR.FL.LEVEL AT REAR)

FIN.GRADE

RIDGE LEVEL

CEILING LEVEL
(TOP OF PLATE)

FIN.FL.

GRADE

FIN.FL.

FIN.BASMT.FL.

2"x 8" RAFTER

2"x 8" JOIST

4" L.S. CAD.

COPPER FLASHING

ASB'S. SIDING SGLS.
10" EXP.

12 PITCH 6

PITCH 12 9

PITCH 9 12

BOTTOM OF SASH

12"CINDER FILL

7'-0" MIN.

18

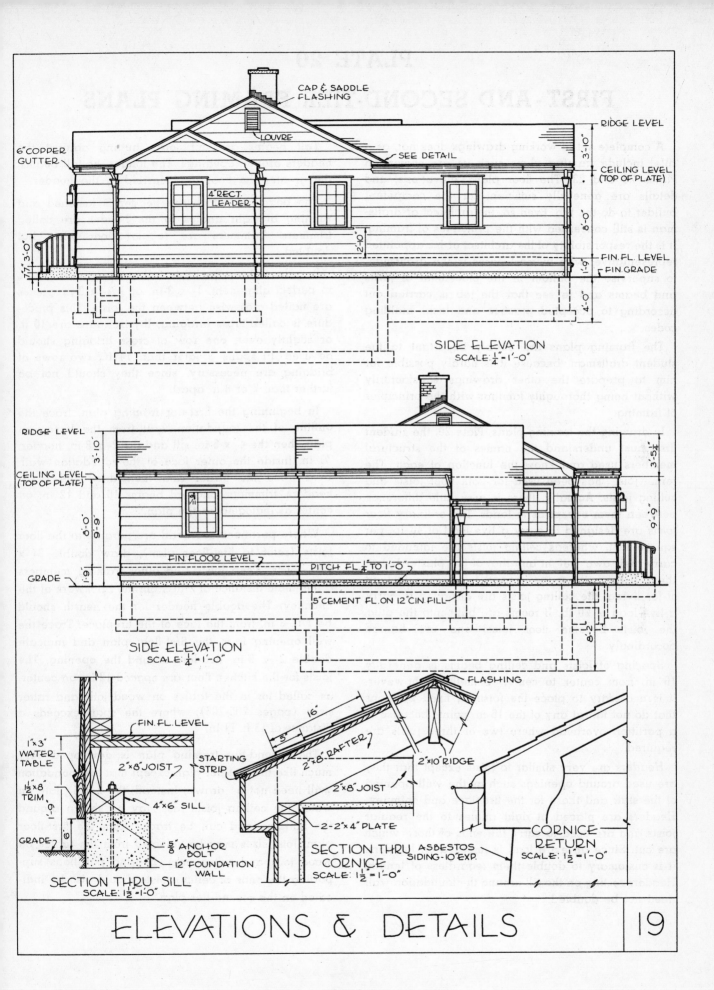

CAP & SADDLE
FLASHING

6" COPPER
GUTTER

LOUVRE

SEE DETAIL

RIDGE LEVEL

3'-10"

CEILING LEVEL
(TOP OF PLATE)

4" RECT.
LEADER

8'-0"

2'-0"

FIN. FL. LEVEL
FIN. GRADE

7'-7"   3'-0"

1'-9"

4'-0"

SIDE ELEVATION
SCALE: 1/4"=1'-0"

RIDGE LEVEL

CEILING LEVEL
(TOP OF PLATE)

3'-10"

3'-5¼"

6'-0"   9'-9"

9'-9"

FIN FLOOR LEVEL

PITCH FL. 1/4" TO 1'-0"

GRADE

1'-9"

5" CEMENT FL. ON 12" CIN. FILL

8'-2"

SIDE ELEVATION
SCALE: 1/4"=1'-0"

FLASHING

16"

5"

2"×8" RAFTER

2"×10" RIDGE

FIN. FL. LEVEL

1"×3"
WATER
TABLE

2"×8" JOIST

STARTING
STRIP

2"×8" JOIST

1½"×8"
TRIM

1'-9"

4"×6" SILL

2-2"×4" PLATE

CORNICE
RETURN
SCALE: 1½"=1'-0"

GRADE

6"

5/8" ANCHOR
BOLT

12" FOUNDATION
WALL

SECTION THRU SILL
SCALE: 1½"=1'-0"

SECTION THRU
CORNICE
SCALE: 1½"=1'-0"

ASBESTOS
SIDING-10" EXP.

ELEVATIONS & DETAILS

19

PLATE 20
FIRST-AND SECOND-TIER FRAMING PLANS

A complete set of working drawings does not, as a rule, include framing plans such as are shown on Plates 20 and 23. The floor plans, elevations, and details are generally sufficient for the competent builder to do the job. Even so, the architect or draftsman is still concerned with the principles of framing. It is the responsibility of the architect or his appointed representative, who in most cases is the draftsman, to supervise the builder in the placement of joists and beams and to see that the job is carried out according to accepted practice and local building codes.

The framing plans are doubly important to the student draftsman, because it is hardly possible for him to prepare the other drawings satisfactorily without being thoroughly familiar with the principles of framing.

In drawing the framing plans, Plate 20, the student first must understand the names of the structural members used and know the function of each. The term "joist" has been used for both floor joists and ceiling joists. Actually, there is very little difference between them except as to loads. The ordinary *floor joists* are designed to carry a live load of 40 lb. per square foot, whereas *ceiling joists* are intended to carry their own weight and that of the plaster below them. If the attic space is used for storage instead of for living, the ceiling joists are designed to carry a live load of 20 lb. If rooms are built into the attic, the joists become floor joists and are figured accordingly.

Spacing of joists and ceiling beams is generally 16 in. from center to center. Sometimes, however, it is necessary to place the joists at fixed positions that do not fall at any of the 16-in. points because of a partition overhead where two or three joists are required.

Headers are very similar to joists except that they are used around openings such as the well opening of the stair and those for the fireplace and chimney. Headers are placed at right angles to the regular joists and are used to carry the ends of those which are cut. Since an extra load is imposed on headers, it is customary to double them regardless of length. Headers resting on the sill around the foundation wall need not be doubled.

Tail beams are cut joists butting against the headers around openings. The longer the tail beams, the greater the floor load carried to the header.

The beams to which the header is fastened and running at right angles to the header are called *trimmers*. Trimmers are regular floor joists but doubled.

In order to keep the joists, tail beams, and trimmers in perfect alignment, 1- x 3-in. or 1¼- x 3-in. pieces are nailed crosswise between the joists. This procedure is called *cross bridging*. If joist spans are 10 ft. or slightly over, one row of cross bridging should be used. In spans greater than 14 ft., two rows of bridging are necessary, since they should not be further than 7 or 8 ft. apart.

In beginning the first-tier framing plan, trace the outline of the foundation wall from the basement plan, then the 4- x 6-in. sill and the 2- x 8-in. header, ⅞ in. inside the outer face of the foundation wall. Next trace the girder and then draw the joists, headers, trimmers, and tail beams 16 and 12 in. on center as indicated on the plan.

Where partitions overhead are parallel to the floor joists (refer to first-floor plan), draw double 2- x 8-in. joists. Keep joists and other framing members a minimum distance of 2 in. from the brickwork of the chimney. The double header for the hearth should be 1 ft. 8 in. from the face of the fireplace. Trace the well opening from the first-floor plan and indicate double 2- x 8-in. headers around the opening. The joists for the kitchen floor are spaced 12 in. on center, as called for in the tables on wood joist and rafter sizes (pages 205-206), where the span exceeds a distance of 13 ft. 11 in.

The second-tier framing plan is developed very much like the first-tier plan except that the foundation wall need not be drawn. Instead, the 2 x 4 plate on which the ceiling joists rest may be shown around the building and can be traced from the first-floor plan. Joist sizes may be selected from the tables on wood joist and rafter sizes. Bearing partitions supporting the ends of ceiling joists should also be indicated on the second-tier plan.

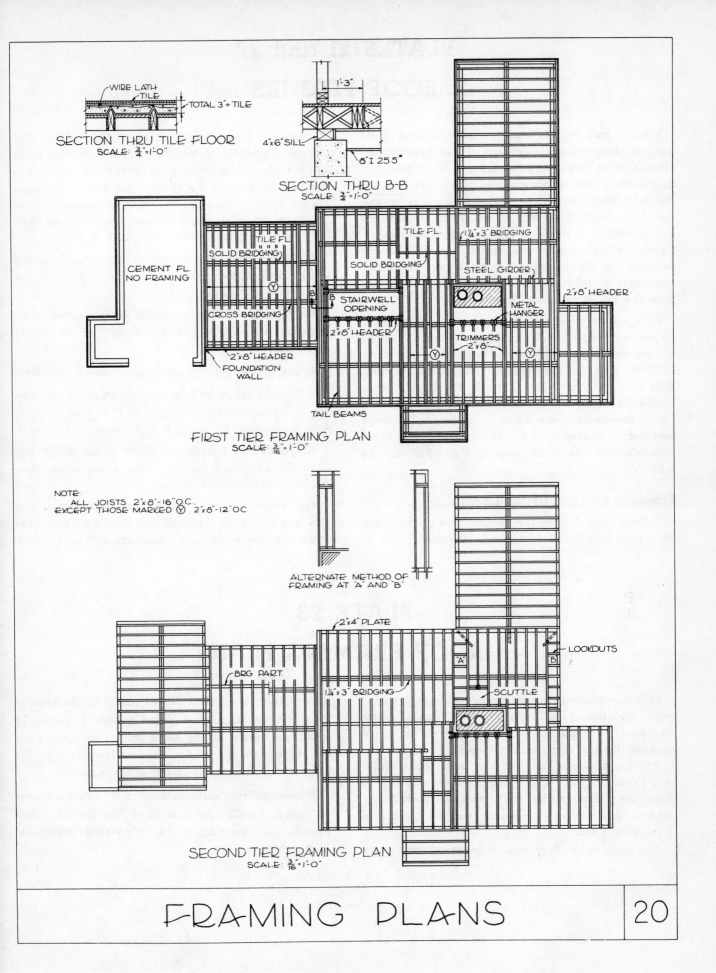

WIRE LATH
TILE
TOTAL 3"± TILE

SECTION THRU TILE FLOOR
SCALE: 3/4"=1'-0"

1'-3"
4"x6" SILL
8" I 25.5"

SECTION THRU B-B
SCALE: 3/4"=1'-0"

CEMENT FL.
NO FRAMING

TILE FL.
SOLID BRIDGING

CROSS BRIDGING

2"x8" HEADER
FOUNDATION
WALL

TAIL BEAMS

TILE FL.
SOLID BRIDGING

1¼"x3" BRIDGING

STEEL GIRDER

2"x8" HEADER

B STAIRWELL
OPENING

2"x8" HEADER

METAL
HANGER

TRIMMERS
2"x8"

FIRST TIER FRAMING PLAN
SCALE: 3/16"=1'-0"

NOTE:
ALL JOISTS 2"x8"-16"O.C.
EXCEPT THOSE MARKED Ⓨ 2"x8"-12"OC

ALTERNATE METHOD OF
FRAMING AT "A" AND "B"

2"x4" PLATE

LOOKOUTS

BRG. PART.

1¼"x3" BRIDGING

"A"

"B"

SCUTTLE

SECOND TIER FRAMING PLAN
SCALE: 3/16"=1'-0"

FRAMING PLANS

20

PLATES 21 and 22

ROOF PITCHES

Various roof heights and roof pitches have been used in drawing the elevations. These heights and pitches have been selected merely for reasons of appearance and proportion with the rest of the building. This standard, however, does not determine the final location of the ridges. Roof pitches are designated as ½ pitch, ⅓ pitch, ¼ pitch, and so on. Select the pitches that come nearest the ridge heights selected for reasons of appearance and determine the exact vertical distance of the top of the ridge from the top of the plate level.

To select the proper pitches, refer to the Schematic Layout of Ridge Levels on Plate 21, which shows the various spans of the roofs. For example, the span of 24 ft. 2 in. for the main building (refer to first-floor plan) shows a 6-to-12 pitch. The 6-to-12 pitch locates the ridge of the main building nearest the height selected for reasons of appearance. The steps involved in finding the 6 ft. 7 in. dimension, the exact distance from the plate level to the ridge, are as follows:

Procedure for Roof-Pitch Layout

1. Draw line A from the outside face of the plate at a pitch of 6 to 12, intersecting the center line of the span at point D (see Plate 22, Roof Pitch Layout and Framing). A 6-to-12 *pitch* means that there are 6 units of rise to 12 units of run. *Run of roof* is half the distance of the span of the roof. A ¼ pitch means that the rise of the rafter is one-quarter as much as the entire span of the roof. It follows then that a 6-to-12 pitch is the same as a ¼ pitch.

2. Draw line B, the bottom of the rafter, parallel to line A, from the inside face of the plate to center the line of the span.

3. Draw line C, the top edge of the rafter, 8 in. from and parallel to line B, intersecting the center line of the span.

4. Draw the ridge board in position as indicated.

5. To find the 6 ft. 7 in. dimension, add the rise, which is one-fourth of the span, or 24 ft. 2 in. ÷ ¼ = 6 ft. 0.5 in. Add 6.5 in. + 6 ft. 0.5 in. = 6 ft. 7 in.

The dimensions from the plate to the ridge can similarly be found for the other roofs when their pitches and spans are known.

The details on Plate 21 are self-explanatory and should be carefully studied and drawn so that their relation to the plans and elevations will be learned.

PLATE 23

ROOF FRAMING PLAN

Before beginning the roof framing plan, it is essential to understand the function of each framing member. First there are the rafters that serve the same purpose for the roof as do the joists for the floors, to provide a support for sheathing and roofing material. These are known as *common rafters* and extend from the ridge to the eave without interruption. Rafters should have a minimum bearing surface of 3 in. on the plate.

The ridge is the horizontal member against which the rafters rest at their upper ends. Its purpose is to aid in the alignment of the rafters. It generally is not necessary to use more than 1-in. lumber for the ridge, except in large houses. The depth of the ridge should equal the depth of the rafters.

Where two roof surfaces meet at an interior corner or valley, a *valley rafter* is used. The shorter rafters running from the ridge to the valley rafter are called *jack rafters*.

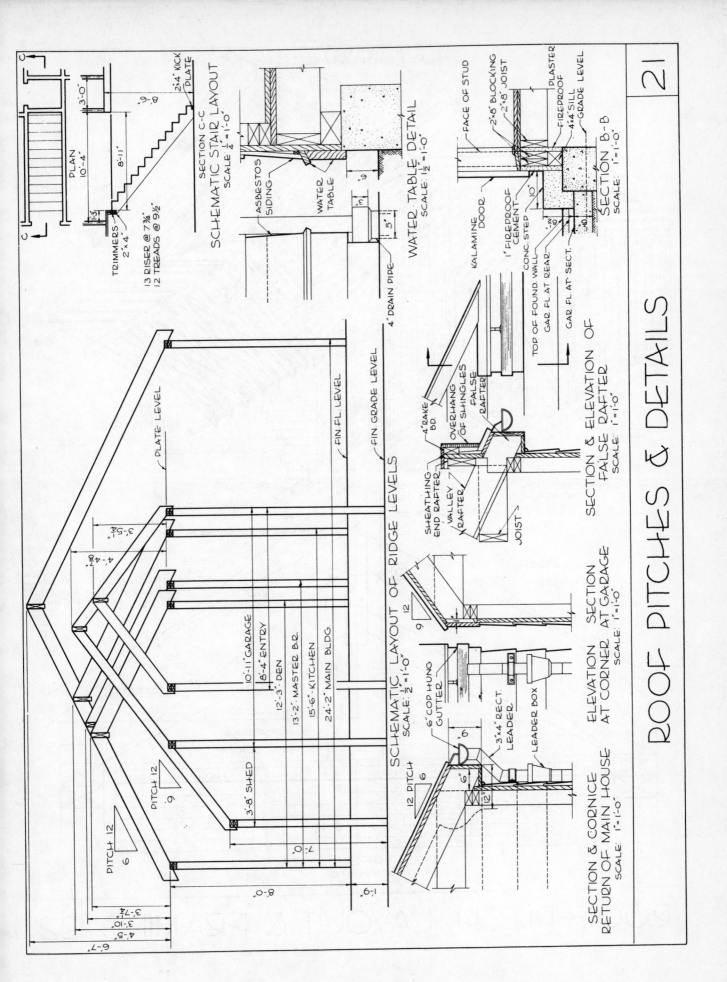

PLAN
10'-4"

3'-0"

2×4 KICK PLATE

8'-11"

8'-9"

1-3"

TRIMMERS 2"×4"

13 RISER @ 7¾"
12 TREADS @ 9½"

SCHEMATIC STAIR LAYOUT
SECTION C-C
SCALE ¼" = 1'-0"

ASBESTOS SIDING

WATER TABLE

4" DRAIN PIPE

WATER TABLE DETAIL
SCALE 1½" = 1'-0"

FACE OF STUD

2×6 BLOCKING

2×8 JOIST

PLASTER

FIREPROOF

4×4 SILL

GRADE LEVEL

KALAMINE DOOR

1" FIREPROOF CEMENT

CONC. STEP

TOP OF FOUND. WALL

GAR. FL. AT REAR

GAR. FL. AT SECT.

SECTION B-B
SCALE 1" = 1'-0"

PLATE LEVEL

3'-5¼"

4'-4⅛"

FIN. FL. LEVEL

FIN. GRADE LEVEL

10'-11" GARAGE

8'-4" ENTRY

12'-3" DEN

13'-2" MASTER B.D.

15'-6" KITCHEN

24'-2" MAIN BLDG.

SCHEMATIC LAYOUT OF RIDGE LEVELS
SCALE ⅛" = 1'-0"

PITCH 12
9

PITCH 12
6

3'-8" SHED

7'-0"

8'-0"

3'-7¼"

3'-10"

4'-5"

6'-7"

6'-1"

4" RAKE BD.

OVERHANG OF SHINGLES

FALSE RAFTER

SHEATHING

END RAFTER

VALLEY RAFTER

JOIST

SECTION & ELEVATION OF
FALSE RAFTER
SCALE 1" = 1'-0"

12
9

SECTION AT GARAGE
SCALE 1" = 1'-0"

6" COP. HUNG GUTTER

3"×4" RECT. LEADER

LEADER BOX

12 PITCH
6

6"

6"

12

ELEVATION
AT CORNER
SCALE 1" = 1'-0"

SECTION & CORNICE
RETURN OF MAIN HOUSE
SCALE 1" = 1'-0"

ROOF PITCHES & DETAILS

21

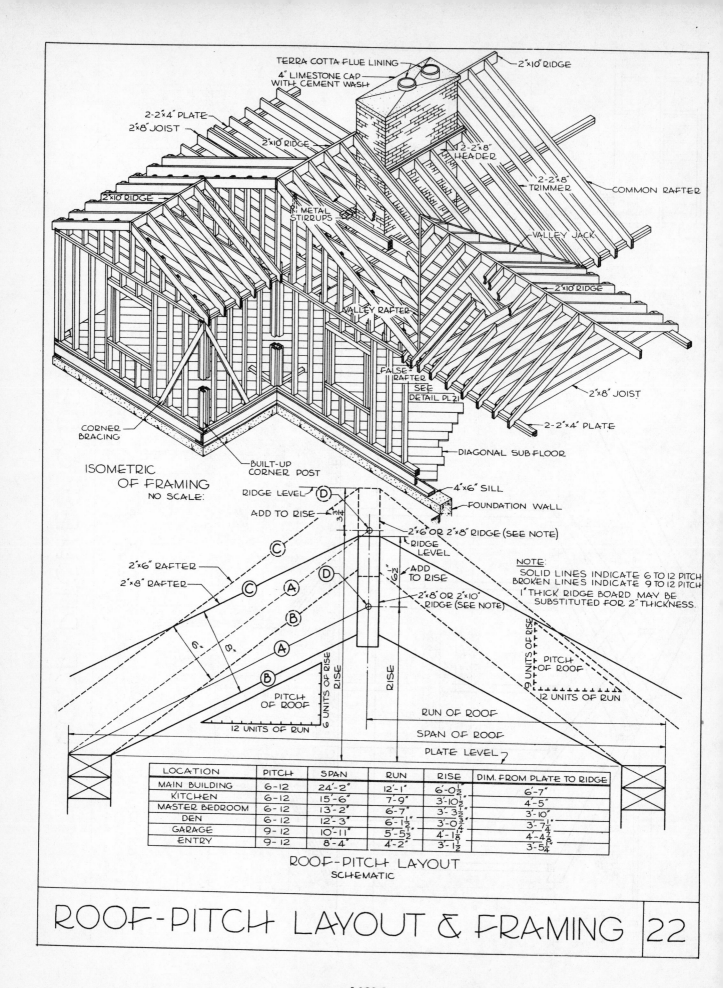

TERRA COTTA FLUE LINING

4" LIMESTONE CAP
WITH CEMENT WASH

2"×10" RIDGE

2-2"×4" PLATE
2"×8" JOIST

2"×10" RIDGE

2-2"×8"
HEADER

2-2"×8"
TRIMMER

COMMON RAFTER

2"×10" RIDGE

R. METAL
STIRRUPS

VALLEY JACK

2"×10" RIDGE

VALLEY RAFTER

2"×10" RIDGE

FALSE
RAFTER
SEE
DETAIL PL.21

2"×8" JOIST

2-2"×4" PLATE

CORNER
BRACING

BUILT-UP
CORNER POST

DIAGONAL SUB FLOOR

4"×6" SILL

FOUNDATION WALL

ISOMETRIC
OF FRAMING
NO SCALE:

RIDGE LEVEL (D)

ADD TO RISE

2"×6" OR 2"×8" RIDGE (SEE NOTE)

RIDGE
LEVEL

ADD
TO RISE

NOTE:
SOLID LINES INDICATE 6 TO 12 PITCH
BROKEN LINES INDICATE 9 TO 12 PITCH
1" THICK RIDGE BOARD MAY BE
SUBSTITUTED FOR 2" THICKNESS.

2"×6" RAFTER

2"×8" RAFTER

C

C   A   D

B

A

B

2"×8" OR 2"×10"
RIDGE (SEE NOTE)

6=

8=

PITCH
OF ROOF

6 UNITS OF RISE

RISE

RISE

9 UNITS OF RISE

PITCH
OF ROOF

12 UNITS OF RUN

RUN OF ROOF

12 UNITS OF RUN

12 UNITS OF RUN

SPAN OF ROOF

PLATE LEVEL

LOCATION	PITCH	SPAN	RUN	RISE	DIM. FROM PLATE TO RIDGE
MAIN BUILDING	6-12	24'-2"	12'-1"	6'-0½"	6'-7"
KITCHEN	6-12	15'-6"	7'-9"	3'-10½"	4'-5"
MASTER BEDROOM	6-12	13'-2"	6'-7"	3'-3½"	3'-10"
DEN	6-12	12'-3"	6'-1½"	3'-0¾"	3'-7½"
GARAGE	9-12	10'-11"	5'-5½"	4'-1⅛"	4'-4⅝"
ENTRY	9-12	8'-4"	4'-2"	3'-1½"	3'-5¼"

ROOF-PITCH LAYOUT
SCHEMATIC

ROOF-PITCH LAYOUT & FRAMING | 22

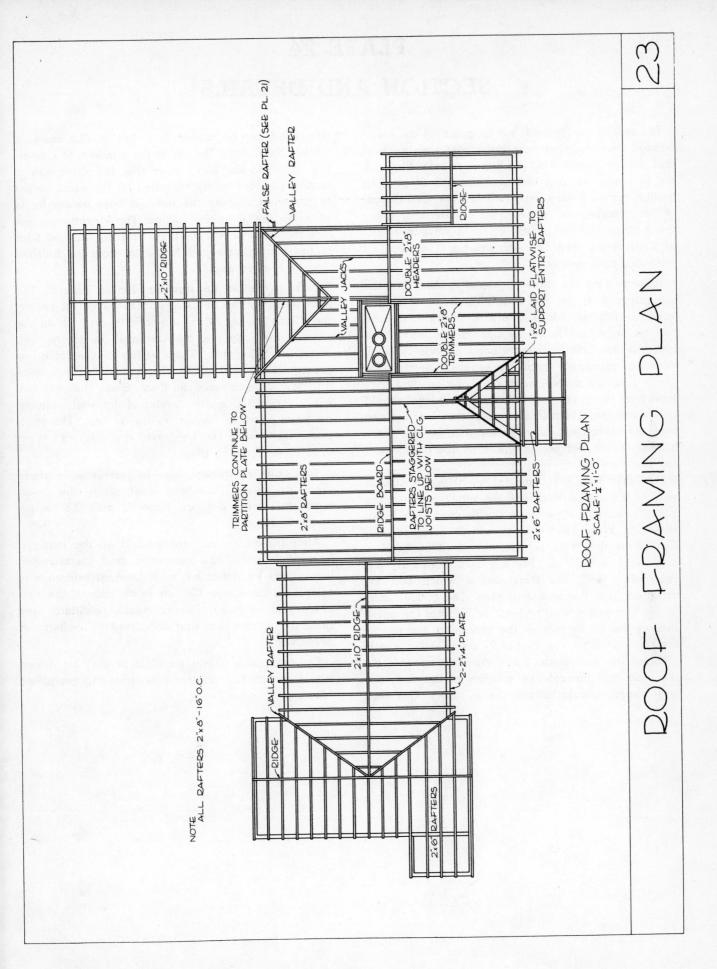

ROOF FRAMING PLAN

ROOF FRAMING PLAN
SCALE: ¼"=1'-0"

NOTE
ALL RAFTERS 2"x8"-16'O.C.

2"x10" RIDGE

VALLEY RAFTER

RIDGE

2"x6" RAFTERS

2"x10" RIDGE

2-2"x4" PLATE

RIDGE BOARD

2"x8" RAFTERS

RAFTERS STAGGERED TO LINE UP WITH CLG. JOISTS BELOW

TRIMMERS CONTINUE TO PARTITION PLATE BELOW

FALSE RAFTER (SEE PL. 21)

VALLEY RAFTER

VALLEY JACKS

DOUBLE 2"x8" HEADERS

DOUBLE 2"x8" TRIMMERS

1"x8" LAID FLATWISE TO SUPPORT ENTRY RAFTERS

2"x6" RAFTERS

RIDGE

23

PLATE 24

SECTION AND DETAILS

The section on Plate 24 is a longitudinal cut taken through the den, living room, hall closet, stair, kitchen, and garage. In checking the first-floor plan, Plate 16, the sectional line A-A indicates this line of cut. The section serves a very important function and is part of the complete set of working drawings. It gives the builder a better picture of the relative positions of floor levels and floor constructions as well as wall and roof details.

In beginning the drawing fasten a sheet of tracing paper over the first-floor plan from which the vertical ends, partitions, doors, windows, and stair can be projected. As in the case of the elevations, the draftsman must have on hand for reference all drawings previously made. To begin the section, the grade line, the correct distance of the finished floor level from the grade line, and the ceiling level should be drawn, the dimensions of which can be obtained from the elevations. First develop that portion of the section which represents the first floor, forgetting for the time the basement and roof structure. At the finished floor level and in line with the outside wall of the den, traced from the plan, construct the box sill, working down from the finished floor level. (Refer to Plate 19 for detail of sill construction.) Next draw the 7/8-in. subfloor, the 2-x-8-in. header, and the 4- x 6-in. sill. The sill is supported by the foundation wall, the thickness of which can be obtained from the basement plan. The outside face of the foundation wall projects 7/8 in. from the outer face of the sill to receive the sheathing. On top of the subfloor draw the double 2- x 4-in. sole, which receives the wall studs. Since the sectional line on the plan cuts through the window of the den, the wall section should include the windows. This sec-

tion need not be drawn in detail at this scale; it is enough to show the sill of the window, the meeting rail, and the head. Note that the draftsman is required to look to the elevation for the exact height of the window from the finished floor before he is able to draw it on the section. The elevations show that the window is 2 ft. 10 in. from the finished floor to the bottom sash and 7 ft. 0 in. from the finished floor to the top sash.

Refer to the first-tier framing plan on Plate 20. The floor joists for the den are spaced 16 in. on center, the living room 12 in. on center and 16 in. in front of the fireplace, and again 12 in. to the well opening of the stair. The spacing of the joists, as previously pointed out, is determined by their span and the loads imposed on them. Since the sectional cut is taken through the center of the well opening, no joists need be shown on the section. The joists under the kitchen can be drawn similarly with reference to the framing plan.

To locate the garage floor in reference to grade level, or finished first-floor level, study the detail marked "section B-B" on Plate 21 and the section on Plate 24.

After the floor joists are worked in, the footings, foundation walls, the excavated and unexcavated levels may be indicated, with constant reference to completed drawings. Ceiling joists, rafters, the fireplace and chimney, interior doors, partitions, and stairs are drawn next and completed in the manner described.

The remaining details on Plate 24 may be drawn with reference to manufacturers' data and completed drawings.

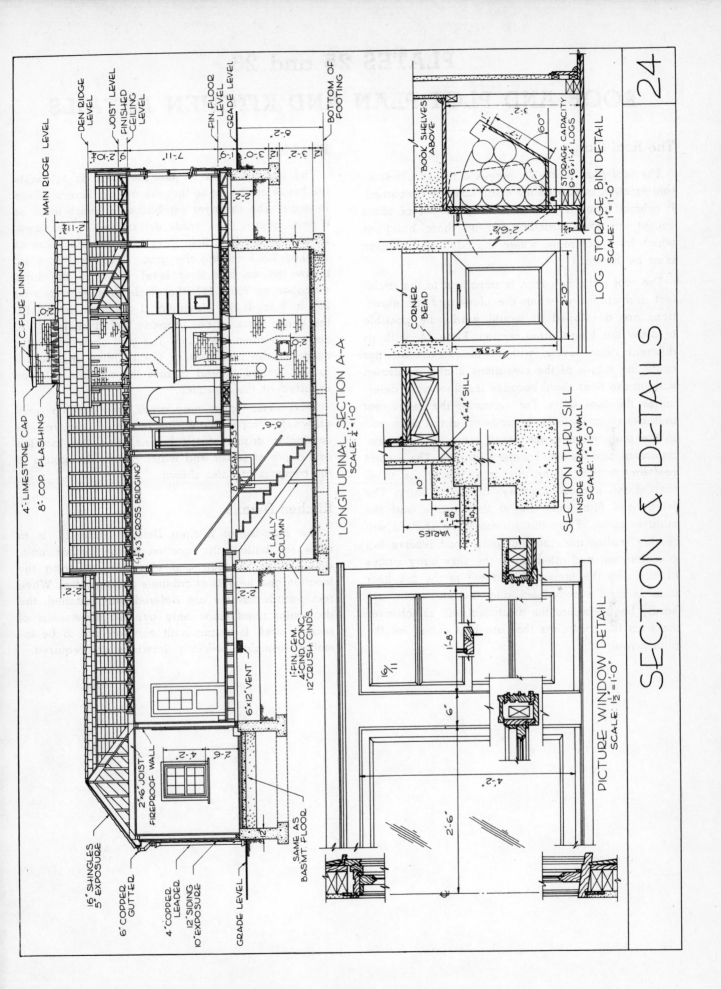

SECTION & DETAILS

24

LONGITUDINAL SECTION A-A
SCALE ¼"=1'-0"

LOG STORAGE BIN DETAIL
SCALE 1"=1'-0"

BOOK SHELVES ABOVE

STORAGE CAPACITY
9-6"×1'4" LOGS

SECTION THRU SILL
INSIDE GARAGE WALL
SCALE 1"=1'-0"

CORNER BEAD

4"×4" SILL

PICTURE WINDOW DETAIL
SCALE 1½"=1'-0"

MAIN RIDGE LEVEL

DEN RIDGE LEVEL
JOIST LEVEL
FINISHED CEILING LEVEL

FIN. FLOOR LEVEL

GRADE LEVEL

BOTTOM OF FOOTING

4" LIMESTONE CAP
8" COP. FLASHING

T.C. FLUE LINING

4"×3" CROSS BRIDGING

8" BEAM 25.5#

4" LALLY COLUMN

6"×12" VENT

1½" FIN. CEM.
4" CIND. CONC.
12" CRUSH. CINDS.

16" SHINGLES 5" EXPOSURE
6" COPPER GUTTER
4" COPPER LEADER
12" SIDING 10" EXPOSURE
GRADE LEVEL

2"×6" JOIST
FIREPROOF WALL

SAME AS BASMT. FLOOR

[105]

PLATES 25 and 26
ROOF AND PLOT PLAN AND KITCHEN DETAILS

The Roof Plan

The roof plan, Plate 25, serves a rather unimportant function insofar as the small home is concerned. It seldom forms a part of a complete set of plans except on large structures, or on those buildings which have flat roofs, where the pitch for drainage must be shown.

The roof plan, however, is important to the architect and draftsman when the plans and the elevations are developed. It would hardly be possible to draw the longitudinal section, Plate 24, with its different ridge levels, without the elevations; nor could the ridges of the elevations finally be drawn without the floor plan, because the floor plan determines the roof units. For example, the main roof unit, shown in Plate 25, is made up of the main unit in the plan, namely, the living room, dining room, bathroom, and the two smaller bedrooms. The second roof unit is that of the master bedroom; the third, that of the kitchen, lavatory, and rear entry. The fourth and fifth units are of the garage and the main entrance. From this summary the student will readily realize that the roof plan must receive full consideration and attention in the very early stages of planning the house. The layout of the first-floor plan is hardly completed and the elevations are hardly begun before the draftsman will sketch over the plan the roof units that are best suited for the plan layout.

Plot Plan

The main function of the plot plan is to locate the house on the lot so that the builder knows where to begin. The surveyor establishes a bench mark or a point from a fixed grade determined by the town. Since the finished floor level on the plot plan is marked 206.5 ft. and the grade level is 1 ft. 9 in. below the finished floor level (refer to the front elevation on Plate 18), the grade level will then be 204 ft. 9 in. If the elevation of the town is 200 ft., the bench mark on our property would be 4 ft. 9 in. above the town elevation. The plot shows also the grade of the first floor of the building in relation to the ground around it, and the number of steps required at the entrance.

Driveways, walks, play areas, and existing trees drawn to proper scale are indicated, as well as conductor drains, catch basins, and the location and depth of sewer and water mains. The points of the compass are also shown.

Kitchen Details

The purpose of Kitchen Details, Plate 26, is to show the builder the location of the kitchen units and fixtures. A plan and elevations showing the location and heights of cabinets are essential. When ready-made fixtures are ordered and installed, the draftsman need show only over-all dimensions of such fixtures. If custom-built cabinets are to be installed, complete working drawings are required.

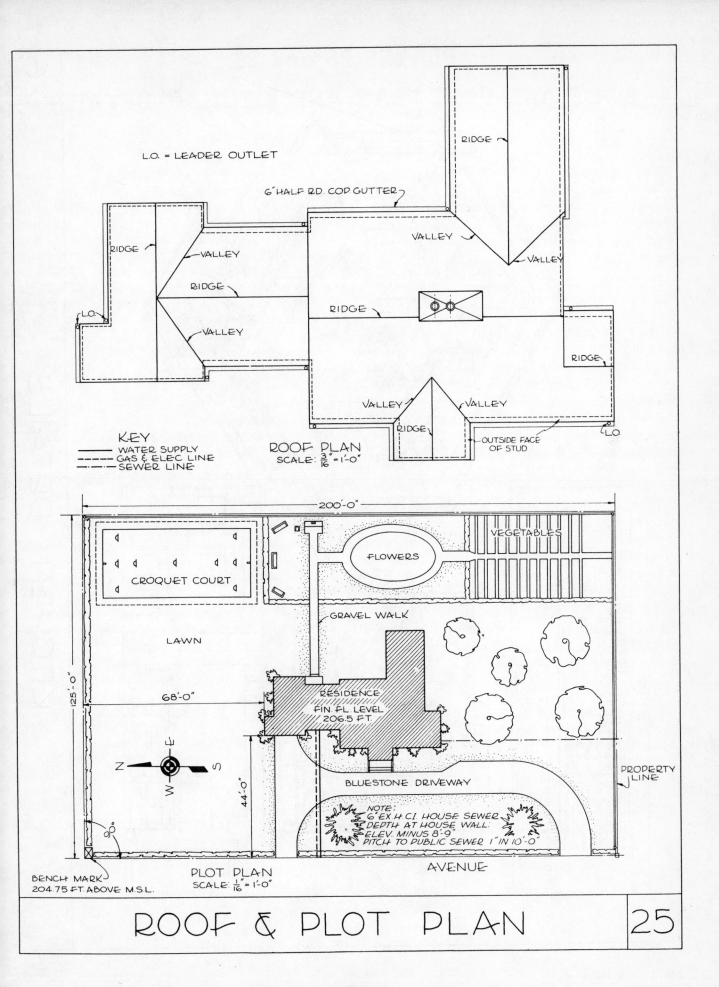

L.O. = LEADER OUTLET

6" HALF RD. COP. GUTTER

RIDGE

VALLEY

VALLEY

RIDGE

VALLEY

VALLEY

RIDGE

RIDGE

L.O.

VALLEY

VALLEY

RIDGE

OUTSIDE FACE OF STUD

L.O.

KEY
—————— WATER SUPPLY
— — — GAS & ELEC LINE
— ·· — ·· SEWER LINE

ROOF PLAN
SCALE: $\frac{3}{16}$" = 1'-0"

200'-0"

VEGETABLES

FLOWERS

CROQUET COURT

GRAVEL WALK

LAWN

RESIDENCE
FIN. FL. LEVEL
206.5 FT.

125'-0"

68'-0"

PROPERTY LINE

N E W S

44'-0"

BLUESTONE DRIVEWAY

NOTE:
6" EX.H.CI. HOUSE SEWER
DEPTH AT HOUSE WALL
ELEV. MINUS 8'-9"
PITCH TO PUBLIC SEWER 1" IN 10'-0"

BENCH MARK
204.75 FT. ABOVE M.S.L.

PLOT PLAN
SCALE: $\frac{1}{16}$" = 1'-0"

AVENUE

ROOF & PLOT PLAN

25

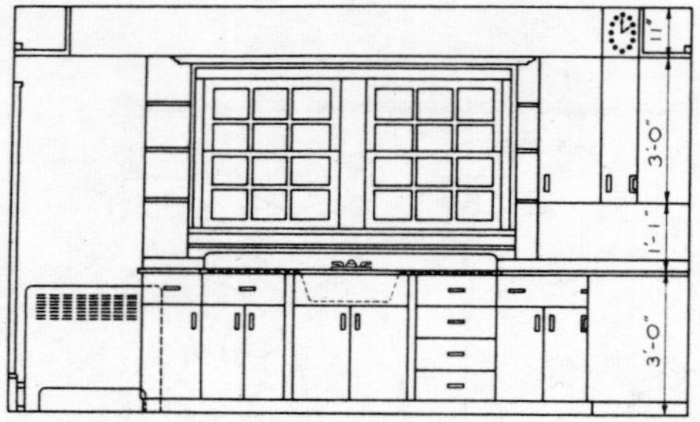

26

KITCHEN DETAILS

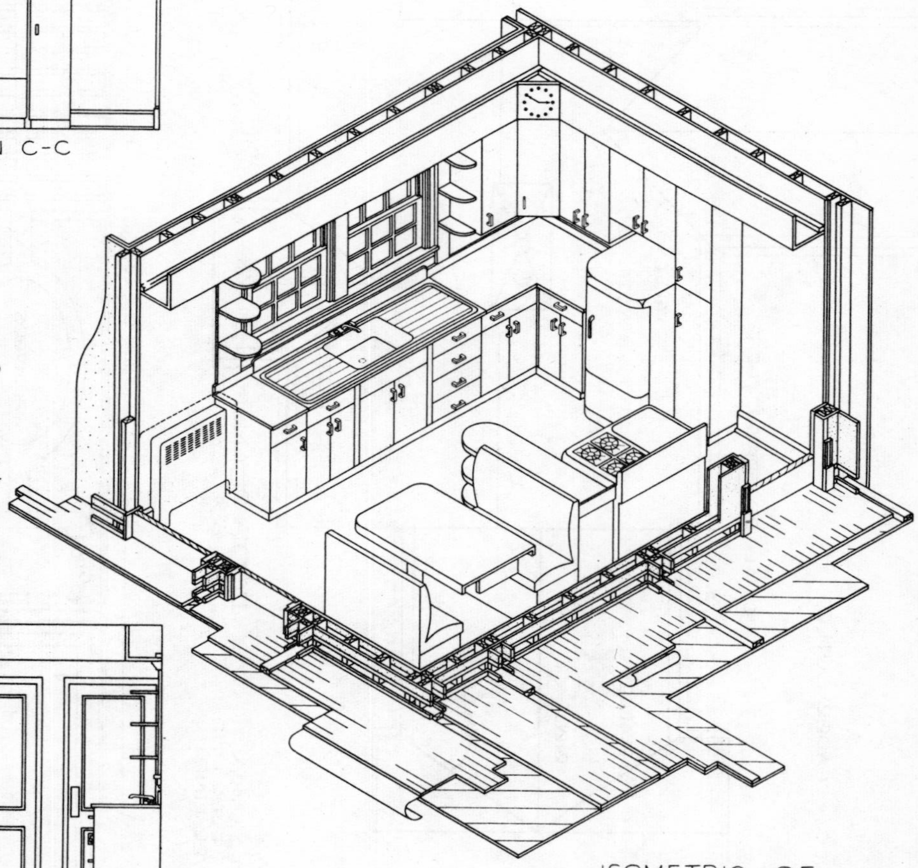

ISOMETRIC OF KITCHEN

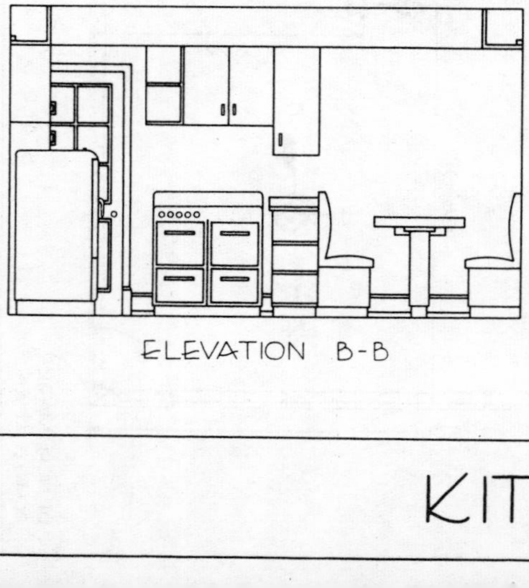

SCALE: $\frac{3}{8}$" = 1'-0"

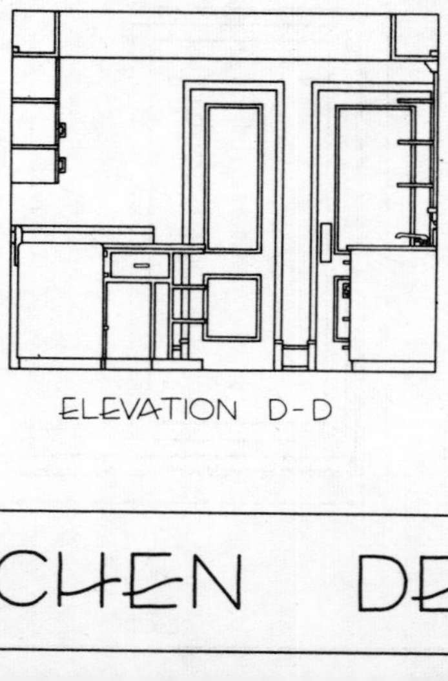

ELEVATION A-A

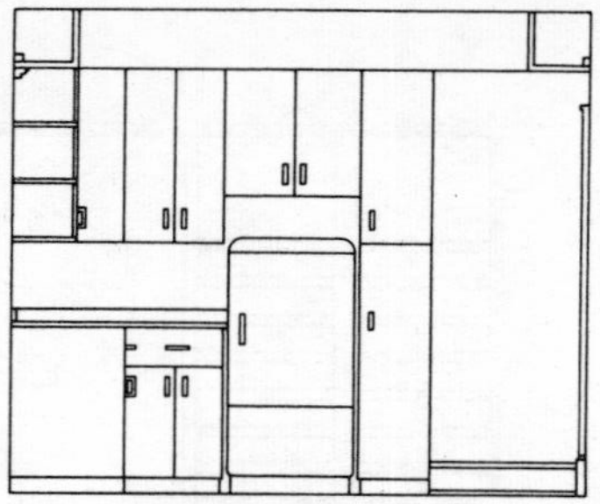

ELEVATION C-C

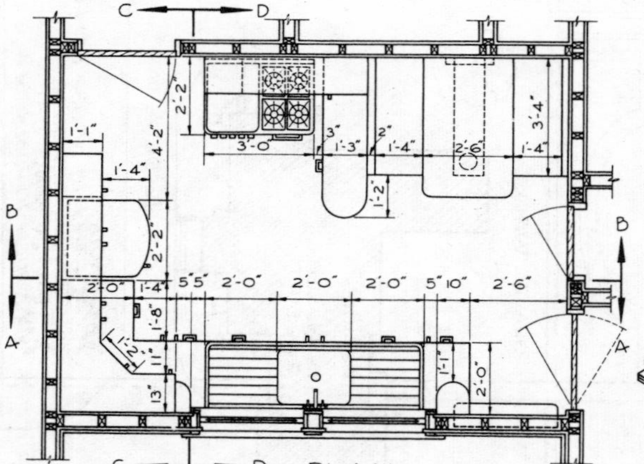

ELEVATION D-D

ELEVATION B-B

PLAN

PLATE 27
TWO-POINT PERSPECTIVE

Objective

To learn the steps involved in the preparation of a simple two-point perspective.

Procedure

1. Draw the plan and front and side elevation of the *block house* in the upper right-hand corner of the drawing sheet, Plate 27, and completely dimension the drawing.

2. Redraw the plan at a scale of ¼ in. = 1 ft. 0 in. at the position shown, one side 60 deg. to the horizontal. (Any desired angle may be used; see Fig. 39c.)

3. Draw the horizontal line known as the *picture plane* through the corner of the plan. Drop a perpendicular from the intersection of the corner of the building and the picture plane.

4. Place the point of the 45-deg. triangle so that the 45-deg. angle is bisected by the perpendicular. In this position move the triangle up or down on the perpendicular until the sides of the triangle encompass the plan or at least a good portion of the plan. This operation will locate the station point (see Fig. 39c).

5. From the station point draw lines to the picture plane, parallel to the sides of the plan (Fig. 39d). From the intersection of the parallel lines with the picture plane drop perpendiculars to the *horizon line*. The ground line may be located at any convenient place on the paper, provided the horizon line or the *eye level* is located the desired distance from the ground line. In this case the distance is 6 ft. 0 in. and represents the height of the person viewing the building.

6. Draw the projection lines from the openings and the corners of the building in plan to the *station point* (Fig. 40). At the intersection of the projection lines with the picture plan, drop perpendiculars locating the widths of windows and the corners of the building. From the ground line, on the line of sight, step off the true height of the building, as well as heights of the windows and door. Vanish the heights to the left and right vanishing points. The intersection of the perpendicular projection lines with the vanishing lines forms the building and its openings.

Problem

Draw the perspective of the block house with the vanishing points (a) 16 ft. 0 in., (b) 1 ft. 0 in. above the ground line.

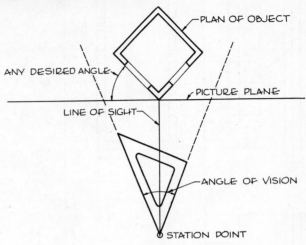

Fig. 39c

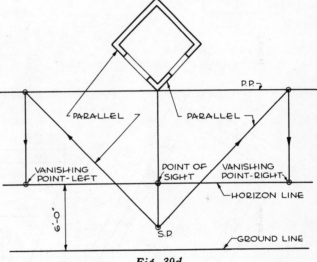

Fig. 39d

Fig. 40

G.L. = GROUND LINE   V.P.R. = VANISHING POINT-RIGHT
H.L. = HORIZON LINE   V.P.L. = VANISHING POINT-LEFT
P.P. = PICTURE PLANE   S.P. = STATION POINT

[109]

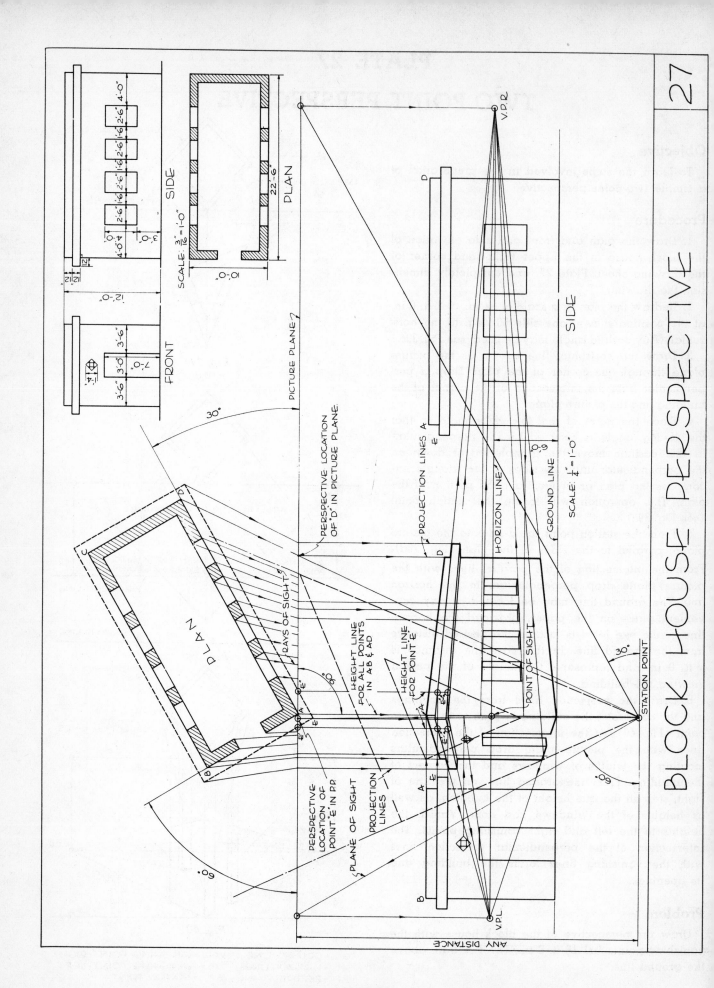

BLOCK HOUSE PERSPECTIVE

27

TWO-POINT PERSPECTIVE

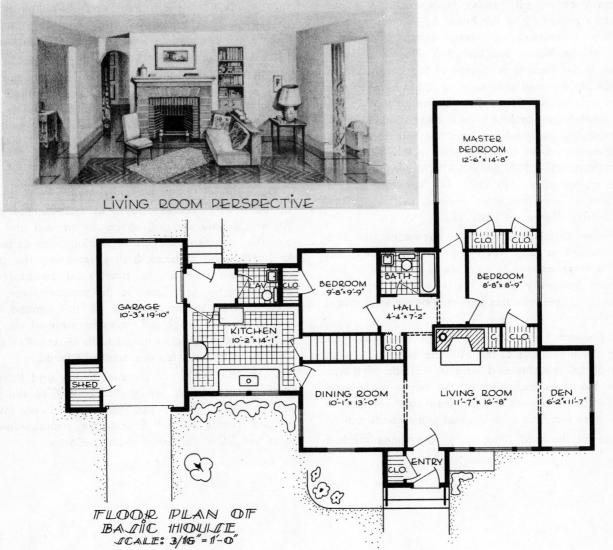

LIVING ROOM PERSPECTIVE

MASTER BEDROOM
12'-6" x 14'-8"

CLO. CLO.

BEDROOM
8'-8" x 8'-9"

CLO.

BEDROOM
9'-8" x 9'-9"

BATH

HALL
4'-4" x 7'-2"

CLO.

LAV. CLO.

GARAGE
10'-3" x 19'-10"

KITCHEN
10'-2" x 14'-1"

SHED

DINING ROOM
10'-1" x 13'-0"

LIVING ROOM
11'-7" x 16'-8"

DEN
6'-2" x 11'-7"

CLO. ENTRY

FLOOR PLAN OF
BASIC HOUSE
SCALE: 3/16" = 1'-0"

BASIC HOUSE RENDERING | 28

PLATE 29
GRIDIRON PERSPECTIVE

Perspective drawing generally forms a very small part of the draftsman's everyday work. Where hundreds of drawings of plans and details are required for a million-dollar project, a comparatively small number of perspectives may be necessary. However, the draftsman working for an architect who specializes in small homes is apt to encounter more perspective work than if he were connected with a large building concern, which would generally employ specialists when perspective drawings and renderings were required. The small-home architect, in many cases, will furnish his client with a perspective rendering of the home he intends to build for him. Sometimes an interior perspective and a plan of the house are included. Plate 28 clearly shows a perspective rendering of the house, including an interior and plan such as might be submitted to its prospective owner. The draftsman working for the small-home architect, will be called upon to prepare the perspectives, and for this reason the fundamentals have been included in this text. Carefully study page 109, the steps in preparing a two-point perspective, and Plate 27, Block House Perspective, in preparation for drawing the basic house perspective shown on Plate 28.

Another form of perspective, known as the gridiron method, is used when a development of homes over a large area is to be shown. This type of perspective generally places the eye level far above the roofs of the buildings and thus becomes a bird's-eye view.

In preparing the Gridiron Perspective, Plate 29, draw the elevations of the building blocks by stepping off the heights and lengths with the dividers, twice the sizes indicated in the upper right-hand and left-hand corners of your drawing sheet. Locate the picture plane on a convenient place on the paper.

Lay out the *grid lines*, or 45-deg. lines marked 1 to 13, to the right of the sheet and the 45-deg. lines marked *A* to *K* to the left of the sheet, beginning at a point where lines 3 and *A* intersect on the picture plane. The intersection of the grid lines will form perfect squares. Draw the plans of the buildings 1, 2, 3, 4, and 5 in their respective locations on the grid.

Establish the station point as described on page 109, and from it draw lines to the picture plane and parallel to the grid lines. Next, draw the ground line at a convenient place on the paper and then the horizon line or eye level well above the ground line so that a bird's-eye view can be obtained. Locate the vanishing points by dropping perpendiculars from the picture plane to the horizon.

Wherever the grid lines in plan intersect the picture plane, drop perpendiculars to the ground line. Through the points thus found, draw lines to vanishing point right (V.P.R.) and vanishing point left (V.P.L.), forming the grid in perspective. Label the grid lines in perspective by numbers and letters corresponding to the grid lines in plan.

The building blocks in perspective may be drawn in the squares corresponding to those in the plan. All heights are stepped off on the ground line and vanished to their respective positions. For example, to find line *ad* of block 5 in perspective, the point representing line *ad* in plan must be projected parallel to the grid lines, to the picture plane, and then carried perpendicularly to the ground line where the true height (*A*) may be stepped off. This height may then be vanished to its perspective position. All other heights are similarly found.

Since line *DE* is not parallel to the grid lines in plan, it is necessary first to find point *E* on the perspective grid. When this point has been found, connect points *D* and *E* with the straightedge to form line *DE* or that side of the building.

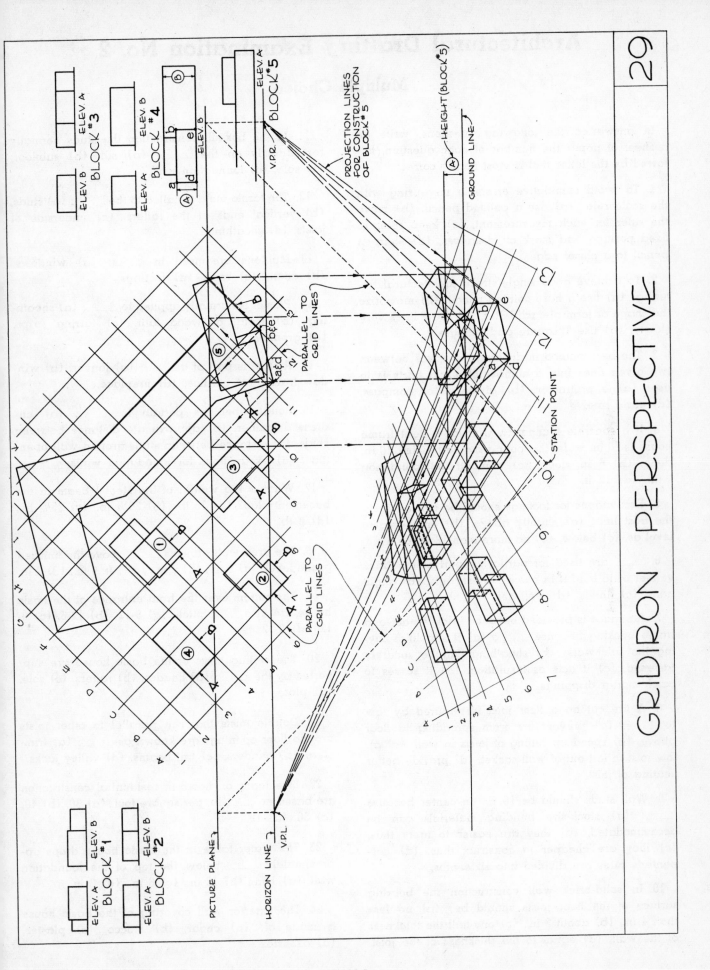

GRIDIRON PERSPECTIVE

Architectural Drafting Examination No. 2

Multiple Choice

In answering the following questions, write on a sheet of paper the number of each question, followed by the letter that is most nearly correct.

1. To avoid cumulative errors in measuring with the scale rule: (a) use a pointed pencil, (b) move the ruler for each measurement, (c) keep ruler in fixed position and mark off distances, (d) sharpen pencil to a chisel edge.

2. To achieve good single-stroke architectural lettering: (a) use a hard-pointed pencil, (b) memorize the shape or form of each letter, (c) draw lines very slowly, (d) use T square and triangle.

3. The best method in dividing the space between two given lines into a number of equal parts is to use: (a) a protractor, (b) dividers, (c) compass, (d) scale rule.

4. If a concrete foundation wall for a light frame house is 10 in. wide, the footing should be: (a) 10 in. deep, (b) 6 in. deep, (c) one-half the foundation wall, (d) 12 in. deep.

5. Excavations for footings should be carried _____ the frost line: (a) slightly above, (b) on the same level as, (c) below, (d) no more than 12 in. below.

6. _____ are used for partial support of the brick veneer or to hold it in place: (a) stirrups, (b) angle irons, (c) lintels, (d) wall ties.

7. Air space is provided between brick veneer and frame backing because _____: (a) it simplifies laying the brickwork, (b) sheathing can be securely fastened, (c) it acts as insulation, (d) it serves to catch mortar drippings.

8. A fire cut on a floor joist is required by law to _____: (a) prevent fire from spreading to floor above, (b) speed up setting of joists in wall, (c) allow joist to fall out of wall socket, (d) provide better seating of joist.

9. Wall studs should be 16 in. on center because _____: (a) stock-size building materials can be accommodated, (b) they are easier to erect thus, (c) they are cheaper to construct thus, (d) carpenter's rules are divided into sixteenths.

10. In solid-brick wall construction the bearing surface of the floor joists should be: (a) no less than 4 in., (b) about 3 in., (c) one-half the thickness of the wall, (d) equal to the thickness of the joist.

11. In the box-sill construction the studs normally rest directly on the _____: (a) sill, (b) subfloor, (c) sole, (d) foundation wall.

12. The fascia mold is nailed to the _____: (a) studs, (b) vertical ends of the rafters, (c) underside of joists, (d) sheathing.

13. Mullions are used in _____: (a) windows, (b) doors, (c) roofs, (d) footings.

14. Plaster is normally applied to _____: (a) sheathing, (b) metal or wood lath, (c) furring strips, (d) grounds.

15. A stool is part of a _____: (a) louver, (b) window frame, (c) cornice, (d) fireplace.

16. Rough openings pertain to _____: (a) undressed lumber, (b) approximate distance between studs, (c) distance between studs around wall openings, (d) excavations for foundation walls.

17. What is the weight of the steel I beam in the basement plan? (a) 15 lb., (b) 20½ lb., (c) 25½ lb., (d) 8 lb.

18. The area wall projects _____ above the finished grade level. (a) 6 in., (b) 3 in., (c) 1 ft. 9 in., (d) 2 in.

19. The rafters over the front entrance of the basic house are at a _____ pitch. (a) 6-12, (b) 12-6, (c) 9-12, (d) 8-12.

20. The ceiling joists of the basic house are supported by the _____: (a) header, (b) rafters, (c) sole, (d) plate.

21. Double joists that run parallel to other joists around floor openings are known as _____: (a) trimmers, (b) headers, (c) tail beams, (d) valley jacks.

22. Live loads on floors in residential construction are based on _____ lb. per square foot. (a) 30, (b) 40, (c) 50, (d) 10.

23. The water table in the basic house drops approximately _____ below the top of the foundation wall. (a) 1 in., (b) 12 in., (c) 6 in., (d) 2 in.

24. The exterior wall covering of the basic house is made of: (a) cedar, (b) stucco, (c) plaster, (d) asbestos.

Architectural Drafting Examination No. 2 (Continued)

True or False

T F 1. In brick-veneer construction the brick veneer serves as a support for the roof rafters in addition to dressing up the exterior of the building.

T F 2. A fire cut should be used in both brick-veneer and solid-brick construction.

T F 3. A 1-in. air space should be allowed between the brick veneer and the stone backing for insulation purposes.

T F 4. Studs are generally spaced 12 or 16 in. on center.

T F 5. In localities subject to earthquakes, anchor bolts may extend from the foundation wall to the plate seating the roof rafters.

T F 6. A lintel is used to support masonry over openings.

T F 7. Tail beams are 2- x 10-in. forming members generally spaced 16 in. on center.

T F 8. A fireplace hearth is normally supported by the surrounding framing members.

T F 9. The symbol for common brick is the same for both section and elevation.

T F 10. Concrete is the only practical material for foundation walls.

T F 11. The sash opening and the rough opening are considered the same thing.

T F 12. Siding may be used on both walls and roofs.

T F 13. The minimum headroom required for the residential stair from the first to the second floor is 7 ft. 0 in.

T F 14. The total run and the well opening of a stair are of the same dimensions.

T F 15. The hearth of the fireplace in a residence should extend a minimum distance of 1 ft. 8 in. from the face of the fireplace.

T F 16. Exterior walls are dimensioned from inside face of stud.

T F 17. In frame construction, openings in exterior walls are normally located from the center of the opening.

T F 18. In ¼-in. scale drawings of frame construction, exterior walls are drawn 6 in. thick.

T F 19. The over-all length of the building on Plate 14, from outside face of one wall to the outside face of the other wall, is 31 ft. 0 in.

T F 20. If the above dimension were taken from outside face of stud to outside face of stud, the dimension would be 30 ft. 10 in.

T F 21. The total height of the brickwork of the chimney on Plate 15 is 25 ft. 6 in.

T F 22. Only one flue is required in the chimney of the basic house.

T F 23. If the distance from the finished first floor to the finished grade is 1 ft. 9 in., three 7¾-in. risers would be required for steps leading to the entrance door.

T F 24. It is not necessary to locate all openings in exterior walls because builders always have architects' scales available.

T F 25. If the floor area of the dining room were 130 sq. ft. one window 3 ft. 0 in. x 4 ft. 6 in. would provide sufficient light.

T F 26. Sheathing that is nailed horizontally will provide greater strength.

T F 27. An angle of 90 deg. in an orthographic projection drawing becomes an angle of 30 or 60 deg. in an isometric drawing.

T F 28. A line that is neither horizontal nor vertical in a projection drawing becomes a nonisometric line in isometric drawing.

T F 29. A horizontal line in a projection drawing forms an angle of 60 deg. from the T square in an isometric drawing.

T F 30. Chimneys should extend a minimum of 3 ft. 6 in. above the ridge.

T F 31. The product of riser and tread for interior stairs should be between 70 and 75.

T F 32. More shrinkage occurs in box-sill construction than solid-sill construction.

T F 33. The lally columns in the basic house are used to support the steel girder and rest upon concrete footings that are 24 in. square and 24 in. deep.

T F 34. Area walls are used to provide light and air to the basement.

T F 35. A venthole is used to provide a passage between excavated and unexcavated portions of a basement.

T F 36. The height of the garage floor at the rear is 6 in. from the grade level.

Short-Answer Type

1. What is flashing used for?

2. Name two types of materials used in flashing.

3. What is the purpose of a bond course in masonry construction?

4. What is meant by "run" in stair construction?

5. What is the nominal size of a common brick?

6. Which end of a draftsman's pencil should be sharpened?

7. What is the floor area of a room that is 11 ft. 6 in. x 9 ft. 6 in.?

8. List the four principal types of lines used in architectural drafting.

9. Explain briefly the difference between plan, elevation, and section.

10. Where are doubled studs used?

11. What instrument would be used in constructing an angle of 23 deg.?

12. In drawing plans to the scale of ¼ in. = 1 ft. 0 in., how thick should the exterior walls and partition walls be made in frame construction?

13. What scale would be used in making a drawing one-quarter full size?

14. What type of lintels, other than angle irons, may be used over masonry openings?

15. Where are headers used?

16. (a) What is a tail beam? (b) What are trimmers?

17. How many joists are required in supporting an 8-ft. stud partition plastered on both sides and running parallel to the floor joists?

18. (a) What are valley rafters? (b) What are jack rafters?

19. How many rows of cross bridging are required for a 16-ft. span?

20. If the span of a roof is 12 ft. 3 in. and a ¼ pitch is used, what is its rise?

21. What is the purpose of the calamine door between the garage and the kitchen entrance?

22. What is the elevation of the garage floor midway between the end walls?

23. Why is it impractical to use a 4- x 6-in. sill on the garage foundation wall instead of a 4 x 4?

24. Why may the rafters over the garage project only 1 in. beyond the outside face of the plate?

25. If the span of a roof is 36 ft. 6 in., what is the run of the roof?

26. If the run of a roof in a frame building is 4 ft. 2 in., what is the span of a joist running from plate to plate?

27. If the span of a roof is 24 ft. 2 in., what is the span of its rafter if a 2-in. thick ridgeboard is used?

28. What is the actual size of a 2 x 4?

29. What does L.O. mean?

30. What is the purpose of a bench mark or surveyor's monument?

31. What do the following abbreviations stand for? (a) G.L., (b) H.L., (c) P.P., (d) V.P., (e) S.P.

32. What two lines in perspective drawing are considered when adjustments are made in the level of sight of an object?

33. On what perspective line do the vanishing points lie?

34. Can a perspective drawing be made by using only one vanishing point?

35. Are perspective drawings ever made with more than two vanishing points?

36. In a two-point perspective drawing, what may a third or fourth vanishing point be used for?

37. Can dimensions be laid off directly anywhere on a perspective drawing?

38. What are rafters that run from the ridgeboard to the plate known as?

39. What are rafters that run from the ridgeboard to a valley rafter known as?

40. How should the three main fixtures in a kitchen be arranged to provide for economy of plumbing?

41. What must be done to certain walls or partitions to accommodate soil and vent stacks?

PART V
HEATING THE HOUSE

Although it is not usually the duty of an architect to design the heating system, he is expected to cooperate with the heating engineer and to coordinate the architectural design with the requirements of the heating system. His draftsmen usually prepare the final drawings and in many cases do the actual computation work. It is therefore advantageous for the student draftsman to familiarize himself with the basic types of heating systems, their advantages, disadvantages, and uses, and methods of calculation. The following pages are included in this text to provide the student with information and data that will enable him to compute heat losses quickly, select radiators and boilers, and lay out an actual heating system.

Heat Loss and How to Compute It

What Is Heat Loss?

Heat loss represents the quantity of heat that the heating system must supply to a given space to maintain the required temperature within that space.

Why Does a Room Have a Loss of Heat?

It is a well-known fact that heat flows downhill, that is, from a high-temperature source to a low-temperature receiver. Thus warm objects lose their heat to colder objects. In the case of a heated structure, the room air acts as the high-temperature source and the outside air as the low-temperature receiver, with the building wall serving as a barrier between the two. Figure 41 shows a typical wall section with heat loss taking place from an inside temperature of 70°F to an outside temperature of 0°F. (A loss of heat will take place as long as a temperature differential exists.) It seems logical to conclude that the amount of heat lost will depend primarily on the following considerations:

1. How much surface is exposed to a cold temperature?
2. How good a heat barrier is this surface?
3. How great is the temperature difference causing the heat flow?

It follows directly, then, that

1. The larger the room, the greater the heat loss.
2. The poorer the wall construction, the greater the heat loss.
3. The colder the outdoor temperature, the greater the heat loss.

What Is the Basic Rule for Computing Heat Loss?

Heat loss = area × wall effectiveness × degree temperature difference

Since heat loss depends on surface, wall construction, and temperature differential, the actual heat loss is expressed in terms of area, wall effectiveness, and degrees temperature difference between inside and outside design temperatures. In the above expression:

Area refers to the square feet of only that surface which is exposed to a temperature less than room temperature. By *surface* is meant wall, glass, door, floor, roof, and partition area that may be exposed to a cold temperature. It should be noted that no heat loss occurs between adjacent rooms if each room is heated to the same temperature. The symbol for area is *A*.

Wall effectiveness expresses the ability of a certain type of material to resist the flow of heat. A heat-flow transmission coefficient has been assigned to every type of commercially used surface. Constructions with low transmission coefficients indicate good insulators; those with relatively high factors indicate poor insulators. These factors are variously referred to in the trade as *heat-transmission coefficients*, *K factors*, or *U factors*. The standard heat-transmission coefficient symbol adopted by the American Society of Heating and Ventilating Engineers is *U*. Figure 42 shows a few typical heat-transmission coefficients.

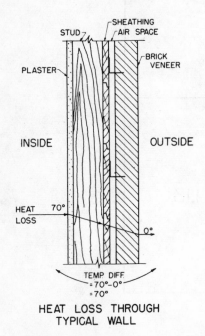

HEAT LOSS THROUGH TYPICAL WALL

Fig. 41

TYPICAL HEAT TRANSMISSION COEFFICIENTS

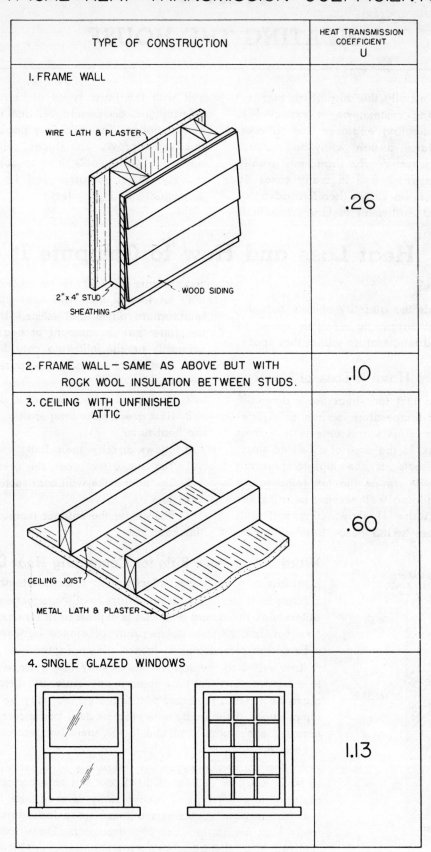

TYPE OF CONSTRUCTION	HEAT TRANSMISSION COEFFICIENT U
1. FRAME WALL — WIRE LATH & PLASTER, WOOD SIDING, 2" x 4" STUD, SHEATHING	.26
2. FRAME WALL — SAME AS ABOVE BUT WITH ROCK WOOL INSULATION BETWEEN STUDS.	.10
3. CEILING WITH UNFINISHED ATTIC — CEILING JOIST, METAL LATH & PLASTER	.60
4. SINGLE GLAZED WINDOWS	1.13

Fig. 42

Figure 42 shows that glass is a poor insulator, because it has a relatively high transmission coefficient. It will be noted that the addition of rock-wool insulation between the studs of the exterior wall shown cuts down the heat loss more than half. Heat-transmission coefficients for ordinary residential constructions vary from 0.07 for well-insulated walls to 1.13 for glass and thin wood doors. Complete tabulations for all building materials may be found in any standard engineering text dealing with heating. (The original source of most data on transmission coefficients is the American Society of Heating and Ventilating Engineers *Guide*, a handbook on heating, ventilation and air conditioning, published yearly by the A.S.H. & V.E., New York.)

Degrees temperature difference is the arithmetical difference between the inside room temperature and the coldest outside temperature likely to occur in a given locality, expressed in degrees Fahrenheit. The symbol for this temperature difference is T. It is common practice to use 70° for the inside design temperature, with the outside design temperature varying with geographical location. The outside design temperature is not the coldest temperature ever recorded in a given locality, since extremely low temperatures exist for only short periods of time and it would be uneconomical to design for such a condition. Table 1 shows that design temperatures in various parts of the country vary considerably.

TABLE 1

OUTSIDE DESIGN TEMPERATURES IN VARIOUS
PARTS OF THE UNITED STATES

Connecticut		*New York*	
Bridgeport	0	New York City	0
Hartford	—5	Albany	—9
New Haven	0	Buffalo	—5
Kansas		*Ohio*	
Concordia	—10	Cleveland	—2
Dodge City	—11	Columbus	—5
New Jersey		*Washington*	
Newark	5	Seattle	18
Paterson	—5	Spokane	—15

For a more comprehensive listing of design temperatures throughout the country refer to the current edition of A.S.H. & V.E. *Guide*.

The basic rule for heat loss may now be stated thus:

$$\text{Heat loss} = A \times U \times T$$

What Unit of Measurement Is Used to Express Heat Loss?

Heat loss requires a unit of measurement, as do length, area, weight, distance, speed and so on. In the United States and Great Britain the unit of heat is the British thermal unit, abbreviated Btu. Unlike the foot, for example, the Btu cannot very well be visualized, but this limitation in no way interferes with its usefulness. As long as heating apparatus is rated in Btu's by the manufacturer and the heat losses are figured in Btu's, then the heating equipment can be selected to match the heat loss.

Actually the Btu is a definite quantity of heat, approximately the heat required to raise the temperature of one pound of water through 1°F. In other words if we heat 1 lb. of water from, say 65° to 66°, or from 86° to 87°, then we shall have to supply an amount of heat equal to 1 Btu. Now if a certain wall has a heat loss of 800 Btu, it is losing heat in an amount which would be equivalent to the heat required to heat 800 lb. of water 1°, 400 lb. through 2°, 100 lb. through 8°, and so on.

Time is also a factor to consider. If a wall has a heat loss of 600 Btu, it is necessary to know whether this loss takes place in one minute, one hour, or one day. It is customary to express all heat losses in terms of Btu per hour, written Btu/hr. The value of U in the heat-loss formula must therefore necessarily be expressed in the units of Btu per square foot of surface per hour per degree of temperature difference.

Is It Possible to Shorten the Heat-Loss Formula for Easy Use?

Yes. Look at the heat loss formula once more:

$$\text{Heat loss} = A \times U \times T$$

For a given construction, U is always the same, and for a given locality the inside and outside design temperatures are fixed. Therefore the product of U and T is always a constant number. If an outside temperature of 70° is chosen and an outdoor design temperature of 0°F is used, then $T = 70° - 0°$. If the known heat-transmission coefficient U is multiplied by 70°, a combined number will be found, which for convenience will be called the K factor. All that is necessary now is to multiply the area in question by the combined K factor to arrive at the heat loss in Btu/hr. Thus:

$$\text{Btu/hr.} = A \times K$$

How Can a Simplified Heat-Loss Table Be Made?

A simplified heat-loss table can be made by obtaining heat-transmission coefficients from any text on the subject, multiplying all coefficients by the desired temperature differential between inside and outside design temperature, and listing all factors thus obtained for all the desired types of construction.

SIMPLIFIED HEAT-LOSS FACTORS

B T U PER HOUR HEAT LOSS = AREA X K

① WALL

NO.	FRAME	K
1	WOOD SIDING OR CLAPBOARD ON SHEATHING, NO INSULATION	18.2
2	SAME, BUT INSULATED WITH ROCK WOOL BETWEEN STUDS	7.0
3	WOOD SHINGLES, NO INSULATION	18.3
4	SAME, BUT INSULATED WITH ROCK WOOL BETWEEN STUDS	7.0
5	STUCCO, NO INSULATION	22.4
6	SAME, BUT INSULATED WITH ROCK WOOL BETWEEN STUDS	8.4
7	BRICK VENEER, NO INSULATION	19.6
8	SAME, BUT INSULATED WITH ROCK WOOL BETWEEN STUDS	9.1

NO.	MASONRY	K
9	8" SOLID BRICK, PLASTERED, NO INSULATION	22.4
10	SAME, BUT WITH 1" RIGID INSULATION UNDER PLASTER	11.2
11	12" SOLID BRICK, PLASTERED NO INSULATION	17.5
12	SAME, BUT WITH 1" RIGID INSULATION UNDER PLASTER	9.8
13	8" HAYDITE CONCRETE BLOCK, PLASTERED, NO INSULATION	17.5
14	SAME, BUT WITH 1" RIGID INSULATION UNDER PLASTER	10.5
15	BRICK VENEER ON 8" CONCRETE BLOCK, PLASTERED, NOT INSULATED	16.1
16	SAME, BUT WITH 1" RIGID INSULATION	9.8

NO.	GLASS	K
17	4" THICK HOLLOW GLASS BLOCK	34.3

② CEILING

NO.	WOOD	K
1	JOISTS & PLASTER, NO FLOOR ABOVE, NO INSULATION	24.1
2	JOISTS & PLASTER, ROUGH FLOOR ABOVE, NO INSULATION	10.5
3	SAME, WITH ROCK WOOL INSULATION	4.0

NO.	CONCRETE	K
4	4" CONCRETE, FURRED & PLASTERED. NO INSULATION, NO FLOORING ABOVE	13.0
5	SAME, WITH 1" RIGID INSULATION	8.8

③ FLOOR (UNHEATED BELOW)

NO.	WOOD	K
1	JOISTS EXPOSED, DOUBLE FLOOR NO INSULATION	5.1
2	PLASTER BOARD BELOW JOISTS, DOUBLE FLOOR. NO INSULATION	3.8
3	SAME, BUT WITH ROCK WOOL INSULATION BETWEEN JOISTS	6.0

NO.	CONCRETE	K
4	4" CONCRETE FLOORING, NO INSULATION	6.0

④ FLOOR (ON GROUND)

NO.	CONCRETE	K
1	4" CONCRETE BASE, NO INSULATION	21.4
2	SAME, WITH 1" RIGID INSULATION	4.4
3	4" CONCRETE, SINGLE WOOD FLOORING, NO INSULATION	17.5
4	SAME, WITH 1" RIGID INSULATION	3.2
5	4" CONCRETE, DOUBLE WOOD FLOORING, NO INSULATION	5.6
6	SAME, WITH 1" RIGID INSULATION	2.8

Fig. 43

SIMPLIFIED HEAT – LOSS FACTORS

(CONTINUED)

⑤ FLOORS (ABOVE GROUND)

NO.	WOOD	K
1	JOISTS, DOUBLE FLOORING, ROCKWOOL & SHEATHING	7.0

NO.	CONCRETE	K
2	4" SLAB, WOOD FLOORING, 1" RIGID INSULATION	12.0

⑥ ROOF

NO.	WOOD	K
1	SHINGLES, SHEATHING AND PLASTER, NO INSULATION	21.7
2	SAME, WITH ROCKWOOL INSULATION BETWEEN RAFTERS	8.0

NO.	CONCRETE	K
3	CONCRETE SLAB, ROOFING & FURRED CEILING, NO INSULATION	28.0
4	SAME, WITH 1" RIGID INSULATION	12.6

⑦ PARTITION (UNHEATED)

NO.	FRAME	K
1	PLASTER ON ONE SIDE OF STUDS, NO INSULATION	22.0
2	SAME, WITH ROCKWOOL INSULATION BETWEEN STUDS	8.0
3	PLASTER, BOTH SIDES, NO INSULATION	12.0

NO.	MASONRY	K
4	8" CINDER BLOCK PLASTER ONE SIDE, NO INSULATION	15.0
5	SAME, WITH 1" RIGID INSULATION	8.0
4	4" HOLLOW CLAY TILE PLASTER ONE SIDE	16.0

⑧ DOORS & WINDOWS

NO.	TYPE	K
1	DOORS, SINGLE GLAZED WINDOWS	79.1
2	STORM DOORS AND WINDOWS	41.0
3	DOUBLE WINDOWS (Thermopane)	43.4

MULTIPLY CUBIC CONTENTS OF ROOM BY FACTOR IN TABLE

⑨ INFILTRATION

WIND PROTECTION	DOORS & WINDOWS WEATHER-STRIPPED	NO WEATHER-STRIPPING
	ONE SIDE EXPOSED	
WITHOUT FIREPLACE	.84	1.4
WITH FIREPLACE	2.24	2.8
	TWO SIDES EXPOSED	
WITHOUT FIREPLACE	1.26	2.1
WITH FIREPLACE	2.66	3.5
	THREE OR FOUR SIDES EXPOSED	
WITHOUT FIREPLACE	1.68	2.8
WITH FIREPLACE	3.08	4.2

⑩ CORRECTION FACTOR

OUTSIDE TEMP.	INSIDE TEMPERATURE						
	50	55	60	65	70	75	80
30	.25	.32	.40	.48	.57	.67	.77
20	.38	.45	.54	.62	.71	.81	.92
10	.50	.58	.67	.76	.86	.96	1.07
0	.63	.71	.80	.90	1.00	1.11	1.23
-10	.75	.84	.94	1.04	1.14	1.26	1.38
-20	.88	.97	1.07	1.17	1.29	1.41	1.54
-30	1.01	1.10	1.21	1.31	1.43	1.55	1.69

Fig. 43 (Cont.)

Figure 43, Simplified Heat-Loss Factors, has been prepared in this manner.

Notice that the K factor shown in Fig. 43, section 1, wall 1, for example, can be obtained by multiplying the heat-loss coefficient U (0.26) shown in Fig. 42, by 70°, thus:

$$K = 0.26 \times 70° = 18.2$$

for frame construction with sheathing and wood siding, wall not insulated.

Likewise the K factor for single-glazed windows shown in Fig. 43, section 8, may be found by multiplying the heat-loss coefficient U (1.13) shown in Fig. 42, by 70°, thus:

$$K = 1.13 \times 70° = 79.1$$

for single-glazed windows.

Enough typical constructions have been included in the Simplified Heat-Loss Factors to cover all generally encountered problems. Sections 1 through 8 (Fig. 43) include walls, ceilings, floors, partitions, doors, and windows; section 9 pertains to infiltrations; section 10 gives correction factors.

What Is Infiltration and What Does it Have to Do with Heat Loss?

Thus far, consideration has been given only to heat loss through walls, floors, window glass, and other members by transmission. There is one more consideration, however. In any room containing windows and doors there is a certain amount of air leakage that seeps inward through the door and window cracks when the wind blows. This leakage is called *infiltration*. Every cubic foot of cold outside air that leaks into the room imposes an additional load on the heating system. It is entirely correct, then, to consider the heat required to warm the infiltrated air to room temperature as an additional heat loss, inasmuch as the heating system has to supply it.

Naturally, infiltration can be lessened by weatherstripping the door and window cracks. Storm windows are not very effective in stopping infiltration, but they do aid in cutting down the transmission heat loss through the glass. See Fig. 43, section 8, and compare items 1 and 2.

A fireplace encourages infiltration when in use since the air used in creating the draft is ultimately sucked in through the cracks around doors and windows.

Another factor to consider when computing infiltration is the number of sides of the room exposed to the weather. A room with one exposed wall will have less infiltration than one with two or three exposed walls. All the above-mentioned factors have been taken into account in computing K factors for Fig. 43, section 9.

Note that the factors listed in Section 9 should be multiplied by the *cubic content of the room*, not by any wall areas.

Cubic content = room length × room width
× ceiling height

When all dimensions are measured in feet, the cubic content is expressed in cubic feet.

What Are Correction Factors?

Section 10 of Fig. 43 shows correction factors which, if used as multipliers, will correct any heat-loss computation as figured from the simplified heat-loss factors, Fig. 43, from the standard design conditions of 70° inside and 0° outside to any other set of design temperatures. Figure 43 includes a range of inside temperatures from 50° to 80°, and outside temperatures from minus 30° to plus 30°F. For example, if a structure has a heat loss of 100,000 Btu/hr based on 0° outside and 70° inside, and the location is Concordia, Kansas, then the corrected heating loss is 100,000 × 1.14 or 114,000 Btu/hr.

What Data Should Be Recorded on a Work Sheet?

Figure 44 shows a work sheet that has proved very satisfactory. With its aid, construction changes and their effect on the heat-loss computations are readily evaluated.

Each vertical column on the work sheet has been numbered for quick reference, as follows:

NAME			DESIGN TEMPERATURE			SHEET		
LOCATION			INSIDE	OUTSIDE		OF		
1	2	3	4	5	6	7	8	9
Room, Cu. Ft.	Item	Area	Section	No.	K	Heat Loss, Btu/Hr.	Corr. Factor	Total

SAMPLE WORK SHEET FOR HEAT-LOSS COMPUTATION
Fig. 44

Column 1 contains the name of the room and its cubic content:

Cubic content = length × width × height

Columns 2 and 3 describe the heat-loss item being considered and its area. All outside wall, regardless of orientation is figured at one time for any given room. It is often convenient to use a pair of dividers and step off the wall lengths, increasing the spread of the instrument by an amount equal to each successive length of wall, until all outside wall is accounted for. Then hold the dividers against the proper scale and read total length of exposed wall. Next multiply by the ceiling height to obtain the total area, including windows and doors. To find the net wall area, subtract the sum of the door and window areas from the total wall area. Always figure on the safe side, but do not attempt to be highly accurate. After all, a heat-loss computation is only approximate; and if ten estimates are prepared by ten different estimators, ten different answers will result. All answers, however, should be reasonably correct. A 10 per cent factor of safety is added to each room to allow for slight discrepancies in calculation and uncertainties in construction.

Column 4 refers to the applicable section in Fig. 43.

Column 5 refers to the particular wall or floor or construction shown in each section of Fig. 43.

Column 6 shows the heat-loss factor *K* listed in Fig. 43.

Column 7 is the product of Column 3 and Column 6. When figuring infiltration, the *K* factor is multiplied by the cubic content shown in Column 1.

Column 8 shows the correction factor for conditions of design other than 0° outside, 70° inside. The correction factor may be found in section 10, Fig. 43.

Column 9 is the product of Column 7 and Column 8. The heat-loss for the entire structure is the sum of the individual room heat losses.

Heat-Loss Computations for Residence

Problem

Calculate the heat loss for the basic house, final stage, shown in Part IV of this text.

Location................................Newark, N. J.
Inside temperature ....70°F.
All floors above unexcavated spaces to be insulated with rock wool.

Procedure

Check type of construction for each wall, floor, ceiling, and other member exposed to a temperature less than 70°F. Compute heat losses for all such surfaces, using the simplified heat-loss factors, Fig. 43. together with the work sheet shown in Fig. 44. See Heat-Loss Computation, Fig. 45.

HEAT – LOSS COMPUTATION

1	2	3	4	5	6	7	8	9

NAME: FRAME RESIDENCE - BASIC HOUSE   LOCATION: NEWARK, NEW JERSEY   DESIGN TEMPERATURE   INSIDE 70° OUTSIDE 5°   SHEET 1 OF 2

ROOM CU. FT.	ITEM	AREA	SECTION	NO.	K	HEAT LOSS BTU / HR.	CORR. FACTOR	TOTAL
LIVING ROOM 12'-0" x 17'-0" x 9'-0" 1830 CU.FT.	EXPOSED WALL 17'-0" x 9'-0" DOOR & WINDOW 20.0 + 34.6 NET WALL CEILING 12'-0" x 17'-0" INFILTRATION ADD 10% F.S.	153 55 98 204	8 1 2 9	1 1 2	79.1 18.2 10.5 2.8	4350 1780 2150 5100 13380 1338 14718	.93	13,700
DINING ROOM 11'-0" x 13'-0" x 9'-0" 1290 CU.FT.	EXPOSED WALL 20'-0" x 9'-0" WINDOWS 12.5 + 12.5 NET WALL CEILING 11'-0" x 13'-0" INFILTRATION ADD 10% F.S.	180 25 155 143	8 1 2	1 1 2	79.1 18.2 10.5 2.1	1980 2820 1500 2700 9000 900 9900	93	9,200
KITCHEN 11'-0" x 14'-0" x 9'-0" 1390 CU.FT.	EXPOSED WALL 14'-0" x 9'-0" WINDOWS 9.5 + 9.5 NET WALL GARAGE PARTITION 11'-0" x 9'-0" FLOOR 11'-0" x 14'-0" CEILING 11'-0" x 14'-0" INFILTRATION ADD 10% F.S.	126 19 107 99 154 154	8 1 7 5 2	1 1 3 1 2	79.1 18.2 12.0 7.0 10.5 1.4	1500 1950 1190 1080 1620 1950 9290 929 10219	.93	9,550

Fig. 45

HEAT – LOSS COMPUTATION (CONTINUED)

NAME: FRAME RESIDENCE – BASIC HOUSE LOCATION: NEWARK, NEW JERSEY
DESIGN TEMPERATURE INSIDE 70° OUTSIDE 5° SHEET 2 OF 2

1 ROOM CU. FT.	2 ITEM	3 AREA	4 SECTION	5 NO.	6 K	7 HEAT LOSS BTU/HR.	8 CORR. FACTOR	9 TOTAL
LAVATORY 5'-0"x6'-0"x9'-0" 270 CU.FT.	EXPOSED WALL 6'-0" x 9'-0"	54						
	WINDOW 2'-0"x3'-2"	6.3	8	1	79.1	500		
	NET WALL	47.7	1	1	18.2	870		
	FLOOR 5'-0" x 6'-0"	30	5	1	7.0	210		
	CEILING 5'-0" x 6'-0"	30	2	2	10.5	315		
	INFILTRATION				1.4	380		
						2275		
	ADD 10% F.S.					227		
						2502	.93	2,330
REAR ENTRY 5'-0"x7'-0"x9'-0" 315 CU.FT.	EXPOSED WALL 7'-0" x 9'-0"	63						
	DOOR-REAR 2'-6"x6'-8"	16.6	8	1	79.1	1310		
	NET WALL	46.4	1	1	18.2	850		
	GARAGE PARTITION	45				SEE NOTE*		
	FIREPROOF DOOR	21	*8	1	39.0	820		
	NET WALL	24	7	3	12.0	290		
	FLOOR 5'-0"x7'-0"	35	5	1	7.0	245		
	CEILING 5'-0"x7'-0"	35	2	2	10.5	366		
	INFILTRATION				1.4	443		
						4324		
	ADD 10% F.S.					432		
						4756	.93	4,420
BATHROOM 6'-0"x8'-0"x9'-0" 430 CU.FT.	EXPOSED WALL 8'-0" x 9'-0"	72						
	WINDOW 2'-0"x3'-2"	6.3	8	1	79.1	500		
	NET WALL	65.7	1	1	18.2	1195		
	CEILING 6'-0"x8'-0"	48	2	2	10.5	505		
	INFILTRATION				1.4	600		
						2800		
	ADD 10% F.S.					280		
						3080	.93	2,860
DEN 7'-0"x12'-0"x9'-0" 760 CU.FT.	EXPOSED WALL 26'-0" x 9'-0"	234						
	WINDOWS 12.5 + 12.5	25	8	1	79.1	1980		
	NET WALL	209	1	1	18.2	3800		
	FLOOR 7'-0"x12'-0"	84	5	1	7.0	588		
	CEILING 7'-0"x12'-0"	84	2	2	10.5	885		
	INFILTRATION				2.8	2130		
						9383		
	ADD 10% F.S.					938		
						10321	.93	9,600
SOUTH BEDROOM 9'-0"x9'-0"x9'-0" 730 CU.FT.	EXPOSED WALL 9'-0" x 9'-0"	81						
	WINDOW 3'-0"x4'-2"	12.5	8	1	79.1	990		
	NET WALL	68.5	1	1	18.2	1250		
	CEILING 9'-0"x9'-0"	81	2	2	10.5	850		
	INFILTRATION				1.4	1020		
						4110		
	ADD 10% F.S.					411		
						4521	.93	4,200
EAST BEDROOM 10'-0"x10'-0"x9'-0" 900 CU.FT.	EXPOSED WALL 12'-0" x 9'-0"	108						
	WINDOW 3'-0"x4'-2"	12.5	8	1	79.1	990		
	NET WALL	85.5	1	1	18.2	1560		
	CEILING 10'-0" x 10'-0"	100	2	2	10.5	1050		
	INFILTRATION				1.4	1260		
						4860		
	ADD 10% F.S.					486		
						5346	.93	4,970
MASTER BEDROOM 13'-0"x18'-0"x9'-0" 2100 CU.FT.	EXPOSED WALL 49'-0" x 9'-0"	440						
	WINDOWS 12.5+12.5+12.5	37.5	8	1	79.1	2950		
	NET WALL	402.5	1	1	18.2	7320		
	FLOOR 13'-0"x18'-0"	235	5	1	7.0	1640		
	CEILING 13'-0"x18'-0"	235	2	2	10.5	2470		
	INFILTRATION				2.8	5900		
						20280		
	ADD 10% F.S.					2028		
						22308	.93	20,700
						GRAND TOTAL HEAT LOSS		81,530

*NOTE: TABULAR VALUE CUT IN HALF, INASMUCH AS TEMPERATURE DIFFERENCE = 35° INSTEAD OF 70° BECAUSE ROOM ADJACENT TO FIREPROOF DOOR IS UNHEATED.

NOTE: FOR COMPUTATION, USE ROOM SIZES TO THE NEAREST WHOLE FOOT. ADD ONE FOOT TO CEILING HEIGHT IN COMPUTING CUBIC CONTENT AND EXPOSED WALL AREA.

What About Insulation?

The homeowner of today is continually reminded that he can save considerable fuel and also have a warmer house in winter and a cooler house in summer if he installs insulation. Let us analyze the heat-loss computation of the previous problem and determine the value of insulation on the given structure. Figure 46 shows how the heat loss of this house is distributed. For instance, 28 per cent of the total heat loss is transmitted through exposed wall, 21.7 per cent through windows and doors, and so on. Notice that insulation alone can be effective on 42.9 per cent (14.9 plus 28 per cent) of the total heat loss. To save an appreciable amount of fuel, weather stripping and storm windows should also be considered. Weather stripping is effective on 23.9 per cent of the heat loss, and storm doors and windows are effective on 21.7 per cent of the heat loss.

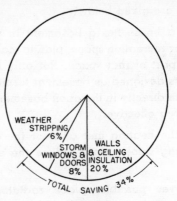

Fig. 47

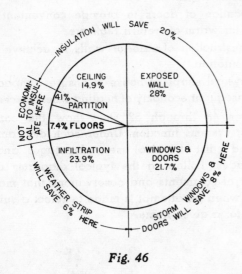

Fig. 46

Fig. 47 is a chart showing the per cent saving by means of insulation and weather stripping, and use of storm door and windows.

The total saving is shown in Fig. 47. Note that in-sulation alone saves 20 per cent of the fuel bill, but in order to capitalize on the greater savings often advertised, it is also necessary to weather-strip all doors and windows and to add storm doors and windows. The total fuel-cost saving for this particular residence would amount to about 34 per cent if storm windows and doors, weather stripping, and insulation were applied.

A complete job of *weatherproofing* a building of this size may easily cost $1000, and the actual fuel saving in dollars may amount to only $50 per season. At this rate the installation would take 20 years to pay for itself, neglecting interest on the principal. There is, however, the factor of increased comfort with insulated homes; and since it is difficult to measure comfort in dollars and cents, this saving is sometimes overlooked.

In the light of the above discussion, the student will no doubt conclude that weatherproofing is a worthwhile long-term investment.

Appropriate factors for common types of insulated walls, floors, ceilings, and roofs, as well as for double-glass windows, and allowances for weather-stripped windows and doors have been included in Fig. 43, Simplified Heat-Loss Factors.

[125]

Practical Considerations — Types of Heating Systems

A few items that deserve careful consideration by the student are given below:

1. When a house has a basement in which there is an open or recreation space, plan to make the heating unit a part of that space. Not only are modern heating units designed as *basement furniture*, but by placing them directly in the open basement area they heat that area effectively.

2. Place the heating unit as near the chimney as possible. Long smoke pipes reduce the efficiency of the unit.

3. Whenever possible, place radiators beneath windows or against cold walls. The best location is underneath a window, because cold air leaking in through the window is warmed before it reaches the interior of the room or floor.

4. If large picture windows extending nearly to the floor are used, it may not be possible to place any radiator beneath the sill. Under these circumstances a forced warm-air system or some form of radiant heat (such as the radiant baseboard) might prove advisable. Sometimes double-glazed windows (Thermopane, for example) are used to make the heating less of a problem.

5. When using warm-air system, always arrange the ductwork so that warm air is blown from the warm walls (partitions) toward the outside walls.

6. Second-floor partitions that line up with those on the first floor are ideal for carrying vertical risers to warm-air outlets on the second floor.

The heating system of any home assumes more and more importance when it is realized just how much of a part it plays in the success of any well-planned project. The design of the heating system may directly affect the following:

1. Shape, size and location of windows, if radiators are to be located beneath them.

2. Location of recreation room in basement, to include heating unit.

3. Location of chimney.

4. Thickness, stud spacing, and location of partition walls where warm-air ducts are used.

5. Construction of floors and ceilings where radiant heat is contemplated.

6. Location of doors to provide convenient wall spaces for warm-air return registers.

7. Construction of exterior walls to achieve good heat insulation.

8. Physical shape of house to ensure compactness and consequent economy of heating where necessary.

Figures 48 through 52 show how the common types of systems function. Under each diagram will be found a list of typical uses, advantages, and disadvantages. Following the typical diagrams are a number of comments and observations that may be helpful when an attempt is made to select a suitable system for a given home.

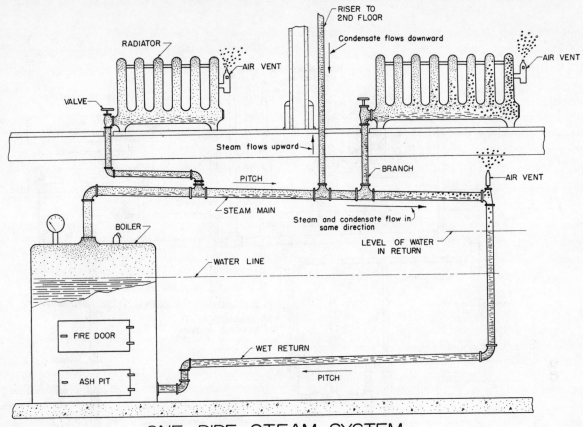

ONE-PIPE STEAM SYSTEM

Fig. 48

WHERE USED

1. Residential structures
2. Apartment buildings
3. Stores
4. Factories
5. Small public buildings
6. Theaters

ADVANTAGES

1. Low cost of material, labor, and maintenance.
2. Easy to install.
3. Very few "steam specialties" required.
4. Existing systems can easily be converted into one-pipe vapor system by addition of vacuum air valves in place of air vents.

DISADVANTAGES

1. Steam and water flow in opposite directions in branches and risers, necessitating large-size pipes.
2. Water hammer sometimes prevalent.
3. Air vented directly into room, carrying any odors.
4. Considerable time and pressure required to vent air from each radiator before heating becomes effective, thereby wasting fuel.
5. Not suitable for use with modern convector-type radiators unless specially designed convectors are used.

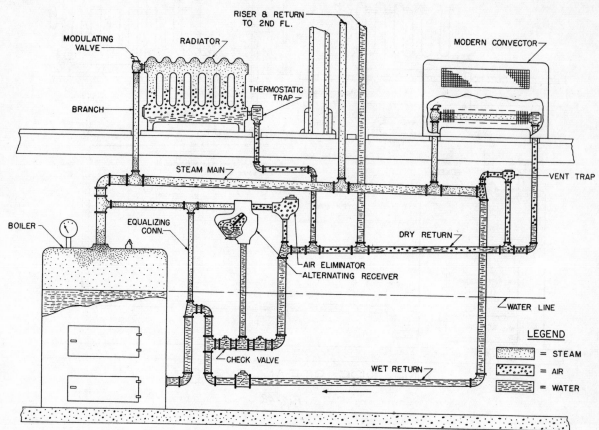

TWO-PIPE VAPOR SYSTEM

Fig. 49

WHERE USED

1. Residential structures
2. Small apartment buildings
3. Small public buildings
4. Stores

ADVANTAGES

1. Extremely low boiler pressure (1 to 2 oz.) and partial vacuum sufficient to circulate steam throughout system, since no air can accumulate in radiators because of thermostatic traps.

2. Modulating-type steam valves may be used, thus making it possible to throttle the radiator. (Not possible with one-pipe system.)

3. No water hammer or odor. Quick heating-up period. Very efficient.

4. System ideal in response to automatic control.

5. May be used with modern convectors.

DISADVANTAGES

1. Higher cost than one-pipe system. Expensive valves, traps, and other steam specialties required.

2. More labor required for installation than with one-pipe system.

One-Pipe Hot-Water Heating System

The most popular type of hot-water radiator system for use in residential work is the one-pipe system (Fig. 49a). In a one-pipe layout, a single main follows the perimeter of the building, usually in the basement, and branches or risers connect the main with the individual radiators. If the house is spread out, two loops or circuits are used, each circuit serving the approximately identical heating load.

The piping system may be wrought iron, black steel, or copper pipe. Joints may be screwed, welded, or sweat-soldered in the case of copper. The size of the main leaving the boiler is usually 1¼ in. or 1½ in. on the average residential job, and the size of the radiator branches to the first floor ½ in. Risers to the second floor seldom exceed ¾ in.

The average circulator pumps about 8 to 10 gallons of hot water per minute through the system and requires a 1/6-hp 110v motor.

A flow valve (Fig. 49b), is located at the first elbow on the main leaving the boiler. It is the purpose of this valve to open under the influence of the velocity pressure of the flowing water when the pump is operating, and to close and prevent gravity flow when the pump is off. If the hot water were allowed to circulate during off-pump periods, the radiators would overheat at a time when the room was already too warm.

Radiators may be of the familiar cast-iron thin-tube design, or may be the more modern convector. The advantage of the convector lies in its streamlined appearance, and in the fact that it may be recessed in the wall. Each convector or radiator is equipped with a control valve and air vent.

In operation, the system is filled slowly with water, with air vents open, until all air is vented from the system. Then the vents are closed, and the control valves adjusted, and the system is ready for continuous operation.

An aquastat, located in the boiler, continually controls the oil burner, or other source of heat, maintaining boiler water at the desired temperature, usually 190° to 200°. A room thermostat, sensing a falling temperature in the room, then starts the circulator, which circulates the hot water throughout the system. When the room has warmed to the desired temperature, the thermostat stops the circulator, the flow valve swings shut, and the system furnishes no further heat until called upon again by the room thermostat.

The advantages of the one-pipe hot-water system lie in its simplicity, flexibility, small pipe sizes, low first cost, negligible maintenance, and ease of installation.

Special Flow Fitting

A special flow fitting at the exit of each convector separates the cooled-off water from the hotter water leading into the next convector.

Use of large glass areas that extend to, or nearly to, the floor, has made it difficult to place radiators or convectors properly in structures of contemporary design. To overcome this difficulty, special metal base-

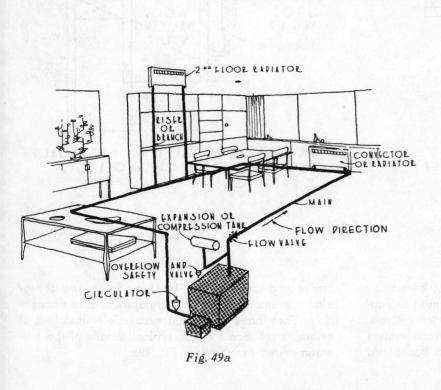

Fig. 49a

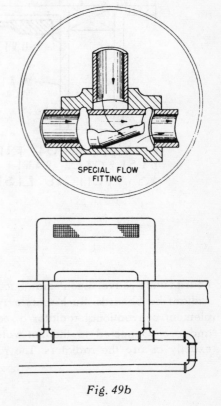

Fig. 49b

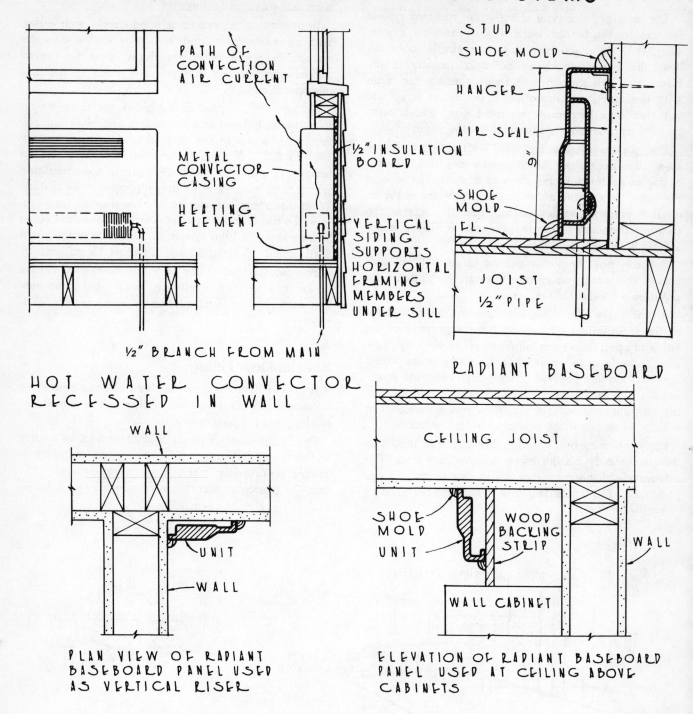

PATH OF CONVECTION AIR CURRENT

METAL CONVECTOR CASING

HEATING ELEMENT

½" INSULATION BOARD

VERTICAL SIDING SUPPORTS
HORIZONTAL FRAMING MEMBERS UNDER SILL

½" BRANCH FROM MAIN

HOT WATER CONVECTOR RECESSED IN WALL

STUD
SHOE MOLD
HANGER
AIR SEAL
SHOE MOLD
EL.
JOIST
½" PIPE

RADIANT BASEBOARD

WALL

UNIT

WALL

PLAN VIEW OF RADIANT BASEBOARD PANEL USED AS VERTICAL RISER

CEILING JOIST

SHOE MOLD
UNIT
WOOD BACKING STRIP
WALL

WALL CABINET

ELEVATION OF RADIANT BASEBOARD PANEL USED AT CEILING ABOVE CABINETS

Fig. 49c

board units have been manufactured, known as radiant baseboards. Such units may be used to supplement conventional radiator or convector systems, and are connected to the hot-water piping system exactly as are the radiators. The radiant baseboard has proved satisfactory in locations where use of regular convectors or radiators is impractical or undesirable. They have also been successfully installed at ceiling level. Some of the typical details of the hot-water system are shown in Fig. 49c.

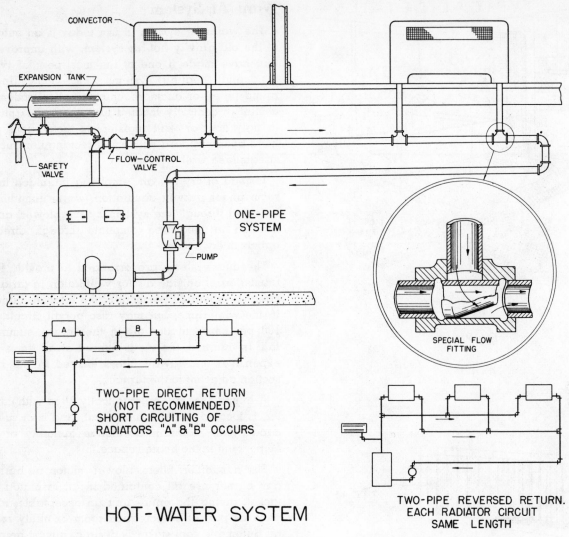

CONVECTOR

EXPANSION TANK

SAFETY VALVE

FLOW—CONTROL VALVE

ONE-PIPE SYSTEM

PUMP

A B

TWO-PIPE DIRECT RETURN (NOT RECOMMENDED) SHORT CIRCUITING OF RADIATORS "A" & "B" OCCURS

SPECIAL FLOW FITTING

TWO-PIPE REVERSED RETURN. EACH RADIATOR CIRCUIT SAME LENGTH

HOT-WATER SYSTEM

Fig. 50

WHERE USED

1. Residential structures
2. Apartment buildings
3. Stores
4. Factories
5. Small public buildings
6. Housing developments
7. Hospitals

ADVANTAGES

1. Extremely efficient because of instant circulation of water.
2. Low-temperature heat for mild weather.
3. Radiators hold heat for a long time.

DISADVANTAGES

1. System always full of water; in cold climates must be drained when not in use.
2. May overheat when weather turns mild suddenly (see 3, Advantages).

[131]

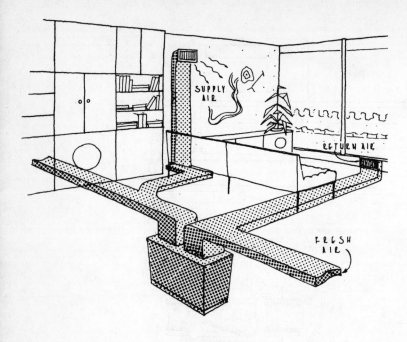

Fig. 50a

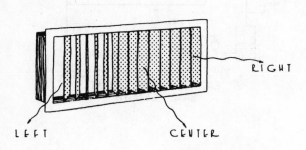

Fig. 50b

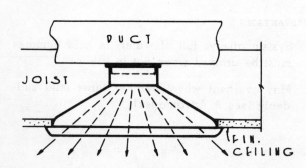

Fig. 50c

Warm-Air System

The warm-air system in use today is an outgrowth of the old gravity hot-air system, with improvements that have made it one of the most popular types of residential heating systems (Fig. 50a). Unsightly round pipes, or ducts, reaching in all directions from a clumsy centrally located furnace, and terminating in ugly floor or wall registers in the various rooms, have been replaced with small rectangular ducts and streamlined wall grilles.

Instead of dry hot air, emptying unguided into the room under gravity circulation, warm humidified air is forced through the system by the blower, and distributed in measured amounts through directional outlets in each room.

The duct systems are arranged to provide for the admission of outside air for ventilation in an amount equal to about 20 per cent of the total air circulated in the wintertime, but may also permit circulation of 100 per cent outdoor air in the spring, summer, or fall. In addition, the air is filtered at all times by inexpensive, throwaway filters located in the blower section adjacent to the furnace.

A humidifier pan, automatically filled with city water, is located in the furnace unit, and is of sufficient capacity to maintain a relative humidity of about 50 per cent in the heated space.

The humidifier, filters, blower, motor, oil burner, or gas burner are all contained in an insulated metal jacket, giving the entire unit an acceptable appearance as part of a recreation room or utility room. If an automatic coal stoker is desired, it must be placed external to the unit, and coal storage space will be required.

This forced-warm-air system for the average sized residence is capable of supplying between 4 and 6 complete air changes per hour within the heated space. Warm, filtered, and humidified air leaves the heating unit at about 155° and arrives at the room grille at about 140°, having lost some of its heat through the metal ductwork.

Modern grilles (Fig. 50b) are designed along clean, simple lines, and may be finished to harmonize with any decorating scheme. The matter of whether to place the supply grille high on the side wall, or near the floor, has received much attention by heating engineers. The results of tests show that the air stream deflected 15 deg. downward toward the floor produces the most uniform temperatures from floor to ceiling. However, this arrangement is unsatisfactory in regard to furniture location, and so the supply grille is usually located with its top edge about 6 in. below the ceiling line. In this location the outlets are high enough to blow air over the heads of the occcupants, and are also ideally placed for cool air supply should

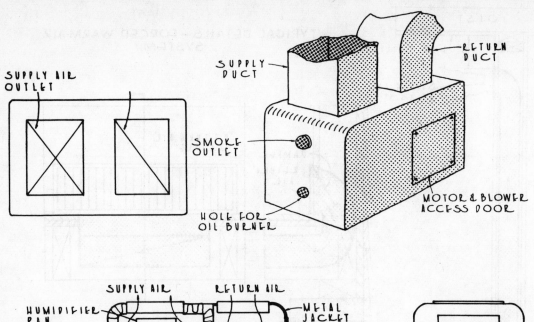

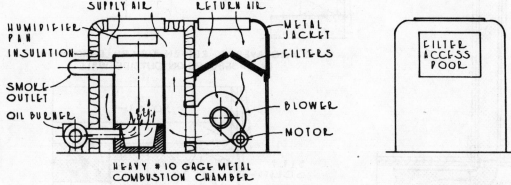

SUPPLY AIR OUTLET

SUPPLY DUCT

RETURN DUCT

SMOKE OUTLET

HOLE FOR OIL BURNER

MOTOR & BLOWER ACCESS DOOR

HUMIDIFIER PAN

INSULATION

SMOKE OUTLET

OIL BURNER

SUPPLY AIR

RETURN AIR

METAL JACKET

FILTERS

BLOWER

MOTOR

HEAVY #10 GAGE METAL COMBUSTION CHAMBER

FILTER ACCESS DOOR

DETAILS OF A TYPICAL WARM-AIR BLOWER-BURNER FURNACE UNIT

Fig. 50d

summer air conditioning be added to the system in the future. Adjustable bars across the face of the grille direct the air in any required direction.

In addition to one or more supply outlets, each area except the kitchen and bathroom contains a return air outlet, for the purpose of recirculating the return air (about 80 per cent of the total). While supply grilles are usually placed high on inside walls, the returns are more efficient if placed in the cold wall at baseboard level, where they can collect down drafts from glazed surfaces and exposed walls.

As a rule, no special construction is required where ducts run through partitions, as the ducts are made to fit the standard stud space. Thus a 3¼- x 14-in. rectangular duct is about the largest size duct that can be run between two studs spaced 16 in. on centers. For rooms larger than about 10 ft. 0 in. x 10 ft. 0 in., two or more ducts are required. A warm air system is only as good as its distribution system, and therefore, it is important to provide for sufficient supply and return air openings.

The furnace unit does not have to be located in the center of the house, and may be placed wherever convenient. Ducts may be run in the basement or in an attic space, or along the ceiling of the space being heated. If ducts are run above the ceiling, air outlets of special design may be mounted on the ceiling (Fig. 50c). Some of the typical details of the warm-air air-blower-burner furnace are shown in Fig. 50d.

The temperature control system for a warm-air job is somewhat similar to that used on a hot-water installation. The room thermostat, upon demand for heat, starts the blower. But the blower can run only if the air temperature at the furnace outlet is between 90° and 175°. This prevents circulation of air which is too cool to heat the room. If the air temperature at the furnace outlet drops below 90°, the burner operates to heat the air to at least 90° before the fan is allowed to start. When the room thermostat is satisfied, the blower and burner unit are inoperative. Further details of the forced warm-air system are shown in Fig. 50e.

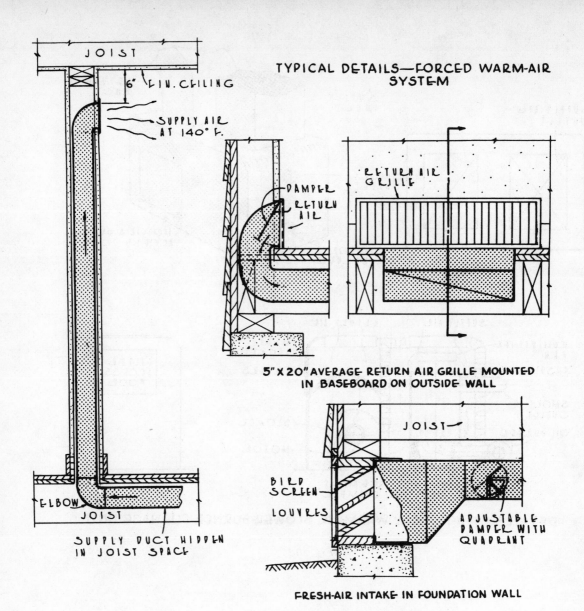

TYPICAL DETAILS—FORCED WARM-AIR SYSTEM

JOIST

6" LIN. CEILING

SUPPLY AIR AT 140° F.

ELBOW

JOIST

SUPPLY DUCT HIDDEN IN JOIST SPACE

DAMPER RETURN AIR

RETURN AIR GRILLE

5"X20"AVERAGE RETURN AIR GRILLE MOUNTED IN BASEBOARD ON OUTSIDE WALL

JOIST

BIRD SCREEN

LOUVRES

ADJUSTABLE DAMPER WITH QUADRANT

FRESH-AIR INTAKE IN FOUNDATION WALL

Fig. 50e

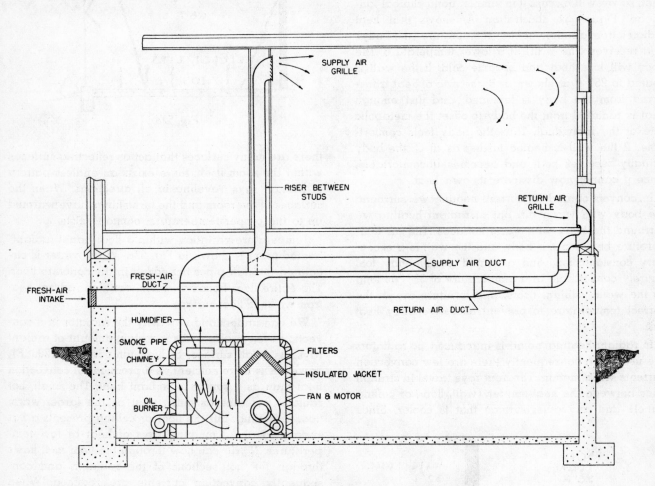

SUPPLY AIR GRILLE

RISER BETWEEN STUDS

RETURN AIR GRILLE

FRESH-AIR DUCT

FRESH-AIR INTAKE

SUPPLY AIR DUCT

RETURN AIR DUCT

HUMIDIFIER

SMOKE PIPE TO CHIMNEY

FILTERS

INSULATED JACKET

FAN & MOTOR

OIL BURNER

FORCED WARM-AIR SYSTEM
Fig. 51

WHERE USED

1. Residential structures

2. Small public buildings

ADVANTAGES

1. This system provides all the requirements of winter air conditioning: heating, humidification, air cleaning, and air circulation.

2. May be converted into year-round air-conditioning system by addition of summer cooling equipment. Same ductwork can be used.

3. System cannot freeze in winter.

4. Can circulate all outdoors in fall and spring.

DISADVANTAGES

1. Cold floor-line temperatures likely if distribution not planned with care.

2. Ductwork sometimes requires additional headroom in basement.

Heating by Radiant Heat

The principle of heating by means of radiant heat is usually not well understood by the average student, so we will discuss it in simple, nontechnical language. Figure 52, illustration *A*, shows that heat radiates from a source of high temperature (the body) to a receiver (the wall) at a lower temperature. The body will lose heat and become cold. If the wall is heated to 85° F as shown at *B*, the rate of heat transferred from the body is lessened, and just enough heat is radiated from the body to offset the metabolic rate of the individual. Thus the body feels comfortable. If the wall is heated further as at *C*, the body actually receives heat and becomes uncomfortable, since it cannot now dissipate its own heat.

In convection and air-current heating we surround the body with warm air, but in radiant heating we surround the body with warm surfaces. The air temperature between the body and the wall is a secondary consideration, and a seated person may feel entirely comfortable in a temperature of 58°, as long as the walls, ceiling, floors, and furniture are at the correct temperature to prevent excessive body heat loss.

In radiant heating, no air is introduced, no radiators are used, and consequently there are few convection currents set in motion. The heat rays travel in straight lines between the heat emitter (wall, floor, or ceiling panel) and any other surface that is cooler. Since

Fig. 52

there are many surfaces that act as reflecting surfaces within the room itself, there exists an endless pattern of radiant rays traveling in all directions. When the surfaces of the room and the furnishings have warmed up to the proper temperature, comfort exists.

Temperature variation within a floor-panel radiant-heated room is shown in Fig. 52a. Warm water is circulated through pipes imbedded in the concrete floor. The entire floor becomes warm, emitting radiant heat from an 85°F floor surface.

We can understand now why the radiator in a convection system also emits a certain amount of radiant rays. Its small surface, at high temperature (200°F), however, is more efficient as a producer of convection heat than as a source of radiant heat. The small, hot radiator contains as much heat as the large, warm floor or ceiling, but the floor or ceiling presents a flat surface ideal for emitting rays of heat at low temperatures. No air can flow through the floor as it flows through the hot sections of the radiator, and consequently convection currents are reduced. When radiant-heat coils are located in the ceiling, there is maximum reduction of convection currents, as the layer of warm air directly under the ceiling cannot rise any higher.

Many times, a student wonders which principle of heating is best, and which type of system utilizing that principle is best. There is no simple answer in this question, because too many variables are involved. A large factor is the human one. Not all people agree on the extent of their comfort or discomfort. Some dislike steam systems and others swear by them. There are some who think that radiant heat is too new to be proved yet. Others think they must have a concrete floor if they want radiant heat.

When it comes to warm-air systems, there are too many who still remember the huge round pipes and octopus arrangement of heat flues that cluttered the basement in the days of the gravity hot-air system. They want no part of such a system today.

Radiant-Heating Coils in Ceiling

Figure 52b shows a typical room with radiant panel

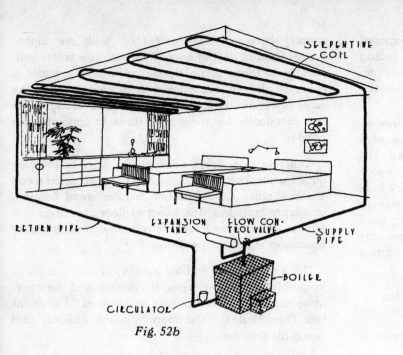

Fig. 52b

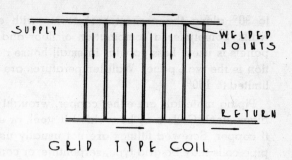

GRID TYPE COIL

located in ceiling. Hot water is circulated through the ceiling coil, which is imbedded in plaster.

Radiant-Heating Coils in Floor

In Fig. 52c is shown a radiant-heating system with pipes imbedded in a concrete floor slab.

Fig. 52c

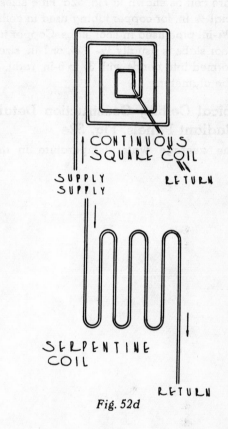

CONTINUOUS SQUARE COIL

SERPENTINE COIL

Fig. 52d

Details Pertaining to Radiant-Heating System

The main part of the system are the boiler, automatic firing device (either coal stoker, oil burner, or gas burner), expansion tank, circulator, flow control valve, imbedded heating coils, and automatic control system.

In operation, the system is completely filled with city water through an automatic feed valve. Air is vented through vent connections located at the high point of the system and at the expansion tank. An outdoor-indoor control device regulates the boiler water temperature in response to the difference between indoor and outdoor temperatures. As the weather grows colder, the boiler water temperature is raised, and vice versa. The circulator, driven usually by a special 1/6-hp single-phase, 110-v motor, starts and stops in response to a room thermostat.

The function of the heating coils, whether located in the floor or ceiling, is to raise the average temperature of all the surfaces enclosing the room, as well as those within the room (such as furniture, pictures, built-in cabinets) to a temperature sufficient to allow normal radiation of body heat. If the average surface temperature is above 70°, the room air temperature may be below 70°, to produce conditions of comfort.

Rooms with large glass areas usually require that the heating coils be placed in the ceiling, because panels can safely be heated to about 120°, and thus more heat may be radiated to the other surfaces.

Floor panels, on the other hand, are usually limited to a temperature of 85° on areas in constant use, and to 90° along the perimeter of rooms with exposed walls. Sometimes a combination of floor and ceiling panels is used. Less popular in small house construction is the wall panel. Wall temperatures are usually limited to 100°.

Piping materials are either copper, wrought iron, or black steel. Coils may be welded if steel, or sweated if copper. Screwed fittings are not usually used. The pipe coils may be grid type, serpentine, or continuous square coil as shown in Fig. 52d. Pipe sizes vary from special ⅜ in. for copper tubing used in ceiling panels, to 1¼-in. pipe used in floor slabs. Copper tubing used in floor slabs is usually ½-, ¾-, or 1-in. size, and may be formed into bends with 3- to 6-in. radii, depending on the diameter.

Typical Ceiling Construction Details for Radiant Panels, Fig. 52e

The average water temperature in the coils is usually between 100° and 150°, with the higher values used in ceiling coils. With such low water temperatures, there is no danger of cracking either a concrete slab or a plaster wall or ceiling, since the rates of expansion for copper, steel and wrought iron are practically identical with those of concrete and plaster.

Concrete slab floors need not be bare to produce good results. They may be floored with cemented wood blocks, linoleum, asphalt tile, regular wood flooring, or simply carpeted. The effect of floor coverings that tend to insulate the floor is to require a slightly higher operating water temperature.

The first cost of a radiant-heating system compares favorably with other types of systems, and the operating costs have been proved as much as 30 per cent less than that for the more familiar radiator and warm-air systems.

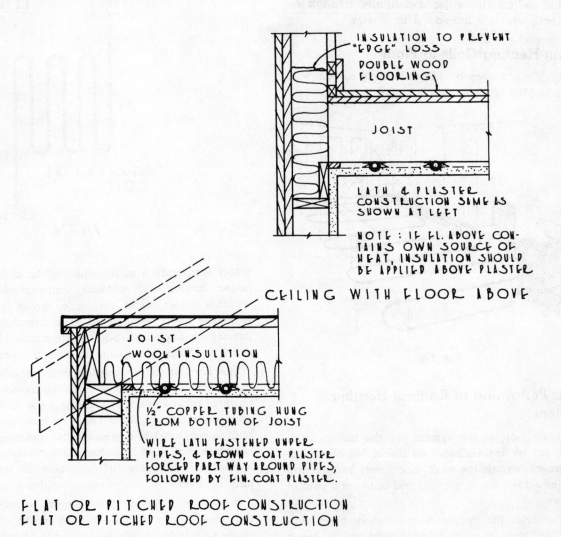

INSULATION TO PREVENT "EDGE" LOSS
DOUBLE WOOD FLOORING
JOIST
LATH & PLASTER CONSTRUCTION SAME AS SHOWN AT LEFT
NOTE: IF FL. ABOVE CONTAINS OWN SOURCE OF HEAT, INSULATION SHOULD BE APPLIED ABOVE PLASTER

CEILING WITH FLOOR ABOVE

JOIST
WOOL INSULATION
½" COPPER TUBING HUNG FROM BOTTOM OF JOIST
WIRE LATH FASTENED UNDER PIPES, & BROWN COAT PLASTER FORCED PART WAY AROUND PIPES, FOLLOWED BY FIN. COAT PLASTER.

FLAT OR PITCHED ROOF CONSTRUCTION

Fig. 52e

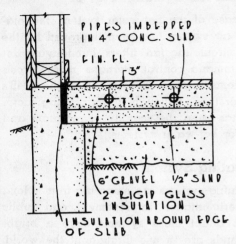

PIPES IMBEDDED
IN 4" CONC. SLAB
FIN. FL.
3"
6" GRAVEL   1/2" SAND
2" RIGID GLASS
INSULATION
INSULATION AROUND EDGE
OF SLAB

AN EXCELLENT CONSTRUCTION FOR CONC. FL. SLAB ON GROUND

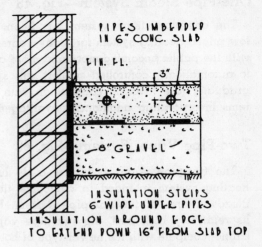

PIPES IMBEDDED
IN 6" CONC. SLAB
FIN. FL.
3"
8" GRAVEL
INSULATION STRIPS
6" WIDE UNDER PIPES
INSULATION AROUND EDGE
TO EXTEND DOWN 16" FROM SLAB TOP

A GOOD CONSTRUCTION FOR CONC. FL. SLAB ON GROUND

PIPES IMBEDDED IN 6" CONC.
SLAB ON 1/2" SAND ON 8" GRAVEL
FIN. FL.

NOTE: WOOD FL. MAY BE
CEMENTED TO CONC. OR MAY
BE SET ON WOOD SLEEPERS.

A COMMON & SATISFACTORY SLAB CONSTRUCTION

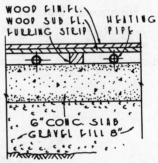

WOOD FIN. FL.
WOOD SUB FL.
FURRING STRIP   HEATING PIPE
6" CONC. SLAB
GRAVEL FILL 8"

DOUBLE WOOD FL. WITH FURRING STRIPS ON CONC. SLAB. PIPES IN FURRED SPACE

Comments Regarding the Heating Systems Shown in Figs. 48 through 52

One-Pipe Steam System—Fig. 48

The one-pipe steam system has been a popular low-priced heating system for many years. However, with the public becoming more and more accustomed to automatically controlled comfort, this system may gradually lose favor in competition with other systems incorporating additional advantages.

Two-Pipe Vapor System—Fig. 49

The two-pipe vapor system is a de luxe steam-heating system intended to overcome the inherent disadvantages of the one-pipe system. Because of its relatively high cost, the two-pipe vapor system cannot compete with the newer type of hot-water and warm-air systems.

One-Pipe Hot-Water System—Fig. 50

The one-pipe hot-water system and the conventional two-pipe systems have been so improved by the addition of the circulating pump, flow-control valves, and other equipment, that they offer the utmost in simplicity, style, efficiency, ease of automatic control, and economy. Hot-water systems share top place in popularity today with the forced warm-air system.

Forced Warm-Air System—Fig. 51

As in the case of the hot-water system, the old-fashioned hot-air system has been improved by the addition of a circulating fan, filters, humidifying device, and automatic control. Perhaps more forced warm-air systems have been installed in the 1940's than any other type, although a contributing factor in this case has been the scarcity of radiators and copper pipe for hot-water systems.

Radiant Heating System

Radiant heating systems are emerging from a long period of experimentation, improvement, and public education. No doubt these systems have a bright future. Thousands are in use throughout the world, and they are fast becoming popular with the small builder. Simple methods of calculation have not yet been devised, however, and unfortunately, the information that is available is highly technical.

All the previously described systems utilize any type of fuel desired, such as coal, oil, or gas. The choice of fuel depends on location, cost, availability, and (naturally) the client's preference. Automatic control devices are an absolute necessity if even temperatures and high efficiencies are to be maintained.

Selection of Equipment

Radiators

Radiators have undergone notable changes in design, appearance, and efficiency during the last 20 years. The old-fashioned cast-iron column-type radiators gave way to the tube type, formerly built in sections 2½ in. on center but now available in narrow slender-tube sections spaced 1¾ in. on center (see Fig. 53).

The Institute of Boiler and Radiator Manufacturers (I-B-R), in cooperation with the Division of Simplified Practice, National Bureau of Standards, has established sizes and ratings of small-tube cast-iron radiators (see Fig. 54, Table of Standard Sizes and Ratings of Cast Iron Radiators for Steam and Hot Water).

The second column of the table in Fig. 54 shows heat output per section in square feet of equivalent direct radiation, abbreviated E.D.R. One square foot of equivalent radiator surface emits 240 Btu per hour when the radiator is filled with steam at 215° and when the room temperature is 70°F. To use the table, divide the Btu per hour heat loss by 240 to arrive at the number of equivalent square feet of radiator surface required. Then select the height and width desired, Columns A and B. Divide the catalogue rating per section into the E.D.R. required to determine number of sections.

EXAMPLE

A certain room has a heat loss of 8,000 Btu/hr. What size of steam radiator should be selected?

SOLUTION

$$\text{Required E.D.R.} = \frac{8000}{240} = 33.3$$

Assume a height of 25 in., which will be satisfactory with a width of $4\frac{7}{16}$ in. A radiator with these dimensions has a catalogue rating of 2 sq. ft. per section.

$$\text{Number of sections} = \frac{33.3}{2} = 16.6 \text{ or } 17 \text{ sections}$$

The over-all dimensions are as follows:

Length $= 17 \times 1\frac{3}{4}$ in. $= 29\frac{3}{4}$ in.

(see note, Fig. 54)

Width $= 4\frac{7}{16}$ in.

Height $= 25$ in.

MODERN SLENDER-TUBE RADIATOR COMPARED WITH OLDER LARGE-TUBE DESIGN. *Courtesy, Burnham Boiler Corp., Irvington, N. Y.*

Fig. 53

TABLE OF STANDARD SIZES AND RATINGS OF CAST-IRON RADIATORS FOR STEAM AND HOT WATER

NUMBER OF TUBES PER SECTION	CATALOG RATING PER SECTION	SECTION DIMENSIONS				
		A	WIDTH (B)		C	D
		HEIGHT	MINIMUM	MAXIMUM	SPACING	LEG HEIGHT
	SQ. FT.	INCHES	INCHES	INCHES	INCHES	INCHES
3	1.6	25	$3\frac{1}{4}$	$3\frac{1}{4}$	$1\frac{3}{4}$	$2\frac{1}{2}$
4	1.6	19	$4\frac{7}{16}$	$4\frac{13}{16}$	$1\frac{3}{4}$	$2\frac{1}{2}$
	1.8	22	$4\frac{7}{16}$	$4\frac{13}{16}$	$1\frac{3}{4}$	$2\frac{1}{2}$
	2.0	25	$4\frac{7}{16}$	$4\frac{13}{16}$	$1\frac{3}{4}$	$2\frac{1}{2}$
5	2.1	22	$5\frac{5}{8}$	$6\frac{5}{16}$	$1\frac{3}{4}$	$2\frac{1}{2}$
	2.4	25	$5\frac{5}{8}$	$6\frac{5}{16}$	$1\frac{3}{4}$	$2\frac{1}{2}$
6	1.6	14	$6\frac{13}{16}$	8	$1\frac{3}{4}$	$2\frac{1}{2}$
	2.3	19	$6\frac{13}{16}$	8	$1\frac{3}{4}$	$2\frac{1}{2}$
	3.0	25	$6\frac{13}{16}$	8	$1\frac{3}{4}$	$2\frac{1}{2}$
	3.7	32	$6\frac{13}{16}$	8	$1\frac{3}{4}$	$2\frac{1}{2}$

NOTE: OVERALL LENGTH EQUALS NUMBER OF SECTIONS TIMES $1\frac{3}{4}$ INCHES

4-TUBE SECTION SHOWN

Fig. 54

When the radiators listed in Fig. 54 are to be used for hot-water systems, the Btu per hour heat loss of the room is not divided by 240 but by the factors shown in Table 2, which depend on the average water temperature in the radiator.

TABLE 2

E.D.R. PER SQUARE FOOT FOR HOT-WATER RADIATORS

Method of Firing	Average Water Temperature in Radiator	E.D.R. per Sq. Ft.
Hand-fired	180° F.	165
Stoker-fired	190° F.	180
Oil or gas-fired	200° F.	200

Convectors

Convectors are radiators consisting of a nonferrous or cast-iron heating element, which is usually finned to increase the heat-transfer rate. The element is placed in a decorative metal enclosure, which may be recessed in the wall, be semi-recessed or left free-standing against the wall.

Figures 55 and 56 show two styles of convectors made for use with steam or hot water. Convectors for hot water are usually rated in thousands of Btu per hour, abbreviated Mbh, whereas steam-convector ratings are expressed in E.D.R.

Figures 57 and 58 give capacities for hot-water and steam convectors, respectively. Dimensions are given in Fig. 59.

TRANE TYPE SK CONVECTOR-RADIATOR.
Courtesy Trane Company, La Crosse, Wis.
Fig. 55

TRANE TYPE A CONVECTOR-RADIATOR.
Courtesy Trane Company, La Crosse, Wis.
Fig. 56

HEIGHT	Av. Water Temp.	6" DEPTH LENGTH										8" DEPTH LENGTH					10" DEPTH LENGTH			
		20"	24"	28"	32"	36"	40"	44"	48"	56"	64"	32"	40"	48"	56"	64"	40"	48"	56"	64"
20	215	3.6	4.4	5.2	6.0	6.8	7.5	8.3	9.1	10.7	12.3	8.0	10.2	12.4	14.5	16.7	11.3	13.6	16.0	18.3
	210	3.4	4.2	4.9	5.7	6.5	7.2	8.0	8.7	10.2	11.7	7.6	9.8	11.8	13.9	15.9	10.8	13.0	15.3	17.5
	205	3.3	4.0	4.7	5.4	6.2	6.9	7.6	8.3	9.7	11.2	7.3	9.3	11.3	13.2	15.2	10.3	12.4	14.6	16.7
	200	3.1	3.8	4.5	5.1	5.8	6.5	7.2	7.9	9.2	10.6	6.9	8.8	10.7	12.5	14.4	9.7	11.7	13.8	15.8
	195	2.9	3.6	4.2	4.8	5.5	6.1	6.8	7.4	8.7	10.0	6.5	8.3	10.1	11.8	13.5	9.2	11.1	13.0	14.9
	190	2.8	3.4	4.0	4.6	5.2	5.8	6.4	7.0	8.2	9.4	6.1	7.9	9.5	11.2	12.8	8.7	10.5	12.3	14.1
	185	2.6	3.2	3.7	4.3	4.9	5.4	6.0	6.6	7.7	8.8	5.8	7.4	8.9	10.4	12.0	8.1	9.8	11.5	13.2
	180	2.4	3.0	3.5	4.0	4.6	5.1	5.6	6.2	7.2	8.3	5.4	6.9	8.4	9.8	11.2	7.6	9.2	10.8	12.4
	175	2.3	2.7	3.2	3.7	4.2	4.7	5.2	5.7	6.7	7.7	5.0	6.4	7.8	9.1	10.4	7.1	8.5	10.0	11.5
24	215	4.2	5.1	6.0	6.9	7.8	8.7	9.6	10.5	12.4	14.2	8.7	11.0	13.3	15.6	18.0	12.8	15.5	18.2	20.8
	210	4.0	4.8	5.7	6.6	7.4	8.3	9.1	10.0	11.8	13.6	8.3	10.5	12.7	14.9	17.2	12.3	14.8	17.4	19.9
	205	3.8	4.6	5.4	6.3	7.1	7.9	8.7	9.5	11.3	12.9	7.9	10.0	12.1	14.2	16.4	11.7	14.1	16.6	19.0
	200	3.6	4.4	5.1	5.9	6.7	7.5	8.2	9.0	10.7	12.2	7.5	9.5	11.4	13.5	15.5	11.1	13.4	15.7	18.0
	195	3.4	4.1	4.8	5.6	6.3	7.0	7.8	8.5	10.1	11.5	7.0	9.0	10.8	12.7	14.6	10.4	12.6	14.8	16.9
	190	3.2	3.9	4.6	5.3	6.0	6.7	7.4	8.0	9.5	10.9	6.7	8.5	10.2	12.0	13.8	9.9	11.9	14.0	16.0
	185	3.0	3.4	4.3	4.9	5.6	6.2	6.9	7.5	8.9	10.2	6.2	7.9	9.6	11.3	13.0	9.2	11.2	13.1	15.0
	180	2.8	3.2	4.0	4.6	5.2	5.9	6.5	7.1	8.4	9.6	5.9	7.4	9.0	10.6	12.2	8.7	10.5	12.3	14.1
	175	2.6	3.2	3.7	4.3	4.9	5.4	6.0	6.6	7.8	8.9	5.4	6.9	8.3	9.8	11.3	8.0	9.7	11.4	13.0
32	215	4.5	5.4	6.4	7.4	8.4	9.5	10.4	11.5	13.4	15.4	9.2	11.7	14.2	16.7	19.1	14.0	16.9	19.8	22.7
	210	4.3	5.2	6.1	7.1	8.1	9.0	9.9	11.0	12.8	14.7	8.8	11.2	13.6	15.9	18.3	13.3	16.1	18.9	21.7
	205	4.1	4.9	5.8	6.8	7.7	8.6	9.4	10.5	12.2	14.0	8.4	10.7	12.9	15.2	17.4	12.7	15.4	18.0	20.7
	200	3.9	4.7	5.5	6.4	7.3	8.1	8.9	9.9	11.5	13.3	8.0	10.1	12.2	14.4	16.5	12.0	14.6	17.1	19.6
	195	3.7	4.4	5.2	6.0	6.9	7.7	8.4	9.3	10.9	12.5	7.5	9.5	11.5	13.5	15.6	11.3	13.7	16.1	18.5
	190	3.4	4.2	4.9	5.7	6.5	7.3	8.0	8.8	10.3	11.9	7.1	9.0	10.9	12.8	14.7	10.7	13.0	15.2	17.5
	185	3.2	3.9	4.6	5.3	6.1	6.8	7.5	8.3	9.6	11.1	6.6	8.4	10.2	12.0	13.8	10.0	12.2	14.3	16.4
	180	3.0	3.6	4.3	5.0	5.7	6.4	7.0	7.8	9.0	10.4	6.2	7.9	9.6	11.2	12.9	9.4	11.4	13.4	15.4
	175	2.8	3.4	4.0	4.7	5.3	5.9	6.5	7.2	8.4	9.7	5.8	7.3	8.9	10.4	12.0	8.7	10.6	12.4	14.2

CAPACITIES FOR HOT-WATER CONVECTORS, EXPRESSED IN MBH (THOUSAND BTU PER HOUR) BASED ON AVERAGE WATER TEMPERATURES SHOWN. *Courtesy Trane Company, La Crosse, Wis.*

Fig. 57

HEIGHT	6" DEPTH										8" DEPTH					10" DEPTH			
	LENGTH										LENGTH					LENGTH			
	20"	24"	28"	32"	36"	40"	44"	48"	56"	64"	32"	40"	48"	56"	64"	40"	48"	56"	64"
20	16.0	19.5	23.0	26.5	30.0	33.4	37.0	40.5	47.5	54.5	35.5	45.5	55.0	64.5	74.0	50.0	60.5	71.0	81.5
24	18.5	22.5	26.5	30.5	34.5	38.5	42.5	46.5	55.0	63.0	38.5	49.0	59.0	69.5	80.0	57.0	69.0	81.0	92.5
32	20.0	24.0	28.5	33.0	37.5	42.0	46.0	51.0	59.5	68.5	41.0	52.0	63.0	74.0	85.0	62.0	75.0	88.0	101.0

CAPACITIES FOR STEAM CONVECTORS. SQ. FT. E.D.R. WITH 215° STEAM AND 65° ENTERING TEMPERATURE OF AIR.
Courtesy Trane Company, La Crosse, Wis.
Fig. 58

EXAMPLE

A certain room has a heat loss of 9150 Btu per hour. The hot-water boiler is oil-fired. Height of convector to be not over 22 in. and not deeper than 6 in. Select a convector of the freestanding type.

SOLUTION

Probable average water temperature in radiator (Table 2) = 200°F.

$$\text{Mbh output} = \frac{9150}{1000} = 9.15$$

Referring to Fig. 57, Capacities for Hot-Water Convectors, for 6-in. depth and 20-in. height, find 9.2 Mbh for 56-in. length.

Overall dimensions (see Fig. 59):

Height = 20 in.
Length = 56 in. + ⅜ in. = 56⅜ in.
    (see notes, Fig. 59)
Depth = 6 in.

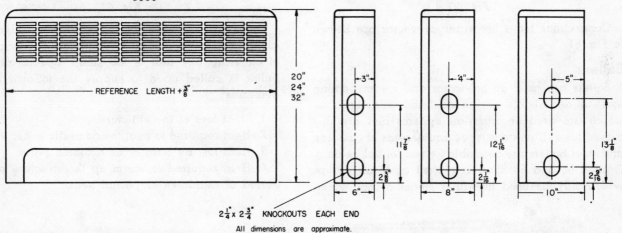

2¼" x 2¾" KNOCKOUTS EACH END
All dimensions are approximate.

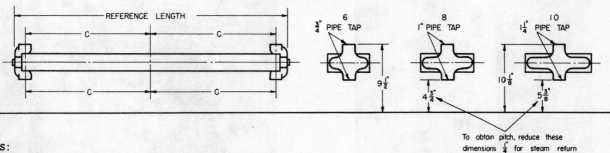

To obtain pitch, reduce these dimensions ¼" for steam return or hot water supply.

NOTES:

Actual cabinet lengths are always ⅜ in. greater than reference length. Heights are exactly 20 in. - 24 in. - 32 in.

Recesses should be constructed ½ in. longer than overall length and ¼ in. higher than height of the unit. If a convector-radiator is recessed into an exposed wall, the back of the unit should be covered with ½ in. insulation.

The two knockouts on each end of the cabinet are located equidistant from front and back of the cabinet. Cabinets can be recessed any distance up to 1¼ in. from the front. This permits easy removal of the front panel.

Side connections should be avoided on recessed installations if a unit with a 6 in. depth is used.

DIMENSIONS FOR FREE-STANDING STEAM AND HOT-WATER CONVECTORS

Fig. 59

Typical piping connections for steam convectors on two-pipe systems are shown in Fig. 60. If it is desired to use a convector on a one-pipe system, a special air vent is required and the return trap is omitted.

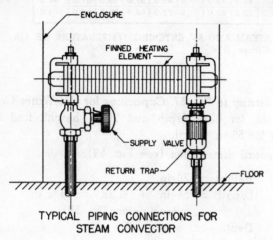

TYPICAL PIPING CONNECTIONS FOR
STEAM CONVECTOR

Fig. 60

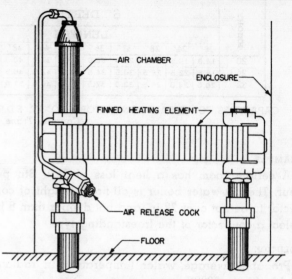

TYPICAL PIPING CONNECTIONS FOR
HOT-WATER CONVECTOR

Fig. 61

COURTESY: THE TRANE CO.
LA CROSSE, WIS.

Connections for a hot-water convector are shown in Fig. 61.

Boilers

Boilers are used on hot-water and steam heating systems and should not be confused with furnaces, which are used on warm-air systems and are discussed later. Numerous types and designs of cast-iron and steel boilers are available for residential heating. Figures 62 and 63 show a typical cast-iron design which may be used for either steam or hot water.

Care must be exercised in selecting a boiler for a given system, especially to avoid the common error of choosing one that is too small. Specifically, the boiler is called upon to supply the following heat demands:

1. Heat loss of the structure.
2. Heat required to heat the domestic water supply.
3. Heat lost by bare or uninsulated pipes.
4. Heat required to warm up the structure after a period of shutdown or partial heat.

Courtesy Crane Co., Chicago, Ill.

Fig. 62

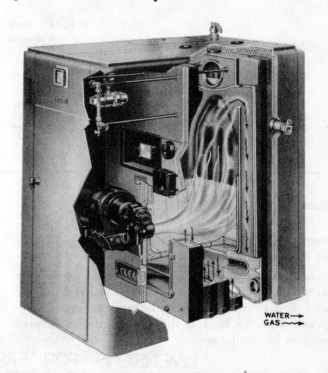

Courtesy Crane Co., Chicago, Ill.

Fig. 63

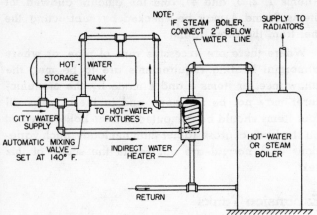

INDIRECT WATER HEATER AND STORAGE TANK

Fig. 64

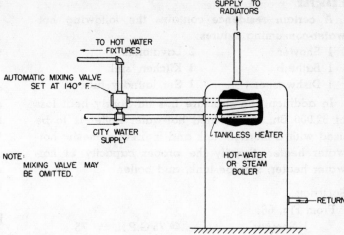

DIRECT OR INSTANTANEOUS WATER HEATER PLACED IN BOILER

Fig. 65

Inasmuch as computations for items 3 and 4 above can usually be expressed as percentages of the boiler load, the only computations required for average installations are items 1 and 2.

A boiler rating based on the sum of these two items is known as a *net rating*. The Institute of Boiler and Radiator Manufacturers, an association of most of the makers of cast-iron radiators and boilers, has agreed on standard ratings for cast-iron boilers, based on items 1 and 2 above, known as *I-B-R net ratings*.

A somewhat similar code of rating steel boilers has been adopted by the *Steel Heating Boiler Institute*. These ratings are also net ratings and no allowance for items 3 and 4 are necessary. They are designated as *S.B.I.* or *S.H.B.I. net ratings*.

Item 1 may be expressed in Btu/hr. or in E.D.R. Manufacturers usually show both ratings. However, in the case of hot-water boilers, standard E.D.R.

ratings are based on 150 Btu per E.D.R., and less confusion will result if the heat loss is expressed in Btu for the purpose of sizing the boiler. (See *Heat Loss and How to Compute It*, beginning on page 117, for a detailed method of computation.

Item 2 refers to the heat that the boiler has to supply to heat the domestic hot water. This amount of heat may be conveniently figured directly in E.D.R., and the equivalent Btu/hr. may be found as follows:

1. Allow 0.5 sq. ft. of 240-Btu radiation for each gallon per hour when an indirect heater is used with a storage tank. (See Fig. 64.)

2. Allow 4 sq. ft. of 240-Btu radiation for each gallon per hour heated with an instantaneous heating coil placed directly in the boiler. In this case no storage tank is required. (See Fig. 65.)

Figure 66 gives hot-water demand per fixture in gallons per hour at 140°F. for residences. By use of this table, both direct and indirect water-heater loads may be figured. The table shown in Fig. 67 gives capacities of round storage tanks in gallons per foot of length.

TABLE OF HOT-WATER DEMAND PER FIXTURE FOR RESIDENCES: GAL. PER HR. AT 140° F.

ITEM	GAL./HR. AT 140° F.
LAVATORY (WASH BASIN)	2
BATH TUB	20
DISHWASHER	15
KITCHEN SINK	10
LAUNDRY	20
SHOWER	75
HOURLY HEATING CAPACITY FACTOR	30%
STORAGE CAPACITY FACTOR	70%

NOTE:
TOTAL G.P.H. x HOURLY HTG. CAPACITY FACTOR = G.P.H. RATING OF TANKLESS HEATER.
TOTAL G.P.H. x STORAGE CAPACITY FACTOR = GAL. CAPACITY OF STORAGE TANK.

FROM A.S.H. & V.E. GUIDE, 1946

Fig. 66

TABLE OF CAPACITY OF ROUND STORAGE TANKS PER FOOT OF LENGTH

DIAMETER	GAL. PER FOOT LENGTH
18	13
20	16
24	24

NOTES:
1. STORAGE TANKS ARE RECOMMENDED FOR MEDIUM- AND LARGE-SIZE JOBS.
2. TANKS SHOULD BE PLACED HORIZONTAL AS FAR ABOVE BOILER AS BASEMENT CEILING WILL PERMIT.
3. ALL TANKS SHOULD BE INSULATED FOR MAXIMUM ECONOMY.

Fig. 67

EXAMPLE

A certain residence contains the following hot-water-consuming fixtures:

1 Shower	2 Lavatories
1 Bathtub	1 Kitchen sink
1 Dishwasher	1 Set laundry tubs

In addition, the structure has an hourly heat loss of 92,000 Btu. An oil-fired hot-water boiler is to be used with a storage tank and indirect domestic hot-water heater. Specify the proper capacity of hot-water heater, storage tank, and boiler.

SOLUTION

From Fig. 66:

1 Shower	@ 75 G.P.H. =	75
1 Bathtub	@ 20 G.P.H. =	20
2 Lavatories	@ 2 G.P.H. =	4
1 Kitchen sink	@ 10 G.P.H. =	10
1 Set laundry tubs	@ 20 G.P.H. =	20
1 Dishwasher	@ 15 G.P.H. =	15
Total		144 G.P.H.

Capacity of storage tank = $144 \times 0.70 = 100$ gal. (approx.)

From Fig. 67:

$$\text{Size of storage tank} = \frac{100 \text{ gal.}}{24 \text{ gal. per ft.}}$$
$$= 4 \text{ ft. 2 in. long}$$
$$(\text{diameter 24 in.})$$

Rating of Water Heater

The indirect water heater shall have sufficient capacity to maintain 140° water in a 100-gal. storage tank.

Note: Manufacturers usually show their heaters rated to match the capacity of the storage tank. Many makes of heaters are available, and current trade literature gives complete catalogue numbers, dimensions, and other data.

Load on Boiler

Item 1: Heat loss of structure...............92,000 Btu/hr
Item 2: Domestic hot-waterload,
$\frac{1}{2} \times 240 \times 144$...............17,280 Btu/hr

Total ....109,280 Btu/hr

Rating of Boiler

If a cast-iron sectional steam boiler is to be used, its net I-B-R rating should be specified as not less than 109,280 Btu per hour. If the boiler is to be of steel construction, its net S.B.I. rating should be specified as not less than 109,280 Btu per hour net.

Any manufacturer's catalogue will list the boiler nearest in capacity to the required Btu per hour.

Such catalogue ratings will also give gross ratings (items 1, 2, 3, and 4), and the amount allowed for items 3 and 4 may be checked by subtracting the net from the gross rating.

Where there are excessive runs of pipe, or where abnormal heating requirements are to be met, the allowance for items 3 and 4 made by the manufacturer may not be sufficient, and in these cases all four items should be computed and the boiler selected on the basis of gross rather than net loads. Such variations from normal are not within the scope of this text.

Expansion Tanks

Expansion tanks are used in hot-water systems to do two things:

1. Provide space for expansion of the hot water in the system.

2. Trap air above their water level and compress it to an extent where all the water in the system will be under sufficient pressure at all times to permit relatively high water temperature to be carried in the boiler without the danger of steam being formed. It is on account of this latter function that these tanks are often called compression tanks.

Note: Although water boils at 212°F under atmospheric pressure, its boiling point may be raised to 270°F when the air pressure in the expansion tank is 30 lb. per square inch. To obtain 215° water in the boiler without danger of boiling, which is necessary in order to have 200° average water temperature in the radiators, a pressure of at least 12 lb. per square inch should be carried in the compression tank.

Table 3 shows the capacity of expansion tanks required for average installations.

TABLE 3

EXPANSION-TANK CAPACITY, GAL.

Up to 500 EDR	18
500 to 1000	24

System Specialties

Devices such as flow fittings, flow-control valve, relief valve, and circulator pump (see Fig. 50) should be sized from manufacturers' data.

Furnaces

As already noted, furnaces and boilers should not be confused. Furnaces contain no water and are used to heat air in warm-air systems. As there is usually no provision for heating the domestic hot-water supply, this may be accomplished in a separate gas or electric automatic water heater. The net load on a furnace therefore is the output at the supply grilles. Between the furnace and the supply grilles there is a heat loss through the sheet-metal ducts carrying the warm air, and consequently more Btu's are needed at the furnace bonnet than are represented by the hourly heat loss. Further, since fresh air is brought in from outside, it must be heated, and this requirement imposes an additional load on the furnace. Manufacturers show a Btu delivery at the bonnet which is in excess of the net Btu by an amount that has been allowed for the duct loss plus the fresh-air load. Here again, when this allowance is not sufficient, because of abnormal amounts of fresh air or excessively long duct runs, the manufacturer should be consulted.

Figure 68 shows the interior of a warm-air furnace, complete with fan, filters, and oil burner (compare with Fig. 51).

Figure 69 shows a smaller model of the same furnace with jacket in place, ready for operation.

Automatic Controls

Temperature and humidity control instruments, safety devices, automatic valves, and similar items are usually not selected by the architect. This highly specialized work is left in the hands of the control manufacturer.

INTERIOR OF FURNACE-BURNER UNIT.
Courtesy International Heater Co., Utica, N. Y.
Fig. 68

ASSEMBLED FURNACE-BURNER UNIT.
Courtesy International Heater Co., Utica, N. Y.
Fig. 69

Design of Heating Systems

Volumes have been written regarding the design of heating systems, and it is not the intent of the material that follows to furnish a substitute for such technical works. This section, necessarily limited in scope and treatment, is written specifically to enable the student of architectural drafting to carry to completion some of the previous material in the form of a heating layout for an average residential structure.

Although it was necessary to describe the operation of the various types of heating systems in the preceding portion of the text, it now becomes inad-

visable to present sufficient technical data for the *complete* design of all these types of systems. The reason for this is obvious: the student cannot design properly those systems which require specialized knowledge and wide experience. Many manufacturers, however, have developed rather simple design procedures that students may use with confidence, and these methods will be presented here.

Table 4 is an attempt to list the different types of heating systems on the basis of the student's ability to design them, with other pertinent information.

TABLE 4

GUIDE TO HEATING-SYSTEM DESIGN

Name of Heating System	Fig. No. in Text	Are Design Data Given in This Text?	If Not, Why Not?	Where Can an Interested Student Get Complete Design Data or Additional Information?
One-pipe steam	48	Yes		A.S.H.&V.E. Guide, published by the American Society of Heating and Ventilating Engineers, 51 Madison Ave., New York 10, N. Y.
Two-pipe vapor	49	Yes		A.S.H.&V.E. Guide
One-pipe hot-water	50	Yes		A.S.H.&V.E. Guide and B. & G. Handbook, published by the Bell and Gossett Co., Morton Grove, Ill. Also trade literature. Consult Sweet's file under Heating Systems, Hot Water.
Two-pipe hot-water	50	No	One-pipe system becoming more popular for small homes	A.S.H.&V.E. Guide; B. & G. Handbook; Trade Literature
Warm-air	51	No	Requires more than elementary knowledge of air handling; considerable experience needed for successful design	A.S.H.&V.E. Guide. Code & Manual (Textbook Section 7), National Warm Air Heating and Air Conditioning Assn. Supplied through local warm-air furnace distributors
Radiant heat		No	A standard code of design has not been agreed upon. At present there are many conflicting methods of calculation, all rather technical.	A.S.H.&V.E. Guide. Trade literature; mostly by piping manufacturers. Consult Sweet's file.

Design Procedures

One-Pipe Steam System

1. Compute Btu/hr. heat loss for each heated room. (See Fig. 43, Simplified Heat-Loss Factors, and Fig. 44, sample work sheet for heat-loss computation.)

2. Select radiators or convectors from manufacturers' data similar to those in Figs. 54 and 58.

3. Determine domestic hot-water requirements from Fig. 66, and choose type of water heater (direct or indirect).

4. Size boiler from data of (1) and (3) above, and select proper unit from manufacturer's catalogue. Give S.B.I. or I-B-R rating.

5. Sketch rough piping layout consisting of supply main with radiator branches, riser to second story if required, and return main. (See Fig. 48 for arrangement of pipes.)

6. Size all supply and return pipes in accordance with the amount of radiation they carry, using the sizes as recommended by the A.S.H.&V.E. Guide. (See Tables 5 and 6.)

7. Prepare finished layout, showing the following:

(a) *Basement Plan*—Locate boiler, water heater, and storage tank, if used, and oil-burner tank where

TABLE 5
SUPPLY-PIPE SIZING TABLE FOR STEAM SYSTEMS

TABLE 5
SUPPLY-PIPE SIZING TABLE FOR STEAM SYSTEMS

Pipe Size, In.	Capacities of Steam Mains and Risers, in. E.D.R. Direction of Condensate Flow			Special Capacities for One-Pipe Systems Only		
	With Steam in One- and Two-Pipe Systems	Against Steam in Two-Pipe Only		Up-Feed Supply Risers	Radiator Valves and Vert. Conns.	Radiator and Riser Runouts*
	1 Oz. Pressure Drop per 100 Ft. Equivalent Run	Vertical	Horizontal			
¾	30	30	....	25		
1	56	56	34	45	28	28
1¼	122	122	75	98	62	62
1½	190	190	108	152	93	93
2	386	386	195	288	169	169
2½	635	635	395	464	....	260

*On radiator runouts over 8 ft. long, increase one pipe size over tabular value.

This table is based on pipe-size data developed through the research investigation of the American Society of Heating and Ventilating Engineers.

oil is to be the fuel. If boiler is to be coal-fired, allow adequate space for coal bin. Check local codes for restrictions. Show supply and return mains, and indicate location of branches and risers, giving all sizes. Be sure to show smoke pipe from boiler to chimney flue. Keep this as short as possible.

(b) *First Floor*—Show location of all radiators. Give radiator ratings in E.D.R. Show schedule of manufacturer's sizes and catalogue numbers or model designations. Show any risers running to upper floors.

(c) *Second Floor*—Same as (b).

Note: It is not necessary to show every valve and fitting, since we are mainly interested in the size and location of the main pipes. If convectors are to be recessed, be sure to show framing details on house framing plans where recesses occur.

TABLE 6
RETURN-PIPE SIZING TABLE FOR STEAM SYSTEMS

Pipe Size, In.	Capacities of Return Mains and Risers (E.D.R.) (1 oz. pressure drop per 100 ft. equivalent run)		
	Mains		Risers
	Wet (below water line)	Dry (above water line)	
¾	....	....	190
1	700	320	450
1¼	1200	670	990

This table is based on pipe-size data developed through the research investigation of the American Society of Heating and Ventilating Engineers.

EXAMPLE

Using Tables 5 and 6, select proper pipe sizes for the one-pipe steam system shown in Fig. 70.

SOLUTION

1. *Compute heat loss.* Assume that this has been done.

2. *Select radiators.* Assume that this has been done. Sizes are shown on Fig. 70.

3. *Determine hot-water requirements.* Assume that this has been done. See Fig. 70.

4. *Size boiler.*

Total radiation = 30 + 50 +
28 + 20 + 40 + 40   = 208 E.D.R.

Heat required to head domestic hot water (Item 2, page 145):

4 E.D.R. × 30 gal. per hour   = 120 E.D.R.
———
Total boiler load (S.B.I. or I-B-R) = 328 E.D.R.

In other words, if a steel boiler is used, it must have an S.B.I. rating of at least 328 E.D.R.; and if a cast-iron boiler is used, it must have an I-B-R rating of not less than 328 E.D.R. (All based on 240 Btu/E.D.R., standard.)

5. *Sketch layout.* See Fig. 70.

6. *Size pipes.* Refer to Table 5. For flow of condensate and steam in same direction, a 2-in. main will carry up to 386 E.D.R. Note that a 1½-in. line will carry 190 E.D.R., which is a little too much undersize.

Continuing around the steam main in the direction of steam flow, we find successive pipe sizes as shown on Fig. 70.

Next, size vertical riser to second floor, and then all radiator runouts. Note that the smallest-size radiator runout allowed by Table 5 is 1 in. Also, it is more economical to use a 1¼-in. main for the last section serving the 40-E.D.R. radiator nearest the boiler than to use the 1-in. size permitted by Table 5, since the runout must be 1¼ in. also.

Next size the dry portion of the return main (above the water line). From Table 6, either a 1-in. or a 1¼-in. pipe may be used. The wet portion (below water line) requires a 1-in. pipe.

If desired, radiator valves of the proper sizes also may be selected from Table 5.

7. *Prepare finished drawings.* This step requires a house plan, which has been omitted here. A complete layout will, however, be shown in a later example covering a hot-water system.

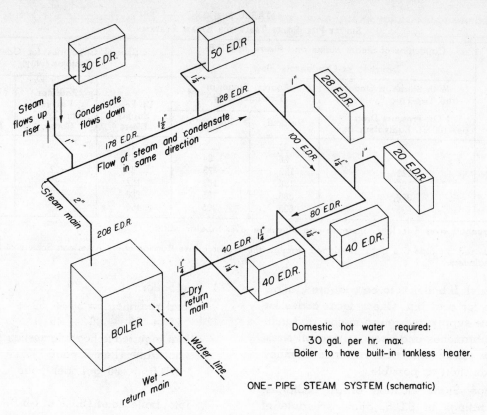

Domestic hot water required:
30 gal. per hr. max.
Boiler to have built-in tankless heater.

ONE-PIPE STEAM SYSTEM (schematic)

Fig. 70

Two-Pipe Vapor System

The two-pipe vapor system may be sized by making use of the proper columns in Tables 5 and 6. The procedure is identical with that described under the one-pipe steam system (refer to Fig. 49 for piping arrangement). Keep in mind that the important thing is to select the proper sizes for the mains, risers, and runouts. The actual scale drawing of the air vent, alternating receiver, and Hartford loop (return connection required by insurance companies to prevent water from backing up in return lines under abnormal boiler pressure) as well as the various fittings around the boiler, is not necessary.

One-Pipe Hot-Water System

1. Compute Btu/hr. heat loss for each heated room. See Fig. 43, Simplified Heat Loss Factors, and Fig. 44, sample work sheet for heat-loss computations.

2. Decide what method of firing the boiler will be used and what kind of fuel will be burned, to determine the probable average water temperature in the radiators. Without some idea of average water temperatures, radiators cannot be selected. (See Table 2.)

3. Sketch rough piping layout, consisting of main supply trunk, two or more circuits, and necessary risers and runouts. Show circulator pump on return side of boiler (see Fig. 50 for arrangement of pipes). Try to balance the load on each circuit.

4. Select radiators or convectors, using data from rating tables similar to Figs. 54 and 57. Add capacity of radiators to sketch, Step 3.

Note: When a group of radiators are connected to the same main, it is natural to assume that each successive radiator receives water a little cooler than that in the preceding unit. For this reason it is desirable to use two or more circuits with about half the radiation on each circuit. Moreover, some engineers add a small percentage to each successive radiator capacity in a single circuit so that the capacity of the last unit on the circuit is about 10 per cent higher than the first. This method will be used here.

To ensure the hottest possible water at each radiator, special flow fittings resembling an ordinary tee in external appearance, are used on the return connection of each unit to the main. Their purpose is to create additional friction in the main, thus causing more water to flow through the radiator. Also, they tend to separate the stream of hot water flowing down the main from the cooler water emerging from each radiator, keeping the hot water on top and the cooler on the bottom of the main (refer to Fig. 50). Some manufacturers employ fittings using the venturi or jet principle, in which the water flowing through the main is accelerated through the venturi-tube flow fitting, thus creating a suction that aids in drawing water through the radiator

5. Determine domestic hot-water requirements from Fig. 66 and choose type of water heater (direct or indirect).

6. Size boiler from data of Steps 1 and 5.

Note: The boiler load should not include the 10 per cent added in Step 4. This is added only to the radiator capacity to compensate for the fact that all the radiators have been selected for a certain water temperature, when actually each successive radiator receives water a little cooler than assumed.

Select proper steel or cast-iron boiler from manufacturer's ratings, specifying minimum S.B.I. or I-B-R rating.

7. Determine size of circulator, trunk line, circuits, radiator branches, and expansion tank. Refer to Fig. 71 and Table 3.

8. Prepare finished layout, showing the following:

(*a*) *Basement Plan*—Locate boiler, water heater, and storage tank, if used, and oil-burner tank where oil is to be the fuel. If boiler is to be coal-fired, allow adequate space for coalbin and check local codes for restrictions. Show circulator, expansion tank, trunk, circuits and radiator supply and return branches, giving all sizes. Be sure to show smoke pipe from boiler to chimney flue. Keep this as short as possible.

(*b*) *First-Floor*—Show location of all radiators or convectors. Give radiator ratings in Mbh (thousands of Btu/hr.). Show schedule of manufacturer's catalogue numbers or model designations. Show any risers running to upper floors.

(*c*) *Second Floor*—Same as (*b*).

EXAMPLE

Using the previously computed heat loss for the basic house (Fig. 45) and the additional data below, design a one-pipe hot-water system and prepare suitable layout.

Additional Data. Domestic hot water suitable for:

2 lavatories	1 kitchen sink
1 Bathtub	1 set laundry tubs
1 shower	

Boiler to be cast iron, gas-fired
Water heater to be indirect
Storage tank to be horizontal, insulated
Convectors to be recessed as far as possible in wall.

SOLUTION

1. *Heat-loss computation.* This has been discussed previously. See Fig. 45.

2. *Average water temperature.* From Table 2, average water in the convectors will be about 200°F, with an equivalent E.D.R. factor of 200 Btu.

3. *Rough piping layout.* Fig. 72.

4. *Selection of convectors.* See worksheet, Fig. 73.

5. *Domestic hot-water requirements.*

Using Fig. 66:

2 lavatories	@ 2 gal./hr. =	4 gal./hr.
1 bathtub	@ 20 gal./hr. =	20 gal./hr.
1 kitchen sink	@ 10 gal./hr. =	10 gal./hr.
1 set laundry tubs	@ 20 gal./hr. =	20 gal./hr.
1 shower	@ 75 gal./hr. =	75 gal./hr.
Total		129 gal./hr.

Storage-tank capacity = gal./hr. × storage-capacity factor

Storage-tank capacity = 129 × 0.70 = 90 gal.

Using Fig 67, we find that a 24-in. diameter tank holds 24 gal. per foot of length.

Therefore

$$\text{required length} = \frac{90 \text{ gal.}}{24 \text{ gal.}} = 3 \text{ ft. } 9 \text{ in.}$$

Total BTU Heat Loss	Total Installed Radiation (E.D.R.)			Trunk + longest circuit + supply and return branches to farthest radiator	Circulator Size	Number of Circuits	Pipe Sizes		Maximum Amount of Radiation per Venturi Fitting for Various BTU Emissions and Water Temperatures (E.D.R.)								
									½" RISER			¾" RISER			1" RISER		
	175° Water	200° Water	215° Water				Trunk	Circuits	175° Water	200° Water	215° Water	175° Water	200° Water	215° Water	175° Water	200° Water	215° Water
60,000	400 sq. ft.	300 sq. ft.	250 sq. ft.	100	1"	1		1"	100	75	63						
				150	1"	2	1¼"	1"	82	61	51						
				200	1"	2	1¼"	1"	66	50	41						
				250	1"	2	1¼"	1"	60	45	38						
75,000	500 sq. ft.⁵	375 sq. ft.	312 sq. ft.	100	1"	2	1¼"	1"	100	75	63						
				150	1"	2	1¼"	1"	82	61	51						
				200	1"	2	1¼"	1"	66	50	41						
				250	1"	2	1¼"	1"	60	45	38						
100,000	670 sq. ft.	500 sq. ft.	416 sq. ft.	100	1¼"	1		1¼"	100	75	63	220	165	137			
				150	1¼"	2	1½"	1¼"	82	61	51	180	135	112			
				200	1¼"	2	1½"	1¼"	66	50	41	145	109	90			
				250	1¼"	2	1½"	1¼"	60	45	38	132	99	82			
125,000	833 sq. ft.	625 sq. ft.	520 sq. ft.	100	1¼"	1		1¼"	100	75	63	220	165	137			
				150	1¼"	2	1½"	1¼"	82	61	51	180	135	112			
				200	1¼"	2	1½"	1¼"	66	50	41	145	109	90			
				250	1¼"	2	1½"	1¼"	60	45	38	132	99	82			
150,000	1000 sq. ft.	750 sq. ft.	625 sq. ft.	150	1½"	2	1½"	1¼"	82	61	51	180	135	112			
				200	1½"	2	2"	1¼"	66	50	41	145	109	90			
				250	1½"	2	2"	1¼"	60	45	38	132	99	82	230	172	144
				300	1½"	2	2"	1½"	50	38	31	110	83	69			

ONE-PIPE HOT-WATER-SYSTEM DESIGN TABLE
Fig. 71

[151]

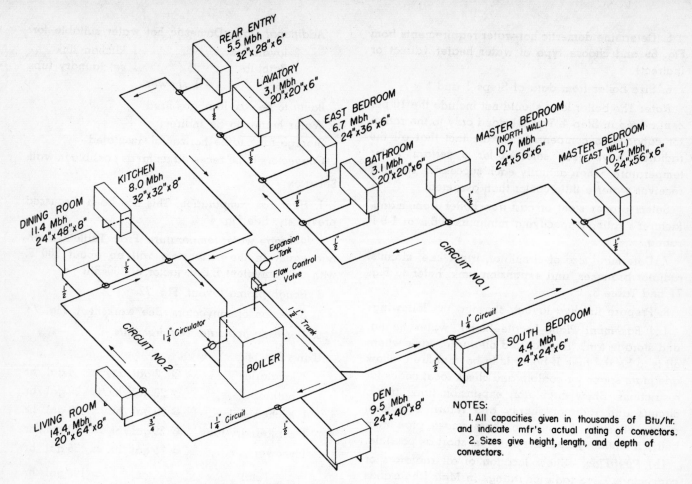

ROUGH PIPING LAYOUT (One-Pipe Hot-Water System)
Fig. 72

NOTES:
1. All capacities given in thousands of Btu/hr. and indicate mfr's actual rating of convectors.
2. Sizes give height, length, and depth of convectors.

6. *Size boiler.*

Boiler load = heat loss + domestic hot-water load

Domestic hot-
   water load = ½ E.D.R. (based on 240 Btu/
   E.D.R.) × gal./hr.

Domestic hot-
   water load = ½ × 240 × 129 = 15,480 Btu/hr.

Heat loss = 81.53 × 1000 = 81,530 Btu/hr.

Total boiler load .... = 97,010 Btu/hr.

This total Btu is equivalent to $\frac{97,010}{200}$ = 486 E.D.R., based on 200° water, which has a heat factor of 200 Btu per E.D.R., or $\frac{97,010}{150}$ = 647 E.D.R., based on 175° water, which corresponds to a heat factor of 150 Btu per E.D.R. This latter rating must be used for specifying the boiler, since boilers are rated on the basis of 175° water.

Therefore, the boiler should be specified as having an I-B-R rating of not less than 647 E.D.R. The student should select such a boiler from manufacturers catalogues and note the over-all dimensions. The required chimney, flue size, and smoke-pipe diameter will also be shown on the dimension sheet.

7. *Size of circulator, trunk line, circuits, radiator*

branches, and expansion tank. Refer to Fig. 71. The following sizes may be read directly from the table in the 100,000-Btu horizontal line (this is nearest to the actual heat loss of 81,530 Btu/hr.) and opposite the 150 ft. length of trunk and longest circuit. Supply and return branches to farthest radiator (this length may be measured from the actual plan with a fair degree of accuracy).

Circulator size .... 1¼ in.
No. of circuits .... 2 (this assumption was made previously)
Size of trunk line .... 1½ in.
Size of each circuit .... 1¼ in.

For size of each convector branch, use E.D.R. equivalents from *Step 4* shown in fourth column when applying Fig. 71. Read values under the 200° column. Record sizes on a rough sketch. It will be seen that a ½-in. branch will handle 61 E.D.R. Only in the living room is this capacity exceeded. Therefore it will be safe to use a ½-in. branch on all convectors except in the living room, where a ¾-in. branch will be required.

From Table 3, the expansion tank will be of 15-gal. size.

8. *Finished layout. See Plate 30.*

CIRCUIT NO.	ROOM	HEAT LOSS MBtu PER HR. ①		E.D.R. EQUIV- ALENT ⑥	PERCENT TO ADD TO EACH RAD. SO THAT LAST RAD. WILL BE INCREASED BY 10% ②	RATING FOR WHICH CONVECTOR IS SELECTED MBtu ③	MANUFACTURER'S ACTUAL RATING SELECTED MBtu ④	HEIGHT (INCHES)	LENGTH (INCHES)	DEPTH (INCHES)
1	SOUTH BEDROOM	4.2		21	0	4.2 × 1.000 = 4.2	4.4	24	24	6
	MASTER BEDROOM EAST WALL	20.7	10.3	51.5	1.7	10.3 × 1.017 = 10.5	10.7	24	56	6
	MASTER BEDROOM NORTH WALL		10.3	51.5	3.4	10.3 × 1.034 = 10.6	10.7	24	56	6
	BATH ROOM	2.86		14.3	5.1	2.86 × 1.051 = 3.0	3.1	20	20	6
	EAST BEDROOM	4.97		24.9	6.8	4.97 × 1.068 = 5.3	6.7	24	36	6
	LAVATORY	2.33		11.6	8.5	2.33 × 1.085 = 2.5	3.1	20	20	6
	REAR ENTRY	4.42		22.1	10.2	4.42 × 1.102 = 4.9	5.5	32	28	6
TOTAL CIRCUIT NO. 1		39.48								
2	DEN	9.6		48	0	9.6 × 1.000 = 9.6	9.5	24	40	8
	LIVING ROOM	13.7		68.5	3.3	13.7 × 1.033 = 14.2	14.4	20	64	8
	DINING ROOM	9.2		46	6.6	9.2 × 1.066 = 9.8	11.4	24	48	8
	KITCHEN	9.55		47.7	9.9	9.55 × 1.099 = 10.4	⑤ 8.0	32	32	8
TOTAL CIRCUIT NO. 2		42.05								
GRAND TOTAL		81.53								

NOTES:

① MBtu/hr means thousands of Btu per hour (Mbh).

② Count all radiators, except the first one, on the circuit. Divide this number into 10 per cent (0.10). The answer is the percentage to add to each radiator capacity so that the last radiator on the circuit will have its capacity increased by about 10 per cent. Note that when 2 per cent is added to a number, the number is multiplied by 1.02.

③ Successive radiator capacities are increased more and more until the last radiator on the circuit is 10 per cent greater than the capacity corresponding to the heat loss served by that unit. This proce-dure compensates for the fact that all radiators are selected for 200° average water temperature, where-as in reality each radiator receives cooler water than the preceding unit.

④ The sum total of the convector ratings will naturally exceed the sum total of the heat-loss fig-ures, since the ratings are based on 200° water for each unit.

⑤ Space does not permit a larger radiator in the kitchen. However, the kitchen is used mainly for cooking, and under these conditions heat is generated by the range. Moreover, the dining-room and rear-entrance convectors are both oversize.

⑥ Based on 200 Btu/E.D.R. (see Table 2).

WORKSHEET FOR SELECTION OF CONVECTORS
Fig. 73

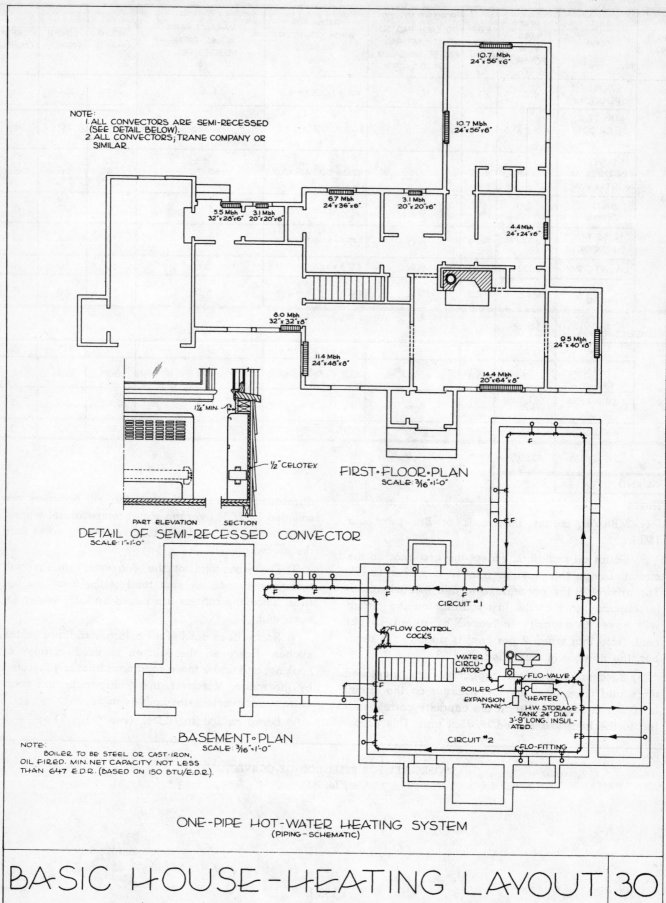

NOTE:
1. ALL CONVECTORS ARE SEMI-RECESSED (SEE DETAIL BELOW).
2. ALL CONVECTORS; TRANE COMPANY OR SIMILAR.

10.7 Mbh
24"x 56"x 6"

10.7 Mbh
24"x 56"x 6"

6.7 Mbh
24"x 36"x 6"

3.1 Mbh
20"x 20"x 6"

4.4 Mbh
24"x 24"x 6"

5.5 Mbh
32"x 28"x 6"

3.1 Mbh
20"x 20"x 6"

9.5 Mbh
24"x 40"x 8"

8.0 Mbh
32"x 32"x 8"

11.4 Mbh
24"x 48"x 8"

14.4 Mbh
20"x 64"x 8"

FIRST·FLOOR·PLAN
SCALE: 3/16"=1'-0"

1¼" MIN.

½" CELOTEX

PART ELEVATION   SECTION

DETAIL OF SEMI-RECESSED CONVECTOR
SCALE: 1"=1'-0"

FLOW CONTROL COCKS

CIRCUIT #1

WATER CIRCU-LATOR

FLO-VALVE

BOILER

EXPANSION TANK

HEATER

H.W. STORAGE TANK 24" DIA x 3'-9" LONG. INSULATED.

CIRCUIT #2

FLO-FITTING

BASEMENT·PLAN
SCALE: 3/16"=1'-0"

NOTE:
BOILER TO BE STEEL OR CAST-IRON, OIL FIRED. MIN. NET CAPACITY NOT LESS THAN 647 E.D.R. (BASED ON 150 BTU/E.D.R.).

ONE-PIPE HOT-WATER HEATING SYSTEM
(PIPING - SCHEMATIC)

BASIC HOUSE-HEATING LAYOUT 30

Architectural Drafting Examination No. 3 (Heating)

In answering the following true-or-false questions, write the number of each question on a sheet of paper, followed by the letter that is most nearly correct.

T F 1. Heat flows from a high-temperature source to a low-temperature receiver.

T F 2. Heat loss is expressed in terms of area, wall effectiveness, and degrees temperature difference between inside and outside design temperatures.

T F 3. Area refers to the square feet of only that surface which is exposed to a temperature equal to room temperature.

T F 4. Heat loss occurs between adjacent rooms if each room is heated to the same temperature.

T F 5. Constructions with low transmission coefficients indicate good insulators.

T F 6. *H* is the standard heat-transmission-coefficient symbol adopted by the American Society of Heating and Ventilating Engineers.

T F 7. It is considered good practice to place the heating unit away from the chimney, because long smoke pipes increase the efficiency of the unit.

T F 8. The best location of radiators is underneath a window, because cold air leaking in through the window is warmed before it reaches the interior of the room.

T F 9. When using a warm-air heating system, always arrange the ductwork so that warm air is blown from the cold walls to the warm partition walls.

T F 10. Second-floor partitions that line up with those on the first floor are not suited for carrying vertical risers to warm-air outlets on the second floor.

T F 11. Water hammer will never occur in the one-pipe steam system.

T F 12. The two-pipe vapor system has a slow heating-up period.

T F 13 The hot-water system is extremely efficient because of its instant circulation of water.

T F 14. The ductwork on a forced warm-air system sometimes requires additional headroom in the basement.

T F 15. Radiant heating is a method of heating whereby room surfaces such as walls, floors, or ceilings are heated by means of steam or hot-water pipe coils, hot air, electricity, or any other practical heating medium.

T F 16. A radiant heating system can easily be converted to summer cooling.

T F 17. Boilers are used on warm-air systems, whereas furnaces are used on hot-water and steam systems.

T F 18. When a group of radiators is connected to the same main, it is natural to assume that each successive radiator receives water a little cooler than the water in the preceding unit.

PART VI
PLUMBING FOR THE TYPICAL DWELLING

Before the actual installation of a plumbing system is begun, the architect, draftsman, or plumbing contractor must lay out the drainage system in accordance with the local sanitary laws and obtain the necessary permits.

In recent years the United States Department of Commerce has published a report entitled *Recommended Minimum Requirements for Plumbing*, based

cast-iron pipe is used, the diameter must not be less than 4 in. Figure 74 shows a typical layout of the house sewer as it empties into the public sewer.

House Trap

Directly inside of the wall of the house and connected to the house sewer is the house trap. Its purpose is to furnish a water seal against the

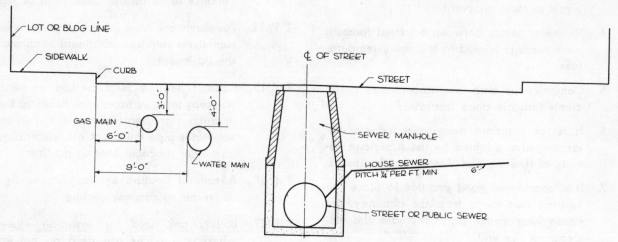

TYPICAL LAYOUT SHOWING PUBLIC SEWER AND SUB-SURFACE STRUCTURES

Fig. 74

on experiments carried out by the National Bureau of Standards. Many of these recommendations, devised to protect the health of the community, have since become part of our plumbing codes all over the country and ensure installations that make for economy and efficiency in all buildings.

In order to understand a typical plumbing system, it is necessary to know the function of each pipe and fitting. The essential equipment of a typical plumbing system is as follows:

1. House sewer
2. House trap
3. Fresh-air inlet
4. House drain
5. Soil and waste stacks
6. Vent stacks
7. Fixture branches
8. Traps

House Sewer

The house sewer is that portion of pipe which extends from the main sewer in the street to the wall of the house. It is generally of vitrified clay with a minimum diameter of 6 in. When laid in the ground, it should have a pitch of ¼ in. to the foot. When

entrance of gases from the public sewer to the piping inside the building. House traps are generally U-shaped with cleanouts at the top of one or both horns (see Fig. 75). Although the house trap serves an important function, occasionally it interferes with the flow of sewage and therefore requires cleanouts. The house trap should be the full diameter of the house drain.

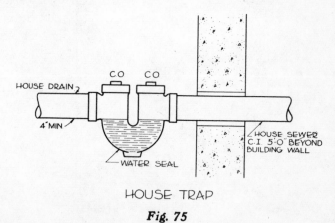

HOUSE TRAP

Fig. 75

Fresh-Air Inlet

The house trap acting as a water seal will cause compression of air or gases in the stacks and house drain if air is driven ahead of a heavy discharge of water. Such compression might force foul gases through the traps in the fixtures and into the living quarters. To prevent this result, a fresh-air pipe (see Fig. 76) is provided directly after the house trap to act as an escape to and avoid compression of gases. The fresh-air inlet, according to codes, should be half the diameter of the house drain, although many plumbers prefer to make it the same diameter as the house drain. When embedded in the wall, it should be furnished with a perforated brass grille at its outer end. The fresh-air outlet should be a minimum of 6 in. from the grade line.

House Drain

The house drain is the horizontal drain inside the house into which the vertical soil and waste stacks discharge (Fig. 77). It must have a minimum diameter of 4 in. and a pitch of at least 1/8 in. to the foot.

The location of the house drain depends upon the depth of the public sewer below grade. Since the sewage of the house generally flows into the public sewer by gravity, the public sewer must of necessity

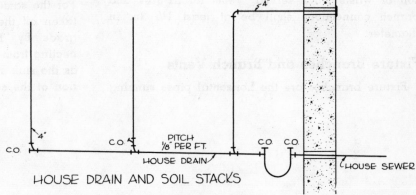

Fig. 76

Fig. 77

HOUSE DRAIN AND SOIL STACKS

be farther below grade than the house drain. The house drain may be embedded in the cellar floor in a concrete trench, it may be suspended by metal straps from the floor joists above, or it may be fastened along the cellar wall by metal straps.

In order to prevent clogging in the house drain, cleanouts (C.O.) must be provided at intervals not more than 50 ft. apart and at the end of the house drain beyond the last vertical stack, and at each change of direction of horizontal run.

Soil and Waste Stacks

Soil and waste stacks (or pipes) are the vertical run of pipe receiving the waste from the branches and fixtures and in turn emptying into the house drain (see Fig. 78). In order to prevent decomposition of the waste matter, a circulation of air throughout the stacks and drains must be provided. The air circulation dilutes poisonous gases, retards pipe corrosion, and maintains balanced atmospheric pressures in the various parts of the system. For purposes of economy, the architect or draftsman must plan for as few stacks as possible, grouping the toilets and other fixtures in the house on one floor or directly above on the next floor.

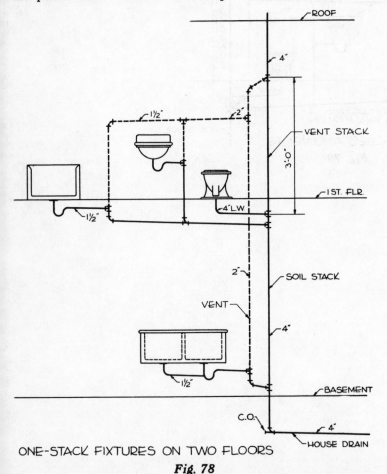

ONE-STACK FIXTURES ON TWO FLOORS

Fig. 78

[157]

Vent Stacks

Vent stacks in the plumbing system are intended to provide air circulation to the soil lines and to prevent the decomposition of the waste matter. They are not to carry waste matter and must be so arranged to render them more effective and to reduce the amount of piping. Figure 78 shows a one-stack soil properly vented. Note that the vent stack carries no waste matter and is connected to the soil line so as to reduce the amount of piping. For example, the soil stack becomes a vent stack above the first floor level and, according to plumbing codes, shall extend undiminished or increased in size above the roof. Vent stacks shall be at least one-half the diameter of the soil or waste stack served. Vents for fixtures and branch connections shall be at least 1½ in. in diameter.

Fixture Branches and Branch Vents

Fixture branches are the horizontal pipes running from the fixture traps to the soil stacks and must have a pitch of ⅛ to ½ in. per foot. If this pitch is to be maintained, the branches must not be too long, especially if they are to be laid between the joists of the floor and ceiling below.

Branch vents are to the horizontal fixture branches as the vertical vent stacks are to the vertical soil stacks. They should be graded so that any moisture that may collect in them can flow back to the branches.

Branch vents must be so arranged so that waste matter flowing through the fixture branches cannot clog and befoul the vents. For this reason branch vents are never connected to the crowns of traps. For the same reason, branch vents should never be taken off the fixture branches below the hydraulic grade. By "hydraulic grade" is meant a line connecting from the high-water level of the fixture, such as the sink shown on Fig. 79, to the branch connection of the soil stack.

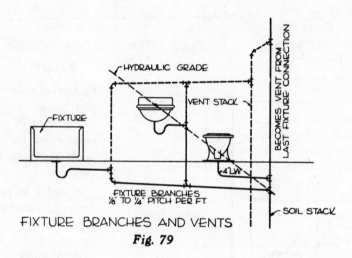

FIXTURE BRANCHES AND VENTS

Fig. 79

General Drainage and Venting Regulations of the New York City Building Code

The following rules and regulations, taken from the New York City Building Code, Article 14, Section 9, should be studied. The figures, indicating paragraph numbers in the code, should be compared with the circled numbers on Plate 31, the Plumbing System for Typical Dwelling. By studying this chart, the student will gain a better understanding of the previous material and will assimilate the facts covered thus far.

3. *Prohibited Connections.* No waste connections shall be made to a bend of a water closet (W.C.) or a similar fixture. Use of soil or waste vents as soil or waste pipe is prohibited.

5. *Grade of Horizontal Drainage Pipes.* At least ⅛ in. per foot.

9. *House Traps and Fresh-Air Inlets.* Every structure in which plumbing fixtures or leaders are installed shall have a house trap on the house drain near the front wall. Each house trap shall have a fresh-air inlet connected to the house drain just ahead of the house trap, with diameter at least half the diameter of the house drain, extending to the outer air and terminating in an open end at least 6 in. above grade. The open end shall be protected by a perforated metal plate fixed in the mouth of the inlet.

14. *Discharge of Water Closets.* The discharge of water closets into a stack less than 3 in. in diameter, and discharge of more than one W.C. into a 3 in. stack, is forbidden.

15. *Minimum Diameter of House Drain.* The minimum size of a house drain receiving the discharge of a W.C. shall be 4 in.

22. *Protection of Traps by Vents.* Each fixture trap shall be individually vented. The topmost fixture, however, may be without vent within 2 ft. of the main stack.

23. *Vent-Pipe Grades.* Vent and branch vent pipes shall be so graded and connected as to drip back to a soil or waste pipe by gravity. Where vent pipes connect to a horizontal soil or waste pipe, the vent branch shall be taken off above the center line of the pipe and the vent pipe shall rise vertically or at an angle of 45 deg. to the vertical before offsetting horizontally or connecting to the branch, main waste pipe, or soil vent.

24. *Distance of Vent from Trap Seal.* The maximum distance from the vent intersection with the waste or soil pipe to the dip of the trap shall be 2 ft. developed length. The vent opening from the soil or waste pipe (except for W.C.'s and similar fixtures) shall be above the dip of the trap. Branch vent lines shall be kept above the tops of all connecting fixtures.

25. *Main Vents to Connect at Base.* Main vents or vent stacks shall connect at their base to the main soil or waste pipe at least 3 ft. below the lowest vent branch and shall extend undiminished or increased in size above the roof, or shall be connected with the main soil or waste stack at least 3 ft. above the highest fixture branch. Where possible, the base of the vent stack shall receive the wash of the adjoining soil or waste.

26. *Required Size of Vents.* Vents shall be at least 1½ in. in diameter. The diameter of every vent stack shall be at least one-half that of the soil or waste stack served.

27. *Roof-Vent Extensions and Terminals.* Roof extensions of soil and waste stacks, or roof vents, shall be run at full size at least 1 ft. above roofs pitched at an angle of more than 30 deg. from the horizontal. Such extensions shall be run full size at least 4 ft. above roofs pitched at an angle of less than 30 deg. from the horizontal and at least 5 ft. where the roof is used for any other purpose than weather protection.

The roof terminal of any vent, soil, or waste pipe, if within 10 ft. of any door, window, scuttle, or airshaft, shall extend at least 3 ft. above such opening.

When soil, waste, or vent pipes are extended through the roof, they shall be at least 4 in. in size. Pipes smaller than 4 in. shall be provided with a proper increaser located just below the roof line.

Article 14, sub article 5, paragraph 7. *Cleanouts.* Easily accessible cleanouts shall be provided at the foot of each vertical waste, soil stack, or inside leader, on all handholes of running traps and of each change of direction of horizontal run. Maximum distance between cleanouts in horizontal soil lines shall be 50 ft.

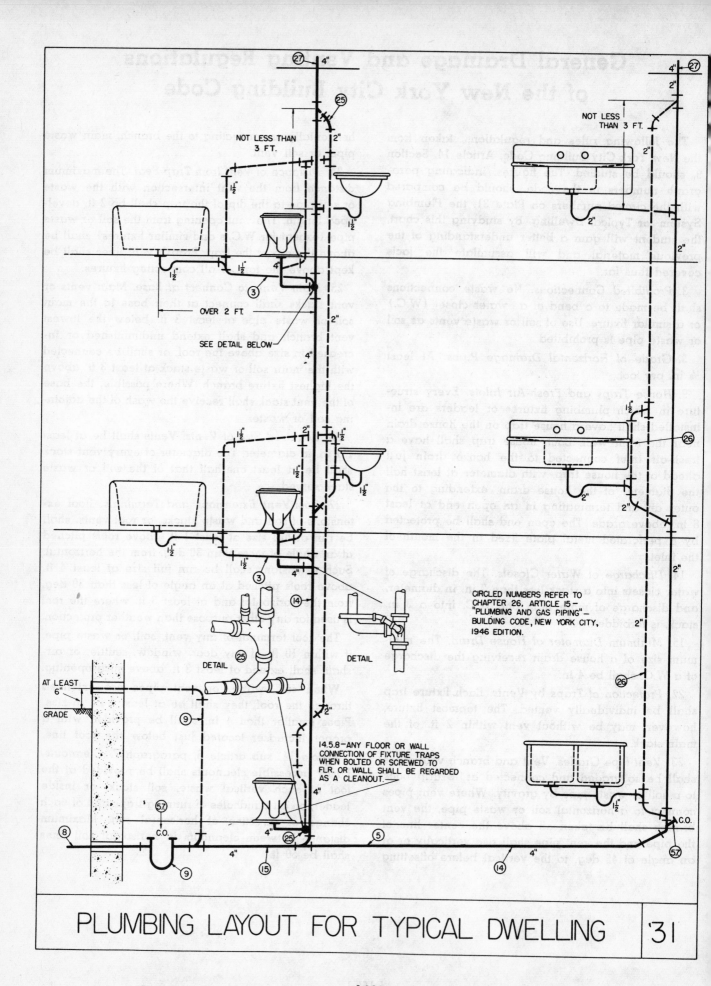

NOT LESS THAN 3 FT.

2"

25

1½"

1½"

1½"

4"

③

OVER 2 FT.

2"

SEE DETAIL BELOW

1½"

2"

1½"

1½"

③

4"

⑭

25

DETAIL

2"

DETAIL

CIRCLED NUMBERS REFER TO CHAPTER 26, ARTICLE 15 – "PLUMBING AND GAS PIPING" – BUILDING CODE, NEW YORK CITY, 1946 EDITION.

AT LEAST 6"

GRADE

⑨

14.5.8-ANY FLOOR OR WALL CONNECTION OF FIXTURE TRAPS WHEN BOLTED OR SCREWED TO FLR. OR WALL SHALL BE REGARDED AS A CLEANOUT.

57

C.O.

8

4"

4"

25

15

⑨

④

5

4"

27

4"

2"

NOT LESS THAN 3 FT.

2"

2"

1½"

26

2"

2"

26

2"

1½"

C.O.

4"

57

PLUMBING LAYOUT FOR TYPICAL DWELLING

'31

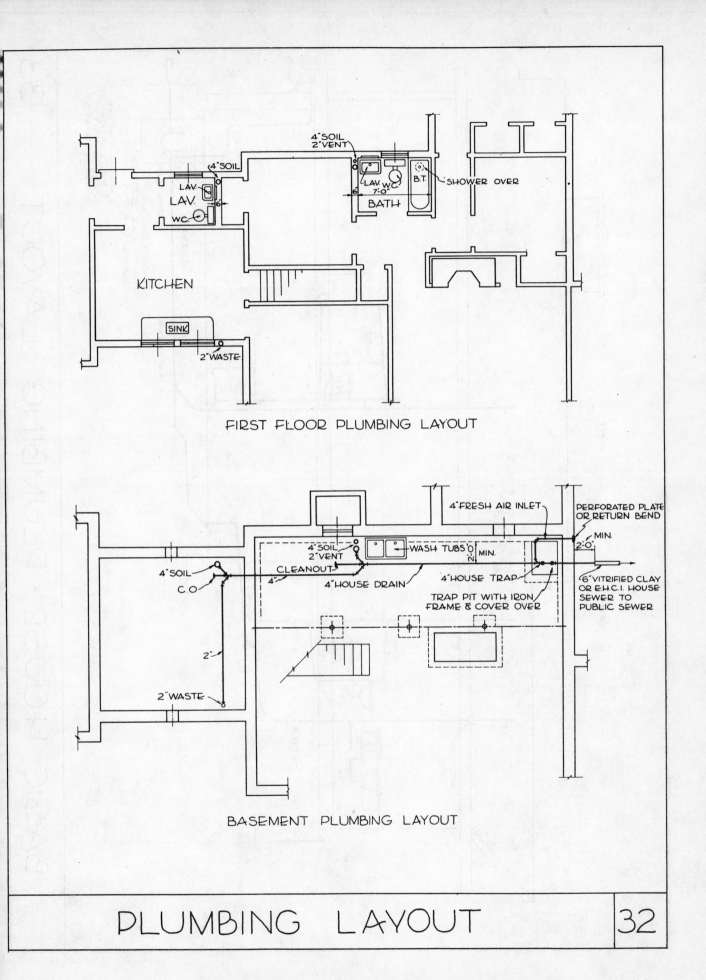

FIRST FLOOR PLUMBING LAYOUT

BASEMENT PLUMBING LAYOUT

PLUMBING LAYOUT

32

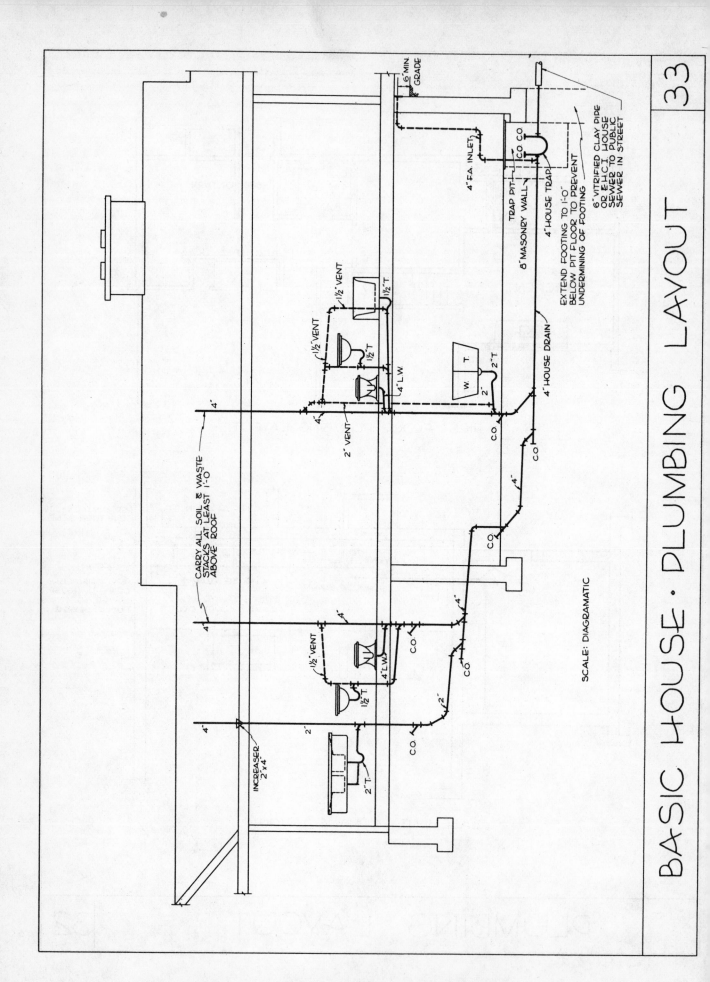

SCALE: DIAGRAMATIC

BASIC HOUSE · PLUMBING LAYOUT

33

Cesspools and Septic Tanks

In the city there are generally public sewers and public water supplies, and the practice of plumbing is under the supervision of competent officials.

In the country, however, these city conveniences do not generally exist, and other means of sewage disposal and water supply must be used. In the absence of public sewers, two types of disposal are in use. These are by means of cesspools or septic tanks.

The Leaching Cesspool

The leaching cesspool is an underground compartment, generally constructed of stone with unfilled joints. It should be not less than 6 ft. 0 in. in diameter, and about 10 ft. 0 in. deep, with its top quite near the surface of the ground. The top is usually dome-shaped, with a 20-in. opening in the top, covered with a cast-iron plate.

In operation, waste material is deposited in the cesspool, with the solid matter retained, and the liquids leaching off through the porous 8-in. walls into the soil. When a cesspool is located in hard soil, or too far below the surface, the leaching action is inhibited.

As would be imagined, there is a chance that the surrounding ground may become contaminated, and consequently no leaching cesspool should be located within 300 feet of a well or within 100 ft. of any watertight cistern.

The use of the leaching type cesspool is looked upon with disfavor since it is often a major cause of water pollution. After a time the joints and crevices become clogged with solid matter, and the liquids overflow and saturate the surrounding soil, and in many ways become a nuisance.

The Watertight Cesspool

The drawing in Fig. 79a shows an approved and recommended type of cesspool known as a watertight cesspool. The compartment on the left is constructed of concrete, and made watertight by a coating of waterproof cement on the inside. Sewage from the house drains into the watertight cesspool, and it fills up finally until the level of the liquid reaches the overflow pipe. The liquid then runs over into a dry well, from which it leaches into the soil. Solid matter remains as a sludge in the watertight compartment, from which it may be cleaned whenever it becomes necessary.

Note that the inlet and outlet connections extend below the liquid level. This is desirable in order to discourage the passing of solid matter into the overflow. Normally these two connections extend about 12 in. below the liquid level.

All cesspools should be vented with a 4-in. pipe, rising 10 ft. 0 in. above the ground. The vent prevents formation of gas pressures in the system.

Watertight cesspools may be located as close as 20 ft. 0 in. to a house, and as close as 30 ft. 0 in. to a well or other source of water supply.

Rain water should never be drained into a sewage cesspool, as it may cause overflowing.

The Septic-Tank Disposal System

Cesspools have been in satisfactory use for many years in our rural areas, but the use of the septic tank has found increasing favor because of its efficiency and sanitary advantages.

Although the term "septic" means the opposite of "sanitary," we say that the septic tank has sanitary advantages because it does not permit polluted waste to enter the soil. The primary function of the septic tank is to hold the sewage, without leakage, to allow thorough digestion of the solid matter, and to retain suspended solids, allowing liquids to overflow into a disposal area.

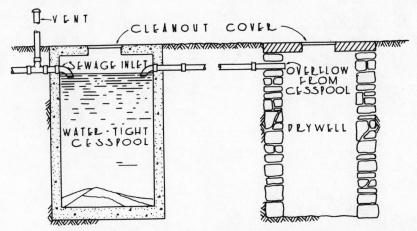

WATERTIGHT CESSPOOL WITH DRY WELL OVERFLOW

Fig. 79a

The septic tank is an improvement over the water-tight cesspool in that it is easily installed and does not have to be constructed 100 per cent watertight. It is movable, contains built-in baffles, and is trouble-free in operation.

The effluent liquid drains to an underground leaching system consisting of field tile, 4 in. in diameter, laid with loose joints which are covered over with metal or tar paper to prevent fill-in by loose earth. Liquid drains from each loose joint and is filtered by the soil. Porous soil makes the best disposal area. Every disposal field should contain at least 100 to 150 lineal feet of tile. Figure 79b shows a typical septic-tank disposal system.

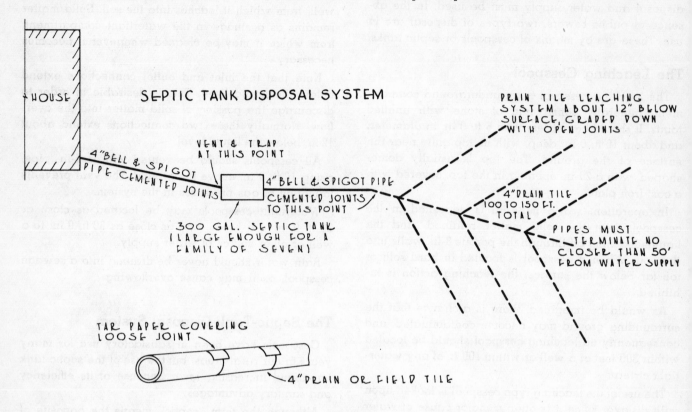

SEPTIC TANK DISPOSAL SYSTEM

HOUSE

4" BELL & SPIGOT PIPE CEMENTED JOINTS

VENT & TRAP AT THIS POINT

4" BELL & SPIGOT PIPE CEMENTED JOINTS TO THIS POINT

300 GAL. SEPTIC TANK (LARGE ENOUGH FOR A FAMILY OF SEVEN)

DRAIN TILE LEACHING SYSTEM ABOUT 12" BELOW SURFACE, GRADED DOWN WITH OPEN JOINTS

4" DRAIN TILE 100 TO 150 FT. TOTAL

PIPES MUST TERMINATE NO CLOSER THAN 50' FROM WATER SUPPLY

TAR PAPER COVERING LOOSE JOINT

4" DRAIN OR FIELD TILE

Fig. 79b

Architectural Drafting Examination No. 4

In answering the following true-or-false questions, write the number of each question on a sheet of paper, followed by the letter that is most nearly correct.

T F 1. The house sewer extends from the public sewer to the outside wall of the building.

T F 2. When cast-iron pipe is used, the house sewer must not be less than 6 in. in diameter.

T F 3. The house trap, directly inside of the wall of the house and connected to the house sewer, serves as a water seal against the entrance of gases from the public sewer to the piping inside the building.

T F 4. The house trap never interferes with the flow of sewage.

T F 5. The fresh-air inlet is that portion of pipe which extends above the roof.

T F 6. The fresh-air inlet must never be less than the diameter of the house drain.

T F 7. The fresh-air inlet should be a minimum of 6 in. from the grade line.

T F 8. The house drain must have a minimum diameter of 4 in. and a pitch of at least ⅛ in. to the foot.

T F 9. The location of the house drain depends on the depth of the public sewer below grade.

T F 10. According to building codes, the house drain may be embedded only in the cellar floor in a concrete trench.

T F 11. Soil and waste stacks are the vertical run of pipe receiving the waste from the branches and fixtures.

T F 12. Vent stacks serve to carry waste matter and must be so arranged as to render them more effective and to reduce the amount of piping.

T F 13. Branch vents are to the horizontal fixture branches as the vertical vent stacks are to the vertical soil stacks.

T F 14. Branch vents must be so arranged that the waste matter flowing through the fixture branches cannot clog and befoul the vents.

T F 15. The minimum diameter of the house drain receiving the discharge of a W.C. shall be 6 in.

PART VII
ELECTRIC WIRING FOR THE HOME

Part of the house planning is concerned with provision of proper illumination in the various spaces. Formerly this did not constitute any problem whatsoever, since the only provision was a center fixture in each room with an occasional wall bracket and base plug receptacle. Today, however, we may take advantage of improved types and styles of luminaries, and of vastly changed concepts and standards of good illumination.

Modern living has likewise brought with it the necessity for literally hundreds of electrical appliances, from hair driers to deep-freeze units, and it is an important part of our electrical planning to provide for their use.

This part describes the electrical characteristics of the important lighting and appliance equipment.

Lighting Equipment

Fluorescent lighting plays an interesting part in today's illumination schemes. With its use, decorative effects as well as good lighting may be obtained. Figures 79c and 79d suggest some uses of fluorescent lighting. Because of the efficiency of this kind of light source, increased illumination may be had without increased operating costs! Fluorescent tubes concealed above frosted glass panels and in vertical columns furnish even illumination in a bathroom (Fig. 79c). Fluorescent tubes concealed behind valences offer subdued lighting as well as decorative effect (Fig. 79d).

In the workshop shown in Fig. 79e, a two-tube fluorescent fixture rated at 80 watts gives as much light as a 150-watt incandescent lamp bulb! And since its wattage consumption is less (it draws about 100 watts from the line) it costs less to operate.

Fluorescent tubes are extremely flexible in application, since they are available in many sizes, shapes, and wattage ratings. Colored tubes are also available for decorative effects. The table at the bottom of page 167 shows the wattage, length, diameter, and color available for illumination.

Incandescent lighting is by no means becoming obsolete. New techniques in spotlighting or projection lighting have opened many possibilities for effective

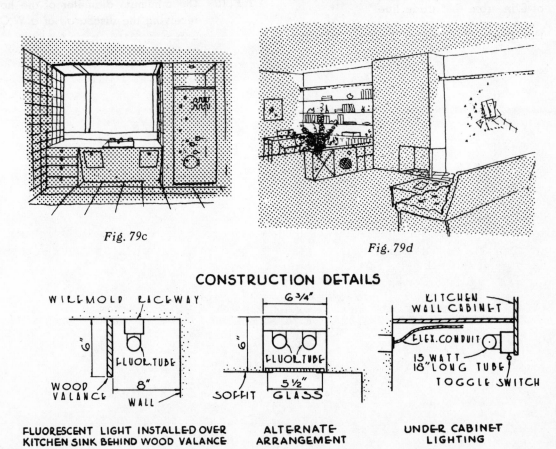

Fig. 79c

Fig. 79d

CONSTRUCTION DETAILS

WIREMOLD RACEWAY

6"

FLUOR. TUBE

WOOD VALANCE

8"

WALL

FLUORESCENT LIGHT INSTALLED OVER KITCHEN SINK BEHIND WOOD VALANCE

6¾"

6"

FLUOR. TUBE

5½"

SOFFIT GLASS

ALTERNATE ARRANGEMENT

KITCHEN WALL CABINET

FLEX. CONDUIT

15 WATT 18" LONG TUBE

TOGGLE SWITCH

UNDER CABINET LIGHTING

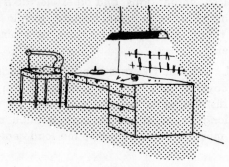

Fig. 79e

PROJECTION LIGHTING USED TO ILLUMINATE THE TABLE IN DINING AREA

ATTRACTIVE AND EFFICIENT LIGHT FIXTURE FOR DINETTE

PROJECTION LIGHTING AS PART OF THE KITCHEN ILLUMINATION. FLUORESCENT LIGHT IS USED UNDER THE CABINET.

Fig. 79f

illumination. In Fig. 79f are shown examples of projection lighting in the home. Outdoor spotlighting also comes under this category. It should be noted that fluorescent tubes do not lend themselves to this kind of lighting, since their light cannot be concentrated in a small area and focused in a beam.

Conventional fixtures are available in any desired style and size. The selection of the proper luminary for each space should be made with care, preferably with guidance from the manufacturer of the lighting equipment.

FLUORESCENT BULBS

Wattage	Length	Tube Diameter	Color
14	15 in.	1½ in.	White, daylight
15	18 in.	1 in.	White, daylight, soft white
15	18 in.	1½ in.	White, daylight, soft white
20	24 in.	1½ in.	White, daylight, soft white
30	36 in.	1 in.	White, daylight, soft white
40	48 in.	1½ in.	White, daylight, soft white
Circular			
20 to 40	8½–12–16 dia.	1 in.	White, daylight, soft white

The following pages deal with the three main features of electric wiring of the house, these are:

I. ELECTRICAL EQUIPMENT. Under this heading are listed the various rooms of the house with their minimum recommended outlets, fixture, and switches, and other types of service outlets. Major fixed appliances for which to plan space and wiring for the average-income house as well as portable appliances such as fans, built-in clocks, etc. are included.

II. ELECTRICAL CIRCUITS. Under this heading are covered the main circuits in the house. These are: the general purpose circuit, which is for lighting the house; appliance circuit, which is for outlets for toaster, electric iron, heater, fans, and other electrical specialties; the individual equipment circuit, which is for the electric range, special room heater, or room air conditioner.

III. CONTROL CENTERS AND FEEDERS. Under this item are covered the control centers from which the circuits are distributed through the house. Circuits must not be too long. For most economical operation, control centers must be placed close to the load centers.

I. Electrical Equipment (Appliances and Lighting)

In order to determine the electrical equipment in the home, the architect or draftsman must first give consideration to the type of home he expects to plan for. Homes may be grouped as follows:

Group A. Covers the lower-priced group: 4 rooms and 1 bath—approximately 800 sq. ft.

Group B. Covers the less expensive units in the intermediate-priced group: 5 rooms and 1 bath—approximately 1200 sq. ft.

Group C. Covers the more expensive units in the intermediate-priced group: 7 rooms and 2 baths—approximately 2000 sq. ft.

Group D. Covers the higher-priced group: 9 rooms and 2 baths—approximately 3000 sq. ft.

For the purposes of our discussion, let us consider Group B.

Tables 7 and 8 following give the minimum fixed appliances requiring electrical connections, and the minimum portable appliances, for the above home group.

TABLE 7

MAJOR FIXED APPLIANCES FOR WHICH TO PLAN SPACE
AND WIRING FOR HOME GROUP B

Appliance	Capacity (approx.)
Utility Room	
Water heater	750–3000 W
Blower, based on heating system being forced warm air	300 W
Furnace motor	400 W
Home freezer	350 W
Laundry	
Conventional washer or Laundromat	
(a) Wringer type normal	375 W
Wringer in operation	450 W
(b) Spinner type normal	375 W
Spinner basket accelerating	800–1600 W
Ironer	1600 W
Clothes drier	4500 W
Kitchen	
Range	7000–14,000 W
Refrigerator	300 W
Dishwasher	500 W
Garbage eliminator	500 W
Baths	
Heater (built in)	1000–1500 W

TABLE 8

PORTABLE APPLIANCES FOR WHICH TO WIRE
IN HOME GROUP B

Appliance	Capacity (approx.)
Ventilating fans in kitchen	90–110 W
Built-in clock in kitchen	2 W

After the designer has determined the fixed and portable appliances required for the home, the next step is to determine the electric lighting outlets, switch controls, convenience outlets, and other types of service outlets.

The following will give the minimum outlet requirements by rooms for the home group in question as recommended by the Westinghouse Electric Corporation, Pittsburgh.

Minimum Outlet Requirements for Home Group B

Living Room (Den, Library)

1. LIGHTING OUTLETS

   Ceiling outlet (rooms twice as long as wide may require more than one outlet). Fixed lighting outlets in rooms may be omitted, provided:

   (a) Wall cove or valance lighting outlets are substituted.

   (b) Switching equivalents to that controlling fixed lighting outlets are provided for one or more convenience outlets.

   (c) Outlet is controlled by switch.

2. SWITCH CONTROLS

   (a) Single-pole switch at entrance door, or three-way switches if commonly used doorways are more than 10 ft. apart.

   (b) Single-pole switch for group of outlets to permit convenience in use.

3. DUPLEX CONVENIENCE OUTLETS

   (a) Place outlets so that no point along floor line on any usable wall space, unbroken by a doorway, is more than 6 ft. from an outlet.

   (b) Outlet in each usable wall space 3 ft. or more in length at floor line.

   (c) Outlet flush in top of mantel shelf, construction permitting; otherwise adjacent to mantel.

4. OTHER TYPES OF SERVICE OUTLETS

   Television or radio outlet (aerial and ground) may be combined with convenience outlet.

Dining Room (Breakfast Room)

1. LIGHTING OUTLETS

   Ceiling outlet or cove lighting.

2. SWITCH CONTROLS

   (a) Single-pole switch at entrance door.

   (b) Three-way switches if commonly used doorways are more than 10 ft. apart.

3. DUPLEX CONVENIENCE OUTLETS

   (a) Place outlets so that no point along floor line on any usable wall space, unbroken by a doorway, is more than 10 ft. from an outlet.

   (b) Outlet in each wall space 3 ft. or more in length at floor line.

   (c) Outlet for portable appliance.

Kitchen

1. LIGHTING OUTLETS

   (a) Ceiling outlet.

   (b) Outlets at each important work area, such as over sink and under wall cabinets, for surface illumination.

2. SWITCH CONTROLS

   (a) Single-pole switch at entrance door.

   (b) Three-way switches if commonly used doorways are more than 10 ft. apart.

   (c) Single-pole switch for group of outlets to permit convenience in use.

3. DUPLEX CONVENIENCE OUTLETS

   (a) Three outlets at work areas (a minimum of one outlet for each work center) to serve refrigerator, waffle baker, mixer, radio, and other appliances.

   (b) For roaster.

   (c) For dishwasher.

4. OTHER TYPES OF SERVICE OUTLETS

   (a) For range.

   (b) For ventilating fan. If fan is built in, it may be wired direct without use of receptacle.

Laundry

1. LIGHTING OUTLETS

   (a) Ceiling outlet at sorting and washing center.

   (b) Outlet at ironing center.

2. SWITCH CONTROLS

   (a) Single-pole switch at entrance door.

   (b) Three-way switches if commonly used doorways are more than 10 ft. apart.

3. DUPLEX CONVENIENCE OUTLETS

   (a) For washer. For the conventional wringer-type washer, a suitable installation is an outlet box at ceiling and about 3 ft. in front of tubs with cord extended within 6 ft. from floor.

   (b) For ironer.

4. OTHER TYPES OF SERVICE OUTLETS

   (a) For hand ironer.

   (b) For water heater.

   (c) For ventilating fan.

Bedrooms

1. LIGHTING OUTLETS

   (a) Ceiling outlet. Rooms twice as long as wide may require more than one outlet. Cove lighting or wall outlets (at least two) may be used in place of ceiling outlet.

   (b) Outlets at vanity table, bed recesses, window valances, and other points where useful.

   (c) In each closet off bedroom having a floor area of 6 sq. ft. or greater—pull chain.

2. SWITCH CONTROLS

   (a) Single-pole switch at entrance door.

(b) Three-way switches if commonly used doorways are more than 10 ft. apart.

(c) Single-pole switch for group of outlets to permit convenience in use.

3. DUPLEX CONVENIENCE OUTLETS

(a) Place outlets so that no point along floor line on any usable wall space, unbroken by doorways is more than 6 ft. from an outlet.

(b) Outlet in each wall space 3 ft. or more in length at floor line.

4. OTHER TYPES OF SERVICE OUTLETS
Radio outlet (aerial and ground) may be combined with convenience outlet.

Baths

1. LIGHTING OUTLETS
(a) Ceiling outlets for baths greater than 60 sq. ft. in area.

(b) Two outlets, one on each side of mirror.

2. SWITCH CONTROLS
Single-pole switch at door.

3. DUPLEX CONVENIENCE OUTLETS
At lavatory, away from tub.

4. OTHER TYPES OF SERVICE OUTLETS
For built-in heater.

Utility Room

1. LIGHTING OUTLETS
(a) Ceiling outlet for every 150 sq. ft. of floor area, as equally spaced as practical.

(b) Outlets at utility equipment, such as furnace, cooling unit, home freezer, at work bench; also for each separately enclosed space.

2. SWITCH CONTROL
(a) Single-pole switch for each outlet or group of outlets to permit convenience in use.

(b) Single-pole switch at entrance door.

(c) Three-way switches if commonly used doorways are more than 10 ft. apart.

3. DUPLEX CONVENIENCE OUTLETS
(a) For home freezer.

(b) At workbench for tool motor, soldering iron, etc.

4. OTHER TYPES OF SERVICE OUTLETS
(a) Heating unit, composed of burner motor, blower motor, and control devices, is generally wired complete, terminating in a junction box provided with a disconnect.

(b) For water heater. This outlet may be located in the utility room, kitchen, or laundry, depending on planning.

Front Entrance

1. LIGHTING OUTLETS
Exterior outlets, number and location depending on architectural treatment of doorway.

2. SWITCH CONTROLS
Single-pole switch inside entrance door. Pilot light may be desirable under certain conditions.

3. OTHER TYPES OF SERVICE OUTLETS
(a) Weatherproof receptacle outlet for decorative lighting.

(b) Push button to call bell, buzzer, or chime (locate outside front entrance door).

Entrance Hall

1. LIGHTING OUTLETS
(a) Outlet for each 15 linear feet of hall or major fraction, if hall is not illuminated by stairway light.

(b) In closet off entrance hall (outlets should be provided in closets 30 in. and over in depth or having a floor area of 6 sq ft or greater).

(c) Exterior outlet over car entrance door.

2. SWITCH CONTROL
(a) Single-pole switch at entrance door.

(b) Three-way switches if commonly used doorways are more than 10 ft. apart.

(c) Pull-chain lampholder in closets off entrance hall.

3. DUPLEX CONVENIENCE OUTLETS
Outlet for each 15 linear feet of hall.

Stairway

1. LIGHTING OUTLETS
One outlet at head and one at foot of each stairway.

2. SWITCH CONTROLS
Separate three-way switches at head and foot of stairs, for controlling each of the two outlets.

Garage

1. LIGHTING OUTLETS
Ceiling outlet over hood end of each car space.

2. SWITCH CONTROLS
(a) Single-pole switch at entrance door. In multiple car groups, no more than two interior outlets should be controlled by the same switch.

(b) Three-way switches if commonly used doorways are more than 10 ft. apart.

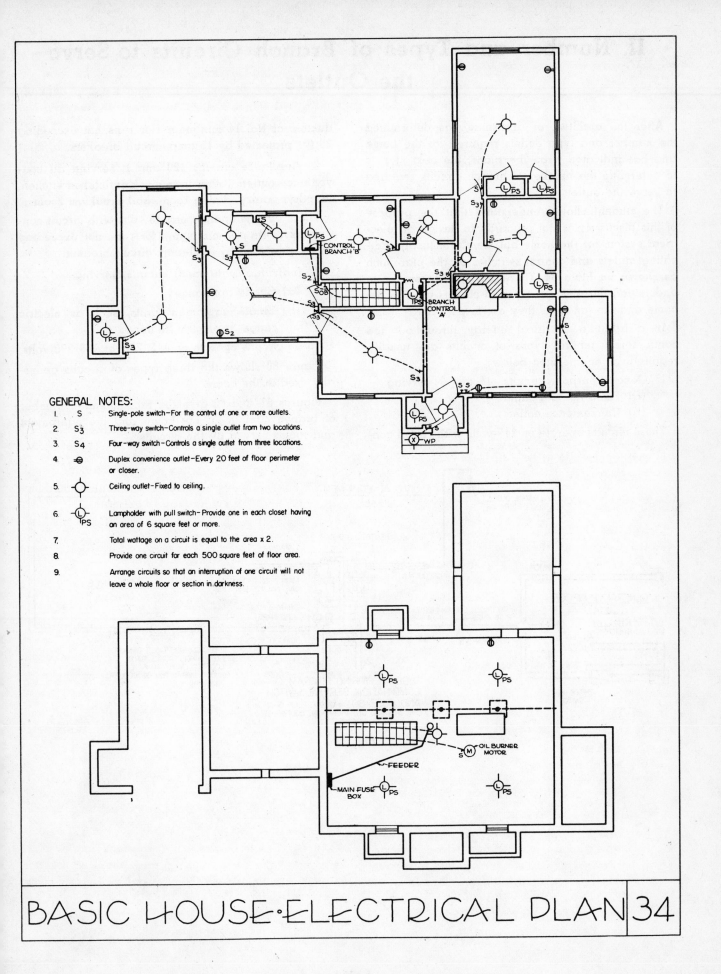

GENERAL NOTES:

1. S   Single-pole switch—For the control of one or more outlets.

2. S₃   Three-way switch—Controls a single outlet from two locations.

3. S₄   Four-way switch—Controls a single outlet from three locations.

4.   Duplex convenience outlet—Every 20 feet of floor perimeter or closer.

5.   Ceiling outlet—Fixed to ceiling.

6.   Lampholder with pull switch—Provide one in each closet having an area of 6 square feet or more.

7.   Total wattage on a circuit is equal to the area x 2.

8.   Provide one circuit for each 500 square feet of floor area.

9.   Arrange circuits so that an interruption of one circuit will not leave a whole floor or section in darkness.

BASIC HOUSE·ELECTRICAL PLAN 34

II. Number and Types of Branch Circuits to Serve the Outlets

After the architect or draftsman has determined the number and type outlets required for the home and has indicated it on the plans, the next step is to determine the number of branch circuits required to serve the outlets.

The student should understand that the purpose of this discussion is not primarily to design an electrical system for the home but merely to justify indicating outlets and control switches on the plan such as shown on Plate 34. Therefore, it is necessary to understand the different types of circuits used in the home and the functions they are to perform.

In distributing electrical energy throughout the home, three general types of circuits are usually required, as enumerated below:

1. *General-purpose circuits* (15 amp.), serving
   (a) Fixed lighting outlets
   (b) Convenience outlets

These circuits operate on 115 volts with circuit conductors of No. 14 minimum (for runs not exceeding 30 ft.) protected by 15 amp. circuit breakers.

2. *Appliance circuits* (20 amp.), serving all convenience outlets (other than clock outlets) in kitchen, laundry, pantry, dining room, and breakfast room.

These circuits operate on 115 volts with circuit conductors of No. 12 minimum (for runs not exceeding 45 ft.) protected by a 20-amp. circuit breaker.

3. *Individual equipment circuits*, serving
   (a) Single appliances
   (b) Single equipment units, such as electric range or electric heater

These circuits operate on 115, 230, or 115/230 volts.

Figure 80 shows the three types of circuits generally used in the home.

Figures 81 and 82 give the recommended number of branch circuits for the home and the equipment and rooms served by the circuits.

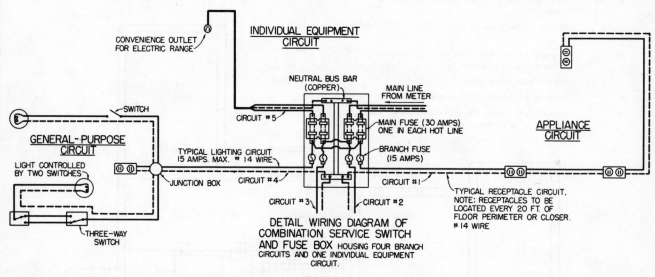

Fig. 80

RECOMMENDED NUMBER OF BRANCH CIRCUITS

GENERAL-PURPOSE CIRCUITS	ONE CIRCUIT IS RECOMMENDED FOR EACH 500 SQUARE FEET OF FLOOR AREA INSOFAR AS IS PRACTICAL, THE TOTAL LOAD SHOULD BE EVENLY PROPORTIONED AMONG THE BRANCH CIRCUITS ACCORDING TO THEIR CAPACITY.			
	FLOOR AREA OF HOUSE (SQUARE FEET)	**NUMBER OF CIRCUITS**		
		KITCHEN AND DINING SPACES	LAUNDRY	UTILITY AND GARAGE SPACES
APPLIANCE CIRCUITS	UP TO 800	1	2	*
	UP TO 1500	2	2	*
	ABOVE 1500	2	2	1
	✱ GENERAL-PURPOSE CIRCUITS MAY SERVE THE UTILITY AND GARAGE SPACES IN HOMES UP TO 1500 SQUARE FEET.			

INDIVIDUAL EQUIPMENT CIRCUITS	IT IS DESIRABLE TO PROVIDE NOT LESS THAN FOUR INDIVIDUAL EQUIPMENT CIRCUITS IN EVEN THE SMALLEST SIZE HOME. THESE FOUR CIRCUITS ARE TO PERMIT THE INSTALLATION OF:
	
	    1. RANGE
	    2. WATER HEATER
	    3. HEATING-AIR CLEANING UNIT
	    4. LAUNDROMAT
	
	ADDITIONAL CIRCUITS SHOULD BE PROVIDED AS FOLLOWS:
	
	FOR HOMES HAVING 1000 SQ. FT. OR MORE—BATHROOM HEATER
	FOR HOMES HAVING 1500 SQ. FT. OR MORE—CLOTHES DRYER AND ELECTRIC SINK
	FOR HOMES HAVING IN EXCESS OF 2500 SQ. FT.—AIR COOLING UNIT			

Fig. 81

EQUIPMENT AND ROOMS SERVED BY CIRCUITS

TYPE OF CIRCUIT	NUMBER OF CIRCUIT	EQUIPMENT	ROOMS SERVED	REMARKS
GENERAL-PURPOSE (15-AMPERE) CIRCUITS	3	(A) LIGHTING (FIXED AND PORTABLE	ALL ROOMS	ARRANGE CIRCUITS SO THAT AN INTERRUPTION OF ONE CIRCUIT WILL NOT LEAVE A WHOLE FLOOR OR SECTION OF THE HOUSE IN DARKNESS. FIXED CLOCKS AND SMALL VENTILATING FANS IN KITCHEN AND LAUNDRY MAY BE CONNECTED TO THESE CIRCUITS.
		(B) SMALL PORTABLE APPLIANCES	LIVING ROOM BEDROOMS BATH	
APPLIANCE (20-AMPERE) CIRCUITS	5	(A) REFRIGERATOR, DISHWASHER, MIXER, FAN, ETC.	KITCHEN	TWO CIRCUITS TO SERVE KITCHEN, DINING SPACE; TWO CIRCUITS TO SERVE LAUNDRY; AND ONE CIRCUIT TO SERVE UTILITY ROOM, ATTACHED GARAGE.
		(B) WAFFLE BAKER, TOASTER, ETC.	KITCHEN DINING SPACE	
		(C) IRONER, HAND IRON, HOT PLATE, ETC.	LAUNDRY	
		(D) HOME FREEZER, TOOL MOTOR, SOLDERING IRON, ETC.	UTILITY ROOM GARAGE	
INDIVIDUAL EQUIPMENT CIRCUITS (FIXED EQUIPMENT)	8	(A) RANGE 9000 W (35 A, 3 WIRE, 115/230 V) (B) WATER HEATER 3000 W (20 A* 2 WIRE, 230 V) (C) HEATING-AIR CLEANING UNIT 800 W (20 A, 2 WIRE, 115 V) (D) LAUNDROMAT 350 W (20 A, 2 WIRE, 115 V) (E) BATHROOM HEATER 1000 W, (20 A, 2 WIRE, 115 V)		EACH APPLIANCE OR EQUIPMENT UNIT SERVED BY AN INDIVIDUAL CIRCUIT.

*ALTHOUGH A 20-AMPERE CIRCUIT WOULD SUFFICE, A 25-AMPERE CIRCUIT IS RECOMMENDED.

Fig. 82

COURTESY OF: WESTINGHOUSE ELECTRIC CORPORATION
PITTSBURGH, PENNSYLVANIA

III. Number and Size of Control Centers and Feeders and the Capacity of the Service Entrance Conductors

In Fig. 80 we have seen the different types of electrical circuits generally required in the home. The place from which these circuits radiate is called the *control center*. A home may be equipped with one main control center from which the branch circuits are carried throughout the house, or a number of control centers, depending on the number of circuits required. The Westinghouse Electric Corporation, Pittsburgh, recommends that:

1. *Main control centers* be restricted to six protective subdivisions. There may be six breakers, either single- or double-pole.

2. *Branch control centers* be restricted to eight poles, that is, eight single poles or four double poles, or four single poles and two double poles.

It follows, then, that the number of circuits required in the home determines the number of control centers.

It has been the custom in the past to locate control centers at one place in the basement. A better practice is to place control centers as near as possible to the load centers. For example, since the greatest electrical load is required for the kitchen, laundry, and utility rooms, a control center should be within this area, resulting in short branch circuits and hence less voltage drop and more efficient operation of the electrical equipment.

Figure 83 shows a schematic layout of branch control centers located near the load centers, and a main control center.

Feeders

Feeders must be of sufficient size to carry the load to which they may be subjected. In very small electrical installations it is quite possible that the total load may be in operation at one time. Therefore, the feeder must be large enough to carry 100 per cent of the electrical load.

In larger installations it is safe to assume that the total load will not be in operation the same time, and hence the feeder may be designed for perhaps 75 per cent of the electrical load. It is considered good practice, however, to use a No. 10 feeder supplying two or more branch circuits.

Service Conductor

The service conductor is that portion of the supply conductor which extends from the street main to the service equipment of the premises supplied. As in the case of the feeders, the service conductor must be of sufficient size to carry the electrical load requirements of the home. It is not, however, absolutely necessary to size the service conductor on the full connected load, because it is very likely that several circuits will be idle.

The common 30 amp., two- or three-wire service installation is rapidly becoming inadequate because of the introduction of new appliances for the home. The latest recommendations of the Westinghouse Electric Corporation are that a three-wire, 70-amp. service entrance installation be the minimum that should be considered in a home.

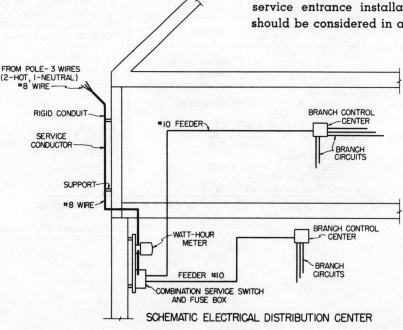

SCHEMATIC ELECTRICAL DISTRIBUTION CENTER

Fig. 83

Architectural Drafting Examination No. 5

In answering the following true-or-false questions, write the number of each question on a sheet of paper, followed by the letter that is most nearly correct.

T F 1. Rooms twice as long as wide require a minimum of three ceiling outlets.

T F 2. A three-way switch controls only one outlet.

T F 3. Duplex convenience outlets should be spaced a minimum of 6 ft. apart, provided the wall space is unbroken by a doorway.

T F 4. The outlet for television or radio may be combined with convenience outlets.

T F 5. The average water heater consumes 750 to 3000 watts.

T F 6. General-purpose circuits serve all convenience outlets in the kitchen, laundry, pantry, dining room, and breakfast room.

T F 7. Appliance circuits serve all fixed lighting outlets and convenience outlets.

T F 8. Individual equipment circuits serve all single appliances and single equipment units such as electrical range or electric heater.

T F 9. The number of circuits required for the home determines the number of control centers.

T F 10. It is considered the best practice to place control centers as far away from the load centers as possible.

T F 11. The longer the branch circuits, the smaller the voltage drop and the more efficient the operation of the electrical equipment.

T F 12. It is considered poor practice to use a No. 10 feeder supplying two or more branch circuits.

T F 13. The service conductor is that portion of the supply conductor which extends from the street main to the service equipment of the premises supplied.

T F 14. A typical lighting circuit of 15 amp. (maximum) requires a No. 14 wire.

T F 15. Circuits must be arranged so that an interruption of one circuit will not leave a whole floor or section in darkness.

T F 16. Recommendations are that one circuit should be used for every 200 sq. ft. of floor area.

T F 17. The total wattage on a circuit is equal to the area (floor area) times 2.

T F 18. A four-way switch controls a single outlet from three locations.

T F 19. Recommendations are that a closet having an area of 6 sq. ft. or more should have a lampholder with pull switch.

T F 20. The problems of electrical wiring for the home today require less attention than they received in the 1920's.

PART VIII
THE MODEL HOUSE

Model House Plans

The plans on pages 177-186 represent a complete set of working drawings and details of a model house designed by Caleb Hornbostel, New York architect.

In order to benefit from such a set of plans, the student draftsman should study them carefully and use them as a model or guide in drawing a similar set of his own design as a final project.

It is interesting to note that the model house plans deviate somewhat from the typical construction principles heretofore discussed. Modern methods with an aim toward simplification seem to be the keynote. The house is a two-level structure with flat roof, canvas deck terrace, stone walls, and red wood siding. The cornice arrangement and sill details (Plate 38) are excellent examples of simplified construction.

Following the model house plans are the written specifications for the various building trades. These specifications are more complete than is generally required for a small house but are typical and can be applied to larger structures. In reading the specifications, the student can readily realize that a set of plans is not sufficient for the builder to erect the house. Information contained in the specifications is generally that which cannot be shown on the drawings.

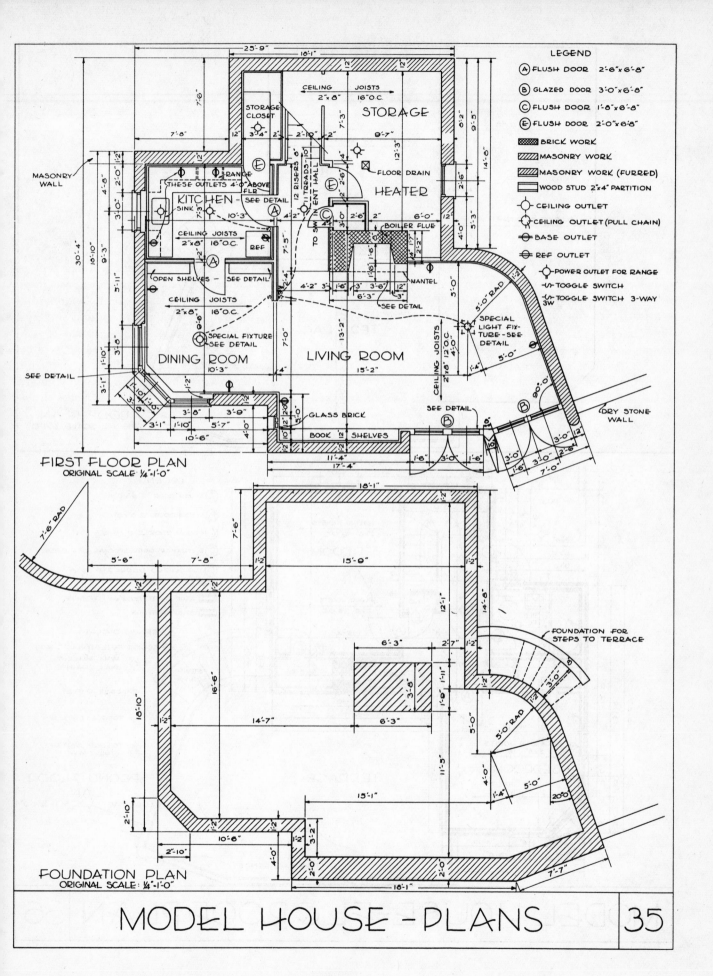

FIRST FLOOR PLAN
ORIGINAL SCALE 1/4"=1'-0"

FOUNDATION PLAN
ORIGINAL SCALE 1/4"=1'-0"

MODEL HOUSE – PLANS

35

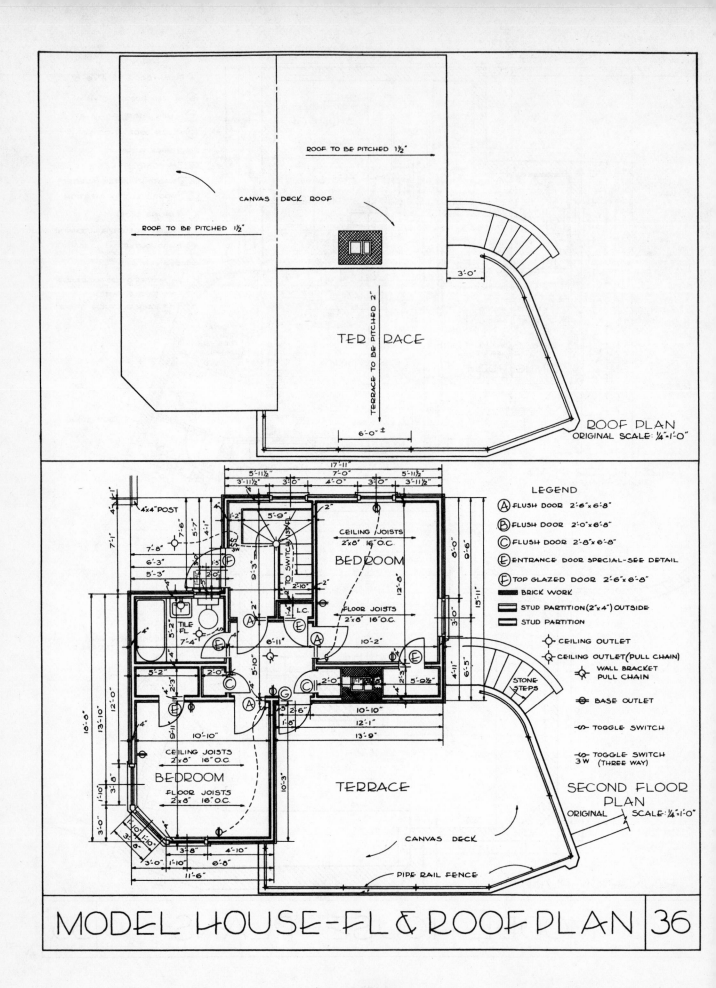

ROOF TO BE PITCHED 1½"

CANVAS DECK ROOF

ROOF TO BE PITCHED 1½"

3'-0"

TERRACE

TERRACE TO BE PITCHED 2"

6'-0" ±

ROOF PLAN
ORIGINAL SCALE: ¼"-1'-0"

LEGEND

Ⓐ FLUSH DOOR 2'-6"×6'-8"
Ⓑ FLUSH DOOR 2'-0"×6'-8"
Ⓒ FLUSH DOOR 2'-8"×6'-8"
Ⓔ ENTRANCE DOOR SPECIAL-SEE DETAIL
Ⓕ TOP GLAZED DOOR 2'-6"×6'-8"
▉ BRICK WORK
▭ STUD PARTITION(2"×4") OUTSIDE
▭ STUD PARTITION

◇ CEILING OUTLET
◈ CEILING OUTLET(PULL CHAIN)
WALL BRACKET PULL CHAIN
⊟ BASE OUTLET
⌁ TOGGLE SWITCH
⌁ TOGGLE SWITCH 3W (THREE WAY)

CEILING JOISTS 2"×8" 16" O.C.
BEDROOM
FLOOR JOISTS 2"×8" 16" O.C.

TILE FL.

L.C.

STONE STEPS

SECOND FLOOR PLAN
ORIGINAL SCALE: ¼"-1'-0"

CEILING JOISTS 2"×8" 16" O.C.
BEDROOM
FLOOR JOISTS 2"×8" 16" O.C.

TERRACE

CANVAS DECK

PIPE RAIL FENCE

4"×4" POST

MODEL HOUSE-FL & ROOF PLAN 36

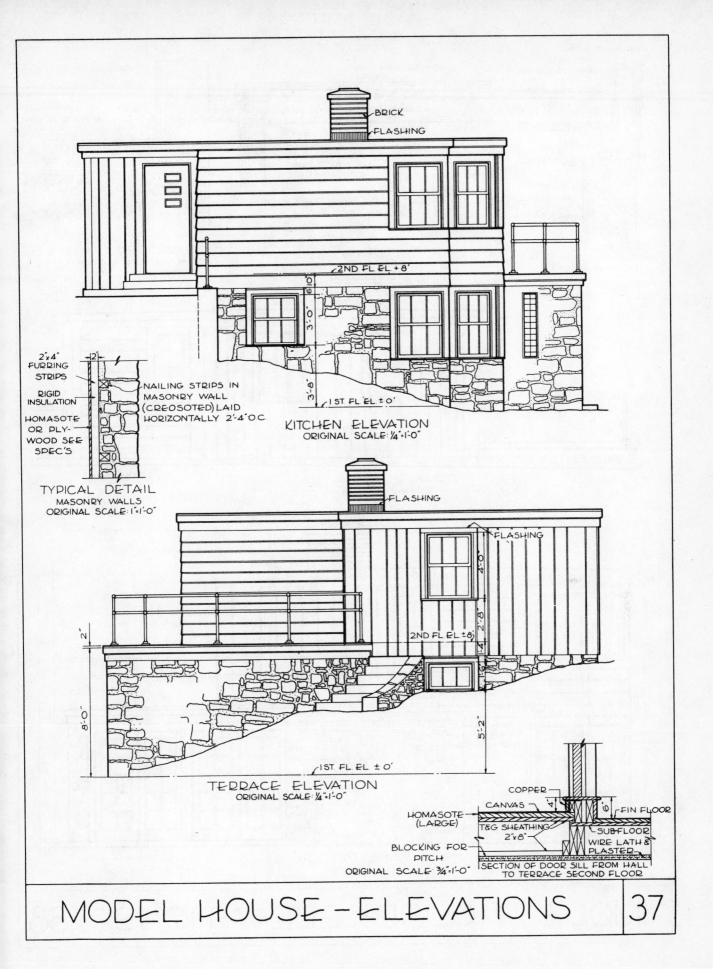

BRICK
FLASHING

2ND FL EL + 8'

6.0

3'-0"

3'-8"

1ST FL EL ± 0'

KITCHEN ELEVATION
ORIGINAL SCALE: ¼"=1'-0"

2"x4"
FURRING
STRIPS

RIGID
INSULATION

HOMASOTE
OR PLY-
WOOD SEE
SPEC'S

2"

NAILING STRIPS IN
MASONRY WALL
(CREOSOTED) LAID
HORIZONTALLY 2'-4" O.C.

TYPICAL DETAIL
MASONRY WALLS
ORIGINAL SCALE: 1"=1'-0"

FLASHING

FLASHING

4'-0"

2ND FL EL ± 8'

2'-8"

4"

2"

8'-0"

5'-2"

1ST FL EL ± 0'

TERRACE ELEVATION
ORIGINAL SCALE: ¼"=1'-0"

COPPER

CANVAS

4"

FIN FLOOR

6"

HOMASOTE
(LARGE)

T&G SHEATHING
2"x8"

SUBFLOOR

BLOCKING FOR
PITCH
ORIGINAL SCALE: ¾"=1'-0"

WIRE LATH &
PLASTER

SECTION OF DOOR SILL FROM HALL
TO TERRACE SECOND FLOOR

MODEL HOUSE – ELEVATIONS | 37

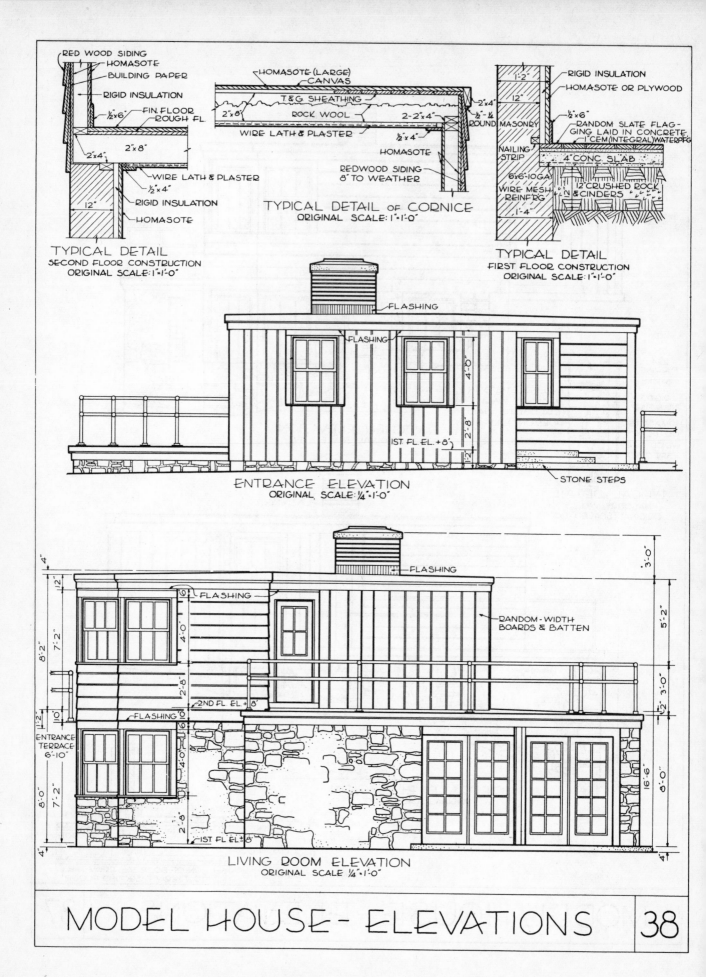

RED WOOD SIDING
HOMASOTE
BUILDING PAPER
RIGID INSULATION
FIN. FLOOR
ROUGH FL.
½"x6"
2"x8"
2"x4"
WIRE LATH & PLASTER
½"x4"
RIGID INSULATION
12"
HOMASOTE

TYPICAL DETAIL
SECOND FLOOR CONSTRUCTION
ORIGINAL SCALE: 1"=1'-0"

HOMASOTE (LARGE)
CANVAS
T & G SHEATHING
ROCK WOOL
WIRE LATH & PLASTER
2"x8"
2-2"x4"
2"x4"
½-1¼ ROUND
½"x4"
HOMASOTE
REDWOOD SIDING
8" TO WEATHER

TYPICAL DETAIL of CORNICE
ORIGINAL SCALE: 1"=1'-0"

RIGID INSULATION
HOMASOTE OR PLYWOOD
½"x6"
RANDOM SLATE FLAG-
GING LAID IN CONCRETE
1"CEM.(INTEGRAL)WATERPFG.
4" CONC. SLAB
12"CRUSHED ROCK
& CINDERS
1'-2"
12"
MASONRY
NAILING
STRIP
6x6-10GA.
WIRE MESH
REINFR'G.
1'-4"

TYPICAL DETAIL
FIRST FLOOR CONSTRUCTION
ORIGINAL SCALE: 1"=1'-0"

FLASHING
FLASHING
4'-0"
2'-8"
1'-2"
1ST FL. EL. +8'
STONE STEPS

ENTRANCE ELEVATION
ORIGINAL SCALE: ¼"=1'-0"

FLASHING
FLASHING
RANDOM-WIDTH
BOARDS & BATTEN
4"
12"
8'-2"
7'-2"
4'-0"
2'-8"
1'-2"
1'-0"
FLASHING
2ND FL. EL. +8'
ENTRANCE
TERRACE
6'-10"
8'-0"
7'-2"
2'-8"
4'-0"
1ST FL EL +8'
4"
3'-0"
5'-2"
1'-2"
3'-0"
8'-0"
16'-6"
4"

LIVING ROOM ELEVATION
ORIGINAL SCALE: ¼"=1'-0"

MODEL HOUSE - ELEVATIONS | 38

VIEW OF TERRACE

VIEW OF MAIN ENTRANCE

MODEL HOUSE—PERSPECTIVES | 39

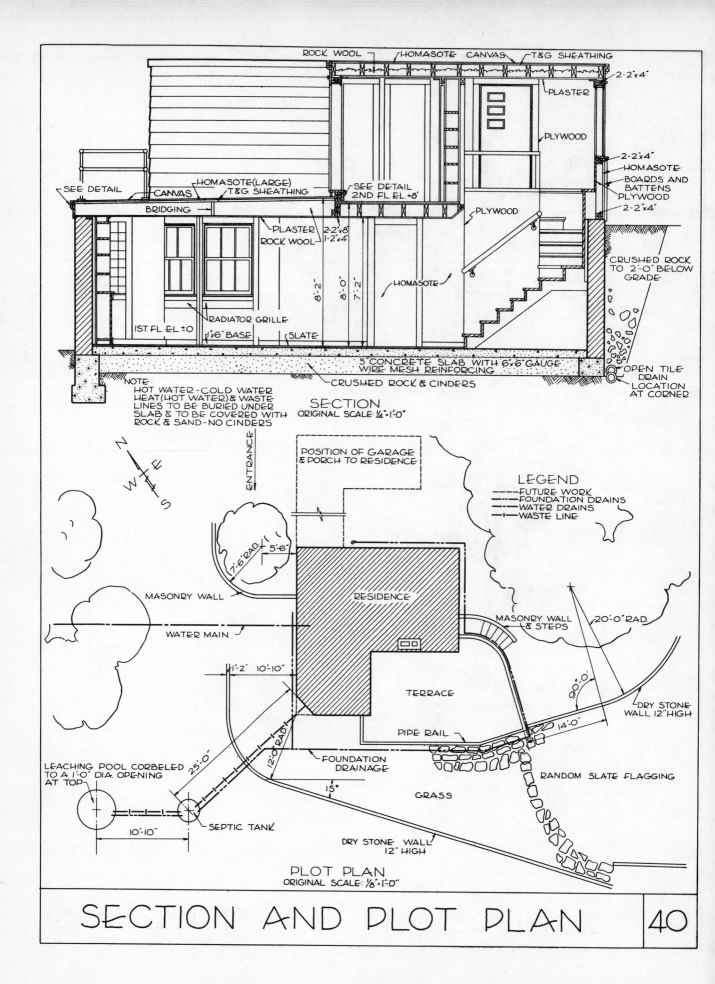

ROCK WOOL — HOMASOTE CANVAS — T&G. SHEATHING

2-2"x4"

PLASTER

PLYWOOD

2-2"x4"
HOMASOTE
BOARDS AND
BATTENS
PLYWOOD
2-2"x4"

CRUSHED ROCK
TO 2'-0" BELOW
GRADE

SEE DETAIL

CANVAS — HOMASOTE (LARGE)
T&G. SHEATHING

SEE DETAIL
2ND FL. EL. +8'

BRIDGING

PLASTER
ROCK WOOL

2-2"x8"
1-2"x4"

PLYWOOD

HOMASOTE

IST. FL. EL. ±0

RADIATOR GRILLE

1"x6" BASE

SLATE

8'-2"   8'-0"   7'-2"

OPEN TILE
DRAIN
LOCATION
AT CORNER

5" CONCRETE SLAB WITH 6"x6" GAUGE
WIRE MESH REINFORCING

CRUSHED ROCK & CINDERS

NOTE:
HOT WATER-COLD WATER
HEAT (HOT WATER) & WASTE
LINES TO BE BURIED UNDER
SLAB & TO BE COVERED WITH
ROCK & SAND-NO CINDERS

SECTION
ORIGINAL SCALE: 1/4"-1'-0"

ENTRANCE

POSITION OF GARAGE
& PORCH TO RESIDENCE

N W E S

7'-6" RAD.   5'-6"

MASONRY WALL

WATER MAIN

LEGEND
------- FUTURE WORK
-·-·- FOUNDATION DRAINS
-··- WATER DRAINS
-···- WASTE LINE

RESIDENCE

MASONRY WALL
& STEPS

20'-0" RAD.

1'-2"   10'-10"

TERRACE

PIPE RAIL

90'-0"

DRY STONE
WALL 12" HIGH

LEACHING POOL CORBELED
TO A 1'-0" DIA. OPENING
AT TOP

25'-0"

12'-0" RAD.

FOUNDATION
DRAINAGE

14'-0"

RANDOM SLATE FLAGGING

15°

GRASS

10'-10"   SEPTIC TANK

DRY STONE WALL
12" HIGH

PLOT PLAN
ORIGINAL SCALE: 1/8"-1'-0"

SECTION AND PLOT PLAN   40

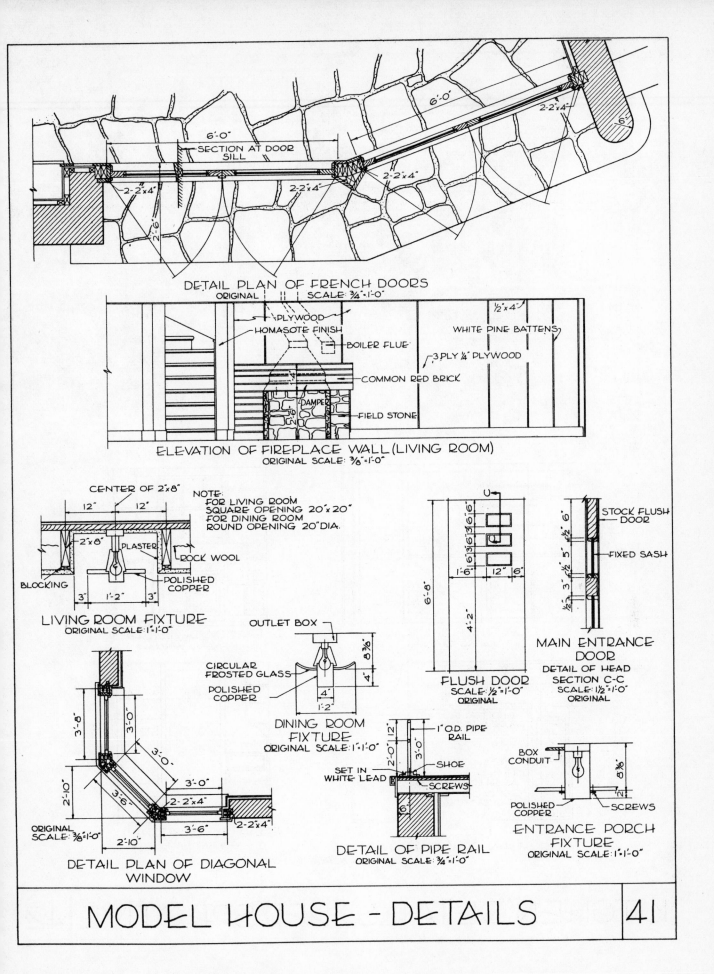

DETAIL PLAN OF FRENCH DOORS
ORIGINAL SCALE: ¾"=1'-0"

ELEVATION OF FIREPLACE WALL (LIVING ROOM)
ORIGINAL SCALE: ⅜"=1'-0"

LIVING ROOM FIXTURE
ORIGINAL SCALE: 1"=1'-0"

NOTE:
FOR LIVING ROOM
SQUARE OPENING 20"x20"
FOR DINING ROOM
ROUND OPENING 20"DIA.

DINING ROOM FIXTURE
ORIGINAL SCALE: 1"=1'-0"

FLUSH DOOR
SCALE: ½"=1'-0"
ORIGINAL

MAIN ENTRANCE DOOR
DETAIL OF HEAD
SECTION C-C
SCALE: 1½"=1'-0"
ORIGINAL

DETAIL PLAN OF DIAGONAL WINDOW
ORIGINAL SCALE: ⅜"=1'-0"

DETAIL OF PIPE RAIL
ORIGINAL SCALE: ¾"=1'-0"

ENTRANCE PORCH FIXTURE
ORIGINAL SCALE: 1"=1'-0"

MODEL HOUSE - DETAILS   41

KITCHEN PERSPECTIVE

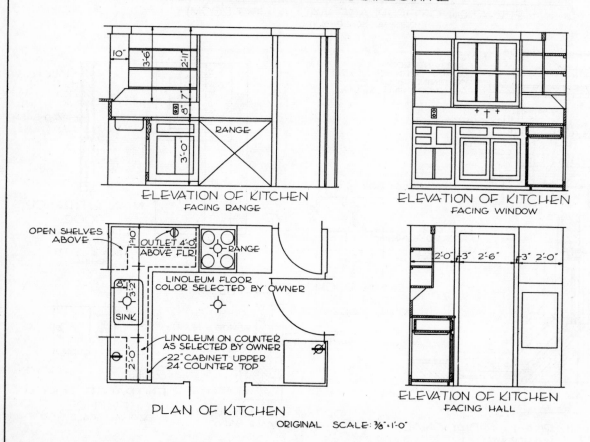

ELEVATION OF KITCHEN
FACING RANGE

ELEVATION OF KITCHEN
FACING WINDOW

PLAN OF KITCHEN

ORIGINAL SCALE: 3/8"=1'-0"

ELEVATION OF KITCHEN
FACING HALL

KITCHEN DETAILS PERSPECTIVE | 42

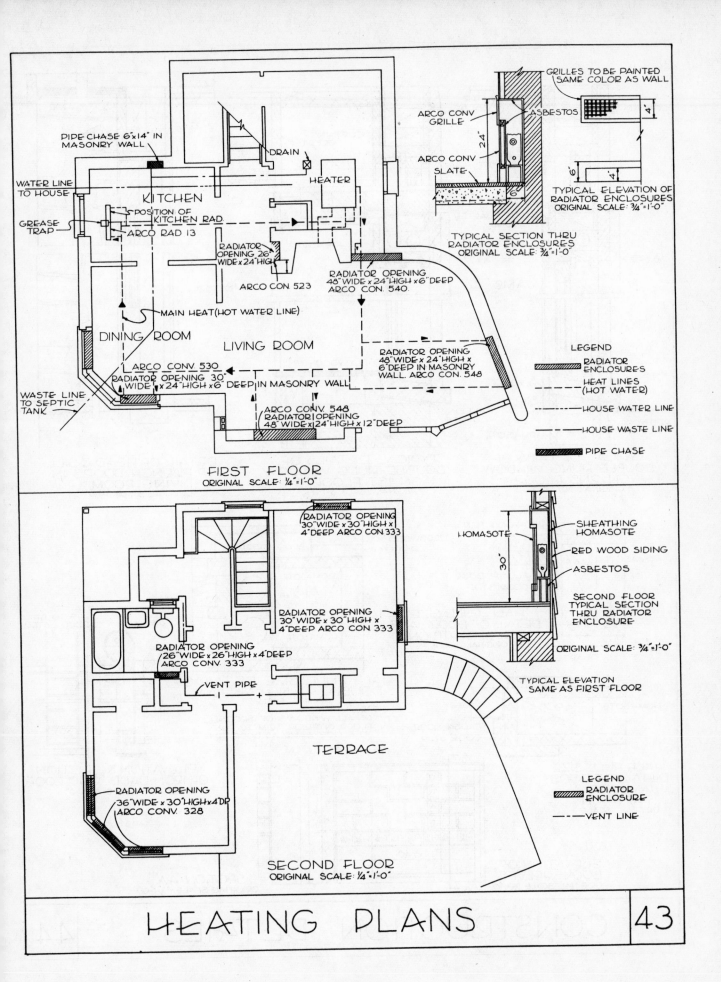

GRILLES TO BE PAINTED
SAME COLOR AS WALL

ARCO CONV
GRILLE

ASBESTOS

ARCO CONV

SLATE

TYPICAL SECTION THRU
RADIATOR ENCLOSURES
ORIGINAL SCALE: ¾"=1'-0"

TYPICAL ELEVATION OF
RADIATOR ENCLOSURES
ORIGINAL SCALE: ¾"=1'-0"

PIPE CHASE 6"x14" IN
MASONRY WALL

DRAIN

HEATER

WATER LINE
TO HOUSE

KITCHEN

POSITION OF
KITCHEN RAD.

GREASE
TRAP

ARCO RAD 13

RADIATOR
OPENING 26"
WIDE x 24" HIGH

RADIATOR OPENING
48" WIDE x 24" HIGH x 6" DEEP
ARCO CON. 540.

ARCO CON. 523

MAIN HEAT (HOT WATER LINE)

DINING ROOM

LIVING ROOM

RADIATOR OPENING
48" WIDE x 24" HIGH x
6" DEEP IN MASONRY
WALL. ARCO CON. 548

ARCO CONV. 530

RADIATOR OPENING 30"
WIDE x 24" HIGH x 6" DEEP IN MASONRY WALL

WASTE LINE
TO SEPTIC
TANK

ARCO CONV. 548
RADIATOR OPENING
48" WIDE x 24" HIGH x 12" DEEP

LEGEND

RADIATOR
ENCLOSURES

HEAT LINES
(HOT WATER)

HOUSE WATER LINE

HOUSE WASTE LINE

PIPE CHASE

FIRST FLOOR
ORIGINAL SCALE: ¼"=1'-0"

RADIATOR OPENING
30" WIDE x 30" HIGH x
4" DEEP ARCO CON. 333

SHEATHING
HOMASOTE

HOMASOTE

RED WOOD SIDING

ASBESTOS

RADIATOR OPENING
30" WIDE x 30" HIGH x
4" DEEP ARCO CON. 333

SECOND FLOOR
TYPICAL SECTION
THRU RADIATOR
ENCLOSURE

RADIATOR OPENING
26" WIDE x 26" HIGH x 4" DEEP
ARCO CONV. 333

ORIGINAL SCALE: ¾"=1'-0"

VENT PIPE

TYPICAL ELEVATION
SAME AS FIRST FLOOR

TERRACE

RADIATOR OPENING
36" WIDE x 30" HIGH x 4" DP
ARCO CONV. 328

LEGEND

RADIATOR
ENCLOSURE

VENT LINE

SECOND FLOOR
ORIGINAL SCALE: ¼"=1'-0"

HEATING PLANS

43

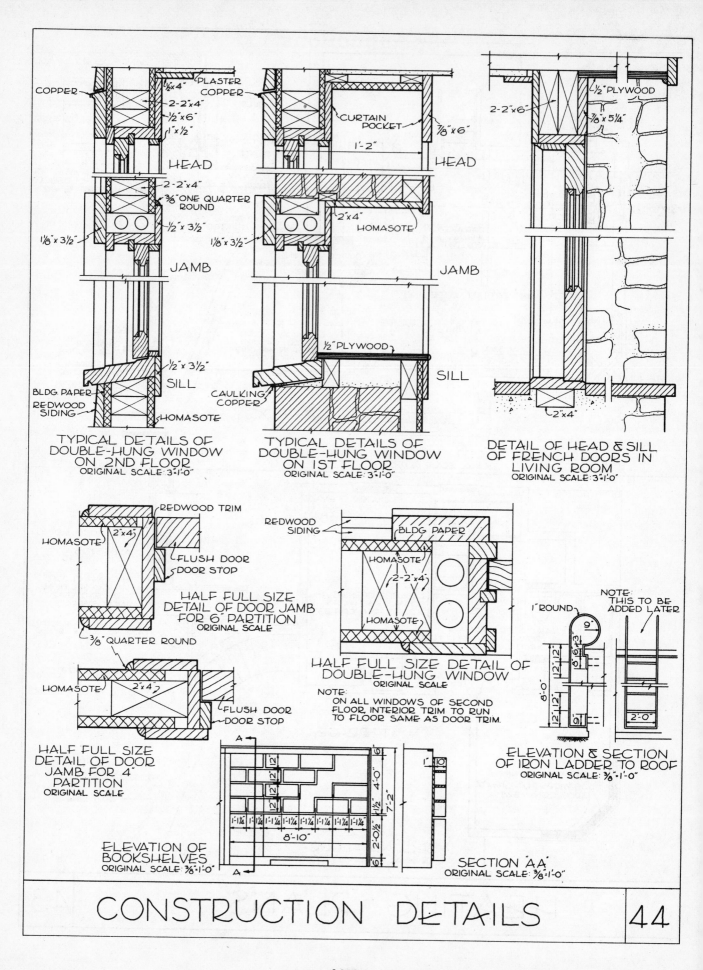

COPPER

¼"x 4" PLASTER
COPPER

2-2"x4"

½"x 6"

1"x ½"

HEAD

2-2"x4"

⅜" ONE QUARTER ROUND

½" x 3½"

⅛" x 3½"

JAMB

½" x 3½"

SILL

BLDG. PAPER

REDWOOD SIDING

HOMASOTE

TYPICAL DETAILS OF DOUBLE-HUNG WINDOW ON 2ND FLOOR
ORIGINAL SCALE: 3"-1'-0"

CURTAIN POCKET

⅞" x 6"

1'-2"

HEAD

2"x 4"

HOMASOTE

⅛" x 3½"

JAMB

½" PLYWOOD

SILL

CAULKING COPPER

TYPICAL DETAILS OF DOUBLE-HUNG WINDOW ON 1ST FLOOR
ORIGINAL SCALE: 3"-1'-0"

½" PLYWOOD

2-2"x6"

⅞" x 5¼"

2"x 4"

DETAIL OF HEAD & SILL OF FRENCH DOORS IN LIVING ROOM
ORIGINAL SCALE: 3"-1'-0"

REDWOOD TRIM

HOMASOTE

2"x 4"

FLUSH DOOR

DOOR STOP

HALF FULL SIZE DETAIL OF DOOR JAMB FOR 6" PARTITION
ORIGINAL SCALE

⅜" QUARTER ROUND

HOMASOTE

2"x 4"

FLUSH DOOR
DOOR STOP

HALF FULL SIZE DETAIL OF DOOR JAMB FOR 4" PARTITION
ORIGINAL SCALE

REDWOOD SIDING

BLDG. PAPER

HOMASOTE

2-2"x 4"

HOMASOTE

HALF FULL SIZE DETAIL OF DOUBLE-HUNG WINDOW
ORIGINAL SCALE

NOTE:
ON ALL WINDOWS OF SECOND FLOOR INTERIOR TRIM TO RUN TO FLOOR SAME AS DOOR TRIM.

1" ROUND

NOTE: THIS TO BE ADDED LATER

9"

8'-0"

12½"

12½"

12½"

2'-0"

ELEVATION & SECTION OF IRON LADDER TO ROOF
ORIGINAL SCALE: ⅜"-1'-0"

ELEVATION OF BOOKSHELVES
ORIGINAL SCALE: ⅜"-1'-0"

1-1¼" 1-1¼" 1-1¼" 1-1¼"

8'-10"

A

12" 12" 12" 12"

6"

4'-0"

1½"

7'-2"

2'-0½"

6"

SECTION "A-A"
ORIGINAL SCALE: ⅜"-1'-0"

CONSTRUCTION DETAILS

44

Specifications

The specifications cover all the features that are not shown on the blueprints, such as the quality and quantity of the materials, and the methods to be used in the construction or the manner in which the work is to be conducted. Like the plans themselves, they are indispensable to the builder. They are generally typed and accompany a set of drawings.

When the general contractor undertakes the task of constructing the building, he is furnished, in addition to a complete set of working plans, all the specifications of the various building trades. Should the general contractor hire a subcontractor in order to perform the work of a particular trade, this subcontractor must be furnished not only the drawings but also the specifications pertaining to his trade.

The following numbered sections represent specifications for the various building trades:

1. Excavation, backfill, and grading
2. Concrete foundations
3. Stonework
4. Rough carpentry
5. Roofing, sheet metal, and waterproofing
6. Concrete fill and cement finish
7. Lathing and plastering
8. Finished carpentry and millwork
9. Finished hardware
10. Glass and glazing
11. Plumbing
12. Heating
13. Painting
14. Electricity

A specification for a particular building trade may be divided as follows:

(a) General conditions
(b) Scope of work
(c) Work not included
(d) Workmanship

General Conditions

Under this heading the contractor is referred to the general conditions of the contract of the American Institute of Architects, which binds him to carry out the work according to standard accepted practice, to adhere to the methods of construction as shown on the approved plans, and to do the work in a professional manner.

Scope of Work

It would not be practical to allow the contractor of a particular building trade to determine for himself, from the blueprints, the work he is to perform. Under this item the contractor is told precisely the work he is to do and the labor, materials, and equipment he is to furnish in order to execute his work properly.

Work Not Included

The work of certain building trades is sometimes so closely related that it becomes necessary to tell the contractor the work that is not to be included in his own. For example, the excavating contractor may be informed not to include in his work the excavation for a septic tank. This task belongs to the plumbing contractor because he is more familiar with this work and hence more efficient in the long run.

Workmanship

Under this item, the contractor is told how to do the work. For example, although the mason contractor knows how to lay the brick, it is still necessary to tell him the type of bond that is desired. The painting contractor knows how to paint, but again it is necessary to tell him the number of coats desired and the colors he is to select.

The following specifications are for the model house, though they are more complete than is generally required for this type of building. The general procedure for a large building is the same.

DIVISION 1
Excavation, Backfill, and Grading

General Conditions

The general conditions of the contract of the American Institute of Architects (current edition) shall form a part of this division, together with the special conditions, to which the contractor is referred.

Scope

The work under this division includes all labor, materials, equipment and appliances required for the complete execution of all excavation, backfill, and grading as shown on the scale and detail drawings, or as may reasonably be inferred to make this division complete, which is generally as follows:

(a) General excavation
(b) Hand excavation
(c) Drain-trench excavation
(d) Excavation and backfill for septic tank and leaching pool
(e) Backfill around walls and under floors
(f) Rough grading (10 ft. from building line)

It is to be assumed that the contractor shall include all items of labor, materials, equipment, and appliances necessary to complete the work, whether specifically mentioned in the specifications or not, except only those items specifically mentioned as omitted from this division of the specifications.

Work Not Included

The following items will be performed under other divisions of this contract, separate contracts, and future work, and will not be included as a part of this division:

(a) Finish grading
(b) Excavation or backfill for plumbing and heating

General Excavation

The contractor shall excavate for occupied spaces in the basement, which shall include the storage and heater room, living room, dining room, kitchen and storage closet, area for terrace steps, and outside area adjacent to kitchen for retaining wall.

The excavation shall be carried down to the underside of the living-room floor construction. The contractor shall make all required allowance beyond the foundation walls and retaining walls for the sloping of banks, sheet piling, forms for foundations, and waterproofing of foundation walls.

All excavated material shall remain on the site to be used for backfill and rough grading herein specified.

Rock excavation is not contemplated in the contract work. Quote unit price for removal of rock encountered in excavation over 27 cu. ft. This unit price is to include the removal of the material from the site.

Hand Excavation

Excavate for all footings under foundation walls and footing for chimney. The excavation shall be made wide enough to allow for the installation of forms for footings.

Drain-Trench Excavation

Where terra-cotta drains to septic tank are shown on the drawings, this contractor shall do all excavation of trenches required for their installation. All trenches shall be 3 ft. below the lowest finished grade level and shall slope toward the septic tank at a pitch of ¼ in. to every foot of length. Trenches shall be of sufficient width to afford proper working conditions. Where required, furnish and install all shoring, sheet piling, and bracing to hold the banks in place.

Excavation for Septic Tank and Leaching Pool

The contractor shall excavate for the septic tank and leaching pool. The excavation of the septic tank shall be 4 ft. below the house sewer inlet. The width of the excavation shall be 6 ft. 6 in. and the length 9 ft.

The excavation for the leaching pool shall be 5 ft. below the inlet and shall be dug to a diameter of 5 ft. 8 in.

After the septic tank and leaching pool have been constructed by others, the contractor shall backfill all trenches and areas around septic tank and leaching pool up to an elevation of the present grade.

Backfill Around Walls and Under Floors

After the footings, foundation, and retaining walls are built and other work required on the exterior of the walls is completed, the contractor shall backfill carefully around these walls with good clean earth up to the level and grades indicated on the drawings.

The backfill under floors shall be spread, sprinkled, and tamped or rolled to a solid and compact condition, ready to receive the cement floor construction installed by others.

Rough Grading

All excavated earth not used for backfill shall be spread around the building to the level or levels to within 6 in. of the finished grade and 10 ft. from the building line.

DIVISION 2
Concrete Foundations

General Conditions

The general conditions of the contract of the American Institute of Architects (current edition) shall form a part of this division, together with the special conditions, to which the contractor is referred.

Scope

The work under this division includes all labor, materials, equipment, and appliances required for the complete execution of all concrete footings and foundations as shown on the scale and detail drawings, or as may reasonably be inferred to make this division complete, which is generally as follows:

(a) Concrete footings

(b) Concrete foundation walls

The contractor shall include all items of labor, materials, equipment, and appliances necessary to complete the work, whether specifically mentioned in the specifications or not, except only those items specifically mentioned as omitted from this division of the specifications.

Work Not Included

The following items will be performed under other divisions of this contract and will not be included as part of this division:

(a) Excavation, backfill, or grading

(b) Reinforced-concrete floor construction

(c) Concrete floor fill

(d) Fieldstone walls

(e) Concrete steps

Materials

Water. All water used shall be clean, free from oil, acid, organic matter, or other deleterious substances. It shall be equal in all physical and chemical properties to potable water.

Sand. All sand used shall be clean and sharp, composed of durable particles, free from mica, loam, organic matter, and suitable in every way to the purpose for which it is intended.

Sand for concrete shall be so graded that when dry 100 per cent shall pass a ¼ sieve; 90 to 100 per cent shall pass a No. 4 sieve; 45 to 75 per cent shall pass a No. 14 sieve; 5 to 25 per cent shall pass a No. 45 sieve; and not more than 6 per cent shall pass a No. 100 sieve.

Cement. Cement shall be an approved brand of Portland cement conforming to all the current standard specifications and tests for Portland cement, serial designations 09, of the American Society for Testing Materials.

Proportion of Concrete. All concrete shall consist of Portland cement, sand, and coarse aggregate in the proportions 1:2:5 by volume. In general, a mixture shall be used which contains the minimum amount of water consistent with the required workability.

Concrete Mixing. All concrete shall be mixed in an approved type of batch mixer. Hand mixing shall not be permitted except for small batches as approved by the architect. Mixing shall be continued for at least 1¼ minutes after all materials are in the mixing drum. Batching or weighing apparatus shall be provided to measure all materials accurately.

All concrete shall be used before initial set has taken place. No retempering will be allowed.

Central mixing or transit may be used, provided the latest requirements of the American Society for Testing Materials' standard specifications for ready-mixed concrete, serial designation C-94, are fully observed.

Forms and Supports

Provide all forms and supports required. Forms shall conform to the shape and dimensions shown on the drawings and shall be sufficiently tight to prevent leakage of mortar and shall be properly braced or tied together so as to maintain position and shape.

No forms shall be removed until the concrete has hardened sufficiently to sustain its own weight and any construction loads liable to come upon it.

DIVISION 3
Fieldstone Walls

General Conditions

The general conditions of the contract of the American Institute of Architects (current edition) shall form a part of this division, together with the special conditions, to which the contractor is referred.

Scope

The work under this division includes all labor, materials, equipment, and appliances required for the complete execution of all fieldstone masonry, as shown on the scale and detail drawings, or as may be reasonably inferred to make this division complete, which is generally as follows:

(a) Fieldstone walls from tops of concrete footings to second-floor level as indicated on drawings

(b) Fieldstone retaining wall near front entry, and fieldstone wall for steps to terrace

(c) Common red brick and fieldstone for fireplace and the furnishing and setting of fireplace cleanout and damper and all brickwork for chimney

(d) Flue linings, thimbles, and cleanouts for chimney

(e) Fieldstone for 12-in. dry walls

(f) Furnish and install all steel railings, bolts, anchors, wood blocking, and all other miscellaneous iron or wood shown on the drawings or otherwise required.

It is to be assumed that the foregoing items and as hereinafter described in this division of the specification are only generally complete.

The contractor shall include all items of labor, materials, equipment, and appliances necessary to complete the work, whether specifically mentioned in the specifications or not, except only those items specifically mentioned as omitted from this division of the specifications.

Work Not Included

The following items will be performed under other divisions of this contract, separate contract, and future work, and will not be included as part of this division:

(a) Furnishing bolts, anchors, or other miscellaneous iron except that specified in Item (f) under Scope of this division

(b) Concrete foundations, fills, and cement finishes on reinforced-concrete slabs.

Materials

Water, Cement, and Sand. Water, cement, and sand shall be as specified in Concrete Foundations, Division 2 of this specification.

Hydrated Lime. Hydrated lime shall be an approved brand of mason's hydrate and shall conform to the specifications for hydrated lime for structural purposes, serial designation 06-31, of the American Society for Testing Materials, current edition.

Common Red Brick. All common red brick shall be made of clay or shale, shall be uniform in size, evenly and not under- or overburned, dense and sound, free from cracks or badly warped surfaces, and shall conform to the latest standard specifications, serial designation C-62, of the American Society for Testing Materials.

Flue Linings. Flue linings shall be of smooth terra cotta of sizes as shown on the drawings and details.

Cast-Iron Cleanout and Damper. Cast-iron cleanout and damper shall be the sizes required and of stock design approved by the architect.

Mortars. Mortars for fieldstone and brickwork shall be cement mortar consisting of 1 part of Portland cement and 3 parts sand, tempered with not more than 1 part of hydrated lime to 10 parts of cement.

Mortar for fieldstone inside of fireplace shall consist of fire clay mixed with water to the proper consistency for proper workability.

Workmanship

Fieldstone walls shall be of the thickness shown on the drawings with 2 x 4 creosoted nailing strips laid horizontally and spaced 2 ft. 4 in. on center with the lowest strip a maximum of 4 in. from the finished floor.

The contractor shall use the Flagg method of building the forms. This instruction generally implies the use of forms only on the inside faces of the fieldstone walls.

He shall provide all the material required for the forms and bracing and shall remove them when the work is completed. The fieldstone shall be laid in full beds and shall be thoroughly slushed up with mortar.

Fieldstone retaining wall near front entry and fieldstone wall for steps to terrace shall require no forms.

Brickwork shall be laid in common bond with headers every sixth course, and shall be laid with a concave joint in full beds and shall be thoroughly slushed up with mortar at every course. Mortar joints shall not exceed ½ in. in thickness. All horizontal and vertical joints shall be straight, true to line, and parallel one with the other.

No brickwork or stonework shall be laid in freezing weather, except as directed by the architect. All brickwork or stonework shall be properly protected at all times during its progress and until completion.

Dry Stone Walls. Dry stone walls shall be laid to the thickness and height as shown on the drawings.

Built-in Work

The contractor shall, as part of his contract, cooperate with the contractors for architectural iron, windows, and doors, mechanical trades, and finished carpentry and with other contractors whose work is to be built in, or to be set, in conjunction with masonry.

DIVISION 4
Rough Carpentry

General Conditions

The general conditions of the contract of the American Institute of Architects (current edition) shall form a part of this division, together with the special conditions, to which the contractor is referred.

Scope

The work under this division includes all labor, materials, equipment, and appliances required for the complete execution of all rough carpentry, as shown on the scale and detail drawings, or as may reasonably be inferred to make this division complete, which is generally as follows:

(a) Wood floor and ceiling beams
(b) Wall plates
(c) Wood stud partitions
(d) 2 x 4 furring strips inside fieldstone walls
(e) 1¼ x 3 cross bridging
(f) Square-edge subflooring
(g) Tongue-and-groove roof sheathing
(h) Outside wall sheathing—Homasote
(i) Furnishing and setting of beam hangers, bolts, ties, anchors, nails, spikes, screws, and similar items required for all rough carpentry
(j) Rock-wool insulation

The contractor shall include all items of labor, materials, equipment, and appliances necessary to complete the work, whether specifically mentioned in the specifications or not, except only those items specifically mentioned as omitted from this division of the specifications.

Work Not Included

The following items will be performed under other divisions of this contract, separate contract, and future work, and will not be included as a part of this division:

(a) Finish wood floors
(b) Wood stairs
(c) Wood forms for concrete work except rough wood floor under deadening in bathrooms

Requirements of Wood

General. Classification of grading, except as otherwise specified, is based on the following grading rules:

West Coast Lumbermen's Association, booklet No. 10, *Standard Grading and Dressing Rules,* Effective July 1934, for Douglas Fir, Sitka Spruce and West Coast Hemlock

Southern Pine Association, *Standard Specifications,* Effective June 1, 1936, for Grades of Longleaf and Shortleaf Southern Pine

Western Pine Association, *Standard Grading Rules,* Effective September 1, 1936, for Ponderosa Pine, Sugar Pine and Idaho White Pine

Materials

Framing. All framing 2 in. and over in thickness shall be No. 1 common or dimension, 15 per cent No. 2 allowed fir or Southern yellow pine.

Two-inch material shall be dressed four sides.

Roof Sheathing Roof sheathing shall be No. 2 common dimension Southern yellow pine, Douglas fir, West Coast hemlock, or Sitka spruce.

Outside Wall Sheathing. Outside wall sheathing shall be ½-in. Homasote panels. Blocking, fillers, bridging, and grounds may be No. 2 dimension Southern yellow pine, Douglas fir, West Coast hemlock, or Sitka spruce.

All materials shall be of the size and thickness as called for on the drawings or as herein specified.

Each piece of lumber shall bear the official grade and the identification mark of the association under whose rules it is graded and the identification mark or number of the mill that manufactured it.

Framing

All work shall be properly framed to the various pitches and levels shown on the drawings, be well braced, closely fitted, thoroughly spiked, accurately set, and rigidly secured in place.

Floor beams under partitions running in the same direction as the beams shall be double.

The contractor shall do all necessary cutting and framing of beams for plumbing and heating pipes in a manner not to impair the carrying capacity of the floor loads. Headers and trimmers at chimney and stair opening shall be doubled and supported by proper side-beam hangers. Trimmers around chimney shall have a 4-in. clearance.

Wall Plates. Wall plates shall be double 2 x 4's set over anchor bolts, built into the masonry walls by the mason contractor, on a full bed of cement mortar. They shall be true and level in their entire length and securely bolted in position. Corners shall be lapped and end joints between pieces of plates shall be staggered and lapped with the other member of the plate. No straight joint entirely through the full width of the plate will be allowed.

Stud Partitions. Stud partitions shall be 2 x 4 in. spaced 16 in. center to center and shall have horizontal sill and cap with one row of block bridging between floor and ceiling. Where a partition acts as a bearing partition, the cap will be doubled. Double all studs around all openings.

Wall Furring. Wall furring shall be 2 x 4's set with 4-in. face against the wall and spaced to fit standard widths of Homasote or plywood panels. Furring shall be securely fastened to the inside face of all exterior fieldstone walls, running vertically from floor to ceiling.

Cross Bridging. Cross bridging shall be placed midway between bearings of all wood floor beams. All bridging shall be cut to fit and shall be securely nailed in place with two nails at each bearing. The nailing at the bottom of the beams shall not be done until after the rough underfloor has been laid.

Rough Underfloor. Rough underfloor shall be 1 x 4 square edge laid diagonally across floor beams and fastened with two nails at each bearing. All joints shall be made on solid bearing and shall be staggered.

In the bathroom where title floor is called for, the underfloor shall be cut between the beams and fastened to cleats secured to the sides of the beams. The top of the beams in this area shall be cut to a thin edge.

Tongue-and-Groove Roof Sheathing

The contractor shall cover the entire roof area with wood sheathing 25/32 in. thick, dressed, tongue-and-groove material not over 9¼ in. wide on face, nailed to each bearing with three nails. All joints shall be made on full solid bearing and all ends shall be nailed down tight.

Joints shall be well broken. All tongue-and-groove material shall be driven up tight. All nailing strips needed to give proper nailing for sheathing shall be provided. All roof sheathing shall be laid at right angles to the supporting members.

Insulation

The contractor shall insulate with rock wool all outside frame walls, all roof areas, and all stone walls as indicated on the scale and detail drawings.

All exterior walls shall be insulated with 2-in. rock-wool batts installed between 2- x 4-in. studs and 2- x 4-in. furring.

The entire roof area of the second floor shall have 4-in. rock-wool batts installed between roof rafters.

The entire ceiling of the living room on the first floor shall have 4-in. rock-wool batts installed between ceiling joists.

Rock-wool shall be batt type as manufactured by Johns-Manville or approved equal.

Outside Wall Sheathing

All outside wall sheathing, from the bottom of the second floor joists up to the underside of the roof boards, shall be covered with ½-in. Homasote standard-size panels. Panels shall join at studs and shall be securely fastened with 8-penny nails, one nail in every 4 to 6 in.

Rough Hardware, Anchors, Joist Hangers

The contractor shall furnish all nails, screws, bolts, ties, hangers, straps, and all other items needed for the proper installation of all carpentry work. All shall be of the proper sizes to hold the members in place securely.

Relation with Other Trades

The contractor shall cooperate with the work of other trades. He shall make sure that all pipes, conduits, outlet boxes, and all other work of other trades are properly located and secured before proceeding with his work.

DIVISION 5

Roofing, Sheet Metal, and Waterproofing

General Conditions

The general conditions of the contract of the American Institute of Architects (current edition) shall form a part of this division, together with the special conditions, to which the contractor is referred.

Scope

The work under this division includes all labor, materials, equipment, and appliances required for the complete execution of all roofing, sheet metal, and waterproofing, as shown on the scale and detail drawings, or as may reasonably be inferred to make this division complete, which is generally as follows:

(a) Canvas roof decks
(b) Copper flashings
(c) Copper gutters and leaders
(d) Dampproofing
(e) Pipe railing for terrace

The contractor shall include all items of labor, materials, equipment, and appliances necessary to complete the work, whether specifically mentioned in the specifications or not.

Materials

Finish for roof and terrace deck shall be extra-heavy canvas laid on ½-in. Homasote according to manufacturer's specification. Copper flashing shall be 16-oz. soft copper, except for leaders and gutters, which shall be 16-oz. hard copper.

Leader connections shall be the flat square type of standard manufacture.

Description of Work

Canvas Roofs. Before proceeding with roofing work of any nature, the roofer shall examine all roof surfaces so intended for application of the canvas and report for correction any and all defects therein that will interfere with the execution of his work and guarantee thereof.

The contractor shall cover all roof surfaces with extra-heavy canvas in the manner set forth by the manufacturer's specifications. The canvas shall be carried over and around the 2 x 4 cornice as indicated on the scale and detail drawings.

Flashings. Flashing around the chimney shall extend 2 in. against the flues.

Base and counter flashing shall be required where pipes and vents pass through the roofs.

The contractor shall supply the carpenter with all flashing for window caps.

Gutters. Gutters shall be of the hanging type. Where joints occur they shall be lapped 1 in., soldered in the direction of flow. Supports shall be at every 3 ft. 0 in., with hangers and braces of standard manufacture. Gutters shall be properly pitched to downspouts.

Leaders. Leaders shall be furnished where required. They shall be of the proper size, soldered at vertical joints. Supports shall be spaced 8 ft. 0 in. apart. They shall be cemented at joints where connecting to underground leaders.

The contractor shall furnish a written guarantee covering a period of 10 years, thereby binding himself to repair or replace faulty work or material completed under this specification. This work is to be done without additional compensation beyond the amount of this contract.

Dampproofing. One coat of pitch shall be applied on all interior faces of stone walls.

Pipe Railing. A railing of 1-in. standard galvanized-steel pipe with elbows, tees, crosses, and shoes shall be installed on perimeter of roof terrace as shown on drawings and details.

DIVISION 6

Concrete Fill and Cement Finish

General Conditions

The general conditions of the contract of the American Institute of Architects (current edition) shall form a part of this division, together with the special conditions, to which the contractor is referred.

Scope

The work under this division includes all labor, materials, equipment, and appliances required for the complete execution of all concrete fill and cement finish as shown on the scale and detail drawings, or as may reasonably be inferred to make this division complete, which is generally as follows:

(a) One inch random slate flagging laid on 1-in. cement on 4-in. concrete slab with 6- x 6-in. No. 10 gauge wire-mesh reinforcing over 12-in. crushed rock and cinders over entire first-floor area and outside area of living-room entrance

(b) One inch cement finish on 4-in. concrete slab on 12-in. crushed rock and cinders for front entry

(c) Concrete steps to terrace

The contractor shall include all items of labor, materials, equipment, and appliances necessary to complete the work, whether specifically mentioned in the specifications or not, except only those items specifically mentioned as omitted from this division of the specifications.

Work Not Included

The following items will be performed under other divisions of this contract, separate contract, and will not be included as a part of this division:

(a) Concrete footings and foundations

(b) Fieldstone walls

Materials

Water, cement, and sand shall be as specified in Concrete Foundations, Division 2 of this specification.

Cinders shall be clean steam-boiler anthracite cinders, properly screened. Ashes will not be permitted. Cinders shall be free from injurious amount of ash, unburned coal, coke, or other harmful materials, and shall pass through a ¾-in. square-mesh screen.

Workmanship

Before placing the dry cinder fill on the entire first-floor level and directly outside the French doors of the living room, the contractor shall level the earth and tamp it solid. Cinders shall be evenly spread to the thickness called for on the drawings, ready to receive the stone concrete.

Over the entire first-floor area, the contractor shall provide a 4-in. stone-concrete floor on the cinder fill. Concrete shall be a 1-3-6 mix composed of 1 part cement, 3 parts sand, and 6 parts broken stone or gravel. Concrete shall be solidly packed to within 2 in. of the finished floor level.

On the 4-in. stone-concrete floor this contractor shall next lay a leveling or screed bed composed of 1 part of Portland cement and 3 parts of sand over the entire first-floor area, including the living-room entry.

Into this bed, while it is still plastic, he shall embed 1 in. of random slate flagging in the living- and dining-room areas, the kitchen, the hall, and the area directly outside the French doors of the living room. No slate flagging is to be laid in the heater room, the closet, and under the stairs.

Floors shall be true and level. Where floor drains are noted, the floor shall pitch to them.

Concrete Steps and Landings

Concrete steps and landing to terrace and main entry step shall be stone concrete and of the same mix as specified for concrete floors over cinder fill. Steps shall have a finish coat and shall be screeded to proper level. They shall be wood-floated and then steel-troweled to a smooth, hard finish.

Relations with Other Trades

The contractor shall cooperate with the work of other trades. He shall make certain that all pipes, conduits, and other mechanical lines are properly located and secured before proceeding with his work.

Protection

Concrete and/or cement finish shall not be placed during rain that would injure the work. Proper precaution shall be taken to prevent premature drying out of concrete and cement finish.

All work shall be protected against freezing, disfigurement, and damage of any kind. The contractor shall provide all coverings, equipment, and other items as needed to protect and carry on the work.

DIVISION 7

Lathing and Plastering

General Conditions

The general conditions of the contract of the American Institute of Architects (current edition) shall form a part of this division, together with the special conditions, to which the contractor is referred.

Scope

The work under this division includes all labor, materials, equipment, and appliances required for the complete execution of all lathing and plastering, as shown on the scale and detail drawings, or as may reasonably be inferred to make this division complete, which is generally as follows:

One coat of plaster and white finish on metal lath on all ceilings of the first and second floors.

The contractor shall include all items of labor, materials, equipment, and appliances necessary to complete the work, whether specifically mentioned in the specifications or not, except only those items specifically mentioned as omitted from this division of the specifications.

Work Not Included

The following items will be performed under other divisions of the contract and will not be included as a part of this division:

(a) Wood furring

(b) Interior wall finish of plywood and Homasote

(c) Temporary heat

Materials

Metal lath shall be expanded metal lath made of open-hearth steel and shall weigh not less than 3.4 lb. per square yard. Lath shall be galvanized after fabrication.

Plaster shall be gypsum neat plaster of an approved brand delivered to the job in the original unbroken package bearing the manufacturer's name and brand.

Finish plaster shall be a prepared white finish that will produce a smooth hard white finish.

Mixing

Plaster shall be mixed in a mixing box made of ample size for proper mixing and sufficiently watertight to prevent water and fine aggregate from leaking away from the mix.

Workmanship

Before proceeding with lathing and plastering, the contractor shall make sure that all plumbing and heating pipes, electric wires, and conduits have been properly installed, inspected, and approved. He shall also be certain that all surfaces are true to line and shall report any improper work or work not installed before applying any lath or plaster.

Metal lath shall be fastened to wood furring with galvanized staples. Staples shall be about 6 in. on centers. Lath sheets shall have side laps of at least ½ in. and end laps of at least 1 in. Lath shall run in opposite direction to its fastenings and shall be stretched tight to eliminate sags.

Patching

The contractor shall do all patching of plasterwork after the work of other trades has been completed or when so directed to do so by the architect or general contractor.

It is understood the patching shall include only the necessary repairs to plaster surfaces previously executed as part of the contract.

Cleaning

After all plasterwork has been completed and approved, the contractor shall remove all scaffolding and tools of every sort used in the execution of his work, and shall exercise reasonable care to avoid soiling, or spattering plaster on, the work of other trades.

DIVISION 8

Finished Carpentry and Millwork

General Conditions

The general conditions of the contract of the American Institute of Architects (current edition) shall form a part of this division, together with the special conditions, to which the contractor is referred.

Scope

The work under this division includes all labor, materials, equipment, and appliances required for the complete execution of all finished carpentry and millwork as shown on the scale and detail drawings or as may reasonably be inferred to make this division complete, which is generally as follows:

(a) Wood stairs, including handrail
(b) Plywood and Homasote walls, where indicated
(c) Exterior and interior millwork
(d) Wood door bucks for French doors
(e) Finished wood floors
(f) Kitchen cabinets

It is to be assumed that the foregoing items and as hereinafter described in this division of the specification are only generally complete.

The contractor shall include all items of labor, materials, equipment, and appliances necessary to complete the work, whether specifically mentioned in the specifications or not, except only those items specifically mentioned as omitted from this division of the specifications.

Work Not Included

The following items shall be performed under other divisions of this contract, separate contract, and will not be included as a part of this division:

(a) Furring strips on interior walls
(b) Rock-wool insulation

Materials

All stair material shall be straight-grained red oak for natural finish, free from wormholes, stains, or other imperfections that would impair its strength, durability, or appearance. All material shall be thoroughly kiln-dried.

Interior wall coverings shall be ½-in. Homasote and ¼-in. plywood panels where shown on the detail and scale drawings. Panels shall be laid vertically. (Vertical joints shall be covered with white-pine battens at windows and doors only.)

Exterior wall coverings shall be redwood beveled siding.

Finished wood flooring shall be. $^{25}/_{32}$ in. thick x 2 in. face select oak flooring, tongued and grooved, and end-matched, furnished, and laid in accordance with the National Oak Flooring Manufacturers' Association. Wood flooring shall be air-dried, kiln-dried, and accurately milled.

Finished flooring shall not be delivered to the building in damp or wet weather, nor shall it be installed in newly plastered rooms or otherwise exposed to dampness. Finished flooring shall not be laid until after all partitions have been erected and Homasote or plywood covering has been applied. Number 15 building paper, lapped 4 in., shall be installed on the underflooring before the laying of any finished wood flooring.

Nails shall be steel-cut 8-penny.

Each piece of flooring shall be well driven into position, blind-nailed, nails spaced 12 in. apart.

Workmanship

Stairs shall be closed string having 1¼-in. treads with ⅞-in. risers housed into the wall stringers. The stairs and landings shall be supported by three 3- x 12-in. carriage beams and 2- x 8-in. floor beams spaced 16 in. on centers.

Carriage beams shall be accurately cut for the rise and tread and adequately supported at the floors and landings in the best manner known to the trade.

Platforms shall be laid with double floors of the same quality specified for floors.

Nosings at floor landings shall be the same detail as the treads.

All material shall be sanded to a smooth surface and all work shall be constructed in the best manner and as approved by the architect. Handrail for stairs shall be stock design approved by the architect.

Interior and exterior wood finish and exposed surfaces and edges shall be finished smooth and be free from marks, blemishes, or defacements of any kind caused by workmanship or manufacture.

All joints shall be neatly and accurately made, fitted tight, blocked, or otherwise put together so as to conceal or avoid any shrinkage.

All work shall be clean and smooth when turned over to the painter. Continuous members of trim shall be in as long pieces as practicable, and joints shall be made only at locations where solid backing for nailing occurs.

All wood finish shall be securely and rigidly fastened in place in an approved manner. As far as practicable, the work shall be blind-nailed. Where this cannot be done, it shall be made as inconspicuous as possible, with nailheads sunk ⅛ in.

Exterior Millwork

Main Entrance. Door shall be flush and of stock design, and shall be as detailed.

Windows. Windows shall be as detailed and the sizes shown. Sash shall be stock design, of the thickness and the number of lights called for. Double-hung windows shall have hard-pine pulley stiles, equipped with approved sash pulleys made for sash chains.

Cornices. Cornices shall be made and constructed in accordance with the detail drawings, fastened to substantial blocking built into masonry or framing. All external corners and end joints shall be mitered, and no joints shall be made except against solid blocking. Members shall be in as long lengths as possible. All members shall be put together with white lead and securely nailed. All nails shall be countersunk.

Wood Door Bucks. Wood door bucks for openings in fieldstone wall shall be the width specified on the detail drawings and shall consist of jambs securely built into the wall at the time of their erection. Three approved wrought-iron anchors shall be used in each jamb to hold the buck securely in position.

Interior Wood Finish

Doors. All shall be flush-type stock doors. Passage doors shall be 1¾ in. thick. Closet doors shall be 1⅜ in. thick. Doors shall be made perfectly flat, square, and true, and so that they will not warp, twist, crack, or develop other defects. Doors shall be accurately fitted, hung, adjusted, and left in perfect condition.

Jambs and Trim. Jambs and trim shall be the thickness as shown or required. Jambs shall be housed together at the head. Trim shall be mitered and spliced together. Jambs and trim shall be put together in the mill as far as is practicable. They shall be erected straight and true with perfect angles and proper alignment.

Wood Base. Wood base shall be as detailed, securely fastened to a true straight line. The base shall be housed together at all interior corners and shall be mitered at all exterior corners and returns.

Wood Stools. Wood stools for windows shall be 1½-in. plywood with bullnose projection beyond the face of the Homasote walls. Apron shall be the same detail as the wood trim. Stools and apron shall have mitered returns back to the face of the Homasote walls.

Priming. All exterior and interior millwork having a painted finish shall be primed on all sides with lead and oil paint. All priming shall be done in the mill before shipment.

Scraping and Surfacing Finished Floors. All flooring, after being laid, shall be swept clean, handscraped, or machine-sanded lengthwise of the grain and rubbed down with No. 1½ sandpaper, again swept, and the dust removed with a soft cloth.

After scraping and cleaning, all finished floors shall be completely protected with heavy building paper. This protection shall be maintained until floors are ready for painting and finishing.

Finishing. All finished wood flooring shall be stained, filled, varnished, rubbed, and waxed.

Interior Millwork

Kitchen Cabinets. Kitchen cabinets shall be tub-built or stock Kitchen Maid or approved equal. Cabinets to consist of base cabinets with drawers, breadboxes, shelves, and so forth, with a linoleum counter top and back splash with required white-metal edgings. Linoleum shall be standard gauge as manufactured by Armstrong Cork Company or approved equal, laid according to manufacturer's directions. Wall-hung cabinets as required. All as shown on the drawings.

Bathroom Accessories. The contractor is to allow a $35.00 cash allowance for bathroom accessories, which will be selected and purchased by the owner.

Bookcase. In living room, install bookcase of clear white pine as shown on drawings and details. All wood-sawed ends to be sandpapered smooth before assembling and all nails to be well countersunk.

Protection

All millwork shall be protected from damage of any kind until it is finally erected in place. Material shall be kept dry at all times and no material shall be shipped from the mill to the job in rain or stormy weather.

Previous to erection, all millwork shall be laid flat as an insurance against warps or twists of any kind.

DIVISION 9

Finish Hardware

General Conditions

The general conditions of the contract of the American Institute of Architects (current edition) shall form a part of this division, together with the special conditions, to which the contractor is referred.

Scope

The work under this division includes all labor, materials, equipment, and appliances required for the complete execution of all finish hardware as required or as may reasonably be inferred to make this division complete, which is generally as follows:

All finish hardware for doors, windows, and so on, including butts, locks, closers, bolts, hooks, and other finished hardware required or specified

It is to be assumed that the foregoing items and as hereinafter described in this division of the specification are only generally complete.

The contractor shall include all items of labor, materials, equipment, and appliances necessary to complete the work, whether specifically mentioned in the specifications or not, except those items specifically mentioned as omitted from this division of the specifications.

Work Not Included

The following items will be performed under other divisions of this contract, separate contract and will not be included as a part of this division:

(a) Rough hardware, such as nails, screws, bolts
(b) Miscellaneous iron, such as beam hangers, beam anchors, bolts, shields, or similar items

Material

All material shall be aluminum, polished finish and similar in quality to that manufactured by the Schlage Company or approved equal.

All lock sets shall be furnished with two keys.

DIVISION 10

Glass and Glazing

General Conditions

The general conditions of the contract of the American Institute of Architects (current edition) shall form a part of this division, together with the special conditions, to which the contractor is referred.

Scope

The work under this division includes all labor, materials, equipment, and appliances required for the complete execution of all glass and glazing as shown on the scale and detail drawings, or as may reasonably be inferred to make this division complete, which is generally as follows:

(a) Clear glass in all windows and doors as called for on the drawings
(b) Glass block where called for on the drawings

Materials

Clear Glass. Clear glass shall be 3/16 in. double-strength quality A, free from blisters over 1/8 in. and from strings, cords, stone, sulphur marks, and burnt spots.

Glass Blocks. Glass blocks shall be 6 x 6 in., obscure, installed according to manufacturer's specification.

Putty. Putty to be of manufacture approved by the architect, composed of proper materials for use with wood or metal sash on frames, and of consistency to remain in perfect condition for a period of 2 years.

Workmanship

All glass in exterior sash or doors shall be thoroughly bedded.

All glass set in wood shall be secured with zinc glazier's points. White-pine blocking shall be used on all sash, to act as cushions at bottom and on sides. The use of felt, rubber, or similar materials will not be permitted.

All putty shall neatly and cleanly run in straight lines, even with the inside edge of sash members, with all corners carefully made.

DIVISION 11

Plumbing

General Conditions

The general conditions of the contract of the American Institute of Architects (current edition) shall form a part of this division, together with the special conditions, to which the contractor is referred.

Scope

The work under this division includes all labor, materials, equipment, and appliances required for the complete execution of all plumbing as shown on the scale and detail drawings, or as may reasonably be inferred to make this division complete, which is generally as follows:

(a) Sanitary drainage
(b) Building of septic tank and leaching pool
(c) Cold-water supply
(d) Hot-water supply and hot-water tank
(e) Plumbing fixtures
(f) Pipe and tank covering

It is assumed that the foregoing items as hereinafter described in this division of the specification are only generally complete.

The contractor shall include all items of labor, materials, equipment, and appliances necessary to complete the work, whether specifically mentioned in the specifications or not, except only those items specifically mentioned as omitted from this division of specification.

Work Not Included

The following items will be performed under other divisions of this contract and will not be included as part of this division:

(a) Piping for heating work
(b) Cutting and patching for any wood framing or masonry work

Drawings

Before any piping and other plumbing is installed, the plumbing contractor shall submit for approval complete plans for plumbing layout, showing all drain, vent, supply lines, including size of all piping, all valves, traps, cleanouts, connections, septic tank, and leaching-pool requirements. No plumbing work shall be started or installed until entire plans are approved by the architect or his authorized representative. All piping shall be concealed when practicable.

Materials

Sanitary drainage pipe such as main stacks, vent stacks, soil pipes, branches, and fittings shall be of cast iron with bonded hubs and of the size shown on the approved drawings.

Pipe lines for leader drains and lines to septic tank and leaching pool shall be of 6-in. salt-glazed tile.

Floor drain shall have body of galvanized cast iron with cast-brass cover.

Valves shall be gate valves unless otherwise specified. Valves 2 in. or smaller shall be of all brass or bronze; valves over 2 in. shall have an iron body, brass mounted.

Water-supply pipe lines and fittings for both hot and cold water shall be of the sizes shown on the approved drawings and shall be of brass conforming to the standard specifications of the American Society for Testing Materials, current edition, with a minimum copper content of 60 per cent, with fitting of cast brass of 125 lb.

Lead bends shall be of the following weight as specified in plumbing code and shall be of 8-lb. lead in all cases:

1½-in. pipe	3 lb. per foot
2-in. pipe	4 lb. per foot
3-in. pipe	6 lb. per foot

Hot-water tank shall be of 40 gal. capacity, steel galvanized inside and out, with convex heads both ends. Seams shall be electrically welded for not less than 100 lb. working pressure.

Fixtures

The following fixtures have been selected from the catalogue of the Crane Company only for the purpose of establishing a basis for quality, design, and size. Fixtures of similar quality from other companies are acceptable if approved.

Lavatory. Lavatory shall be wall type, rectangular, with concealed hanger similar to Crane Rhodile C-2151 or approved equal. Trimmings shall be chromium plated, consisting of faucets and waste fixture similar to Crane V-12. Also cast brass-chromium-plated P trap with cleanout plug.

Bathtub. Bathtub shall be the size shown and shall be one-piece acid-resisting enamel on cast iron, complete with chromium-plated trimmings. The tub shall be equipped with ½-in. over-rim fixtures,

1½-in. access waste, shower-head mixing valve, and curtain rod with hooks, eyes, and curtain.

Kitchen Sink. Kitchen sink shall be medium-size, flat-rim, one-piece acid-resisting enamel on cast iron. Sink shall be equipped with chromium fittings, consisting of faucets, waste, and trap, and shall be installed in kitchen-cabinet counter top.

Workmanship

Main stacks, vent stacks, and soil lines shall be of material specified and the sizes indicated, and shall run as shown to discharge into the sewer lines. Vent line shall be carried up through the roof with proper collar and flashings. Connections in cast-iron pipe shall be made with picked oakum gasket and pig lead. Y fitting shall be used wherever possible.

Install all traps and cleanouts as necessary or required in accordance with plans and with all applicable sanitation laws of the locality.

Service piping shall be of material specified for the complete hot- and cold-water system and shall be installed in a workmanlike manner with proper fittings. All junctions shall be painted with red lead and screwed tight to resistance. All piping shall be installed in accordance with all sanitary laws governing same.

Tests

The entire plumbing system shall be tested for leaks by an approved method to the satisfaction of all local authorities. No plumbing work shall be covered by the work of other trades before a certificate, issued by the proper authorities, stating that the work had been accepted, is received.

DIVISION 12
Heating

General Conditions

The general conditions of the contract of the American Institute of Architects (current edition) shall form a part of this division, together with the special conditions, to which the contractor is referred.

Scope

The work under this division includes all labor, material, equipment, and appliances required for the complete execution of a hot-water heating system necessary to heat all occupied spaces to 70°F. in zero weather, and which is generally as follows: boiler, radiators, pipes, fittings, breechings, dampers, thermostats, domestic hot-water heating unit (Taco or approved equal), and covering for boilers, pipes, and fittings.

It is assumed that the foregoing items, as hereinafter described in this division of the specifications, are only generally complete.

The contractor shall include all items of labor, material, equipment, and appliances necessary to complete the work whether specifically mentioned in this division or not, except only those items mentioned in this division under Work Not Included.

Work Not Included

The following items will be performed under other divisions of this contract, separate contract, and will not be included as a part of this division:

(a) Plumbing
(b) Hot-water tank
(c) Painting of radiators

Materials

Boiler. Boiler shall be an oil burner with clock thermostat similar to Burnham Furnace Company's Yellow Jacket or its approved equal.

Radiators. Radiators shall be the concealed type similar to those manufactured by the American Radiator Company or the approved equal.

Grilles. Grilles to be by the American Foundry and Furnace Company or approved equal.

Pipes and Fittings. All pipes shall be full-weight wrought steel. All fittings shall be of standard lengths and thickness, right-hand thread. Pipe sleeves shall be heavy galvanized iron.

Smoke-Pipe Connections. Smoke-pipe connections between boiler and chimney shall be made of heavy-gauge sheet metal with locked joints and of proper size required.

Pipe Coverings. Pipe coverings shall be of air-cell type, 7/8 in. thick, jacketed with 6-oz. canvas. Bands shall be of brass, 18 in. apart, of not less than 36 Brown & Sharpe gauge and not less than 3/4 in. in width.

Drawings

Contractor shall furnish drawings showing complete piping layout, size of piping, capacity and make of boiler, hot-water heater, size and type of radiators, and other necessary information. They shall be submitted for approval before the work is proceeded with.

Guarantee

The contractor shall make, at his own expense, all necessary repairs and adjustments required because of faulty material on installations for a period of 5 years after completion of the work.

DIVISION 13
Painting

General Conditions

The general conditions of the contract of the American Institute of Architects (current edition) shall form a part of this division, together with the special conditions, to which the contractor is referred.

Scope

The work under this division includes all labor, materials, equipment, and appliances required for the complete execution of all finished painting as shown on the scale and detail drawings, or as may reasonably be inferred to make this division complete, which is generally as follows:

(a) Two coats of lead and oil paint on all exterior woodwork and interior sash

(b) Two coats of approved boat deck paint on all canvas

(c) One finish coat of aluminium paint on roof and deck

(d) One coat of approved primer and sealer on ceilings, walls, trim, bookcase, and kitchen cabinets

(e) Two coats of casein paint on ceilings and walls

(f) One coat of lead and oil paint on all interior trim, bookcase, and kitchen cabinets

(g) One coat of filler, shellac, and spar varnish, and one coat of wax rubbed on all wood floors

(h) One finish coat of enamel paint on kitchen cabinets

(i) Two coats of metal paint on all exterior and interior ironwork.

It is to be assumed that the foregoing items as hereinafter described in this division of the specification are only generally complete.

The contractor shall include all items of labor, materials, equipment, and appliances necessary to complete the work, whether specifically mentioned in the specifications or not, except only those items specifically mentioned as omitted from this division of the specifications.

Work Not Included

The following items will be performed under other divisions of the specifications and will not be included as part of this division:

(a) Priming of exterior woodwork

(b) Priming of all exterior ironwork

Materials

White lead, red lead, casein paints, linseed oil, turpentine, aluminum paint, and other materials shall be the best products of approved manufacturers and shall conform to the specifications of the American Society for Testing Materials, current edition.

Workmanship

The contractor shall examine all surfaces to be treated by him and report any damaged or impaired surfaces that would affect the satisfactory appearance or the permanency of this work. His failure to report such inferior surfaces shall not relieve him of his responsibility under his guarantee.

The contractor shall remove all dirt, dust, grease, or other foreign particles from all surfaces to be treated by him before applying any material to those surfaces.

The priming coat for plaster ceilings shall be an approved primer and sealer as specified in the contract and shall be brushed on evenly with all surfaces fully covered.

All woodwork shall be sanded smooth before work is proceeded with. Fillers shall be applied and allowed to penetrate the wood fully before the surplus material is wiped off. All surfaces shall be wiped thoroughly clean, free from streaks and clouded spots.

DIVISION 14

Electricity

General Conditions

The general conditions of the contract of the American Institute of Architects (current edition) shall form a part of this division, together with the special conditions to which this contractor is referred.

Scope

The words under this division include all labor, materials, equipment, and appliances required for the complete execution of all electrical wiring as shown on the plans, or as may reasonably be inferred to make this division complete, which is generally as follows:

(a) Furnish and install complete wiring system for lighting where shown
(b) Furnish and install all outlets, receptacles, switches, etc., where shown on the drawings
(c) Furnish and install bell system

All work done under these specifications shall be executed in strict accordance with the rules and requirements of the National Board of Fire Underwriters and shall conform to all local ordinances governing the work.

Materials

General Electric Supr-KODE grade or equal.

Conduit or Cable. From lot line to the house as required by ordinance.

Armored Wire. BX flexible cable shall be used throughout the house for electrical wiring. Run wiring concealed.

Rigid Conduit. In the utility and heat room for electrical wiring where exposed on concrete walls.

Outlet Boxes. Round boxes for ceiling outlets, rectangular type for wall outlets.

Switches. Tumbler switches 4 ft. 0 in. from floor.

Convenience Outlets. Double outlets set in the baseboard except in the kitchen, other service rooms, and bath where they will be on wall.

Lighting Fixtures. Owner will furnish lighting fixtures to electrician. Electrician shall hang same.

Bell System. Install a small button at the front door to ring the bell in the kitchen. Two-tone combination bell flush with plaster in the kitchen for front door. Install a bell-ringing transformer mounted on a wood meter board.

The electrical contractor shall take all necessary measures to avoid delays in construction because of refusal of the local Electrical Workers Union to work with certain materials or equipment. The contractor shall be responsible for having delivered to the job only such materials and equipment as the union will not refuse to install.

MAXIMUM SPANS FOR FLOOR JOISTS Nº 1 COMMON

LIVE LOAD OF 60 LBS. PER SQ. FT.
UNIFORMLY DISTRIBUTED WITH & WITHOUT PLASTERED CEILING

AMERICAN STANDARD LUMBER SIZES		DIST. ON CENTER	MAXIMUM CLEAR SPAN BETWEEN SUPPORTS					
			SO. PINE & DOUGLAS FIR		WESTERN HEMLOCK		SPRUCE	
NOMINAL	NET		UNPLAST'D	PLASTERED	UNPLAST'D	PLASTERED	UNPLAST'D	PLASTERED
3" x 6"	2 5/8" x 5 5/8"	12"	12'-7"	10'-6"	12'-1"	10'-1"	11'-6"	9'-7"
		16"	11'-0"	9'-7"	10'-6"	9'-3"	10'-0"	8'-9"
2" x 8"	1 5/8" x 7 1/2"	12"	13'-4"	12'-0"	12'-9"	11'-6"	12'-2"	10'-11"
		16"	11'-8"	11'-0"	11'-2"	10'-6"	10'-8"	9'-11"
3" x 8"	2 5/8" x 7 1/2"	12"	16'-8"	14'-0"	16'-0"	13'-4"	15'-2"	12'-9"
		16"	14'-6"	12'-10"	14'-0"	12'-3"	13'-4"	11'-7"
2" x 10"	1 5/8" x 9 1/2"	12"	16'-10"	15'-2"	16'-1"	14'-6"	15'-4"	13'-9"
		16"	14'-8"	13'-10"	14'-0"	13'-3"	13'-4"	12'-7"
4" x 8"	3 5/8" x 7 1/2"	12"	19'-10"	15'-5"	18'-11"	14'-10"	18'-1"	14'-0"
		16"	17'-4"	14'-1"	16'-8"	13'-6"	15'-11"	12'-11"
3" x 10"	2 5/8" x 9 1/2"	12"	20'-11"	17'-7"	20'-0"	16'-10"	19'-1"	15'-11"
		16"	18'-4"	16'-1"	17'-6"	15'-5"	16'-9"	14'-7"
2" x 12"	1 5/8" x 11 1/2"	12"	20'-2"	18'-3"	19'-4"	17'-6"	18'-5"	16'-8"
		16"	17'-8"	16'-8"	16'-11"	16'-0"	16'-2"	15'-2"
3" x 12"	2 5/8" x 11 1/2"	12"	25'-0"	21'-1"	24'-0"	20'-3"	22'-10"	19'-3"
		16"	22'-0"	19'-4"	21'-1"	18'-6"	20'-1"	17'-7"
3" x 14"	2 5/8" x 13 1/2"	12"	29'-1"	24'-7"	27'-10"	23'-7"	26'-7"	22'-5"
		16"	25'-8"	22'-7"	24'-6"	21'-7"	23'-5"	20'-6"

• NOTE:- DEFLECTION LIMITED TO $\frac{1}{360}$ OF THE SPAN.
DEAD LOAD FIGURED TO INCLUDE WEIGHT OF JOISTS, LATH, AND PLASTER
CEILING (10 LBS) AND SUB-FLOOR AND FINISH FLOOR.

MAXIMUM SPANS FOR FLOOR JOISTS Nº 1 COMMON

LIVE LOAD OF 75 LBS. PER SQ. FT.
UNIFORMLY DISTRIBUTED WITH & WITHOUT PLASTERED CEILING

AMERICAN STANDARD LUMBER SIZES		DIST. ON CENTER	MAXIMUM CLEAR SPAN BETWEEN SUPPORTS					
			SO. PINE & DOUGLAS FIR		WESTERN HEMLOCK		SPRUCE	
NOMINAL	NET		UNPLAST'D	PLASTERED	UNPLAST'D	PLASTERED	UNPLAST'D	PLASTERED
2" x 8"	1 5/8" x 7 1/2"	12"	12'-0"	11'-4"	11'-6"	10'-10"	11'-0"	10'-3"
		16"	10'-6"	10'-4"	10'-0"	9'-10"	9'-7"	9'-5"
3" x 8"	2 5/8" x 7 1/2"	12"	15'-2"	13'-2"	14'-6"	12'-8"	13'-10"	12'-1"
		16"	12'-2"	12'-1"	12'-8"	11'-7"	12'-5"	11'-0"
2" x 10"	1 5/8" x 9 1/2"	12"	15'-3"	14'-3"	14'-7"	13'-8"	13'-11"	12'-11"
		16"	13'-3"	13'-0"	12'-8"	12'-5"	12'-1"	11'-10"
4" x 8"	3 5/8" x 7 1/2"	12"	17'-7"	14'-7"	16'-11"	14'-0"	16'-2"	13'-3"
		16"	15'-5"	13'-4"	14'-10"	12'-9"	14'-1"	12'-2"
3" x 10"	2 5/8" x 9 1/2"	12"	19'-0"	16'-8"	18'-3"	15'-11"	17'-5"	15'-2"
		16"	16'-8"	15'-2"	15'-11"	14'-7"	15'-3"	13'-9"
2" x 12"	1 5/8" x 11 1/2"	12"	18'-4"	17'-2"	17'-6"	16'-5"	16'-9"	15'-8"
		16"	16'-0"	15'-9"	15'-2"	15'-1"	14'-7"	14'-3"
4" x 10"	3 5/8" x 9 1/2"	12"	22'-1"	18'-4"	21'-2"	17'-7"	20'-1"	16'-8"
		16"	18'-5"	16'-10"	18'-7"	16'-2"	17'-9"	15'-3"
3" x 12"	2 5/8" x 11 1/2"	12"	22'-10"	20'-1"	21'-11"	19'-2"	20'-8"	18'-2"
		16"	20'-1"	18'-4"	19'-3"	17'-7"	18'-4"	16'-8"
3" x 14"	2 5/8" x 13 1/2"	12"	26'-7"	23'-5"	25'-3"	22'-3"	24'-3"	21'-3"
		16"	23'-4"	21'-6"	22'-4"	20'-6"	21'-4"	19'-6"

• NOTE:- DEFLECTION LIMITED TO $\frac{1}{360}$ OF THE SPAN.
DEAD LOAD FIGURED TO INCLUDE WEIGHT OF JOISTS, LATH, AND PLASTER
CEILING (10 LBS) AND SUB-FLOOR AND FINISH FLOOR.
DATA SUPPLIED BY NATIONAL LUMBER MANUFACTURERS ASSOCIATION.

WOOD JOIST SIZES

MAXIMUM SPANS FOR FLOOR JOISTS No 1 COMMON

LIVE LOAD FOR RESIDENTIAL USE OF 40 LBS PER SQ. FOOT
UNIFORMLY DISTRIBUTED WITH & WITHOUT PLASTERED CEILING

AMERICAN STANDARD LUMBER SIZES		DIST. ON CENTER	MAXIMUM CLEAR SPAN BETWEEN SUPPORTS					
			SO. PINE & DOUGLAS FIR		WESTERN HEMLOCK		SPRUCE	
NOMINAL	NET		UNPLAST'D.	PLASTERED	UNPLAST'D.	PLASTERED	UNPLAST'D.	PLASTERED
2" x 6"	1 5/8" x 5 5/8"	12"	12'-0"	10'-0"	11'-6"	9'-6"	10'-11"	9'-1"
		16"	10'-6"	9'-1"	10'-0"	8'-8"	9'-6"	8'-3"
3" x 6"	2 5/8" x 5 5/8"	12"	15'-0"	11'-8"	14'-4"	11'-2"	13'-8"	10'-6"
		16"	13'-1"	10'-8"	12'-6"	10'-2"	12'-0"	9'-8"
2" x 8"	1 5/8" x 7 1/2"	12"	15'-11"	13'-3"	15'-3"	12'-8"	14'-6"	12'-0"
		16"	13'-11"	12'-1"	13'-4"	11'-7"	12'-8"	11'-0"
3" x 8"	2 5/8" x 7 1/2"	12"	19'-8"	15'-4"	18'-10"	14'-8"	17'-11"	13'-11"
		16"	17'-4"	14'-0"	16'-7"	13'-5"	15'-9"	12'-9"
2" x 10"	1 5/8" x 9 1/2"	12"	19'-11"	16'-8"	19'-1"	16'-0"	18'-3"	15'-2"
		16"	17'-4"	15'-3"	16'-8"	14'-7"	15'-11"	13'-10"
3" x 10"	2 5/8" x 9 1/2"	12"	24'-7"	19'-3"	23'-6"	18'-5"	22'-5"	17'-6"
		16"	21'-8"	17'-8"	20'-9"	16'-11"	19'-9"	16'-1"
2" x 12"	1 5/8" x 11 1/2"	12"	23'-11"	20'-1"	22'-11"	19'-3"	21'-10"	18'-3"
		16"	20'-11"	18'-5"	20'-1"	17'-7"	19'-3"	16'-9"
3" x 12"	2 5/8" x 11 1/2"	12"	29'-4"	23'-1"	28'-1"	22'-1"	25'-5"	20'-11"
		16"	25'-11"	21'-3"	24'-10"	20'-4"	22'-5"	19'-4"
2" x 14"	1 5/8" x 13 1/2"	12"	27'-8"	23'-5"	26'-6"	22'-6"	25'-3"	21'-2"
		16"	24'-4"	21'-5"	23'-4"	20'-6"	22'-3"	19'-6"
3" x 14"	2 5/8" x 13 1/2"	12"		26'-11"		25'-9"	30'-0"	24'-5"
		16"		24'-10"		23'-9"	27'-6"	22'-6"

* NOTE:- DEFLECTION LIMITED TO $\frac{1}{360}$ OF THE SPAN.
DEAD LOAD FIGURED TO INCLUDE WEIGHT OF JOISTS, LATH AND PLASTER
CEILING (10 LBS) AND SUB-FLOOR AND FINISH FLOOR.

MAXIMUM SPANS FOR RAFTERS No 1 COMMON

ROOF LOAD OF 30 LBS PER SQ. FT. UNIFORMLY DISTRIBUTED
FOR SLOPES OF 20° OR MORE

AMERICAN STANDARD LUMBER SIZES		DIST. ON CENTER	MAXIMUM CLEAR SPAN - PLATE TO RIDGE					
			SO. PINE & DOUGLAS FIR		WESTERN HEMLOCK		SPRUCE	
NOMINAL	NET		UNPLAST'D.	PLASTERED	UNPLAST'D.	PLASTERED	UNPLAST'D	PLASTERED
2" x 4"	1 5/8" x 3 5/8"	16"	7'-8"	6'-10"	7'-4"	6'-6"	7'-0"	6'-2"
		24"	6'-3"	6'-0"	6'-0"	5'-8"	5'-9"	5'-5"
2" x 6"	1 5/8" x 5 5/8"	16"	11'-9"	10'-6"	11'-3"	10'-1"	10'-9"	9'-7"
		24"	9'-8"	9'-3"	9'-3"	8'-10"	8'-10"	8'-5"
3" x 6"	2 5/8" x 5 5/8"	16"	14'-10"	12'-3"	14'-1"	11'-9"	13'-6"	11'-1"
		24"	12'-3"	10'-10"	11'-9"	10'-4"	11'-1"	9'-10"
2" x 8"	1 5/8" x 7 1/2"	16"	15'-7"	14'-0"	15'-0"	13'-4"	14'-3"	12'-9"
		24"	12'-10"	12'-3"	12'-4"	11'-9"	11'-9"	11'-2"
3" x 8"	2 5/8" x 7 1/2"	16"	19'-5"	16'-1"	18'-7"	15'-5"	17'-9"	14'-7"
		24"	16'-1"	14'-3"	15'-5"	13'-7"	14'-9"	12'-11"
2" x 10"	1 5/8" x 9 1/2"	16"	19'-7"	17'-6"	18'-9"	16'-10"	17'-11"	15'-11"
		24"	16'-3"	15'-6"	15'-6"	14'-10"	14'-10"	14'-0"
2" x 12"	1 5/8" x 11 1/2"	16"	23'-6"	21'-2"	22'-6"	20'-3"	21'-6"	19'-3"
		24"	19'-6"	18'-8"	17'-10"	17'-10"	17'-10"	17'-0"

* NOTE:- DEFLECTION LIMITED TO $\frac{1}{360}$ OF THE SPAN.
DEAD LOAD FIGURED TO INCLUDE WEIGHT OF RAFTERS, ROOF SHEATHING AND 2.5 LBS. FOR WOOD SHINGLE OR 3-PLY READY-
MADE ROOFING. FOR HEAVIER ROOF FINISHES USE RAFTER NEXT SIZE LARGER.
DATA SUPPLIED BY NATIONAL LUMBER MANUFACTURERS ASSOCIATION.

WOOD JOIST & RAFTER SIZES

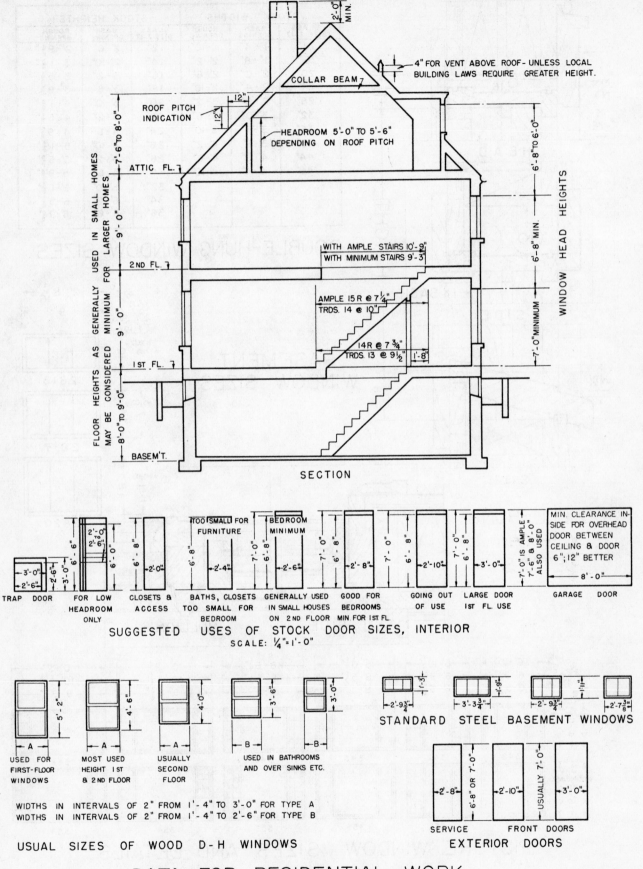

2'-0" MIN.

4" FOR VENT ABOVE ROOF- UNLESS LOCAL BUILDING LAWS REQUIRE GREATER HEIGHT.

COLLAR BEAM

ROOF PITCH INDICATION

12"

12"

HEADROOM 5'-0" TO 5'-6" DEPENDING ON ROOF PITCH

7'-6" TO 8'-0"

ATTIC FL.

9'-0"

2ND FL.

WITH AMPLE STAIRS 10'-9"
WITH MINIMUM STAIRS 9'-3"

AMPLE 15 R @ 7$\frac{1}{4}$"
TRDS. 14 @ 10"

14R @ 7$\frac{3}{4}$"
TRDS. 13 @ 9$\frac{1}{2}$" 1'-8"

9'-0"

1ST FL.

8'-0" TO 9'-0"

BASEM'T.

FLOOR HEIGHTS AS GENERALLY USED IN SMALL HOMES MAY BE CONSIDERED MINIMUM FOR LARGER HOMES

6'-8" TO 6'-0"

6'-8" MIN.

7'-0" MINIMUM

WINDOW HEAD HEIGHTS

SECTION

TRAP DOOR
3'-0"
2'-6"

FOR LOW HEADROOM ONLY
2'-0" TO 2'-6"
6'-6"

CLOSETS & ACCESS
6'-8"
2'-0"

BATHS, CLOSETS TOO SMALL FOR BEDROOM
TOO SMALL FOR FURNITURE
6'-8"
2'-4"

GENERALLY USED IN SMALL HOUSES ON 2ND FLOOR
BEDROOM MINIMUM
7'-0"
6'-8"
2'-6"

GOOD FOR BEDROOMS MIN. FOR IST FL.
7'-0"
6'-8"
2'-8"

GOING OUT OF USE
7'-0"
6'-8"
2'-10"

LARGE DOOR IST FL. USE
7'-0"
6'-8"
3'-0"

7'-6" & 8'-0" ALSO USED
7'-0" IS AMPLE

MIN. CLEARANCE IN-SIDE FOR OVERHEAD DOOR BETWEEN CEILING & DOOR 6"; 12" BETTER

GARAGE DOOR
8'-0"

SUGGESTED USES OF STOCK DOOR SIZES, INTERIOR
SCALE: $\frac{1}{4}$"=1'-0"

USED FOR FIRST-FLOOR WINDOWS
A
5'-2"

MOST USED HEIGHT 1ST & 2ND FLOOR
A
4'-6"

USUALLY SECOND FLOOR
A
4'-0"

USED IN BATHROOMS AND OVER SINKS ETC.
B
3'-6"
B
3'-0"

WIDTHS IN INTERVALS OF 2" FROM 1'-4" TO 3'-0" FOR TYPE A
WIDTHS IN INTERVALS OF 2" FROM 1'-4" TO 2'-6" FOR TYPE B

USUAL SIZES OF WOOD D-H WINDOWS

1'-3"
2'-9$\frac{3}{4}$"

1'-9"
3'-3$\frac{3}{4}$"

1'-1"
2'-9$\frac{3}{4}$"

2'-7$\frac{3}{8}$"

STANDARD STEEL BASEMENT WINDOWS

SERVICE
2'-8"
6'-8" OR 7'-0"

FRONT DOORS
2'-10"
USUALLY 7'-0"
3'-0"

EXTERIOR DOORS

DATA FOR RESIDENTIAL WORK

COURTESY OF JOHN WILEY & SONS INC., NEW YORK

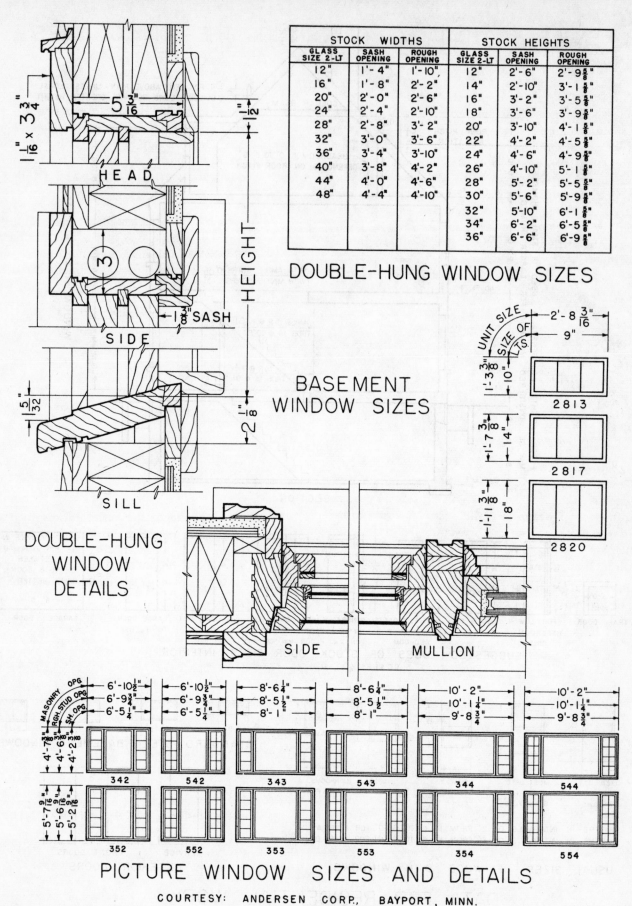

HEAD

$1\frac{1}{16}$ x $3\frac{3}{4}$

$5\frac{3}{16}$"

$1\frac{1}{2}$"

SIDE

3

$1\frac{3}{8}$" SASH

HEIGHT

SILL

$\frac{5}{32}$"

$2\frac{1}{8}$"

DOUBLE-HUNG
WINDOW
DETAILS

STOCK WIDTHS			STOCK HEIGHTS		
GLASS SIZE 2-LT	SASH OPENING	ROUGH OPENING	GLASS SIZE 2-LT	SASH OPENING	ROUGH OPENING
12"	1'-4"	1'-10"	12"	2'-6"	2'-9$\frac{5}{8}$"
16"	1'-8"	2'-2"	14"	2'-10"	3'-1$\frac{5}{8}$"
20"	2'-0"	2'-6"	16"	3'-2"	3'-5$\frac{5}{8}$"
24"	2'-4"	2'-10"	18"	3'-6"	3'-9$\frac{5}{8}$"
28"	2'-8"	3'-2"	20"	3'-10"	4'-1$\frac{5}{8}$"
32"	3'-0"	3'-6"	22"	4'-2"	4'-5$\frac{5}{8}$"
36"	3'-4"	3'-10"	24"	4'-6"	4'-9$\frac{5}{8}$"
40"	3'-8"	4'-2"	26"	4'-10"	5'-1$\frac{5}{8}$"
44"	4'-0"	4'-6"	28"	5'-2"	5'-5$\frac{5}{8}$"
48"	4'-4"	4'-10"	30"	5'-6"	5'-9$\frac{5}{8}$"
			32"	5'-10"	6'-1$\frac{5}{8}$"
			34"	6'-2"	6'-5$\frac{5}{8}$"
			36"	6'-6"	6'-9$\frac{5}{8}$"

DOUBLE-HUNG WINDOW SIZES

BASEMENT WINDOW SIZES

UNIT SIZE
SIZE OF LTS.

2'-8$\frac{3}{16}$"
9"
$1'-3\frac{3}{8}$"
10"
2813

$1'-7\frac{7}{8}$"
14"
2817

$1'-11\frac{3}{8}$"
18"
2820

SIDE

MULLION

MASONRY OPG. 6'-10$\frac{1}{2}$"
RGH. STUD OPG. 6'-9$\frac{3}{4}$"
SH. OPG. 6'-5$\frac{1}{4}$"

6'-10$\frac{1}{2}$"
6'-9$\frac{3}{4}$"
6'-5$\frac{1}{4}$"

8'-6$\frac{1}{4}$"
8'-5$\frac{1}{2}$"
8'-1"

8'-6$\frac{1}{4}$"
8'-5$\frac{1}{2}$"
8'-1"

10'-2"
10'-1$\frac{1}{4}$"
9'-8$\frac{3}{4}$"

10'-2"
10'-1$\frac{1}{4}$"
9'-8$\frac{3}{4}$"

4'-7$\frac{3}{16}$"
4'-6$\frac{3}{8}$"
4'-2$\frac{3}{8}$"

342   **542**   **343**   **543**   **344**   **544**

5'-7$\frac{3}{16}$"
5'-6$\frac{3}{8}$"
5'-2$\frac{3}{8}$"

352   **552**   **353**   **553**   **354**   **554**

PICTURE WINDOW SIZES AND DETAILS

COURTESY: ANDERSEN CORP., BAYPORT, MINN.

ENGINEERING DATA FOR DETERMINING THE CORRECT SIZES OF WOOD GIRDERS AND POSTS

GIRDERS. To determine the size of a girder: (1) Find the distance between girder supports (span). (2) Find the "girder load width." A girder must carry the weight of the floors on each side to the midpoint of the joists that rest upon it. (3) Find the "total floor load" per square foot carried by the joists and bearing partitions to the girder. This will be the sum of the sum of the loads per square foot listed in the diagram below, with the exception of the roof loads, which are carried on the outside walls unless braces or partitions are placed under the rafters, in which case a portion of the roof load is carried to the girder via joists and partitions. (4) Find the total load on the girder. This is the product of (a) "girder span" (b) "girder load width" (c) "total floor load." (5) Select proper size of girder from table below, which indicates safe loads on standard-size girders for spans from 6 ft. to 10 ft. Shortening the span is usually the most economical way to increase the load that a girder will carry.

SPECIAL CASES. Continuous joists, concentrated loads caused by framing one girder into another or by bearing partition at right angles to a girder, etc., are not usual in smaller house construction and are not considered here.

GIRDERS	SAFE LOAD IN LBS. FOR SPANS FROM 6 TO 10 FEET				
SIZE	6 FT.	7 FT.	8 FT.	9 FT.	10 FT.
6 x 8 SOLID	6,875	5,893	5,156	4,583	4,125
6 x 8 BUILT UP	6,100	5,220	4,575	4,065	3,663
6 x 10 SOLID	8,575	8,667	8,273	7,354	6,618
6 x 10 BUILT UP	9,795	8,385	7,345	6,525	5,865
8 x 8 SOLID	9,285	8,036	7,031	6,250	5,625
8 x 8 BUILT UP	8,145	6,960	6,125	5,425	4,880
8 x 10 SOLID	11,690	11,820	11,281	10,028	9,025
8 x 10 BUILT UP	13,050	11,180	9,775	8,700	7,825

POSTS. For ordinary posts (not longer than 9 ft. 0 in. or smaller than 6 x 6 in.), it will be safe to assume that a post whose greatest dimension is equal to the girder that it has to support will carry the girder load. Thus, for a girder 6 in. wide, use 6 x 6 in. posts; for a girder 8 in. wide, use 6 x 8 in. or 8 x 8 in. posts, etc.

RAFTERS. The size of roof rafters will depend upon three factors: (1) the span (2) the weight of roofing material, and (3) the snow and wind loads (live loads).

The span of a rafter is the horizontal distance between the supports (see Fig. 1). Note also how the effective span is shortened by the use of collar ties (Fig. 2). Since the collar tie acts as a strut, it is important that it be fastened securely to the rafters (see illustration).

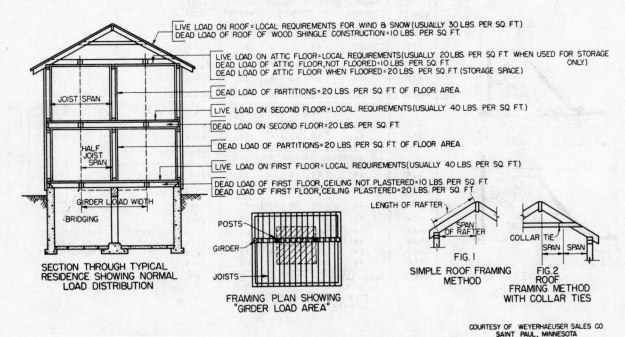

LIVE LOAD ON ROOF = LOCAL REQUIREMENTS FOR WIND & SNOW (USUALLY 30 LBS. PER SQ. FT.)
DEAD LOAD OF ROOF OF WOOD SHINGLE CONSTRUCTION = 10 LBS. PER SQ. FT.

LIVE LOAD ON ATTIC FLOOR = LOCAL REQUIREMENTS (USUALLY 20 LBS. PER SQ. FT. WHEN USED FOR STORAGE ONLY.)
DEAD LOAD OF ATTIC FLOOR, NOT FLOORED = 10 LBS. PER SQ. FT.
DEAD LOAD OF ATTIC FLOOR WHEN FLOORED = 20 LBS. PER SQ. FT. (STORAGE SPACE)

DEAD LOAD OF PARTITIONS = 20 LBS. PER SQ. FT. OF FLOOR AREA.

LIVE LOAD ON SECOND FLOOR = LOCAL REQUIREMENTS (USUALLY 40 LBS. PER SQ. FT.)

DEAD LOAD ON SECOND FLOOR = 20 LBS. PER SQ. FT.

DEAD LOAD OF PARTITIONS = 20 LBS. PER SQ. FT. OF FLOOR AREA.

LIVE LOAD ON FIRST FLOOR = LOCAL REQUIREMENTS (USUALLY 40 LBS. PER SQ. FT.)

DEAD LOAD OF FIRST FLOOR, CEILING NOT PLASTERED = 10 LBS. PER SQ. FT.
DEAD LOAD OF FIRST FLOOR, CEILING PLASTERED = 20 LBS. PER SQ. FT.

JOIST SPAN

HALF JOIST SPAN

GIRDER LOAD WIDTH

BRIDGING

SECTION THROUGH TYPICAL RESIDENCE SHOWING NORMAL LOAD DISTRIBUTION

POSTS
GIRDER
JOISTS

FRAMING PLAN SHOWING "GIRDER LOAD AREA"

LENGTH OF RAFTER
SPAN OF RAFTER
FIG. I
SIMPLE ROOF FRAMING METHOD

COLLAR TIE
SPAN   SPAN
FIG. 2
ROOF FRAMING METHOD WITH COLLAR TIES

COURTESY OF WEYERHAEUSER SALES CO.
SAINT PAUL, MINNESOTA

POKER CONTROL NUMBER	ROTARY CONTROL NUMBER	THROAT BOT. T	THROAT TOP A	THROAT OPG. O	OVERALL LGTH. L	OVERALL BACK B	OVERALL WIDTH W	WIDTH A	HEIGHT B	DEPTH C	BACK D	VERT. BACK E	SLOPE BACK F	THROAT G	WIDTH H	DEPTH I	SMOKE CHAMB J	SLOPE SM. CH. K	RECT. FLUE LINING L M	ROUND FL. LIN Ø	R'TRY NO.	POKER NO.
224	324	24	17 5/16	4 1/4	28 1/2	21	9 7/8	26	24	16	13	14	14	8 3/4	39	20	24	15	8 1/2 × 8 1/2	10	330	230
230	330	30	23 5/16	4 1/4	34 1/2	27	9 7/8	28	28	16	15	14	18	8 3/4	42	20	25	14 1/2	8 1/2 × 13	10	330	230
233	333	33	26 5/16	4 1/4	37 1/2	30	9 7/8	30	30	16	17	14	20	8 3/4	42	20	25	14 1/2	8 1/2 × 13	10	330	230
236	336	36	29 5/16	4 1/4	40 1/2	33	9 7/8	32	28	16	19	14	20	8 3/4	44	20	26	15 1/2	8 1/2 × 13	10	333	233
242	342	42	35 5/16	4 1/4	46 1/2	39	9 7/8	34	30	16	21	14	20	8 3/4	46	20	28	16 1/2	8 1/2 × 13	12	336	236
248	348	48	41 5/16	4 1/4	52 1/2	45	9 7/8	36	30	16	23	14	20	8 3/4	46	20	28	16 1/2	13 × 13	12	336	236
254	354	54	42 1/2	7	58 1/2	46	14 5/8	40	30	16	27	14	20	8 3/4	50	20	32	18 1/2	13 × 13	12	342	242
260	360	60	49 1/2	7	64 1/2	53	14 5/8	42	30	16	29	14	20	8 3/4	54	20	35	20 1/2	13 × 13	12	342	242
272	372	72	60 1/2	7	76 1/2	64	14 5/8	48	33	18	33	14	23	8 3/4	59	22	40	23	13 × 13	15	348	248
284	384	84	73 1/2	7	88 1/2	77	14 5/8	54	36	20	37	14	26	13	67	24	42	24 1/2	13 × 18	15	354	254
296	396	96	85 1/2	7	100 1/2	89	14 5/8	60	39	22	42	14	29	13	71	26	45	26 1/2	18 × 18	18	360	260
								72	40	22	54	14	30	13	83	26	56	32 1/2	18 × 18	18	372	272

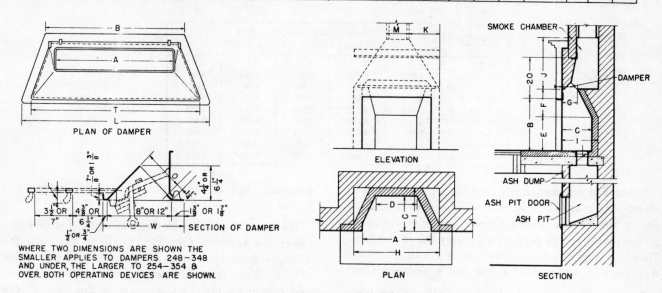

PLAN OF DAMPER

SECTION OF DAMPER

WHERE TWO DIMENSIONS ARE SHOWN THE SMALLER APPLIES TO DAMPERS 248—348 AND UNDER, THE LARGER TO 254—354 & OVER. BOTH OPERATING DEVICES ARE SHOWN.

ELEVATION

PLAN

SMOKE CHAMBER — DAMPER — ASH DUMP — ASH PIT DOOR — ASH PIT

SECTION

DONLEY THROAT AND DAMPER

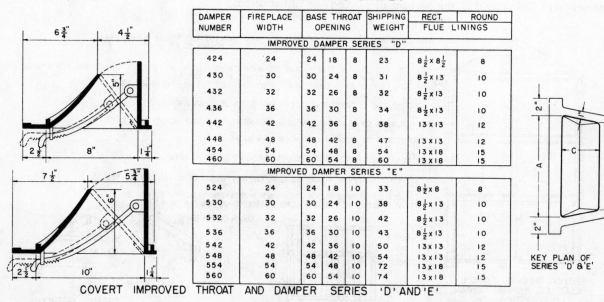

DAMPER NUMBER	FIREPLACE WIDTH	BASE THROAT OPENING			SHIPPING WEIGHT	RECT. FLUE LININGS	ROUND
IMPROVED DAMPER SERIES "D"							
424	24	24	18	8	23	8 1/2 × 8 1/2	8
430	30	30	24	8	31	8 1/2 × 13	10
432	32	32	26	8	32	8 1/2 × 13	10
436	36	36	30	8	34	8 1/2 × 13	10
442	42	42	36	8	38	13 × 13	12
448	48	48	42	8	47	13 × 13	12
454	54	54	48	8	54	13 × 18	15
460	60	60	54	8	60	13 × 18	15
IMPROVED DAMPER SERIES "E"							
524	24	24	18	10	33	8 1/2 × 8	8
530	30	30	24	10	38	8 1/2 × 13	10
532	32	32	26	10	42	8 1/2 × 13	10
536	36	36	30	10	43	8 1/2 × 13	10
542	42	42	36	10	50	13 × 13	12
548	48	48	42	10	54	13 × 13	12
554	54	54	48	10	72	13 × 18	15
560	60	60	54	10	74	13 × 18	15

KEY PLAN OF SERIES 'D' & 'E'

COVERT IMPROVED THROAT AND DAMPER SERIES 'D' AND 'E'

DAMPERS

ELECTRICAL EQUIPMENT

SYMBOL	DESCRIPTION	ILLUSTRATION
S	SINGLE-POLE SWITCH 10 AMPS, 125 VOLTS — For the control of one or more lighting or convenience outlets	
S₃	THREE-WAY SWITCH 10 AMPS, 125 VOLTS — For the control of a single outlet from two different locations - e.g. at head and foot of stairs to control a hall outlet.	
S₄	FOUR-WAY SWITCH 5 AMPS, 125 VOLTS — For the control of a single outlet from three different locations—one four-way and two three-way switches must be used	
* S_OB	SINGLE-POLE SWITCH WITH OIL BURNER COVER — For use where codes require an additional switch near head of basement stairs for emergency control of an oil burner	
* S_MBC * S₃MBC	SINGLE-POLE SWITCH WITH METAL BOX COVER — For use in basements, garage and utility rooms where a finished appearance is not required. May also be used for three-way operation.	
S_P	COMBINATION DOUBLE-POLE SWITCH WITH PILOT LIGHT 15 AMPS, 125 VOLTS — For use in conjunction with a pilot light, e.g., top of basement stairs for control of basement lights (Seldom used in residential work).	
S without pilot S_P with pilot	COMBINATION SWITCH, PILOT LIGHT AND OUTLET — For use with appliances, such as iron, toaster, etc. Both pilot and outlet controlled by switch. May be used without pilot where outlet may be always hot or controlled by switch.	with pilot
duplex / single / triplex / floor	CONVENIENCE OUTLET 15 AMPS, 125 VOLTS — Receptacle for appliances, or table and floor lamps, where a finished appearance is required.	duplex

*Not A.S.A. symbols.

SYMBOL	DESCRIPTION	ILLUSTRATION
* MBC	DUPLEX CONVENIENCE OUTLET WITH BOX MOUNTING FOR GARAGE 15 AMPS, 125 VOLTS — For use where a finished appearance is not required.	
C	CLOCK HANGER OUTLET 15 AMPS, 125 VOLTS — For use with wall hung clock. Recessed to house surplus cord.	
R	RANGE OUTLET 50 AMPS, 250 VOLTS — Receptacle for connecting special range plug.	
L (wall / ceiling)	LAMPHOLDER—KEYLESS 660 WATTS, 250 VOLTS — Designed with shade or globe holder groove—for holding lamp bulb.	
L (wall / ceiling)	GENERAL-PURPOSE OUTLET — For use as a ceiling or wall outlet; permits attachment of a variety of globes or lighting fixtures.	
L_PS ceiling / L_PS wall	LAMPHOLDER—PULL CHAIN 250 WATTS, 250 VOLTS — Same as above, furnished with chain and cord. Used in closets, basements, attic, garage, etc.	
T outlet / apparatus	TELEPHONE OUTLET — To receive connection for telephone apparatus.	

[211]

TABLE A—LINTELS WITH WALL LOAD ONLY

SIZE OF LINTEL		CLEAR SPAN OF LINTEL FT.	BOTTOM REINFORCEMENT	
HEIGHT IN.	WIDTH IN.		NO. BARS	SIZE OF BARS
$5\frac{3}{4}$	8	UP TO 7	2	$\frac{3}{8}$-IN. ROUND DEFORMED
$5\frac{3}{4}$	8	7 TO 8	2	$\frac{1}{2}$-IN. ROUND DEFORMED
$7\frac{3}{4}$	8	UP TO 8	2	$\frac{3}{8}$-IN. ROUND DEFORMED
$7\frac{3}{4}$	8	8 TO 10	2	$\frac{1}{2}$-IN. ROUND DEFORMED

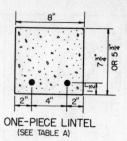

ONE-PIECE LINTEL
(SEE TABLE A)

TABLE B—SPLIT LINTELS WITH WALL LOAD ONLY

SIZE OF LINTEL		CLEAR SPAN OF LINTEL FT.	BOTTOM REINFORCEMENT—EACH SECTION	
HEIGHT IN.	WIDTH IN.		NO BARS	SIZE OF BARS
$5\frac{3}{4}$	$3\frac{3}{4}$	UP TO 7	1	$\frac{3}{8}$-IN. ROUND DEFORMED
$5\frac{3}{4}$	$3\frac{3}{4}$	7 TO 8	1	$\frac{1}{2}$-IN. ROUND DEFORMED
$7\frac{3}{4}$	$3\frac{3}{4}$	UP TO 8	1	$\frac{3}{8}$-IN. ROUND DEFORMED
$7\frac{3}{4}$	$3\frac{3}{4}$	8 TO 10	1	$\frac{1}{2}$-IN. ROUND DEFORMED

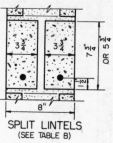

SPLIT LINTELS
(SEE TABLE B)

TABLE C—LINTELS WITH WALL AND FLOOR LOADS
(FLOOR LOAD ASSUMED TO BE 85 LBS. PER SQ. FT. WITH 20-FT. SPAN)

SIZE OF LINTEL		CLEAR SPAN OF LINTEL FT.	REINFORCEMENT		WEB REINFORCEMENT NO.6 GAGE WIRE STIRRUPS. SPACING FROM END OF LINTEL—BOTH ENDS THE SAME
HEIGHT IN.	WIDTH IN.		TOP	BOTTOM	
$7\frac{3}{4}$	8	3	NONE	$2-\frac{3}{8}$-IN. ROUND	NO STIRRUPS REQUIRED
$7\frac{3}{4}$	8	4	$2-\frac{3}{8}$-IN. ROUND	$2-\frac{1}{2}$-IN. ROUND	3 STIRRUPS, SP: 2,3,3 IN.
$7\frac{3}{4}$	8	5	$2-\frac{3}{8}$-IN. ROUND	$2-\frac{5}{8}$-IN. ROUND	5 STIRRUPS, SP: 2,3,3,3,3 IN.
$7\frac{3}{4}$	8	6	$2-\frac{3}{4}$-IN. ROUND	$2-\frac{3}{4}$-IN. ROUND	7 STIRRUPS, SP: 2,3,3,3,3,3,3 IN.
$7\frac{3}{4}$	8	7	$2-1$-IN. ROUND	$2-1$-IN. ROUND	9 STIRRUPS, SP: 2,3,3,3,3,3,3,3,3 IN.

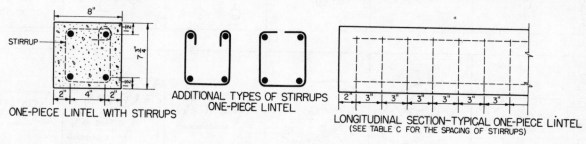

ONE-PIECE LINTEL WITH STIRRUPS

ADDITIONAL TYPES OF STIRRUPS
ONE-PIECE LINTEL

LONGITUDINAL SECTION—TYPICAL ONE-PIECE LINTEL
(SEE TABLE C FOR THE SPACING OF STIRRUPS)

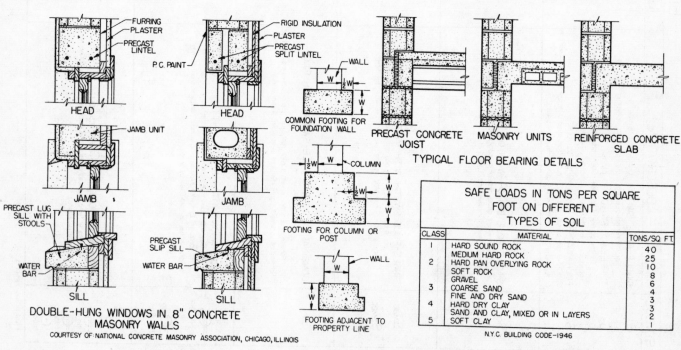

HEAD — FURRING, PLASTER, PRECAST LINTEL, P. C. PAINT

HEAD — RIGID INSULATION, PLASTER, PRECAST SPLIT LINTEL

JAMB — JAMB UNIT

JAMB

SILL — PRECAST LUG SILL WITH STOOLS, WATER BAR

SILL — PRECAST SLIP SILL, WATER BAR

DOUBLE-HUNG WINDOWS IN 8" CONCRETE MASONRY WALLS

COMMON FOOTING FOR FOUNDATION WALL

FOOTING FOR COLUMN OR POST

FOOTING ADJACENT TO PROPERTY LINE

PRECAST CONCRETE JOIST

MASONRY UNITS

REINFORCED CONCRETE SLAB

TYPICAL FLOOR BEARING DETAILS

SAFE LOADS IN TONS PER SQUARE FOOT ON DIFFERENT TYPES OF SOIL

CLASS	MATERIAL	TONS/SQ. FT.
1	HARD SOUND ROCK	40
2	MEDIUM HARD ROCK	25
	HARD PAN OVERLYING ROCK	10
	SOFT ROCK	8
3	GRAVEL	6
	COARSE SAND	4
	FINE AND DRY SAND	3
4	HARD DRY CLAY	3
	SAND AND CLAY, MIXED OR IN LAYERS	2
5	SOFT CLAY	1

N.Y.C. BUILDING CODE—1946

COURTESY OF NATIONAL CONCRETE MASONRY ASSOCIATION, CHICAGO, ILLINOIS

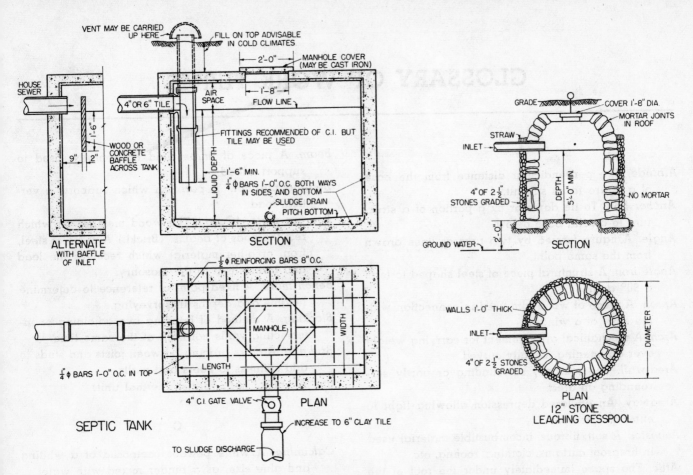

SEPTIC TANK

VENT MAY BE CARRIED UP HERE — FILL ON TOP ADVISABLE IN COLD CLIMATES

MANHOLE COVER (MAY BE CAST IRON)

2'-0"
1'-8"
FLOW LINE
AIR SPACE
4" OR 6" TILE
HOUSE SEWER
FITTINGS RECOMMENDED OF C.I. BUT TILE MAY BE USED
LIQUID DEPTH
1'-6" MIN.
¼" ∅ BARS 1'-0" O.C. BOTH WAYS IN SIDES AND BOTTOM
SLUDGE DRAIN PITCH BOTTOM

WOOD OR CONCRETE BAFFLE ACROSS TANK
1'-6"
9" 2"

ALTERNATE WITH BAFFLE OF INLET

SECTION

½" ∅ REINFORCING BARS 8" O.C.
MANHOLE
WIDTH
LENGTH
¼" ∅ BARS 1'-0" O.C. IN TOP
4" C.I. GATE VALVE
PLAN
INCREASE TO 6" CLAY TILE
TO SLUDGE DISCHARGE

GRADE — COVER 1'-8" DIA.
MORTAR JOINTS IN ROOF
STRAW
INLET
4" OF 2½" STONES GRADED
2'-0"
DEPTH 5'-0" MIN.
NO MORTAR
GROUND WATER
SECTION

WALLS 1'-0" THICK
INLET
4" OF 2½" STONES GRADED
DIAMETER
PLAN 12" STONE
LEACHING CESSPOOL

DESIGN OF SEWAGE DISPOSAL SYSTEMS

NO. OF PERSONS SERVED	SEPTIC TANKS								LEACHING CESSPOOL DISPOSAL											
	SEPTIC TANK					CONCRETE THICKNESS			FOR RAPID ABSORPTION				FOR MEDIUM ABSORPTION				FOR SLOW ABSORPTION			
	GALS WORKING CAP	LENGTH	WIDTH	AIR SPACE	LIQUID DEPTH	WALLS	TOP	BOTTOM	NO. OF CESS- POOLS	DIA.	DEPTH	ABSORPTIVE AREA PER PERSON	NO. OF CESS- POOLS	DIA.	DEPTH	ABSORPTIVE AREA PER PERSON	NO. OF CESS- POOLS	DIA.	DEPTH	ABSORPTIVE AREA PER PERSON
1-4	325	5'-0"	2'-6"	1'-0"	3'-6"				1	5'-0"	5'-0"	24.5 □'	1	6'-0"	6'-0"	35 □'	2	5'-0"	5'-0"	49 □'
5-9	450	6'-0"	2'-6"	1'-0"	4'-0"	6"	4"	6"	1	6'-0"	6'-0"	15.7 □'	2	6'-0"	6'-0"	31.3 □'	2	8'-0"	7'-0"	48 □'
10-14	720	7'-0"	3'-6"	1'-0"	4'-0"	6"	4"	6"	1	8'-0"	6'-0"	14.4 □'	2	8'-0"	6'-0"	28.7 □'	2	10'-0	8'-0"	46.7 □'
15-20	1000	8'-0"	4'-0"	1'-0"	4'-0"	6"	4"	6"	2	6'-0"	6'-0"	14.1 □'	2	9'-0"	7'-0"	26.14 □'	3	10'-0"	8'-0"	49.5 □'
21-25	1250	9'-0"	4'-6"	1'-0"	4'-3"	7"	5"	6"	2	7'-0"	6'-0"	13.6 □'	2	10'-0"	8'-0"	27.1 □'	4	9'-0"	8'-0"	46.4 □'
26-30	1480	9'-6"	4'-8"	1'-3"	4'-6"	8"	5"	6"	2	8'-0"	6'-0"	13.4 □'	2	9'-0"	7'-0"	26.14 □'	4	10'-0"	8'-0"	43.6 □'
31-35	1720	10'-0"	5'-0"	1'-3"	4'-8"	8"	5"	6"	1	8'-0" / 9'-0"	7'-0"	13.6 □'	1 / 2	9'-0" / 10'-0"	7'-0" / 8'-0"	26.1 □'	5	10'-0"	8'-0"	46.7 □'
36-40	1950	10'-6"	5'-3"	1'-3"	4'-9"	9"	5"	6"	1	9'-0" / 9'-0"	7'-0" / 8'-0"	13.7 □'	4	9'-0"	7'-0"	26.1 □'	4	12'-0	10'-0	48.9 □'
41-45	2175	11'-0"	5'-6"	1'-3	4'-10"	9"	5"	6"	3	8'-0"	6'-0"	13.4 □'	4	9'-0"	8'-0	25.7 □'	5	12'-0"	10'-0"	54.3 □'
46-50	2400	11'-6"	5'-9"	1'-3"	5'-0"	9"	5"	6"	3	10'-0"	8'-0"	13.0 □'	4	10'-0"	8'-0"	26.1 □'	5	12'-0"	10'-0"	48.9 □'

CAPACITY OF ABOVE CESSPOOLS BASED ON 50 GALLONS FLOW OF SEWAGE PER PERSON PER 24 HOURS, AND IS FOR RESIDENTIAL WORK.

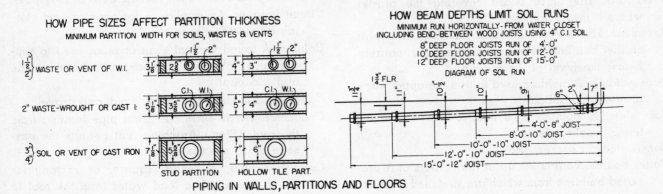

HOW PIPE SIZES AFFECT PARTITION THICKNESS
MINIMUM PARTITION WIDTH FOR SOILS, WASTES & VENTS

1½" 2" WASTE OR VENT OF W.I.
3⅜" 2½" — 4" 3"

2" WASTE—WROUGHT OR CAST I.
C.I. W.I. 5⅛" 3⅝" — C.I. W.I. 5" 4"

3" 4" SOIL OR VENT OF CAST IRON
7⅛" 5⅝" — 7" 6"
STUD PARTITION — HOLLOW TILE PART.

PIPING IN WALLS, PARTITIONS AND FLOORS

HOW BEAM DEPTHS LIMIT SOIL RUNS
MINIMUM RUN HORIZONTALLY—FROM WATER CLOSET INCLUDING BEND—BETWEEN WOOD JOISTS USING 4" C.I. SOIL

8" DEEP FLOOR JOISTS RUN OF 4'-0"
10" DEEP FLOOR JOISTS RUN OF 12'-0"
12" DEEP FLOOR JOISTS RUN OF 15'-0"

DIAGRAM OF SOIL RUN

1¾" FLR.
4'-0"—8" JOIST
8'-0"—10" JOIST
10'-0"—10" JOIST
12'-0"—10" JOIST
15'-0"—12" JOIST

GLOSSARY OF WORK TERMS

A

Altitude. The perpendicular distance from the base of a figure to its summit.

Anchor bolt. To tie down or fix a portion of a structure to a solid base below.

Angle. A figure formed by two rays or lines drawn from the same point.

Angle iron. A structural piece of steel shaped to form a 90° angle.

Apron. A piece of wood trim used in connection with the stool of a window.

Arch. A mechanical arrangement for carrying weight over an opening. Usually curved.

Area-wall. The masonry surrounding or partly surrounding an area.

Areaway. An enclosed depression allowing light to enter a basement.

Asbestos. A soft, fibrous, incombustible material used in fireproof curtains, clothing, roofing, etc.

Attic. The space immediately under the roof of the house.

B

Backfill. Earth used to fill in around exterior foundation walls.

Backhearth. That part of the hearth inside the fireplace.

Backing, wall. That portion of the wall giving additional strength to the face of the wall.

Baluster. One of a set of small pillars that support the handrail of a parapet or balustrade.

Base (Carp). A horizontal band of interior wood finish next to the floor. (Brickl.) The lowest part of building pier or wall.

Baseboard. The finish board covering the plaster where it meets the floor.

Basement. The lowest story of a building. That part of the building which is partially or entirely below the level of the ground.

Base molding. A molding used to trim the upper edge of interior baseboards.

Base shoe. A molding used next to the floor in interior baseboards.

Bat. A piece of broken brick.

Batter boards. Boards set up at the corners of a proposed building from which are stretched the lines marking off the walls.

B

Beam. A piece of timber laid horizontally, used to support a load.

Bearing partition. A partition which supports a vertical load.

Bearing plate. (Carp.) The wood member on which rest the ends of beams. (Brickl.) A piece of steel, iron, or other material which receives the load and transmits it to the masonry.

Bench mark. A fixed point of reference to determine heights and depths in surveying.

Blocking. A method of bonding two adjoining or intersecting walls not built at the same time.

Bridging. A cross bracing between joists and studs to add stiffness to floors and walls.

Btu. A unit of heat (British thermal unit).

C

Calcimine. A white powder composed of a whiting and glue size, as a binder mixed with water.

Carriage. The horizontal part of the stringers of a stair that supports the treads.

Casement. A glass frame which is made to open by turning on hinges affixed to its vertical edges.

Casing. A metal or wooden member around door and window openings to give a finished appearance.

Catch basin. A cast-iron, cement, or wooden receptacle into which the water from a roof, floor, etc., will drain. It is connected with a sewer or draintile.

Center-to-center. Measurements taken from the center of one joist to another, or from one rafter to another, or from one stud to another.

Channel. A structural-steel shape.

Circuit. A path over which electric current may pass.

Circuit breaker. An appliance for opening and closing an electric circuit.

Column. A round vertical shaft or pillar used to support an entablature. It consists of a base, a shaft, and a capital.

Concrete. A mixture of cement, sand, and gravel.

Conductor. (Arch. Draft.) A drain pipe leading from the roof. (Elec.) Anything that permits the passage of an electric current.

Conductor pipe. A round, square, or rectangular metal pipe used to lead water from the roof to the sewer.

Contractor. A person offering to do work for a specified sum of money.

Convector. A heat-transfer surface designed to transfer its heat to surrounding air largely or wholly by convection currents.

Corbel. One of a series of brackets, often ornamental, projecting from the face of a wall.

Cornice. The part of the roof that projects from the wall.

Cross hatch. Lines drawn closely together, generally at an angle of 45 degrees, to denote a sectional cut.

D

Damper. A movable plate which regulates the draft of a stove, a fireplace, or a furnace.

Detail. The separate items of a structure broken down into its component parts.

Dimension line. A line with arrowheads at either end to show the distance between two points.

Dimension lumber. Lumber of any length which is between 2 and 5 in. thick.

Dividers. An instrument used for stepping off equal distances.

Double-hung window. A window with two sashes, one made to raise and the other to lower.

Drain. A means of carrying off waste water. A sewer or other pipe used for conveying ground, surface, or storm water, or sewage.

Drip cap. A molding designed to prevent rain water from running down the face of a wall. Used also on doors and windows.

Dry well. A pit located on porous ground walled up with rock which allows water to seep through the pit. Used for the disposal of rain water or the effluent from a septic tank.

E

Eave. That part of the roof that extends beyond the wall line.

Elevation. Drawing of front, sides, or rear face of a building, usually made as though the observer were looking straight at it.

Ellipse. A curve that is longer than it is wide.

Enamel. Paint with a considerable amount of varnish. It produces a hard, glossy surface on wood or other materials.

Excavation. A pit or hole formed by digging out earth.

F

Face brick. A brick used on the outside face of a wall to give it an attractive appearance.

Fascia. A vertical board nailed on the ends of the rafters. It is part of the cornice.

Fire brick. A brick that is especially hard and heat-resistant. Used in fireplaces.

Fire clay. A grade of clay that can withstand a large quantity of heat. Used for fire brick.

Fire cut. The angular cut at the end of a joist, designed to rest on a brick wall.

Fire door. A door that will resist fire.

Fire stop. A projection of brickwork on the walls between the joists to prevent the spread of fire.

Fixture. A receptacle attached to a plumbing system, in which water or other waste may be collected for ultimate discharge into the plumbing system.

Flashing. Sheet-metal work over windows and doors and around chimneys to prevent leakage.

Floor plan. A horizontal cut through a building showing rooms, partitions, windows, doors, and stairs.

Flue. An aperture in a chimney to allow the passage of smoke.

Footing. That part of the building resting on the bearing soil. Generally somewhat wider than the foundation wall.

Foundation. The base or lowest part of the structure. Also the footing.

Framing. The wood skeleton of a building. The act of building a frame for a door or window.

Frieze. That part of the wall board directly under the cornice.

Furring. The leveling-up or building-out of a part of a wall or ceiling by wood strips.

Fuse. A strip of soft metal inserted in an electric circuit, designed to melt and open the circuit should the current exceed a predetermined value.

G

Gable roof. A roof sloping up from two walls only.

Girder. A large, horizontal, structural member used to support the ends of joists and beams or to carry walls over openings.

Girt. The horizontal double 2 x 4's carrying the second-floor joists in a braced-frame building.

Grade. The level of the ground around the building.

Grounds. Strips of wood of plaster thickness nailed to the framing. They aid the plasterer and later act as nailing strips for the baseboard.

Guide lines. Lines drawn very lightly to act as a guide for lettering.

Gutter. A trough for carrying off water.

H

Hangers. Iron straps for supporting joists or beams.

Header. One or more pieces of lumber supporting ends of joists. Used in framing openings of stairs and chimneys.

Hearth. That portion of the flooring directly in front of the fireplace made of vitreous material. Also the floor inside the fireplace on which the fire is built.

Hip rafter. The rafter at the junction of two sloping roofs that form an exterior angle.

Hip roof. A roof sloping up from four walls of the building.

Horizon line. An imaginary line parallel to the ground line. Used in perspective work.

Horizontal. Parallel to the line where the earth meets the sky.

House drain. That part of the horizontal sewer piping inside the building receiving waste from the soil stacks.

Humidifier. A mechanical device which controls the amount of water vapor to be added to the atmosphere or any material.

I

I-B-R. Institute of Boiler and Radiator Manufacturers.

Initial set. The first-setting section of mortar.

Insulation. A special preparation placed between floors and walls to reduce the conductivity of sound and heat.

Isometric. A picture drawing in three-dimensional form having no perspective.

J

Jack rafter. A short rafter placed between the hip rafter and the plate of the roof framing, or between the valley rafter and the roof ridge.

Jamb. The innermost or exposed surfaces between the two wall lines of an opening.

Joist. A small timber which supports the floor, its ends resting on walls.

K

Kalamine door. A fireproof door with a metal covering.

L

Lally column. A vertical support for beams, made of iron pipe filled with concrete.

Landing. A platform at the head or top of a flight of stairs.

Lath. (Wood). A wooden strip about 4 ft. long nailed to studding and joists to which plaster is applied. The lath holds the plaster. (Metal). Made of sheet metal pierced with holes and nailed to studding and joists to which plaster is applied.

Lavatory. A place for washing hands and face.

Lineal foot. A measurement of 1 ft. along a straight line.

Lining. A covering placed over the interior surface of an object, such as a flue lining inside the brick chimney.

Lintel. A horizontal member, of wood, steel, or concrete, placed over an opening to support the load above.

Longitudinal. Pertaining to length.

Lot lines. The limits of a lot.

Louvres. A series of shutters used for the circulation of air.

Lower case. Small letters of the alphabet.

M

Manhole. An opening constructed in a sewer to allow access for a man.

Mantel. The shelf over a fireplace.

Masonry. A material such as brick, stone, etc., used by the mason in constructing a building.

Mastic. A waterproof material used to seal small openings in building construction.

Meeting rail. The horizontal rails of window frames that fit together when the window is closed.

Members. The various structural parts of a building or the parts of one unit of a building.

Metal wall ties. Strips of corrugated metal used to tie a brick veneer wall to framework.

Miter. A beveled surface cut on the ends of moldings so that they may fit at points where they change direction.

Mortar. A mixture of sand and cement, or lime, sand, and cement, used as a bonding material.

Mullion. A vertical bar in a window separating two windows.

Muntin. Small bars in a window separating the glass panes.

N

Newel. The post of a handrail of a stair used where the handrail starts or changes direction.

Nonferrous. Not containing iron. Said of a metal such as brass or copper.

Nominal size. A term used to express the sizes of fittings (e.g. ½ in., 1 in., 1½ in.) although the dimensions by which they are called are not exact.

Nosing. The rounded edge of a stair tread.

O

Orthographic projection. The drawing of an object in two or more views. Orthographic projection is a special case of parallel projection in which the projections are perpendicular to the plane of projection.

Outlet. The point where a lamp, fixture, heater, motor, or other current-consuming devices are attached to a wiring system.

P

Panel. A piece of flat wood framed in by other wood.

Parallel. Pertaining to lines that are equally distant at all points.

Partition. A wall separating two rooms or areas and not over one story in height.

Party wall. A wall common to two buildings or to two adjoining properties.

Perpendicular. A line or plane at right angles to another line or plane.

Perspective drawing. Drawing of an object in a three-dimensional form on a plane surface. An object drawn as it would appear to the eye.

Picture plane. An imaginary plane between the eye and the object drawn. Used in perspective drawing.

Pilot light. A small flame, used in gas-heating devices, which burns constantly. A small electric light of very low wattage indicating a closed circuit.

Pitch. The amount of rise of a pipe line per unit of length.

Plangier. That part of the cornice at right angles to the wall.

Planks. Pieces of timber 1½ in. and more in thickness.

Plate. The horizontal 2- x 4-in. member on top of a row of studs.

Primary coat. The first coat of paint.

Priming. Preparing a surface by applying a coat of paint to seal all the pores of the surface.

Protractor. An instrument used to measure angles.

Purlin. A structural member spanning from truss to truss and supporting the rafters of a roof.

R

Rafter. A beam running from the ridge of the roof to the cornice plate. Used to support the roof.

Rebate. A groove or recess cut into the edge of a board to receive the edge of another piece.

Rendering. The art of shading or coloring a drawing.

Ribbon. A support for joists. A board set into studs that are cut to support joists.

Ridge. The top edge of the roof where two slopes meet.

Rise. The vertical distance from the center of a span to the ridge of the roof.

Riser. One of the vertical pieces of a stair.

Rocklath. A plaster base made of a gypsum composition.

Ruling pen. An instrument with which ink lines are drawn.

S

Saddle. A small double-sloping roof designed to carry water from the back of chimneys, etc.

Sash. A frame in a door or window for holding glass.

S.B.I. Steel Boiler Institute.

Scale drawing. A drawing made to a size other than the actual size of the object represented.

Schedule. An inventory of parts or details.

Section. A drawing of an object cut lengthwise to show the interior.

Septic tank. A concrete tank, embedded in the earth, into which sewage is allowed to drain.

Sheathing. The rough boarding on the outside walls or roof of a house.

Shingles. Specially cut pieces of wood used as a roof or wall covering.

Shoring. Timbers braced against a wall to form a temporary support where it is necessary to remove the wall below.

Siding. The boarding on the outside walls of the house.

Sill. A wood or stone member across the bottom of a door or window opening. The timber resting directly on top of the foundation wall.

Sleepers. Timbers embedded in a concrete floor to act as nailing strips for a wood-floor covering.

Smoke chamber. That part of the flue directly above the fireplace.

Soffit. The underside of an arch.

Soil stack. The vertical pipe in the house into which sewage from fixtures and branches discharges.

Sole. The horizontal member in framing on which the studding rests.

Specifications. The written description of workmanship, etc., that accompanies a set of drawings.

Stile. The vertical member of a built-up part, such as a door, a window, a panel, etc.

Stirrups. A U-shaped metal strap used to support framing members.

Stool. The wood shelf across the bottom and inside of a window.

Stratification. The formation of layers one upon another; e.g. layers of air or heat.

Stringer. The main support of a stairway.

Studs. The vertical members that form the skeleton of a frame building.

Subflooring. The flooring nailed directly on the floor joists. The subfloor receives the finished floor.

Symbol. An arbitrary sign used to represent an object, a quality, etc.

T

Tail beams. Joists or framing members that are supported by headers or trimmers at one or both ends.

Tangent. A straight line or a curve that touches another curve at only one point but does not cut or cross it.

Temperature. Heat or cold recorded in degrees on a thermometer.

Terra-cotta. A composition of baked clay and sand.

Terrazzo. A combination of marble chips and cement, used in floor construction, ground and polished to a high finish.

Thermostat. An automatic device for controlling the supply of heat.

Throat. A passage directly above the fireplace opening upon which a damper is usually set.

Tie beam. A framing member connecting opposite rafters in roof construction, used to strengthen or shorten an excessive rafter span, or to provide a ceiling.

Tier. A single row or layer in a rising series of rows, as a framing tier of joists.

Tongue. A projection on the edge of wood flooring that joins with a similarly shaped groove.

Total run. The total of all the tread widths in a stair.

Tracing. The duplication of an original drawing by following lines seen through a transparent paper, vellum, or cloth.

Transmission. Sending or transferring a substance (e.g. heat or cold) through a material of construction.

Trap. A U-shaped device filled with water and located beneath plumbing fixtures to form a seal against the passage of foul odors or gases.

Tread. The step or horizontal member of a stair.

Triangle. A plane geometric figure with three sides and three angles.

Trimmers. Single or double joists or rafters that run around an opening in floor or roof construction.

Truss. A braced arrangement of steel or wood framework over openings or between supports, as in roof and bridge construction.

T-square. A T-shaped instrument of metal or wood used in drafting.

U

Undressed lumber. Lumber that is not squared or finished smooth.

Upper case. Capital letters of the alphabet.

V

Valley jacks. Rafters that run from a ridge board to a valley rafter.

Valley rafter. A rafter used to form the intersection of two gables in roof construction.

Valve. A device designed to regulate the direction of flow of fluids or gases, e.g. a steam or water valve on a radiator.

Veneer. A thin layer of wood over other wood, or a layer of masonry material over wood or other masonry; e.g. brick veneer over frame backing.

Vent pipe. A vertical pipe used to ventilate plumbing systems and to provide a release for pressure caused by flushing.

Vent stack. The upper portion of a soil or waste stack above the highest fixture.

Venturi. A restriction in a pipe designed to increase the rate of flow of a liquid.

Vertical. Perpendicular to a line or a plane that is parallel to the earth's surface.

Vitreous. Pertaining to a composition of materials that resembles glass; e.g. lavatories or drain pipe.

Volume. The amount of space occupied by an object. Usually measured in cubical units.

Volute. A line or surface starting at a point and moving around and outward from the point in a spiral-like manner.

Vanishing point. A point in perspective drawing toward which a series of parallel lines recede.

W

Wall string. A board running along the wall side of a stair into which the treads and risers are usually housed.

Waste stack. A plumbing pipe used to receive liquid discharge from lavatories, sinks, and bath tubs.

Waterproof. To treat a material to resist the passage of water or moisture.

Water table. A construction directly beneath the outside wall covering of a building designed to direct the flow of rain water away from the structure.

Weatherstripping. A strip of fabric or metal inserted in window and door edges to keep out cold and rain.

Well opening. The opening in a floor for access to a stair.

Working drawing. A technical drawing used to guide workers in the erection of a building or structure.

Workmanship. The art or skill of a worker in manufacturing or construction.

Index